HUMAN RE_____T

HUMAN RESOURCES MANAGEMENT

Ninth Edition

H T Graham
DPA, Dip Soc Stud, FIPM, MBIM

Roger Bennett
BA, MSc(Econ), DPhil
London Guildhall University

London • Hong Kong • Johannesburg • Melbourne • Singapore • Washington DC

PITMAN PUBLISHING
128 Long Acre, London WC2E 9AN
Tel: +44 (0)171 447 2000
Fax: +44 (0)171 240 5771

A Division of Pearson Professional Limited

Ninth edition published in Great Britain 1998

© Pearson Professional Limited 1998

The right of H T Graham and Roger Bennett to be identified
as authors of this work has been asserted by them in accordance
with the Copyright, Designs, and Patents Act 1988.

ISBN 0 273 63401 1

British Library Cataloguing in Publication Data
A CIP record for this book is available from the British Library.

10 9 8 7 6 5 4 3 2 1

Typeset by WestKey Limited, Falmouth, Cornwall
Printed and bound in Great Britain by Redwood Books, Ltd
The Publisher's policy is to use paper manufactured from sustainable forests

CONTENTS

PREFACE

The subject of human resources management combines elements of work psychology, personnel management, law, business organisation, training and industrial relations. This wide range of subject matter causes problems for the student in that the core reading for a human resources management unit is usually scattered over numerous text books and articles in disparate fields. Accordingly this book attempts to bring together in a single volume all the key points of the subject and to present them in a concise and understandable way.

This new edition represents a comprehensive expansion and restructuring of material included in earlier versions of the text. Among the numerous fresh topics appearing are:

- Learning theory and the learning organisation
- The four Cs model and the new approach to HRM
- Chaos theory and its implications for personnel management
- The latest EU Directives and thinking in relation to HRM: equal opportunities, parental leave, race discrimination, agism, the Working Time and Works Council Directives, etc.
- The Disability Discrimination Act
- Motivation and wages
- Teamworking and team development
- The problems of bullying and sexual harassment at work
- Self-leadership and self-managing teams.

Sections on flexible working, the free movement of workers within the EU, empowerment, re-engineering and the evaluation of personnel departments have been updated, as have all legal references. Information on personnel management in Austria, Finland and Sweden has been incorporated into the chapters concerned with international and European comparisons of HRM.

Roger Bennett

Part One

BACKGROUND TO HUMAN RESOURCES MANAGEMENT

1

NATURE OF HUMAN RESOURCES MANAGEMENT

INTRODUCTION

1. Definition

Human resources management (HRM) concerns the human side of the management of enterprises and employees' relations with their firms. Its purpose is to ensure that the employees of a company, i.e. its human resources, are used in such a way that the employer obtains the greatest possible benefit from their abilities and the employees obtain both material and psychological rewards from their work. Human resources management is based on the findings of work psychology and uses the techniques and procedures known collectively as 'personnel management', i.e. that part of human resources management concerned with staffing the enterprise, determining and satisfying the needs of people at work, and the practical rules and procedures that govern relationships between employees and the organisation. Differences between personnel management and HRM are discussed in **3**.

Everyone who has control over others shares in human resources management; it is not a function which the individual manager can avoid and leave to specialists. Human resources are much more difficult to manage than material resources, partly because conflict often occurs between the employer's and employees' wishes and partly because, to an increasing extent, employees try to share in making decisions about their working environment.

History of HRM

Human resources management emerged from personnel management which, in Britain, itself developed from the activities of 'industrial welfare workers' in the latter half of the nineteenth century. Throughout the history of HRM, however, a single common factor has been paramount – namely the needs of people at work. The first stage of development involved a handful of employers and philanthropists who, driven by the desire to improve the conditions of working people, initiated various programmes for bettering physical work-

3

ing environments and the quality of working life. Stage two may be said to have emerged during the First World War when, faced with acute labour shortages and the urgent need to increase industrial productivity, governments in Europe and the USA actively encouraged the systematic study of employer–employee relations and the human aspects of industrial work. This led to a fresh understanding of labour management problems and hence to a more technical and sophisticated approach to the personnel officer's role. The third stage was characterised by the advancement in the 1930s and 40s of various academic theories of management and the integration of management studies into general 'social science'. By the 1960s, specialisations had developed within the personnel function, which itself had become recognised as a valuable discipline in its own right, applicable to *all* forms and sizes of business and work situation. Company personnel policies and procedures now encompassed recruitment and selection, training, industrial relations, labour planning, salary administration, and employee appraisal.

Intense business competition in the 1980s and 90s, the introduction of new production technologies which depended heavily on multiskilled flexible working practices (frequently involving teamworking), and changing cultures at both the national and individual enterprise levels, catapulted personnel management to increasingly critical positions within firms. Personnel work became associated with wider business functions, and with business strategy 'in the round'. Inevitably, therefore, personnel managers were more and more involved with general business management and concerned with profit-maximising activities such as staff motivation, performance management, empowerment of workers (*see* 2:**13**), total quality management (TQM), organisational modification, and so on. *Human resourcing* decisions had to be taken at the very top level of management within a company.

2. Personnel management

The Institute of Personnel and Development has published the following definition:

> 'Personnel management is that part of management concerned with people at work and with their relationships within an enterprise. Its aim is to bring together and develop into an effective organisation the men and women who make up an enterprise and, having regard for the well-being of the individual and of working groups, to enable them to make their best contribution to its success.
>
> In particular, personnel management is concerned with the development and application of policies governing:
>
> - Human resources planning, recruitment, selection, placement and termination
> - Education and training; career development
> - Terms of employment, methods and standards of remuneration
> - Working conditions and employee services

- Formal and informal communication and consultation both through the representatives of employers and employees and at all levels throughout the enterprise
- Negotiation and application of agreements on wages and working conditions; procedures for the avoidance and settlement of disputes.

Personnel management is also concerned with the human and social implications of change in internal organisation and methods of working, and of economic and social changes in the community.'

Further personnel management responsibilities are:

(a) Conducting research into local wage levels to ensure that the firm's reward system is competitive with those in other companies.

(b) 'Incentivating', i.e. devising remuneration systems to stimulate workers into enhanced effort and efficiency.

(c) Administration of superannuation schemes (in conjunction with finance department) and advising employees about their pension and other entitlements.

(d) Maintenance of personnel records and statistics.

(e) Preparation of accurate job descriptions and other recruitment aids.

(f) Implementation of health and safety regulations, accident prevention and the provision of first-aid facilities.

(g) Management training, development and succession planning.

(h) Employee communications, transmitting information of interest to employees *via* newsletters, notice boards, briefing sessions, etc.

Another way of defining personnel management is to regard it as a range of policies, institutions and procedures which enable the principles of work psychology to be put into practice. Its purpose is not only to make effective use of people at work and develop satisfactory relationships among them but to motivate them both by providing them with jobs which are satisfying in themselves (if this is practically possible) and by offering them financial and other rewards.

Accordingly, personnel management may be re-defined as that part of management which deals with people at work as regards:

(a) *Utilisation* – recruitment, selection, transfer, promotion, separation, appraisal, training and development.

(b) *Motivation* – job design, remuneration, fringe benefits, consultation, participation, negotiation and justice.

(c) *Protection* – working conditions, welfare services, safety, implemenation of appropriate legislation.

5

These three divisions are not separate and self-contained. For example, an employee who has been well selected and trained for his or her job will be more motivated in it than someone who has been carelessly selected and untrained. The use of consultation and participation, besides motivating employees, will often show how they can be better utilised. A well-designed and safe working environment will enable better use to be made of people's abilities and will in most cases help to provide satisfaction of human needs.

3. Personnel management and human resources management

Personnel management is an important element of the broader subject of human resources management, although in practice the two terms are frequently used interchangeably – emphasising the fact that the people employed in a company are resources which are at least as important as financial or material resources and must be given careful and expert attention.

Employees will not submit passively to manipulation or dictatorial control by management but more and more expect and demand some influence in the way they are employed. Research in the behavioural sciences shows that an appropriate response by management will benefit the company. Personnel management techniques in, for example, appraisal, training and job evaluation can only be successfully applied with the consent and support of the employees.

The following relationships and differences between human resources management (HRM) and personnel management may be distinguished:

(a) Personnel management is practical, utilitarian and instrumental, and mostly concerned with administration and the *implementation* of policies. Human resources management, conversely, has *strategic* dimensions and involves the total deployment of human resources within the firm. Thus, for example, HRM will consider such matters as:

(*i*) The aggregate size of the organisation's labour force in the context of an overall corporate plan (how many divisions and subsidiaries the company is to have, design of the organisation, etc.).
(*ii*) How much to spend on training the workforce, given strategic decisions on target quality levels, product prices, volume of production and so on.
(*iii*) The desirability of establishing relations with trade unions from the viewpoint of the effective management control of the entire organisation.
(*iv*) Human asset accounting, i.e. the systematic measurement and analysis of the costs and *financial* benefits of alternative personnel policies (e.g. the monetary consequences of staff development exercises, the effects of various salary structures, etc.) and the valuation of the human worth of the enterprise's employees.

The strategic approach to HRM involves the integration of personnel and other HRM considerations into the firm's overall corporate planning and strategy formulation procedures. It is proactive, seeking constantly to discover new ways of utilising the labour force in a more productive manner thus giving the business a competitive edge. Practical manifestations of the adoption of a strategic approach to HRM might include:

(*i*) Incorporation of a brief summary of the firm's basic HRM policy into its mission statement.

(*ii*) Explicit consideration of the consequences for employees of each of the firm's strategies and major new projects.

(*iii*) Designing organisation structures to suit the needs of employees rather than conditioning the latter to fit in with the existing form of organisation.

(*iv*) Having the head of HRM on the firm's board of directors.

More than ever before, human resource managers are expected to contribute to productivity and quality improvement, the stimulation of creative thinking, leadership and the development of corporate skills.

(b) HRM is concerned with the wider implications of the management of change (*see* Chapter 6) and not just with the effects of change on working practices. It seeks proactively to encourage flexible attitudes and the acceptance of new methods.

(c) Aspects of HRM constitute major inputs into organisational development exercises (*see* 22:**14**).

(d) Personnel management is (necessarily) reactive and diagnostic. It *responds* to changes in employment law, labour market conditions, trade union actions, government Codes of Practice and other environmental influences. HRM, on the other hand, is *prescriptive* and concerned with strategies, the initiation of new activities and the development of fresh ideas.

(e) HRM determines general policies for employment relationships within the enterprise. Thus, it needs to establish within the organisation a *culture* that is conducive to employee commitment and co-operation. Personnel management, on the other hand, has been criticised for being primarily concerned with imposing *compliance* with company rules and procedures among employees, rather than with loyalty and commitment to the firm.

(f) Personnel management has short-term perspectives; HRM has long-term perspectives, seeking to *integrate* all the human aspects of the organisation into a coherent whole and to establish high-level employee goals.

(g) The HRM approach emphasises the needs:

(*i*) for direct communication with employees rather than their collective representation

(*ii*) to develop an organisational culture conducive to the adoption of flexible working methods

(*iii*) for group working and employee participation in group decisions

(*iv*) to enhance employees' long-term capabilities, not just their competence at current duties.

7

A contentious view of the difference between HRM and personnel management is the proposition that whereas the latter is 'pluralistic' in orientation, HRM has a 'unitaristic' approach (*see* below).

4. Pluralistic and unitary frames of reference

A frame of reference is the totality of all the attitudes, preassumptions and psychological influences that determine how a person perceives and interprets issues and events. In the industrial relations context, people with 'unitary' frames of reference regard both sides of industry (management and employees) as having identical interests and, in consequence, believe that workers should naturally co-operate with management, should work together as a team, and actively seek to assist management achieve its objectives. Human resources management, therefore, needs to involve (*i*) the unification of effort, (*ii*) the implementation of measures designed to inspire and motivate the workforce, (*iii*) the communication to workers of details of the organisation's wider goals, and (*iv*) the construction of policies for securing employees' loyalty and commitment to the firm.

The problems with unitarism are:

(a) It cannot comprehend the motives of individuals who do not regard everyone in the organisation as 'being in the same boat'.

(b) Arguably, it fails to recognise the *inevitability* of conflicts of interest in certain management/employee situations.

(c) It can impair the efficient resolution of disputes.

Hence, 'pluralism' has been suggested as a more effective approach. A pluralistic frame of reference is one which sees conflicts of interest and disagreements between managers and workers over the distribution of the firm's profits as the normal and inescapable state of affairs. Realistically, therefore, management should accept that conflicts will *necessarily* occur, and thus should seek to resolve them by establishing sound procedures for settling disputes. Pluralism assumes that the best way to achieve consensus and long-term stability in management/worker relations is for management to recognise conflicting interests, to negotiate compromises, and to balance the demands of various groups. This implies the need for grievance procedures, joint-negotiation committees, union-recognition agreements, arbitration arrangements, and so on, i.e. all the mundane, practical and utilitarian devices traditionally associated with *personnel management*.

5. The 'new approach' to HRM

Although the term 'human resources management' has been in use since the 1960s, the work of a number of US academics (notably those connected with the 4Cs model – *see* 6) led to the term assuming a new meaning in certain contexts in the 1980s and 1990s. This 'new' perspective on HRM emphasised:

- Individualism rather than collectivism (resulting from the long-term decline in the number of employees belonging to trade unions)
- Wage systems based on personal contracts (*see* 20:**9**) wherein a worker's pay is set through individual negotiation with the firm, as opposed to collective bargaining involving trade unions
- Increasing levels of casual and part-time employment
- The idea that managers and workers have *common interests* of management and workers in achieving company goals (*see* **4**)
- The need for cost-cutting and 'lean production' methods consequent to ever-increasing international business competition
- Interpersonal relationships and management/worker communications systems appropriate for 'high-tech' industries using the latest management techniques
- 'Flexible' labour practices (*see* 9:**1**)
- Teamwork, the implementation of corporate values, company-wide (rather than individual) learning, and the idea of 'putting the customer first'. Pluralistic concerns with conflict management are put to one side, with HRM specialists concentrating more on wide-ranging cultural and leadership issues than on detailed procedures and rules.

There are of course many close similarities between the 'new' HRM and conventional personnel management. Both recognise that personnel/HRM specialists occupy an advisory role in relation to line managers; both are concerned with the needs of people at work; and both deal with the same range of practical matters (recruitment, training, etc.).

Criticisms of the 'new approach' to HRM

A number of criticisms have been levelled against the transformation of personnel management into the 'new approach' to HRM:

(a) Although the strategic orientation of HRM reflects management's *hopes* and *aspirations*, this new approach to personnel matters is in reality ambiguous and lacking in concrete policy prescriptions. There is no single rigorous underlying theory uniting the various elements of 'new' HRM practice.

(b) The mixing up of 'directive' management processes (performance management, quality control, etc.) with the conventional personnel management function gives the latter a bad name, leading to the downgrading of vital personnel activities.

(c) This wider management-orientated approach to HRM can cause employees to perceive HRM as little more than an unfair set of devices designed to make them work harder for less money.

(d) Power (*see* 2:**2**) in employer–employee relationship situations in fact lies predominantly in the hands of management. Employees may regard HRM policies as one-sided.

(e) Workers are expected to display commitment to their employing firms, but what in practice does this actually mean?

(f) An employee's individuality might be overlooked in a business dominated by a strong corporate culture.

(g) Workers may become 'brainwashed' into doing whatever the organisation wants them to do, without question and regardless of what is best for the individual.

(h) Constant exposure to management persuasion and propaganda could cause employees to feel they are being manipulated.

(i) Implementation of 'new' HRM approaches requires trained, competent and committed managers. In reality many executives are simply not up to the task, and attempts by incompetent line managers to interfere with personnel matters can lead to worse results than if they were not involved in HRM at all.

(j) At the end of the day, production and profitability considerations are bound to override HRM considerations.

(k) It is difficult to apply the ideas associated with the new HRM in organisations that lack a coherent strategic direction.

THE FOUR Cs MODEL OF HUMAN RESOURCES MANAGEMENT

The Four Cs model was developed by researchers at the Harvard Business School as a means of investigating HRM issues in a wider environmental context than the mundane and instrumental tasks of recruitment and selection, training, appraisal, maintenance of employee records, and so on. According to the Harvard model (Beer *et al* 1985) HRM policies need to derive from a critical analysis of:

- the demands of the various stakeholders in a business
- a number of 'situational factors'.

6. Stakeholder theory

This asserts that since organisations are owned and operated by differing interest groups (stakeholders), management's main task is to balance the returns to various group interests. Examples of stakeholders are shareholders, different categories of employee, customers/users of the product, creditors (including banks), unions, and (possibly) local or national government.

Managers, therefore, need to be politicians and diplomats. They must establish good relations with each group, develop persuasive skills, create alliances, represent one faction to others, etc.

Stakeholder theory implies the recognition that each interest group possesses certain basic rights. Thus, for example, management should consider workers' interests as well as those of shareholders when taking important decisions.

Stakeholders may or may not hold formal authority, although each will have invested something in the organisation, whether this be work, finance or other resources. Accordingly, every stakeholder will expect a reward from the enterprise and normally will wish to influence how this is determined. Management must:

- Identify the stakeholders in the organisation
- Determine the minimum return each stakeholder is willing to accept
- Seek to influence stakeholders' perceptions of the organisation (e.g. by persuading shareholders that a high dividend is not in a company's best long-term interest or convincing workers that a high wage settlement is not possible during the current year)
- Identify key individuals in specific stakeholder groups and establish good relations with these people.

7. Situational factors

These include the state of the labour market, the calibres and motivation of employees, management style (which itself depends in part on the culture of the local community), the technologies used in production and the nature of working methods (e.g. whether specialisation and the division of labour are required). Labour markets situations are crucial to the analysis. The labour market comprises all the people seeking work and all the companies, government bodies and other organisations that require employees. Labour markets operate at regional, industry sector, national and (increasingly) international levels. There are sub-markets for various categories of occupation, skill, educational background and other employee characteristics and for different types of task.

Further situational factors that might be relevant are:

- Form of ownership of the organisation (and hence to whom management is accountable)
- Influence of trade unions and employers' associations
- Laws and business practices of the society in which the organisation operates
- The competitive environment
- Senior management's ability to coordinate and control.

Stakeholder expectations and situational factors need to be taken into account when formulating human resources strategies, and will affect HRM policies concerning such matters as remuneration systems, degree of supervision of workers, use of labour-intensive rather than capital-intensive methods, etc. An increase in the intensity of business competition may cause a firm to improve labour productivity, discard employees, restructure administrative systems, and so on. A change in the age structure of the population could lead an organisation to hire more women. Rising educational standards might make it appropriate to redesign jobs in order to give workers more autonomy.

Outcomes to human resources management

According to the Harvard researchers, the effectiveness of the outcomes to human resources management should be evaluated under four headings: commitment, competence, congruence and cost-effectiveness.

(a) **Commitment** concerns employees' loyalty to the organisation, personal motivation and liking for their work. The degree of employee commitment might be assessed via attitude surveys, labour turnover and absenteeism statistics, and through interviews with workers who quit their jobs.

(b) **Competence** relates to employees' skills and abilities, training requirements and potential for higher-level work. These may be estimated through employee appraisal systems and the preparation of skills inventories. HRM policies should be designed to attract, retain and motivate competent workers.

(c) **Congruence** means that management and workers share the same vision of the organisation's goals and work together to attain them. In a well-managed organisation, employees at all levels of authority will share common perspectives about the factors that determine its prosperity and future prospects. Such perspectives concern the guiding principles that govern the organisation's work; how things should be done, when, by whom, and how enthusiastically.

   To some extent these perceptions may be created by management via its internal communications, style of leadership, organisation system and working methods; but they can only be sustained and brought to bear on day-to-day operations by the organisation's workers. Staff should *feel* they possess a common objective. They need to experience a sense of affinity with the organisation and *want* to pursue a common cause. Congruence is evident in the absence of grievances and conflicts within the organisation, and in harmonious industrial relations.

(d) **Cost-effectiveness** concerns operational efficiency. Human resources should be used to the best advantage and in the most productive ways. Outputs must be maximised at the lowest input cost, and the organisation must be quick to respond to market opportunities and environmental change.

Problems with the four Cs approach

The Harvard model suggests that human resources policies should seek to increase the level of each of the four Cs. For example, commitment might be enhanced through improving the flow of management/worker communication, while competence could be increased through extra training. Problems with the four Cs approach are:

- How *exactly* to measure these variables
- Possible conflicts between cost-effectiveness and congruence (especially if the drive for the former generates low wages).
- The huge variety of variables potentially relevant to any given HRM situation. Often it is impossible to distinguish the key factors defining the true character of a particular state of affairs.
- The fact that sometimes a technology or set of working conditions make it virtually impossible to increase the levels of some of the Cs. Certain jobs are inevitably dirty, boring and repetitive; yet they still have to be done.

PRACTICAL ASPECTS OF PERSONNEL WORK

8. Roles of the personnel manager

The mundane tasks of writing copy for job advertisements, organising training courses, personnel records, operating wages systems, looking after the firm's health and safety at work arrangements, etc., are known collectively as the *service* function of the personnel role. Other major personnel management functions are as follows:

(a) The *control* function, comprising:

(*i*) analysis of key operational indices in the personnel field: labour turnover, wage costs, absenteeism and so on
(*ii*) monitoring labour performance (staff appraisal, for example)
(*iii*) recommending appropriate remedial action to line managers.

(b) The *advisory* function, whereby the personnel department offers expert advice on personnel policies and procedures, for example:

(*i*) which employees are ready for promotion
(*ii*) who should attend a certain training course
(*iii*) how a grievance procedure should be operated
(*iv*) interpretation of contracts of employment, health and safety regulations, etc.

So wide-ranging are the many tasks that personnel managers may be called upon to undertake that special problems are attached to personnel work, including the following:

13

(a) Line managers may interpret personnel department initiatives as unwarranted challenges to their authority.

(b) It is difficult to define the boundaries of the personnel role. To what extent should personnel considerations figure in normal operational decisions?

(c) Personnel department represents management; yet individual personnel managers – who through their duties communicate directly with the firm's employees – may sympathise more with labour than with management on certain issues. Consequently, a personnel manager may be called upon to implement policies with which he or she does not wholeheartedly agree.

It follows that the personnel officer has to be a *diplomat*; mediating between management and worker, between manager and manager, and among various groups of employee. He or she must gather and assess facts, *diagnose* situations and prescribe solutions. Thus a personnel manager has to be an effective planner, analyst, team worker and communicator, capable of presenting proposals and arguing a case at all levels within the organisation – from the board room to the employees' workplaces.

9. Organisation of the personnel department

The personnel officer is necessarily a generalist, since the variety of issues typically dealt with in a personnel department is so diverse that no one person could master all aspects of the job. Thus, a personnel manager requires a working rather than a detailed knowledge of:

- The firm, its products and the industry in which the business operates
- Production methods and company organisation structure
- Pension schemes, wage and bonus arrangements
- Law relating to employment
- The fundamentals of management theory and practice.

Consequently, the personnel manager requires wide-ranging knowledge and skills, in contrast to the highly specialised qualifications and experiences of many of the line managers whom the personnel manager will advise. This might cause reluctance among line managers to accept advice from a personnel manager who does not possess their detailed knowledge of specific functions.

The structure of a personnel department should depend on the relative importance of the various tasks it performs, which in turn depends on the organisation of the firm – its size and complexity, production technology, degree of bureaucracy and historical tradition. Some personnel departments employ a number of personnel officers who share work equally, operating a 'single-door' policy whereby any problem that arises (no matter how serious or complex) is assigned to the first officer who becomes free. This recognises the generic nature of personnel work, and it ensures that personnel department staff acquire experience of all personnel tasks. Alternatively, a personnel department might be segmented according to particular functions, with separate staff and sections responsible for recruitment, industrial relations, welfare services, personnel records, etc. Such 'functional' organisation enables staff to specialise in a certain area and hence develop great expertise in that field, but it has the disadvantage of encouraging narrow and introspective attitudes among personnel department staff.

Status of the personnel department

Personnel managers sometimes complain of a cultural separation between themselves and managers in other departments, and that the importance of HRM is not properly understood. Negative perceptions of the role of a personnel department might arise from the latter's (inevitable) involvement in the implementation of redundancies, dismissal and grievance procedures, rejections of union requests for pay increases, and other disagreeable aspects of life at work. Widespread interest in quality assurance and quality management among business people has led a number of firms to 'market' the personnel function within their organisations. This can be done through:

(a) Conducting surveys to discover the expectations of other departments (i.e. the personnel department's 'customers') *vis-à-vis* the personnel manager's role

(b) Educating line managers about what the personnel department can and cannot do

(c) Involving other departments when formulating personnel policies

(d) Training personnel staff to understand customer needs

(e) Communicating with customers on an on-going basis

(f) Relating the personnel function to the overall corporate strategy of the firm (*see* **3**)

(g) Making the services of the personnel department user friendly.

Practical devices for enhancing the status of a personnel department include the issue of professionally produced leaflets and brochures explaining each of its main activities, briefing sessions conducted by personnel staff in other departments by, for example, the inclusion of a prominent and attractive logo on all literature, memoranda, etc., arising from the personnel function. It is important moreover that the personnel department be *seen* to be efficient, as the personnel function is sometimes accused of having a vested interest in creating hierarchical and bureaucratic organisation structures and employee grading systems in view of the extensive opportunities for devising job evaluation schemes, staff development programmes, appraisal checklists, etc., that they create. All these duties enhance the role of the personnel department, possibly to the extreme annoyance of managers in other sections.

Evaluating the effectiveness of a personnel department

Effective personnel management should feed through into improved organisational performance, higher productivity among employees, better customer service and hence increased long-term sales. Measuring the value of the short-run activities of a personnel department, however, can be problematic. Specific difficulties attached to the evaluation of the personnel function are that:

(a) Since organisations operate in widely disparate commercial environments, wide differences in labour turnover, absenteeism, etc. are to be expected among firms engaged in similar lines of work.

(b) Personnel management is such a wide-ranging activity that it might not be appropriate to select just a handful of variables for appraisal.

Quantitative indices of a personnel department's work may be available in relation to:

- Unit labour costs compared to those in competing companies
- Staff turnover
- Absenteeism rates
- Incidence of invocations of grievance procedures
- The proportion of the personnel department's staff that obtain professional qualifications
- Number of days lost through strikes
- How long it takes to recruit a new employee
- Successes achieved in the implementation of equal opportunities policies.

Subjective criteria include employee motivation, team spirit and willingness to accept change; the extent to which proposals emerging from the personnel department are accepted by senior management; quality of relationships with trade unions; calibres of job applicants' responses to job advertisements; usefulness of documents drafted by the department (job descriptions and person specifications for example), and so on. Staff from other parts of the firm may be questioned in order to ascertain how they rate the personnel department in terms of such matters as:

- How promptly it responds to requests for information or advice
- The quality of advice given by personnel department staff
- Politeness and approachability of the department's members
- Individual knowledge of technical personnel matters
- The department's overall contributions to the work of other sections.

Senior management may evaluate a personnel department's contributions on the basis of its ability to handle satisfactorily sensitive human relations problems arising from downsizing, organisational restructuring and the implementation of change. Also the personnel/human resources officer will be expected to make meaningful contributions to top management team decisions and to assist with strategic issues such as the formulation of mission statements, determination of corporate cultures, facilitation of technological change, and so on.

10. Personnel policies

Well-constructed personnel policies are essential for the well-being and long-term survival of the firm. Conflicts between management and labour can be minimised through:

(a) Giving workers security of employment

(b) Offering promotion to suitably qualified staff

(c) Consultation and negotiation with employees' representatives on all issues affecting terms and conditions of employment and working environments

(d) Avoidance of discrimination in recruitment and/or promotion on the grounds of sex, ethnic origin, religion, marital status, age or physical disability

(e) Providing opportunities for retraining and the acquisition of new skills

(f) Establishing codes of practice for dealing with redundancies and dismissals, and grievance procedures for complaints against management by staff.

Personnel management is difficult because human relations problems are complex and difficult to solve, and there are many constraints that restrict the personnel manager's capacity to improve conditions at work. For instance, physical working conditions in some jobs (routine assembly-line work, for example) are unavoidably unpleasant, causing boredom and ill temper; or current economic conditions may be so poor that the firm is unable to pay workers the wage increases they feel they deserve.

Human resources management and competitive advantage

There are a number of reasons why the effective management of human resources can give a business a competitive edge over rival firms:

(a) Contented and hard-working employees are more likely to produce excellent work that genuinely adds value to the enterprise.

(b) The stability of a company that possesses sound employee relations will encourage outside investors to buy shares in the business, so that it becomes easier for the company to raise funds.

(c) The existence of common values upheld throughout the organisation facilitates the development of long-term strategies and plans.

(d) Company resources should be used in the most efficient way (via the recruitment of the best people, use of high-level skills developed through top class training programmes, etc.).

(e) An organisational culture conducive to quality performance is likely to prevail.

(f) Change can be implemented with less disruption.

(g) The organisation's core competencies are strengthened and enhanced.

11. Ethical issues in human resources management

Ethics concerns moral principles and how people should conduct themselves in social affairs. Personnel officers are perhaps more likely to confront ethical dilemmas in the course of their duties than most other executives, since in many respects the personnel manager occupies a 'mediative' role between management and the workforce, balancing the interest of employees against the needs of the overall organisation. Examples of ethical problems that might arise in the course of a personnel officer's work include:

(a) Conflicts between a personnel manager's desire to improve the quality of employees' working lives (*via* job extension (*see* 4:**20**), improvement of conditions, increased participation, etc.) and the insistence of other managers that the division of labour be applied as extensively as possible, and/or that pay and conditions be kept constant.

(b) Senior management demanding that the personnel officer deliberately misrepresent unsound personnel policies in order to promote them to workers.

(c) Awareness that certain employees are not receiving fair rewards for their efforts; that equal opportunities legislation is not being obeyed; that there is unfair discrimination preventing the promotion of certain individuals, etc.

(d) Having to decide whether to report to the police illegal acts of employees (e.g. theft) or of the employing firm (e.g. serious and deliberate contravention of health and safety legislation).

There are two basic approaches to the resolution of such moral dilemmas:

(1) The personnel manager predetermines for him or herself a strict code of behaviour and adheres to this always – regardless of extenuating circumstances. Advantages to this approach include consistency in behaviour (the people with whom the personnel officer deals always know what to expect) and the fact that the individual does not have to wrestle with his or her conscience every time an ethical problem arises. The difficulties with the approach are that it can lead to obstinacy and intolerance of human weaknesses, and that the manager's credibility will be totally destroyed if that person is seen to break his or her self-imposed moral principles.

(2) Alternatively, the individual consciously chooses to vary behaviour according to the requirements of each and every situation. Here the manager changes his or her moral outlook as circumstances alter. This creates scope for flexibility in decision making and could lead to fairer decisions but might also result in inconsistency and in the person never being entirely sure whether he or she behaved correctly. Also those affected by a manager's ethical inconsistency might resent and retaliate against decisions.

12. Use of consultants

Human resources management consultants are increasingly engaged by organisations to undertake specialist personnel assignments and/or to advise on personnel policies. Typically, consultants are used when an unusual human resources problem arises within the firm and the existing management has little idea of its nature and implications. An outsider can analyse the issue objectively and explain how similar difficulties have been dealt with in other organisations. Advantages to using an HRM consultant include:

(a) It can be cheaper than employing a full-time personnel specialist; no overheads need be incurred; and there are no costs of training and staff development. Internal staff might not be fully employed throughout the year.

(b) Consultants should possess detailed and expert knowledge of the latest specialist techniques and of complex personnel matters (the legal aspects of job evaluation, for instance).

(c) The independence of the consultant, who can question *anyone* within the organisation without concern for internal politics.

(d) Senior management may prefer to discuss sensitive HRM issues with an outside consultant than with its own subordinate staff.

(e) The consultant's wide experience should enable him or her quickly to identify the critical factors affecting a situation and to analyse all the available options.

(f) In-house staff may lack the specialist skills needed to complete unusual or difficult HRM projects. Also, in-house employees are not subject to penetrating expert criticism, and security of tenure could lead to lack of effort and innovation.

(g) Outside consultants should have numerous contacts with other external specialists in the personnel field.

(h) Managements can learn a lot simply through observing a high-calibre consultant at work.

   The disadvantages to using external consultants are that:

(a) They lack intimate knowledge of the firm's day-to-day operations.

(b) Vital information might be concealed from them by employees suspicious of their work.

(c) Consultants are not accountable in the long term for the consequences of their recommendations (they usually move on to another organisation immediately an assignment is completed).

(d) Their careers do not depend on achieving success on a particular *ad hoc* project undertaken for a specific client firm.

(e) Consultants might not be instantly available (as are in-house staff).

Effective control of a consultant requires the detailed specification of the assignment, clear objectives (accompanied by concrete criteria for determining whether they have been achieved), and the predetermination of how much information the consultant must gather independently and how much will be collected by the client's own staff.

Consultancy costs should not normally be assigned to the budget of any one department (especially not the personnel department) because the benefits of the consultant's efforts should eventually be felt throughout the firm. Rather, consultancy costs should be absorbed generally, as happens with the salary of a managing director or company secretary.

CURRENT TRENDS

13. Recent developments in human resources management

A number of important factors have altered the scope and nature of human resources management in recent years, notably the following:

(a) Greater involvement of line managers in personnel management and a general decentralisation and devolution of the function. Increasingly, line managers are required to undertake duties previously completed by personnel specialists. This results in part from firms seeking to cut costs through reducing the sizes of their personnel departments, and partially in consequence of the view that line managers *ought* to be able to complete this work (see below).

(b) Economic recession in the early 1990s, the downsizing of organisations and a shift in the nature of the relationship between management and labour.

(c) New working methods based on flexible labour practices.

(d) Recognition of the importance of the development of a firm's human resources as a means for securing competitive advantage, spurred on by the successes achieved by Japanese companies which pay great attention to the personnel role.

Decentralisation and devolution

Many personnel and HRM functions can be undertaken by managers in local units rather than through a central personnel department (decentralised collective bargaining [*see* 20:**10**] for example). Note that the individuals completing such duties in subsidiaries, divisions, etc., might *themselves* be personnel specialists rather than general line managers, although in practice this is rare because of the duplication of effort involved. The main problem with devolution of personnel and/or HRM work to non-specialist line managers is that they may be neither competent nor interested in personnel or HRM issues, and might not be motivated to complete HRM duties properly so that critically important personnel tasks are neglected. Bad HRM decisions lead to a poor corporate image, higher long-run costs and loss of output due to industrial conflict. Also line managers might focus all their attention on immediately pressing personnel problems, at the expense of long-term HRM planning, and it could result in HRM considerations not influencing strategic management decisions.

Effective devolution requires:

(a) The provision of back-up services in relation to technical problems arising from contracts of employment, legal aspects of redundancy and dismissal, union recognition, etc. An outside consultancy (*see* **10**) might assume this role.

(b) Acceptance by everyone that line managers' workloads will have to increase following their assumption of personnel responsibilities.

(c) Training of line managers in HRM techniques and concepts.

14. The future of human resources management

A number of issues seem likely to be increasingly important for UK personnel management in the future, notably:

(a) EU interventions in matters affecting employee protection and employee relations and the need for personnel (and other) managers to adopt international orientations towards their work

(b) Growing concern for the application of ethical approaches to personnel management

(c) Implementation of equal opportunities policies

(d) The human resources management implications of flexible workforces (*see* 9:**7**)

(e) Heightened awareness (following the example of successes achieved by Japanese companies in Britain) of the need for effective employee participation in company production systems

(f) The consequences for personnel management of the demographic time bomb (*see* below)

(g) Changing attitudes among trade union leaders and members (partly due to the higher levels of unemployment experienced over the last 15 years) which give managements a wider range of policy options in industrial relations matters

(h) Greater involvement of the law in personnel issues, including laws on hiring, firing, equal opportunities, and the conduct of industrial relations.

15. The demographic time bomb

This refers to the fact that the average age of the workforce is increasing, creating thereby a shortage of younger workers. The latter are often preferred by employers for a number of reasons:

(a) Young workers have completed their education more recently and are thus more up to date than older colleagues.

(b) On the whole, younger employees tend to be more flexible in their attitudes and less resistant to change than older workers, who might have a vested interest in maintaining the *status quo*.

(c) The family commitments of older employees are typically more extensive than for young people, so that older workers usually expect higher levels of remuneration.

(d) Since young recruits have recent experience of the learning process (attending lessons, taking notes, concentrating on the key points of lectures, reading and absorbing instructional materials, etc.), they can usually be trained faster than older workers, who may have forgotten the basic techniques of 'how to learn'.

The demographic time bomb will cause recruitment difficulties for firms wishing to engage young workers, and will create skills shortages in certain areas and occupations. Another consequence will be an oversupply of people in middle management and hence the need for more extensive outplacement procedures (*see* 10:**9**). Further effects of the demographic time bomb could involve the following:

(a) Greater female participation in the labour force with employers offering women:

(*i*) financial assistance towards childcare
(*ii*) flexible benefits packages that allow them to trade off, e.g. pension rights against increased maternity leave and payments
(*iii*) guaranteed re-entry to jobs following time out from the labour force for child raising, etc.

(b) Retraining of older workers in new technologies.

(c) Greater equality of opportunity for young people from disadvantaged ethnic minorities.

(d) A higher level of immigration of young people from other countries.

(e) Higher wages and benefits for young workers, with employers competing for their services by offering training schemes, career development packages, large bonuses for remaining with a firm for a certain number of years, etc.

(f) A reduction in age discrimination ('agism') by employers. Justifications sometimes given for age discrimination are that older workers are slow, have low productivity and are poor learners. Currently there is no UK law forbidding agism, which is frequently criticised as unfair on the grounds that older employees may in fact make extremely good workers. Older employees have lower-than-average absenteeism, lateness and labour turnover, and it has been demonstrated that older employees tend to be more satisfied with their jobs (possibly because their expectations are lower and because they are better adjusted to work routines than younger workers). Age-related decreases in individual productivity are likely to be very marginal, and outweighed by the benefits of experience. Training difficulties might be due more to older people being out of practice than to lack of ability, and training programmes can be adapted to take this into account.

Specific problems confronted by older workers include:

- Early loss of employment because of age
- Difficulties in finding fresh employment
- Targeting of older people in company downsizing exercises
- What are in effect compulsory early retirement schemes
- Exclusion from government retraining programmes and, where such programmes exist, the training materials used to reskill older workers being based (unsuitably) on those applied to the training of very young people
- Loss of statutory protection against unfair dismissal once an employee has reached a certain age.

Note that companies which recruit large numbers of older employees might become unattractive to young people because of the consequential loss of immediate short-term promotion prospects for young workers. Also, since older employees are less likely to quit their jobs, reduction of the size of a firm's labour force through natural wastage can become extremely difficult. This is because a freeze on recruitment means that younger people (who tend to leave their employers more frequently) are not replaced, thus increasing the average age of remaining workers. Consequently staffing crises arise when older cohorts simultaneously retire.

No EU country has constitutional provisions barring age discrimination, although Belgium, Italy, the Netherlands, Portugal and Spain have constitutional clauses from which the impropriety of age discrimination may be inferred. Italy's constitution, for example, states that all citizens must be treated equally regardless of 'personal and social conditions'. France and Sweden ban the use of maximum age limits in job advertisements, while decisions of the Irish Labour Court have held that specification of maximum ages can amount to indirect sex discrimination. Germany, Finland and Sweden have *ad hoc* laws that outlaw age discrimination *within* employment. In Ireland and Italy it is illegal to dismiss an employee on the grounds of age. Austria and France have laws that make it inconvenient and costly (though not illegal) to dismiss older workers, while in Sweden the minimum period of notice to be given to employees is age rather than service-related.

Reference

Beer, M., Spector, B.A., Lawrence, P.R. and Walton, R.E. (1985), *Human Resource Management*, The Free Press.

Progress test 1

1. Define personnel management.
2. What is the meaning of the term human resources management?
3. What is a pluralistic frame of reference?
4. Define the service role of the personnel department.
5. What are the implications of the demographic time bomb?
6. 'Human resource management is just a fashionable name for traditional personnel management.' Discuss this statement.
7. 'The pluralistic framework for industrial relations is now completely dead, and the power of unions is insignificant.'
   Discuss the accuracy of this remark (both today and in the foreseeable future) and its implications for the personnel function.
8. 'The distinction between policy and strategy is not clear.' Explain this statement, with particular reference to personnel policy and strategy.
9. Your organisation is proposing to make extensive changes involving the introduction of new technology. The Chief Executive has asked you to prepare a report outlining the advantages and disadvantages of using external consultants for the purpose of advising what changes are required and the appropriate strategies for their implementation. Outline the points you would probably make.

2

LEADERSHIP AND PARTICIPATION

UNOFFICIAL AND OFFICIAL LEADERS

1. The unofficial leader

Leadership is the ability of a person to influence the thoughts and behaviour of others. In psychological studies, a leader is usually defined in terms of the group he or she leads; the leader is the person who directs and controls the group so that the purposes of the group are achieved. When a group forms spontaneously by a process of social interaction, it quite frequently has more than one leader at any one time. The leaders in such a situation may be rivals, but more frequently share between themselves the various leadership functions of planning, directing, reviewing, etc. Different circumstances may bring about a change in leadership, different leaders emerging who seem more capable of dealing with the new situation.

In commerce and industry the unofficial leader can be a very important person, particularly when the working group is strongly united. Hence, unofficial leaders are often given special and privileged treatment by management. However, the importance of the unofficial leader tends to be intermittent, becoming active at times of crisis and quiescent in more placid circumstances. On the other hand, the official leader, the person given formal authority over others, is always important because of his or her function of seeing that a certain area of the firm's business is effectively dealt with.

2. The official leader

Extending the definition in the preceding section, an official leader is a person who motivates and controls subordinates to work towards goals which are regarded by the organisation as desirable and possible. The subordinates must therefore be led in such a way that they value the rewards they are able to obtain from their work; these may be money, friendship, status, approval, a sense of achievement or a mixture of these.

The official leader, who may be called, for example, supervisor, section leader or manager, possesses *authority* partly because he or she has been appointed by the owners of the company (or their representatives) and partly because of his or her competence to hold the post. Subject to employment law, official leaders have *power* over subordinates, i.e. such leaders can get them to do things they would otherwise not do, through their right to punish or reward, control of resources, knowledge of the job, skills in handling people, etc. The way they combine these factors is called their *management style*, and a great deal of research has been carried out to try to identify the style which a manager should adopt to bring the best results from subordinates.

Note that authority and power need not coincide. Authority is the *right* to control, as determined by a person's position in the official management hierarchy. It is associated with taking decisions, giving orders, allocating work, and assigning rewards (pay rises, for instance) and penalties (e.g. demotion, suspension) to subordinates. Nevertheless, a person does not have to occupy an official management position in order to exercise power. Individuals can be powerful in consequence of their charisma, ability to satisfy other group members' needs, or their control over information or resources. Other determinants of power include:

(a) The extent to which a person is known, liked, trusted and respected by the group

(b) Whether group members identify with that individual

(c) Group members' perceptions that the person has expert knowledge of the activities on which the group is engaged, and/or their feelings that the person's position is legitimate – say because of seniority within the group.

LEADERSHIP STUDIES

3. Research on leadership

Early writers on leadership took the view that the *personality* of the leader was all important; they said that leaders were born, not made, perhaps coming from a certain class of society. They compiled lists of the personal qualities (intelligence, integrity, steadfastness, etc.) that were needed in a successful leader. These lists reflected of course the writers' own prejudices and were not based on careful observation and research. It was not an approach which could lead to any ways of improving leadership behaviour.

Later work on leadership has been conducted from a *behavioural* point of view; leaders and their subordinates are studied in actual work situations in order to discover whether certain kinds of leadership behaviour are more effective than others. Research of this kind has obvious difficulties, e.g. the presence of observers may distort normal behaviour, effectiveness is often difficult to measure, leaders' behaviour may be influenced by the quality of their subordinates, and descriptions of different management styles easily become very subjective. However, quite consistent results have been obtained from many hundreds of studies, two of the most important being summarised below.

4. Empirical studies

Systematic empirical research into leadership style began in the USA in the late 1940s. One of the first of the major studies occurred in the offices of the Prudential Life Insurance Company. Researchers divided the firm into relatively high-producing and relatively low-producing departments, using the available records of the clerical time taken to deal with a certain amount of work. The supervisors of all the departments were then interviewed to find out how they approached their jobs and their attitudes towards the company, their subordinates and their colleagues. As a result of these interviews it was possible to divide the supervisors into two classes:

(a) *Employee-centred*, in which emphasis was given to relationships within the department, and to the preferences, needs and capacities of individual subordinates. The supervisor believed in helping subordinates to get promotion and in giving them general rather than close supervision.

(b) *Production-centred*, in which the subordinates were closely supervised and controlled, both as to the pace and the method of work. The need to get the work done on time was continually emphasised.

When the productivity of the departments and the management styles of the supervisors were compared, it was found that there was a very strong tendency for the high-producing departments to be run by employee-centred supervisors and for the low-producing departments to be under production-centred supervisors, the efforts of the latter to push the work through being apparently self-defeating.

This pioneering study was followed by a wide-ranging investigation into management style conducted by researchers from Ohio State University, who collected a large amount of information about leadership approaches by means of interviews, observation and questionnaires. Two major factors emerged by which managerial style could be described:

(a) *Consideration* – including emphasis on mutual trust and respect between manager and subordinate, consideration for subordinates' feelings, and two-way communication.

(b) *Initiating structure* – the close definitions of the jobs of subordinates, great activity by the manager in planning, controlling, initiating new ideas and criticising subordinates.

It will be seen that these definitions of two independent dimensions of management behaviour are very similar to the definitions of employee-centredness and production-centredness of the Prudential studies. For convenience and clarity, the two dimensions will be called emphasis on task and emphasis on the people.

In the first the manager regards subordinates as factors of production at his or her disposal for performing a certain task. The manager will direct and control them in precise terms, their reward for accepting this being monetary payment. It is improbable that they would obtain satisfaction of ego or self-actualisation needs in these circumstances.

Managers who put the emphasis on people regard subordinates almost as equals and do not exercise strict authority over them. The manager assumes that they have ideas to contribute and that it is part of the leadership function to draw out these ideas. Another assumption is that they will produce good work without close or detailed supervision, i.e. that the job itself provides part of the motivation, perhaps by the satisfaction of the higher needs.

Another part of the Ohio State University study was concerned with the relationship between management style and employee satisfaction, as expressed in the rate of labour turnover and the number of grievances. It was found that both turnover and grievances were highest when the management style showed low consideration, irrespective of the degree of initiating structure that was shown. The lowest rates of turnover and grievances were found when the management style showed medium to high consideration with low initiating structure. Thus the degree of consideration seems to be the dominant factor in determining this area of employee behaviour. The research did not, however, show a similar clear relationship between a particular management style and productivity.

5. Subsequent research

Subsequent research has confirmed the Ohio findings, though the dimensions are often given other names.

(a) The analysis of leadership behaviour worked out by Blake and Mouton (*see* below) and known as the managerial grid uses the terms concern for people and concern for production.

(b) Another approach, by W. J. Reddin, calls the dimensions relationships orientation and task orientation, but adds a third dimension, effectiveness.

(c) F. E. Fiedler, in his research into leadership, uses the terms permissive, non-directive and task-controlling, directive.

(d) Douglas McGregor's theory X and theory Y which are described in 11 are similar in that theory X has a resemblance to initiating structure and theory Y to consideration.

(e) R. Likert uses the terms co-operative-motivation system and job-organisation system.

Other important studies were those of:

(a) K. Lewin, R. Lippitt and R. K. White, who investigated the effects of autocratic, democratic and *laissez-faire* leadership styles in boys clubs in Iowa in the USA, concluding that democratic approaches were generally more effective. Use of autocratic styles caused test subjects to become aggressive, discontented, and to lack initiative and commitment when completing tasks.

(b) R. Tannenbaum and W. H. Schmidt, whose researches led them to argue that managers should consider three sets of factors when choosing a leadership style:

(*i*) the background, values and experiences of the leader (including his or her abilities and attitudes towards employee participation)

(*ii*) the characteristics of subordinates (their competence, experience, interests, etc.)

(*iii*) the nature of the situation (type of task, extent of group cohesion, time available for taking decisions, and so on).

(c) W. W. Soujanen, who suggested that organisations which regularly experienced crisis situations tended to adopt authoritarian management styles, whereas 'routine-orientated' firms (i.e. normal, conventional businesses) usually opted for participative approaches.

Recent research into leadership has drawn a distinction between *transactional* and *transformational* leaders. Transactional leaders organise work efficiently, provide subordinates with the assistance and resources necessary for them to complete their duties, but do not attempt to transform employees' attitudes in order to increase their commitment to the firm. Transformational leaders, conversely, possess charisma, vision, and the ability to inspire subordinates towards *transcending* their immediate goals. This and other aspects of leadership theory are discussed in *Organisational Behaviour* in this series.

EFFECTIVE LEADERSHIP

6. The managerial grid

Robert Blake and Jane Mouton devised a 'managerial grid' illustrating degrees of concern for human relations and for efficiency. The grid is a taxonomy of management styles classified according to the manager's interest in subordinates as people in comparison with his or her concern for production. Each concern is rated on a scale from one to nine so that a 9,9 manager, for example, is one who possesses both a very high concern for people and a high concern for production. A 1,9 manager, who has a low concern for production but who greatly emphasises human relations, will pay careful attention to subordinates' human needs, but will exert little effort to ensure that work is actually done. Such a manager is likeable, enjoys satisfactory relations with subordinates and generates a friendly atmosphere in his or her department. The 9,1 manager arranges work as efficiently as possible, with scant regard for subordinates' feelings. Other potential combinations are 1,1

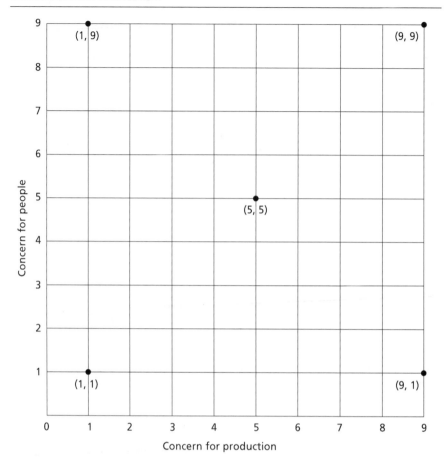

Figure 2.1 Blake and Mouton's managerial grid

managers, who make little effort to get work done or develop close personal relationships, and 5,5 managers who balance task performance with human relations considerations. Best of all is the 9,9 manager who achieves high production from committed, satisfied subordinates. The various positions on the grid are illustrated in Fig. 2.1.

7. Management style and effectiveness

Although reductions in labour turnover and grievances are very valuable, the principal aim of the research into management style is to establish its relation to effectiveness, that is the degree to which it facilitates adequate or high productivity.

An important factor determining which particular management style is effective is the task structure – the extent to which the work is defined or programmed. Task structure in most cases depends on the technology, and is best illustrated by describing its two extremes:

(a) Structured or highly-programmed work, e.g. assembly-line work in a mass-production factory, is strictly defined as to method and time. Each individual job is specialised and must be carried out as defined in order that it may fit into a complex production system. There are few work decisions the subordinate can make.

(b) Unstructured or loosely-programmed work, e.g. as found in a research laboratory, is defined in very broad terms and gives the subordinate a large number of decisions regarding methods and sequence. Sometimes the task itself is rather vague, and there may be many possible ways of accomplishing it. The subordinate is often given the freedom to choose the way he or she prefers.

In highly-programmed work the manager will almost inevitably emphasise the *task*, for it is his or her responsibility to ensure that jobs are done according to their precise specification. There is little purpose in asking employees for their suggestions about the way the work should be done, and it is impracticable to allow them to work at their own pace; such deviations would certainly upset the efficiency of the process, and might indeed be dangerous.

In contrast, the manager of unstructured work will as a rule obtain the best results by emphasising *people*, because most employees prefer to control and arrange their own work rather than be closely supervised, and they often welcome the opportunity to contribute suggestions and ideas. When the work is loosely-programmed, close supervision is unnecessary and tends to be resented. The manager's job should be to see that subordinates are self-motivating and self-directing.

In this analysis, individual differences among subordinates should not be overlooked; some do not expect or wish to contribute suggestions or take responsibility, while others (probably an increasing proportion) expect management to emphasise the people dimension and arrange jobs so that they will be less structured. The manager must therefore use his or her judgement to decide whether the attitudes of subordinates must override the requirements of the process.

8. Fiedler's theory of leadership effectiveness

The American psychologist F. E. Fiedler has put forward a theory, based on several studies, which modifies the simple relationship which has just been described. Fiedler suggests that although in general the task-centred approach is best for structured work, it may also be effective when the work is unstructured, relations between the manager and subordinates are poor and the manager's formal powers, e.g. of dismissal or promotion, are weak. In other words, when conditions are unfavourable for the manager the best plan is to take firm control of subordinates.

The theory goes on to confirm that in general the people-centred approach is best for unstructured work, but adds that this approach may also be

31

effective when the work is structured and the manager powerful but not well-liked. Fiedler's analysis thus uses four variables:

Emphasis on task or people
Task structure
Manager–subordinate relationships
Powers of the manager.

It shows that management style, to be effective, should take account of technology, social relationships and the place of the manager in the organisation.

Fiedler's work together with that of Tannenbaum and Schmidt and W.W. Soujanen formed the basis for the *contingency approach* to leadership, which asserts that there is no single management style that can be relied on to be completely effective in *all* situations. Rather, a leader's style should be varied to meet the needs of the particular situation to hand. Thus, leaders must be prepared to adjust their behaviour as circumstances change. This enables leaders to adopt management styles appropriate for specific groups and situations (e.g. using an autocratic approach when quick and unpopular decisions are needed). However, it could also lead to unpredictable and inconsistent behaviour on the leader's part. Moreover, managers require leadership training and experience to enable them to apply the contingency approach.

Further contingency approaches are those of P. Hersey and K.H. Blanchard, and J. Adair. Hersey and Blanchard developed a 'situational' model of leadership based on the 'maturity' of subordinates. Maturity is taken to mean an employee's work experience, technical competence, ability to assume responsibility, self-confidence and self-respect. According to the model, directive leadership is necessary for the control of freshly-recruited workers. Gradually, however, subordinates 'learn the ropes' and a participative management style becomes appropriate. Eventually, workers are able to act independently so that the need for close direction ends. A *laissez-faire* approach can now be applied.

John Adair suggests that, to be more effective, a leader must simultaneously satisfy three sets of interconnecting needs: task, group and individual. Task needs relate to the job being completed and involve planning, setting objectives, performance appraisal, work scheduling, etc. Group needs refer to the maintenance of team spirit, group cohesion, discipline, and other means for ensuring the group does not disintegrate. Individual needs concern the personal requirements of each group member and how these can be satisfied. Examples of measures for meeting individual needs are counselling (*see* 16:**16**), coaching (*see* 22:**8**), motivating and staff development.

9. Changing managers

It may sometimes be quite obvious that a manager's style is quite unsuitable for the work he or she is responsible for, and that the manager would be more effective if his or her style were to change.

The most usual example is the authoritarian, task-centred manager, in charge of relatively unstructured work. Because attitudes of this kind are deeply rooted in the manager's personality, they are very difficult to change, except superficially and temporarily. Since the style of many managers cannot be changed, it may be necessary in order to make the best use of their abilities to transfer them to work more appropriate to their style. Another possibility might be to change the degree to which the work is structured, but this would have great difficulties in practice.

10. Self-leadership and self-managed teams

Arguably there is little need for formal leadership in the modern workplace situation, which is increasingly likely to involve working in a team. According to this view, employees are quite capable of motivating themselves to perform unattractive as well as appealing tasks and to determine which group members are best qualified to complete particular duties. Advantages to self-managed teams include lower supervision costs, higher levels of employee interest in the work of the organisation as a whole, and hopefully the optimum use of human resources.

According to S. Kerr and J.M. Jermier, the need for leadership can be mitigated in many workplace situations by a number of factors:

(a) *Organisational characteristics* such as cohesive work groups that remove the need for supportive leadership, and the formalisation of working procedures (which results in group members not needing to ask a leader how to perform duties).

(b) *Job characteristics* e.g. routine duties, feedback within a task and/or interesting and satisfying work.

(c) *Employee characteristics*. It is unlikely that workers who are experienced, trained, willing and able will need to be led. Professionally qualified employees are normally capable of looking after themselves.

To the extent that work groups do not need to be led, the particular style of leadership applied by the group's formal supervisor is largely irrelevant, explaining perhaps the very mixed results that have been obtained from many empirical studies in the leadership behaviour field.

PARTICIPATION

Worker participation is the inclusion of employees in the decision-making process of the organisation. It implies also that the employees have access to sufficient information on which to base their share in decisions. In many companies in Great Britain, however, participation may merely consist of the management informing employee representatives of decisions that have already been made, and asking for their comments.

11. Theory X and Y

The American writer Douglas McGregor described two contrasting assumptions about the behaviour of employees, called theory X and theory Y.

(a) Theory X takes the view that the average employee dislikes work, will try to avoid responsibility, and will only be made to work by a mixture of close control and threats.

(b) Theory Y assumes that work is a natural and welcome activity which need not be externally controlled if the employee is adequately motivated, that employees will seek responsibility and that they can give valuable help in solving work problems.

McGregor took the view that theory Y was the correct assumption to make, and that firms should be organised on that basis. He said that theory X gave employees the opportunity to satisfy only basic and security needs at work, but a theory Y management attitude would enable them to satisfy higher needs, in particular ego and self-actualisation needs (*see* 4:2). A person's job should be so constructed that it gave the opportunity for full self-development.

There are similarities between theory X and task-centred management on the one hand, and theory Y and people-centred management on the other, and the comments made in the previous section about styles of management apply to a large extent to theories X and Y. Most employees would no doubt welcome the opportunity to have more control over their work and to put into practice their own ideas. There is undoubtedly a large fund of valuable expertise, experience and originality among employees that is often untapped by management.

Unfortunately some jobs are so closely limited, defined and integrated into a complex production process that opportunities to satisfy the higher needs at work are completely absent. Workers in jobs like these must quite often be treated in a theory X manner, i.e. coerced and controlled, if adequate effort is to be obtained. Moreover, there are many employees who do not expect to take responsibility at work and avoid it if they can. Therefore, management is sometimes justified in making theory X assumptions about employees.

12. Quality circles

A quality circle is a departmental workers' discussion group that meets regularly to consider, analyse, investigate and resolve production and quality problems. The group is trained in problem-solving techniques and, importantly, is given resources and (limited) authority to implement decisions. Circle leadership might be assumed by an existing departmental supervisor or by someone directly elected from the group. In their Western form, circles meet during working hours and participation may or may not be compulsory. If membership is voluntary, management might encourage participation *via* group bonuses, generous payments for expenses, hints of promotion for enthusiastic members, etc. Circles normally concentrate on mundane practical (rather than organisational) problems, and solve them using ideas and methods developed by circle members. Typically, circle activities are initiated by the circle, although management might occasionally refer problems to it for analysis and resolution. The advantages of quality circles are:

(a) Improved morale as workers become involved in departmental decision-taking

(b) Workers apply their skill, personal knowledge and experience to quality and productivity issues

(c) Circle decisions are taken by the people who must implement them so there is a high probability they will be carried out.

The problems with quality circles are:

(a) Apathy may arise among circle members who might feel they are undertaking (unpaid) extra duties the benefits of which will accrue entirely to the firm and not to circle members.

(b) Frustrations may result from the circle's inability to solve problems the sources of which are beyond its control.

(c) Antagonisms might develop between circle leaders and other managers about how particular difficulties should be overcome and over the extent of the resources and executive authority the circle should command.

(d) Within the group, friction may occur as low-status, low-paid employees offer more and better solutions to problems than do appointed supervisors and other higher-paid departmental superiors.

(e) The circle acquires experience of participative decision making, and may wish to apply this to other areas of the organisation's work (industrial relations or welfare, for example) – even though management might oppose employee participation apart from in quality circles.

13. Participation, empowerment and the quality of working life

Participation is an important ingredient of any programme intended to improve the quality of working life (QWL) of a firm's employees. Other elements of a QWL scheme might include the improvement of environmental conditions, increasing the flow of communication within the organisation, employee involvement in target setting, job design, introduction of staff development systems, having employees solve workplace problems, better leadership styles and interpersonal relationships, stress-reduction programmes, and generally enhancing the culture of the workplace. The rationale for improving the quality of working life is that employees will normally be more productive if, rather than just tolerating their lives at work, they actively enjoy the work experience.

35

Empowerment

An employee's feeling of being in control and of significantly contributing to an organisation's development can be greatly enhanced by 'empowering' that person to complete tasks and attain targets independently, without constantly having to refer back to management for permission to take certain actions. The employee is *trusted* to take sensible decisions. Hence, for example, salespeople might be empowered to offer special discounts to prospective customers, production operatives can be empowered to decide the speed of an assembly line, and work teams may be empowered to determine the extent and intensity of the use of robots within a section of a firm. The aim is to enable employees who actually have to deal with problems to implement solutions quickly and without recourse to supervisors and/or higher levels of management. This is increasingly necessary as large and bureaucratic organisations 'delayer' management hierarchies in the search for administrative efficiency and lower costs. Removal of one or more entire layers of the management pyramid is a fast and sometimes highly effective means for streamlining management communication and control.

Empowerment differs from 'delegation' in that whereas the latter is the devolution of duties from boss to subordinate (albeit with the authority to implement decisions), empowerment is a general *approach* to operational management, requiring not just the passing down of power and responsibility through a hierarchy but also that the individual worker actively contributes to improving the performance of tasks.

Benefits to empowerment include:

- The encouragement of individual creativity and initiative, commitment to the enterprise and team spirit
- Decision-taking at the most suitable levels
- Facilitation of performance management (*see* 17:**13**)
- Faster and more flexible responses to customer requirements
- Higher levels of self-confidence and motivation among employees
- Better relations between management and front-line (customer contact) employees
- A 'meetings of minds' *vis-à-vis* customers and the firm's staff regarding what constitutes product quality
- Receipt of valuable ideas for new products from front-line employees
- Provision of an early warning system regarding customer dissatisfaction
- Immediate correction of mistakes.

Problems with empowerment are that greater care has to be exercised when hiring employees, who then need more training than in conventional circumstances. Staff might take bad decisions, and customers may be treated differently, leading to resentments among those not receiving favours. The entire organisation might need to be redesigned in order to make empowerment operationally effective.

If empowerment is to succeed, employees need to receive:

- Information concerning the organisation's performance
- Power to make decisions that genuinely influence the direction and performance of the organisation
- Knowledge enabling them to understand and contribute to organisational performance
- Rewards that are based on the organisation's performance.

14. Participation in company-level decisions

All the above are concerned with employees' participation in decisions affecting them directly and in the short term. There is plenty of evidence that most, though not all, employees are more than willing to take part in decisions of this type, but not very much evidence about their willingness to be involved in decisions at the highest level, e.g. manufacturing or investment policy.

In the great majority of UK organisations there is very little participation by employees in policy decisions; sometimes there are varying degrees of *consultation*.

(a) Employees are consulted before a decision is made, but the management is not bound by their views, though it usually tries to take them into account.

(b) Employees are informed of decisions and are consulted about their effects. The decisions may be modified in detail.

(c) Employees are informed of decisions, and negotiations take place between them and the management about implementation. The detailed application of a redundancy decision is an example.

(d) There is a company suggestion scheme.

In many companies there is neither participation nor consultation, but merely information to employees about the decisions that have been made. Note however that the situation is entirely different in most other European Union countries, where there is statutory provision for employee participation in management decision-making in most countries, either through compulsory employee representation on company boards or through 'works councils' (see below). Details of national differences in representation schemes are given in Chapter 24.

15. Works councils

Works councils are bodies comprising representatives of management and employees who meet regularly to discuss matters of mutual interest. Under an EU Directive (*see* 24:4) works councils are compulsory for certain sizes of firm (measured in terms of number of employees) in all European Union nations. In addition to the minimum requirements laid down by the Directive, some EU countries have laws which require large companies to delegate to their works councils the authority to *take decisions* on particular topics, effectively giving employee representatives the right of veto on management's proposals in specific fields. The range of issues involved differs substantially from country to country. Decision-making powers vary from internal works rules (e.g. the operation of grievance procedures) to recruitment methods and whether the firm is to take on part-time or temporary workers. In Germany and the Netherlands, employee representatives on works councils have the legal right to delay certain important management decisions (on company mergers for instance). Examples of issues that are subject to decision-making by works councils are given in Chapter 24.

16. Advantages and drawbacks of works councils

Works councils are said to possess several advantages:

(a) Management is compelled to seek a consensus with unions on fundamental issues, hence avoiding many possible sources of conflict.

(b) Works councils come to execute certain management functions (allocation of overtime, decisions on working methods, determination of promotion criteria, etc.) that otherwise would have to be undertaken by alternative (and perhaps more costly) management committees. Employees assume *obligations* for the operation of the business as well as rights of consultation.

(c) Discussions between management and labour encourage the latter to propose new ideas, offer alternative solutions to problems and generally adopt constructive and useful perspectives.

(d) Change can be introduced more easily, since a works council provides a useful forum for explaining the needs for and implications of new methods.

(e) Management benefits as it is quickly made aware of any problems related to intended developments that are likely to provoke hostile opposition from the workforce and hence can alter its plans in order to remove or minimise employee resistance.

Although it is known that employee apathy frequently results in works councils not operating within many companies in countries where employee representative is legally mandatory, the *existence* of legislative procedures itself can create an environment in which managers are sensitive to the need to consult with and gain the confidence of the workforce, leading perhaps to greatly improved management/labour relations. The latter will facilitate co-operation and the smooth running of an enterprise. At the national level, moreover, stable employee relations contribute significantly to a country's competitive advantage. There are fewer costly stoppages and delivery dates are met (an important point for countries extensively committed to international trade).

Note however that stability has a price: wages and conditions tend to be higher in countries where compulsory participation applies. Other disadvantages of works councils include:

(a) Efficiency improvements that involve shedding labour might be impeded.

(b) They are financially expensive to operate (time costs, rooms, secretarial support, etc.).

(c) Decision-taking can be slow, and many employee representatives will not have the technical knowledge upon which they can base decisions.

(d) Employees may adopt short-term perspectives, and might oppose decisions that would benefit the company in the long run but do not offer many rewards to employees in the immediate future. Innovation and enterprise may be discouraged.

(e) Councils can easily degenerate into vehicles for plant-level collective bargaining, undermining normal management/union negotiating machinery.

17. Supervisory boards

In Belgium, Germany and the Netherlands there is a legal requirement that large companies have two-tier boards of directors. The lower tier is an 'executive board', comprising managerial employees of the firm responsible for day-to-day operational management. Above this is a 'supervisory board', which takes strategic decisions in relation to the overall direction of the enterprise. By law, employee representatives must sit on the supervisory boards of companies in these countries. The functions of supervisory boards include:

(a) The appointment and dismissal of executive managers and the determination of their remunerations

(b) Deciding the overall direction of the enterprise (its products, markets, major new investments, etc.)

(c) Matters concerning mergers and takeovers and how the company is to be financed.

The rationale for the system is that general policy-making is undertaken objectively and independently without interference from executives with vested interests in outcomes, and that employee interests may be considered in the absence of line managers who control workers. Also, tough decisions that adversely affect senior line managers can be taken more easily.

18. Worker directors on supervisory boards

The basic argument in favour of having worker directors is that since employees spend much of their lives working for and making valuable contributions

39

to employing organisations they should be entitled, through elected representatives, to some say in how their employers' businesses are run. Also, worker directors can criticise management's intentions and put new interpretations on issues and events. The counterargument is that since firms are owned by entrepreneurs or shareholders who put their personal capital at risk, it is inappropriate for anyone other than directors selected by owners to control a company's assets. Worker directors, moreover, may face substantial difficulties which prevent their being effective in this work.

The problems confronting worker directors include:

(a) Possible reluctance of other board members to disclose confidential information to employees' representatives in case it is passed on to union negotiators.

(b) Potential hostility and social ostracism from other directors, who might conduct secret board meetings to decide key issues without the presence of employee representatives.

(c) The possibility of special privileges afforded to worker directors – higher status, preferential treatment, expenses, time off for board meetings – might cause them to lose contact with basic-grade workers.

Nevertheless, worker directors can voice criticism of management's stated intentions and express the workplace point of view. Management is confronted with new and different interpretations of issues. Also, the presence on the board of employee representatives underlines senior management's commitment to employee welfare, and a climate of mutual confidence and co-operation between management and labour may emerge.

Specific implications of having worker directors on supervisory boards are:

(a) The knowledge and experience of employee representatives can be directly applied to *strategic* decisions without employee representatives having to argue with line managers.

(b) Matters concerning human relations are automatically elevated to the highest level of decision-making within the organisation. Note that since the supervisory board appoints and dismisses senior managers then the latter will be highly sensitive to worker director's views, and to human relations issues generally.

(c) Arguably, the presence of employee representatives on a supervisory board facilitates the financial stability of the company, because worker directors' concerns for employees' continuity of employment invariably cause them to argue in favour of profit retention and the accumulation of reserves to guard against temporary economic downturns. Also, employee representatives will oppose any merger or takeover that could result in redundancies.

19. The Fifth Draft Directive on Company Law

Under this European Commission proposal all EU based companies with more than 1,000 workers would be required to have a two-tier board or a single board with a majority of non-executive directors empowered to appoint and dismiss executive directors. Between one third and one half of a single or supervisory board would have to consist of employee representatives. Alternatively, worker participation could be achieved via a separate works council with proper representation on the board. A number of objections have been raised against the proposal, including the following:

(a) Agendas of board meetings could become dominated by personnel management and industrial relation issues, at the expense of considering strategic and operational matters.

(b) Businesses affected by the Directive would need to train employee representatives in the principles of management, company structure, finance, market environments, etc., in order to enable them to understand board-room discussions.

(c) Companies operating in several EU countries would experience severe practical problems resulting from their boards having to include employee representatives from several countries, speaking different languages (thus requiring the presence of interpreters at board meetings), from widely disparate trade union backgrounds, and with contrasting cultural perspectives.

(d) Conflicts might be created between agreements reached by worker and other directors at the board level, and settlements concluded via plant-level collective bargaining in divisions and subsidiaries of the firm.

20. Participation – a summing up

In such a controversial subject, influenced so much by individual attitudes, it is impossible to come to a clear conclusion. Readers might like to make their own judgments, based on the following arguments, firstly in favour of participation and secondly against it.

In favour of participation

(a) It makes use of the knowledge and experience of employees, which are usually at least as valuable as a manager's.

(b) Employees are more motivated in their work if they can take part in decisions affecting their work. If they think that decisions are unfair to them, they will be less motivated.

(c) The greater the number of people involved in a decision, the less the possibility of important factors being overlooked.

(d) Unworkable impracticable decisions are avoided.

(e) Many decisions impinge directly on employees' lives; it is only right that they should help to make them.

(f) Employees by their efforts contribute to the prosperity of the company; it is right that their voice should be heard.

(g) Modern educational methods and policies encourage independent, informed thinking. Employees should be encouraged to apply this to their work.

Against participation

(a) Involving the employees in decisions is time-consuming; many decisions have to be made urgently.

(b) Most employees do not have the technical knowledge on which to base the majority of decisions.

(c) Employees have no responsibility for making the best use of the company's assets and maximising profits; the managers of the company have this responsibility and their decisions must recognise it.

(d) Employees tend to take the short-term view, and may oppose decisions which may benefit the company in the long run but do not offer many rewards to employees in the immediate future. Innovation and enterprise may be discouraged.

(e) Employee participation at company policy level needs such cumbersome machinery that it is only possible and genuine in small companies.

(f) Many employees take the view that they are not paid to make decisions, and will only become involved in decisions which affect them directly.

(g) There is a fundamental conflict of interests between employers and employees; negotiation is more realistic than participation.

The arguments against participation are much weaker, some would say non-existent, when the employees are also the owners of the company. There are a few companies, usually rather small, of this type in the UK; they seem to be both commercially successful and stable. Most have been created and built up by a single owner who has then given them away to the firm's employees. Possibly the number of such companies is too small for reliable conclusions to be drawn.

References

Adair, J. (1983), *Effective Leadership*, Gower.
Blake, R.R. and Mouton, J.S. (1964), *The Managerial Grid*, Gulf Publishing.
Fiedler, F.E. (1967), *A Theory of Leadership Effectiveness*, McGraw-Hill.

Kerr, S. and Jermier, J.M. (1978), Substitutes for leadership; Their meaning and measurement, *Organisational Behaviour and Human Performance*, Dec. 1978, 375–403.

Lewin, K., Lippit, R. and White, R.K., Patterns of aggressive behaviour in experimentally created social environments, *International Journal of Social Psychology*, Vol. 10.

Likert, R. (1961), *New Patterns of Management*, McGraw-Hill.

Reddin, W.J. (1970), *Managerial Effectiveness*, McGraw-Hill.

Soujanen, W.W. (1966), *The Dynamics of Management*, Holt, Rinehart and Winston.

Tannenbaum, R. and Schmidt, W.H. (1958), How to choose a leadership pattern, *Harvard Business Review*, March-April 1958.

Progress test 2

1. What is the difference between an unofficial and an official leader?
2. Define employee-centred and production-centred leadership.
3. What is the managerial grid?
4. What is worker participation?
5. Summarise theories X and Y. Is theory Y always preferable to theory X?
6. What is empowerment?
7. Describe the problems attached to quality circles.
8. Summarise the arguments for and against worker participation.
9. What are the functions of a supervisory board?
10. Many organisations nowadays are involved in quality improvement programmes or customer-care initiatives. What is the role of the personnel function in promoting and reinforcing these activities?

3

GROUPS

THE BEHAVIOUR OF WORKING GROUPS

1. The formation of a working group

Work is rarely an activity carried out in solitude; most of us have colleagues whose wishes and personalities we have to learn to understand because we work closely with them. When we work with others, merely understanding them is not enough; it is necessary for us to modify our behaviour to some extent, acting in ways which are acceptable to them rather than completely satisfying to ourselves.

After people have worked closely and continuously with each other for some time, the mutual adjustments of behaviour settle down into a fixed pattern, a set of mental attitudes becomes established which all share, and very often certain customs become so strongly entrenched that they are almost compulsory. A collection of individuals has now been transformed into a *working group*, which is a special type of *social group*.

A group is a collection of two or more people who possess a common purpose. Work groups may be created by management to perform specific functions, or can emerge naturally by themselves. The formation of groups at work is at once a natural consequence of the division of labour and an important means of fulfilling individual social needs. Work groups may be primary or secondary, formal or informal. A primary group consists of members who come into direct face-to-face contact. Secondary groups are larger, less personal, and lack immediate direct contact between members. Examples of primary groups are small departments within a firm, project teams, families, sports teams or other direct-contact recreational associations. Secondary groups might be factories, communities, long assembly lines where workers do not come into contact with each other, or geographical divisions of a firm. These groups will be less solid and cohesive than primary groups, though interactions between members will still occur. Within primary groups, communications are rapid and direct. Membership will often provide social and psychological support during times of stress.

Formal and informal groups

Formal groups are deliberately created by management for particular predetermined purposes. Management selects group members, leaders and methods of doing work. A formal group may be defined with respect to a task, function, status within the managerial hierarchy (such as members of the board of directors), or length of service with the firm (long-serving employees might receive privileges not available to others and hence constitute an identifiable group). Formal groups are characterised by a high degree of managerial involvement in co-ordinating, controlling and defining the nature of the activities they undertake. Group structures are clearly defined, and their tasks are carefully delineated.

Informal groups can form without management support. They are established by people who feel they possess a common interest. Members organise themselves and develop a sense of affinity to each other and a common cause. Often, it is an informal group that actually determines how much work is done.

Hopefully, the aims of the informal group that spring up within an organisation will correspond to the objectives of its management, but they might not. Indeed, informal groups could form specifically to oppose the wishes of management. Formal groups are created to meet the needs of an organisation; informal groups arise to satisfy the needs of its individual members. Management must recognise the importance of informal groups for organisational efficiency and their potential for disrupting organisational plans.

Group norms

A group norm is a shared perception of how things should be done, or a common attitude, feeling or belief. Norms may relate to working methods, to how much work should be done and how enthusiastically it should be done; quality of output, relations with management (and trade unions); how various people should be addressed and treated; and a whole range of other issues. Group norms are particularly important in determining workers' attitudes towards change, since norms can create or overcome resistance to new methods and ideas.

As norms emerge, individuals will start to behave according to how they feel other group members expect them to behave. Initially, an entrant into an existing group will feel isolated and insecure and hence will actively seek out established norms that will act as a guide to how that person ought to behave. Norms, therefore, facilitate the integration of an individual into a group, and thus will be eagerly accepted by new members.

2. The work of Elton Mayo

The importance of the working group was first shown clearly by Elton Mayo and his colleagues in a detailed study of worker behaviour at the Western

Electric Company factory at Hawthorne, near Chicago, between 1924 and 1932.

Mayo had been called in by the management because production at the factory was thought to be too low. At first Mayo experimented with the illumination, following the current belief that if physical conditions were suitable and the pay adequate there was no reason why employees should not work hard. A puzzling result of the experiment was that output increased even when lighting was made worse. Because definite conclusions were difficult to draw from the behaviour of a large department when its working conditions were varied, he eventually segregated five female operators into a separate room so that their behaviour could more easily be controlled and observed.

3. The relay assembly test room

During the period 1927 to 1929 variations in rest pauses and working hours were made and compared with the output of the five women. Throughout the period, even during the times when working conditions had been made worse, output steadily increased. When the women were interviewed to find an explanation for this unexpected result they said:

(a) They enjoyed working in the test room, and worked harder there than in the factory because they felt special.

(b) They did not regard the observer who was present in the room with them as a normal supervisor because he explained things to them and reassured them.

(c) The experiment seemed to show that management was interested in them.

(d) They helped each other at work and had developed close friendships with each other away from work.

(e) They felt united and had a common purpose.

4. The bank wiring room

Between November 1931 and May 1932 a group of men were put into a special room but in other respects continued working under their usual conditions. The group, which was engaged in the assembly of banks for use in telephone exchanges, consisted of nine wiremen, three soldermen and two inspectors. An observer also sat in the room but did not participate in any way, the men sometimes being interviewed outside the room by another member of Mayo's staff. A supervisor was formally in charge of the men, but was present in the room only part of the time. Payment was made according to a rather complicated piece-work scheme. The following observations were made:

(a) The men worked to an unofficial level of output; if anyone worked harder than this he was abused by the others.

(b) Reported figures for output and delay time (when stoppages occurred for reasons beyond a worker's control) were false; they showed a constant, instead of a variable, output week by week.

(c) The men often exchanged jobs, contrary to management instructions. They often helped each other.

(d) The supervisor knew about these practices, but did not try to stop them. He was not regarded by the group as their leader.

(e) One wireman, though conforming with the unofficial norms of production, used to tell the foreman about irregular practices. He was the outcast of the group, and was called 'squealer'.

(f) Unofficial leaders in the group were more influential than the official leader, the foreman.

5. Conclusions from the Hawthorne studies

The steadily increasing level of output in the relay assembly room was ascribed by Mayo to the beneficial effects of a united working group outweighing the deteriorating physical working conditions. The bank wiring room study had shown, however, that a united working group could oppose management interests by restricting its output. Thus the working group was shown to be powerful enough to override working conditions on the one hand and a payment-by-results scheme on the other.

When the Hawthorne results were published the relay assembly room received most attention, and the human relations movement which appeared soon afterwards emphasised the encouragement of united working groups because it was thought that good performance would follow. This advice did not always bring the hoped-for result, firstly because it is not always possible to manipulate employees into cohesive groups, and secondly because it is never certain that the groups, if formed, would agree that their own objectives coincided with those of management, i.e. they might resemble the bank wiring room rather than the relay assembly room.

6. Working groups – benefits to the employee

An individual at work can derive certain benefits from becoming a member of a group:

- Satisfaction of social needs
- The benefits of shared experience, e.g. an experienced worker showing the ropes to a newcomer
- Mutual support, e.g. colleagues backing up someone who is having a dispute with management

- A basis for self-expression, because the security afforded by the group often encourages creativity.

GROUP FORMATION AND DEVELOPMENT

7. Formation of working groups

A collection of individual employees does not automatically become a working group. The conditions which will cause a group to form and make it cohesive are:

(a) The employees must be near enough to each other for easy face-to-face communication.

(b) The work they are doing must be related; e.g. they form parts of a chain (like a progressive assembly line), are doing similar jobs (as in the relay assembly room), or have the same purpose (like a committee organising a works outing).

(c) The individuals must be compatible, without great differences in status, skill or education.

(d) The total number should not exceed about twelve, though this depends on physical arrangements in the workplace.

(e) An external threat will often cause a collection of individuals to form themselves into a group.

Group development

According to B.W. Tuckman, groups develop through four stages as follows:

1 Members learn about each other, about the nature and purpose of the group and the constraints that limit its activities. Group structures, status hierarchies and patterns of interaction among members are determined. Rules of behaviour are established and individuals tell each other about their perceptions of the group's structure and objectives. This stage is sometimes referred to as the 'orientation' or *'forming'* phase.
2 Disputes and power struggles arise. There is internal group conflict, criticism and open questioning of the group's goals. This is the 'confrontation' or *'storming'* phase.
3 Conflicts are resolved and a division of work and responsibilities among group members is tentatively implemented. Specialisations develop; individual differences are recognised and 'who does what' disputes disappear. Group norms (*see* **1** above) emerge. This is the 'differentiation' or *'norming'* phase.
4 Eventually, group productivity increases, there is much collaboration among members and commitment to the group. Individuals value the contri-

butions of their colleagues and accept their idiosyncrasies. A decision-making system acceptable to all the group's members is established. People get on with their work. This is the 'collaboration' or *'performing'* phase of the process.

Resistance to change

A group is something to lean on when things go wrong. It acts to support and reinforce the individual's view of the outside world. Such benefits greatly encourage conformity to group norms. Membership of a group provides individuals with companionship, social experience, opportunities for self-expression and social intercourse. Against these benefits, however, individuals must be prepared to modify their behaviour to fit in with group norms. The more valuable group membership is perceived as being, the more the individual will want to conform. Feelings of attachment will be greater, and the power of the group to compel obedience to established norms is enhanced. Eventually group behaviour will settle down to a fixed routine: conformity is demanded of new entrants who must demonstrate their willingness to abide by group norms. The group will continue to function despite changes of personnel. It becomes a self-perpetuating identity.

In consequence, groups are often resistant to change. Members become set in their ways and attitudes; they come to believe the group norm is right – no matter what the circumstances – and of course any deviation from the norm would have to be explained and justified by the individual to other members. And if the deviation is not accepted by the group the deviant member is liable to face social ostracism.

8. Behaviour of working groups

When a working group has come into existence it will behave in certain characteristic ways, very much as if it had a life of its own independent of the lives of the individuals included in it.

(a) The group will produce a settled system of personal relationships and customs.

(b) These customs sometimes include restrictions on output.

(c) Individuals will often behave more in the way the group expects than as they would if left to themselves.

(d) The group exerts great pressure on all its members to conform to its own standards of behaviour.

(e) Newcomers to the group are often made to feel unwelcome. Groups vary in this respect just as individuals vary in their ability to become easily accepted by a group.

(f) The group tends to resist change imposed on it, and will react to it slowly because of the threat to its existence, its security, its customs and its pattern of relationships.

(g) Unofficial leaders emerge in the group, changing according to the needs of the situation at the time. When the group is in open conflict with the management, for example, it may choose as its leader a person whom normally its members would describe as an agitator. When conditions settle down, a new leader might emerge who would be a more diplomatic person.

(h) A group often seems to follow the same motivation process as an individual – searching for and eventually perceiving satisfying goals. It can be frustrated and show the negative reactions of aggression, regression, resignation and fixation.

(i) The character of a group will not change because one person leaves it or joins it, unless that person is extremely influential.

(j) An external threat or the competition of another group will increase the cohesiveness of a group.

9. Group cohesiveness

The extent to which individuals feel that they are members of a group, and the strength of their attachment to the group, is called cohesiveness or morale. It is shown by the frequent use of the word 'we' instead of 'I', the help group members give each other and the perseverance and enthusiasm they show. Cohesive working groups usually have low rates of labour turnover and absence.

Many factors contribute to the creation of group cohesion, including the following:

(a) How often group members come into contact with each other.

(b) How enthusiastically members support group aims.

(c) The extent to which members feel they belong to an exclusive and special group.

(d) Whether members share common interests.

(e) Whether members have a common background, education, age, outlook, or ethnic or social origin.

(f) The existence of external threats to the group.

(g) How easily group members can communicate.

(h) Whether members are engaged on similar work.

A high degree of cohesiveness is not always linked with high productivity. Restriction of output by working groups is widespread, and is usually found in groups cohesive enough to be able to rely on the observance of limits of output by its members. On the other hand when organisation structure or work methods are rearranged to facilitate the formation of working groups, productivity is sometimes increased.

It is possible to find any combination of cohesiveness and productivity; no doubt many people have encountered happy united groups which do very little work, or sections composed of workers who dislike each other but nevertheless show above-average rates of output. The relationship between cohesiveness and productivity is similar to that between individual job satisfaction and productivity, that is it depends on the group's perception of its own interests. However, although the effect of group cohesiveness on output is uncertain, an employer's costs will nearly always be reduced by the presence of cohesive working groups because labour turnover and absence will be comparatively low.

10. Working groups: implications for management

Research shows that working groups can be powerful forces within an organisation. Sometimes their presence is beneficial to management, e.g. the relay assembly room, and sometimes the reverse, e.g. the bank wiring room, because there is no reliable connection between the cohesiveness of a group and its rate of production.

The working group must also be considered in relation to the formal structure of the organisation; does the group coincide with an official section or department, or does it draw its membership from several of them? Frequently a company is organised by function, i.e. production workers belong to one department, maintenance workers to another and clerks to a third. An informal working group, consisting of people working near each other on the same task, could possibly include members of each of these three departments. A somewhat similar situation occurs when the unofficial leader of the group and the officially appointed foreperson or manager are rivals for the allegiance of the group, creating confusion and lack of control.

If management wishes to make constructive use of informal working groups, and minimise the difficulties they can sometimes bring, the following measures are often recommended:

(a) By ensuring that working conditions are good, that employment policies are fair and by taking a personal interest in the employees, encourage groups to perceive the company's interests as coinciding with their own, thus increasing productivity.

(b) In any case, making it easier for cohesive groups to form because labour turnover and absenteeism will be reduced.

(c) When making changes, remember the instinctive opposition of the working group.

(d) Arrange for competition between groups, so that cohesiveness will increase. Greater output may also occur.

(e) Examine incentive schemes to see if they can be based on the output of the group instead of the individual.

(f) If practicable, make the working group coincide with the official section or department. In some cases the functional division of authority may have to be abandoned.

(g) If it is not possible to give the unofficial leader an official post, give some sort of recognition perhaps by including that person in joint consultation procedures. Train forepeople and managers in human relations skills so that the group will be more satisfied with its official leadership.

TEAMWORKING

11. Teams

A team is a special sort of group. All teams are groups, but groups do not necessarily behave as teams. The defining characteristic of a team is that its members *voluntarily* co-ordinate their work in order to achieve group objectives. Team members are highly interdependent, and each individual must to some extent interpret the nature of his or her particular role. Teams have leaders who may or may not be appointed by an outside body (higher management, for example), but the authority of the leader of a team – as distinct from any working group – is fully accepted by all its members.

The team leader represents the group to the outside world and is formally answerable for its behaviour. Within a team there will be a high degree of group cohesion, much interaction, mutual support and shared perceptions of issues. Team members will be willing to interchange roles, share workloads and generally help each other out. Typically, each team member will hold other members in high regard, and will experience much satisfaction from belonging to the team. The leader of a team can improve team spirit through:

- Representing and defending the team in the outside world, e.g. by fighting for extra resources on their behalf
- Clarifying 'territorial divisions' among team members, hence ensuring that all members are fully aware of their individual and collective responsibilities
- Encouraging members to suggest new working methods.

Other causes of good team spirit are:

- A fair distribution of work and responsibilities within the group, especially of unpleasant or exceptionally demanding tasks
- Well-designed work programmes with realistic completion dates
- Compatibility of the personal characteristics of participants.

Symptoms of poor teamwork are easily recognised: absenteeism, latecoming, high staff turnover, bad temper, deprecatory remarks about other team members, and so on. Staff lose confidence in the team's ability to achieve its objectives; comment is interpreted as criticism, the quality of work declines, staff lack effort, and petty grievances arise. Causes of such problems may include bad physical working conditions, wage levels and relativities, terms and conditions of employment (feeling of job insecurity, for example) or poor interpersonal relations within the group. Further problems might relate to the status of the group in the hierarchy of the total organisation.

Reasons for teamworking

These include the introduction of modern management methods such as cell-based manufacturing, just-in-time production, total quality management, etc., and/or the consequences of delayering (*see* 6:**13**), empowerment (*see* 2:**13**), business process re-engineering (*see* 6:**13**), downsizing and the use of flexible working practices. Most of these techniques involve a slimming down of the organisation and the need, therefore, to concentrate the expertise of the remaining people into distinct units rather than their being scattered around the firm. Also the majority of the methods previously mentioned demand *cross-functional* working that only multi-disciplinary teams can provide (*via* the pooling of skills, ideas and experience).

Implementation of teamworking

Simply setting up teams to complete particular tasks will not improve organisational effectiveness of *itself*: supportive management structures and personnel practices (*vis-à-vis* recruitment, training, reward systems, etc.) are also required. Indeed, a major cultural shift among employees might be needed.

If it is to succeed, teamworking must be accompanied by a shift in the focus of the firm's management style away from individuals and towards teams. Also the company will need to revise its human resource management policies in order to facilitate teamworking.

Specific problems that could be experienced during implementation include:

- Lack of clear definition of team roles
- Bad selection and/or inadequate training of team leaders
- Failure to modify the firm's reward system to accommodate teamworking
- Absence of proper procedures for evaluating team performances
- Constructing teams from existing employees who are not suitable for teamworking
- Allocation to individuals of personal as well as team duties, so that they do not have enough time to complete either (bearing in mind the extra meetings and communications that teamwork involves)
- Certain team members not pulling their weight, leading to resentments among other participants who feel they are 'carrying' the people

concerned. Appraisal of team performance needs to identify individual contributions to a team's failure or success.

Rewards

The main options available for rewarding team members are:

(a) A flat rate wage paid to each member of the team.

(b) Group payment-by-results systems.

(c) Individual wage rates paid to team participants plus team bonuses.

(d) Flat rate wages as in **(a)** accompanied by individual bonuses for exceptional contributions to team performance (though note how individual performance related pay might create internal competition that disrupts the work of a team).

12. Team building

In the 1970s, R Meredith Belbin and colleagues developed a theory of team building which suggested that certain types of individual do not perform well when working together in the same team. Belbin argued that people have different psychological characteristics which cause them to adopt particular roles at work, and that an appropriate combination of persons assuming various roles is essential for the creation of a well-balanced team. Nine team roles were identified, each of which needed to be fulfilled within a successful team (although they did not have to be present in equal measure). Team members would instinctively adopt specific roles according to their psychological make-ups, defined in terms of their intelligence, extroversion/ introversion, dominance, and degree of stability or anxiety. The nine team roles were as follows:

1 *Co-ordinator*. The co-ordinator is a mentally stable individual, extrovert and dominant, and makes an ideal chairperson. He or she is self-confident, mature, a good speaker and listener, and adept at clarifying issues and facilitating group decisions. Unfortunately, other team members may perceive the person as manipulative and as someone who personally avoids completing tasks.

2 *Team worker*. This person is also mentally stable and extrovert, but low in dominance. The team worker is perceptive, able to identify problems, and promotes harmony within the group. However, he or she will avoid confrontation and tends to be indecisive.

3 *Specialist*. The specialist is a dedicated professional who provides technical skills and knowledge. He or she may fall into any personality category.

4 *Plant*. A 'plant' is a major source of a team's ideas and creativity, although the person might not be a good communicator. Plants are imaginative problem solvers: intelligent, introvert and dominant.

5 *Shaper*. This personality type is dynamic, outgoing, extrovert, dominant and highly strung. The shaper is task-orientated, argumentative, and thrives on pressure. He or she will overcome obstacles, albeit at the expense of other team members' feelings.

6 *Completer-finisher*. The completer-finisher is an unassertive introvert who is reluctant to delegate, and inclined to worry unduly. Strengths of this personality type are that such people are painstaking, conscientious and have a permanent sense of urgency.

7 *Implementer*. An implementer is practical, stable and controlled, and capable of turning ideas into action. He or she is disciplined and reliable, but prone to inflexibility and rigid attitudes.

8 *Monitor-evaluator*. This person is a critic rather than a creator: stable, intelligent, introvert, and capable of deep analysis of issues. Such individuals lack warmth, are rarely able to inspire others, yet are usually correct in their assessments.

9 *Resource investigator*. The resource investigator is a relaxed, positive and enthusiastic person who goes outside the group to discover new ideas and information. He or she is a dominant extrovert who inclines towards over-optimism and tends to lose interest in projects once his or her initial enthusiasm has passed.

Problems with the Belbin approach include its subjectivity (there is little empirical evidence concerning the personal characteristics of members of highly successful teams) and the difficulty of appraising *team* as opposed to individual performance. There is little hard evidence that any one mix of team types is any more effective than others.

A somewhat similar categorisation of team roles was developed in the 1980s by C Margerison and D McCann. According to these authors there are three aspects of team performance:

1 The extent of the functions that need to be carried out by the team. Margerison and McCann measured this by a 'types of work index' (TWI).

2 Individual preferences concerning the way each person works. Typically, people concentrate on things they enjoy doing and neglect or perform badly tasks they dislike. A 'team management index' (TMI) was constructed to analyse personal preferences.

3 Communications and interactions within the team, as measured by a 'linking skills index' (LSI).

Eight major team roles were identified:

1 The *creator-innovator* who obtains and experiments with new ideas.

2 The *explorer-promoter* who looks for and informs others of fresh opportunities.

3 The *assessor-developer* who tests the applicability of various ideas.

4 The *thruster-organiser* who devises and implements new ways of making things work.

5 The *concluder-producer* who is best at operating existing systems and practices.

6 The *controller-inspector* who checks and audits systems.

7 The *upholder-maintainer* who ensures that standards are upheld.

8 The *reporter-adviser* who gathers and disseminates information.

Additionally all team roles must perform linking activities, in order to co-ordinate and integrate the work of the other eight roles.

Relative needs for the fulfillment of the various roles within a particular team were assessed using the TWI, a 64-item questionnaire. The personal preferences of the individuals who would undertake particular jobs were evaluated *via* the TMI, which categorises people under four headings:

1 Extrovert/introvert.

2 Practical/creative.

3 Analytical/believing. An analytical person uses objective criteria when taking decisions, whereas the other personality type pays more attention to personal beliefs and principles.

4 Structured/flexible. Someone who is 'structured' is well-organised, neat and tidy, and likes to take decisions quickly. A 'flexible' individual prefers to spend time thinking over a problem and will not reach conclusions until all relevant information has been considered.

Comparison of the TWI and TMI supposedly indicates overlaps between job demands and personal preferences. Differences between the two indices might suggest needs for job redesign, training, reallocation of duties or changes in team membership. The LSI diagnoses team members' individual strengths and weaknesses in terms of eleven key linking skills: listening; communicating with others; team development; work allocation; respecting, trusting and understanding colleagues; delegation; maintenance of quality standards; target setting; representing the team to outsiders; problem solving and counselling; and participation in team activities. Note the questionable reliability of the three indices used in the analysis, as they are largely based on self-reporting.

ROLES

13. Roles

A 'role' is a self-contained pattern of behaviour considered typical of a person who occupies a certain social position, e.g. husband, mother, office boy, senior manager, etc. Role theory concerns how individuals behave, how they feel they ought to behave, and how they believe other people should respond to their actions. For example, a supervisor might be expected to behave (perhaps even dress and speak) in a particular manner – distinct standards and norms of conduct may be anticipated from those who occupy a supervisory role.

The term 'role category' describes a complete class of person belonging to a specific social division ('leader', 'old person', 'senior executive', etc.). Through experience, individuals eventually form role categories into which people of the various occupational classes they encounter may be placed. A company welfare officer, for instance, may be expected always to behave in a sympathetic manner – regardless of his or her personality, background or general approach to management affairs. Such generalisations simplify social interrelationships, since once stereotypes are established it is no longer necessary for the individual to analyse every situation he or she confronts.

A person's actual role behaviour may or may not conform to expectations; it might deviate significantly, or be quite irrelevant to the situation in hand. Thus, for example, a high-ranking executive might be an extremely bad organiser, despite the ability to organise being a major assumption of a senior manager's role. Ideally, an individual's perceptions of 'correct' behaviour in a job will correspond to senior management's interpretation of what the worker ought to be doing and thinking about his or her occupational role. Sometimes, however, these perceptions differ – possibly resulting in 'role strain', which occurs when the demands of a role overtax its occupant's ability to cope to the extent that he or she does not behave in accordance with the expectations attached to the role. Consider, for example, the supervisor whose subordinates expect him or her to represent them to senior management but whose own superiors insist on that person implementing all management decisions regardless of their industrial relations effects.

Individuals who cannot live up to role expectations may experience feelings of inadequacy, embarrassment and guilt. Interactions with others become difficult, and could eventually collapse.

A person might be unclear about the exact nature of his or her role. The more explicit and specific the expectations attached to a role the easier it is to conform to its requirements. Role ambiguity can cause stress, insecurity and loss of self-confidence. An example might be a newly-appointed head of department, who is not entirely clear about how much authority he or she commands.

Serious problems occur when role occupants and others disagree fundamentally about the contents of a role, i.e. the duties it covers, ranges of acceptable behaviour, whether certain actions are voluntary or mandatory and (importantly) which of the role occupant's obligations should assume priority.

In setting role priorities, a person might select for priority those role behaviours which:

(a) correspond to his or her personal ethical standards and perceptions of moral worth

(b) are expedient

(c) bring the greatest personal reward and/or avoid personal cost

(d) avoid controversy or unpleasant relationships with people the individual particularly respects.

14. Jobs and careers

A career is a related series of jobs in an ascending order of status and responsibility. Career development may occur within a single (usually large) organisation; through a person moving between organisations; or by a mixture of the two. Advantages to *organisations* of having employees who are pursuing careers (rather than holding *ad hoc* jobs) are:

(a) Individuals might be motivated to work hard in order to further their careers.

(b) Employees have definite career targets at which to aim.

(c) Workers' loyalties to their occupations and/or employing organisations might be enhanced.

(d) Employees' competence will increase systematically over time.

(e) Management succession schemes can be drafted more easily.

(f) Career planning can be directly related to the firm's performance appraisal and management by objectives systems.

Advantages to *individuals* of following a career include:

(a) Feelings of security resulting from the likelihood that his or her job opportunities will increase as the person's career progresses.

(b) Enhanced self-awareness resulting from being forced to analyse personal strengths and weaknesses and the career options available.

(c) Acquisitions of useful experience as the employee selects jobs in organisations, departments, divisions, etc., that will best promote his or her career.

(d) Having a tangible long-term objective.

To plan a career a person needs to establish career priorities, closely observe the behaviour and attitudes of individuals who have already succeeded in the field, select jobs which build on personal strengths and minimise the effects of personal weaknesses, obtain the appropriate training, and if possible find a 'sponsor' who is an existing senior manager in the occupation or organisation concerned and who can assist and advise the junior person. Thereafter, the individual must regularly monitor his or her career achievements and carefully analyse the reasons for any shortcomings. Some organisations provide career counselling to assist employees in these respects. For more information on careers and career planning see *Organisational Behaviour*, Chapter 11, published in this series.

References

Belbin, R.M. (1981), *Management Teams: Why they Succeed or Fail*, Butterworth-Heinemann.

IRRR (Industrial Relations Review and Reports) (1994), Team building and development, *Employee Development Bulletin*, 55, July 1994, 2–11.

Mayo, G.E. (1945), *The Human Problems of an Industrial Society*, Harvard University Press.

Progress test 3

1. Summarise the results of the experiment in the relay assembly test room at Hawthorne.
2. What were the main observations made in the bank wiring room at Hawthorne?
3. What benefits does an employee obtain from membership of a working group?
4. Under what conditions is a working group likely to form?
5. Describe some of the main characteristics of a working group.
6. What is the relationship between group cohesiveness and productivity?
7. How can the existence of working groups affect management policy?
8. What is a role expectation?
9. What is a career?
10. How does a 'team' differ from an ordinary working group?
11. Explain the importance to the working group within industry and commerce of: (a) attitudes; (b) leadership; (c) motivation.

4

MOTIVATION IN WORK

MOTIVATION

1. Definition

An employee's motivation to work consists of all the drives, forces and influences – conscious or unconscious – that cause the employee to want to achieve certain aims. Managers need to know about the factors that create motivation in order to be able to induce employees to work harder, faster, more efficiently and with greater enthusiasm. Employees are motivated in part by the need to earn a living and partly by human needs for job satisfaction, security of tenure, the respect of colleagues, and so on. The organisation's reward systems (pay, fringe benefits, job security, promotion opportunities, etc.) may be applied to the first motive and job design to the latter. Much research has sought to discover the sources of motivation at work, but the theory of motivation is tentative and no definite conclusions can be advanced.

Early approaches to motivation

Social philosophers such as Jeremy Bentham and John Stuart Mill defined motivation in hedonistic terms. Humans, they asserted, are driven by the desire to obtain pleasure and avoid pain. As the science of psychology developed, this approach gave way to the view that innate instinctual differences in humans caused individuals to be motivated in different ways. It was believed that people were born with unique predispositions towards various motivating influences.

Sigmund Freud suggested that a person's motivations could be greatly influenced by his or her unconscious mind. Individuals, he argued, are frequently unaware of their true desires and the forces which cause them to behave in particular ways. Often, repressed sexual motives were the actual cause of behaviour. B.F. Skinner's theory of operant conditioning implied that motivation emerges from the interplay of stimulus and response. For example, poverty causes the search for work and, once the individual obtains employment, to work hard in order to maximise income. Immediate rewards (high wages) are obtained for correct behaviour (working energetically). Effort is regarded as the product of drive and learned behaviour. Modern theories focus on the relationship between motivation and human need. The latter is regarded as central to the motivation process.

Biological approaches to motivation

In the early years of the twentieth century Clark Hull suggested that humans possess certain biological drives – gained over the centuries through the Darwinian process of natural selection – which largely explain individual predispositions towards certain actions. Initially Hull considered just the primary drives of hunger, thirst, sex, and pain avoidance. Deprivation of a physiological need would produce a drive to initiate behaviour aimed at satisfying the need, e.g. lack of water creates thirst and hence the search for liquid refreshment. Variability in actions taken depended on differences in the intensity of the drive, which itself depended on the degree of deprivation. Need satisfaction reinforced the behaviour patterns that led to fulfilment, so that these behaviour patterns would become habitual. 'Secondary reinforcers' were defined as factors that, while not of themselves satisfying primary needs, would nevertheless help obtain things that did indeed satisfy primary requirements. Money is an example of a secondary reinforcer. The concept of secondary reinforcement enabled Hull to attempt explanations of complex aspects of human behaviour. Consider for instance the motivation to achieve. In infancy a person's needs for food are satisfied by his or her mother, who also provides most of the infant's social contact. Hence the child learns to associate the reduction of hunger with maternal attention and approval, which becomes a secondary reinforcer. Over time the child thus becomes motivated to perform activities that have the mother's approval, e.g. achieving success at school. Eventually the quest for success might assume a permanent role in the person's motivational system.

Problems with the biological approach to motivation include:

(a) The theory is extremely difficult to test empirically. How for example can the extent of habitual behaviour be measured? Most experiments in the field have been conducted on rats. This has generated large amounts of information on rat psychology, but may have little to do with human motivation.

(b) Unlearned drives are not restricted to hunger, thirst, sex and the avoidance of pain.

(c) Biological approaches fail to explain many forms of human behaviour.

(d) Arguably the theory is very naive in its assertion that complex behavioural processes can be understood by examining just a handful of variables.

(e) Altruistic motives are ignored.

NEEDS AND THEIR SATISFACTION

2. Human needs

Psychologists make these basic assumptions when interpreting human behaviour.

(a) All human behaviour has a *cause*, which itself is the consequence of the combined effects of heredity and environment.

(b) At the root of human behaviour are *needs*, or wants or motives. Need is the term usually employed in this connection.

(c) Human behaviour is *goal-seeking*; people try to achieve objectives or goals which, when reached, will satisfy their needs. For example, food will satisfy the hunger need.

The hierarchy of needs

The American psychologist, A. H. Maslow, has divided human needs into the following classes:

(a) *Physiological or basic needs* – people must satisfy these needs just to keep alive. They include, for example, hunger, thirst and sleep. In the work environment, the fundamental purpose of a wage or salary is to provide the means of satisfying basic needs.

(b) *Security or safety needs* – these are concerned with self-protection, with the avoidance of harm and, to some extent, with provision for the future. Examples are the needs for shelter, warmth and self-defence. At work the wish for security of tenure, the existence of restrictive practices, and many aspects of trade unionism show how employees try to satisfy needs of this kind.

(c) *Belonging or affection needs* – everyone, in various degrees, wishes to give and receive friendship. Companionship and association with others for recreational purposes are examples of these needs. Note that, for example, people may join with others partly to satisfy affection needs and partly for greater security.

(d) *Esteem or ego needs* – these include the needs to become independent, to receive the esteem of others, to dominate and to acquire possessions. As it is possible for needs of this kind to be satisfied through social activity, there is again overlapping between needs of groups **(c)** and **(d)**. At work a position of authority, a company car, an office carpet or a special type of overall are means by which these needs are satisfied.

(e) *Self-actualisation needs* – this final group comprises the needs to make the fullest use of one's capabilities, to develop oneself and to be creative. In the working environment the majority of employees find few opportunities to satisfy needs in this class; skilled operatives, professional workers and managers are the most likely to be satisfied in this way.

Maslow has suggested that the classes of needs, in the order shown, form a hierarchy; people tend to satisfy their needs in a certain order of precedence. In general, when physiological and security needs have been satisfied, the higher needs (belonging, esteem and self-actualisation) become important, usually, according to Maslow, in the order of the hierarchy. For example, a manager who receives a substantial salary, and thus adequately satisfies his or her lower needs, regards status symbols like a well-furnished office as important, but a former manager who has been unemployed for a long time will eventually take any available job that brings a reasonable income, even though it is of low status.

3. Modifications to Maslow's theory

Maslow's theory is widely accepted, easy to understand and can be used to explain much, but not all, behaviour at work. Alderfer has proposed instead a modification of the theory, consisting of three levels of need:

(a) *Existence needs* – approximately equivalent to Maslow's physiological and security needs.

(b) *Relatedness needs* – including affection needs and that part of esteem needs which is concerned with personal relationships.

(c) *Growth needs* – including self-actualisation needs and that part of esteem needs which is concerned with individual effort.

The theory (often known as the ERG theory) agrees with Maslow in saying that as one level becomes satisfied the level above becomes important, but adds a further proposition that if one level is not sufficiently satisfied the level below becomes more important, e.g. a disappointment in promotion (growth needs) may produce a greater wish for social involvement (relatedness needs). Alderfer claims that his theory provides a more comprehensive explanation of behaviour than Maslow's.

4. Discussion of Maslow's work

Maslow's theory has been criticised on the following grounds:

(a) The theory asserts that people seek to achieve higher-level needs *after* lower-level ones have been fulfilled. Yet some individuals feel strong desires to gratify higher-level needs *before* lower-level needs have been fully satisfied. For instance, a poor person may yearn for status symbols even though his or her immediate physical and security requirements have not been properly met.

(b) Individuals might not rank the various types of need in the manner suggested. For some men and women, esteem needs are more important than needs for affection. Indeed, some of the needs in Maslow's hierarchy might not exist in certain people; and what is considered essential by one person might be trivial to someone else.

Note, moreover, that whether someone feels the need for something depends greatly on that person's perceptions, which themselves depend critically on the traditions, cultures and life-styles of the society in which he or she lives. Many desires are actually learned responses to environmental pressures with societal rather than physiological origins. For example, advertising can cause people to feel needs for things they never previously considered.

5. Individual differences in need-satisfaction

People differ in the way they satisfy their needs in a variety of ways:

(a) *Cultural* – the manner in which for example hunger and sex needs are satisfied is surrounded by many customs and laws.

(b) *Perceptual* – in general, people perceive the world in terms of their least-satisfied needs; their perceptions tend to recognise goals which will help satisfy their needs. A starving person perceives an apple orchard as a source of food rather than an attractive feature of the countryside.

(c) *Individual* – people have different physical and intellectual capabilities and aptitudes; they also have different personalities. These are reflected in the various ways in which needs are satisfied; one person might achieve self-actualisation by an intellectual feat, another by sporting prowess.

ACHIEVEMENT NEEDS

According to David McClelland, the need to achieve is a primary motivating factor. Other important needs, he suggested, are the needs for power and affiliation. Achievement-oriented people were said to (*i*) prefer tasks for which they had sole responsibility, (*ii*) avoid risk, and (*iii*) monitor continuously the effects of their actions. 'Need achievers', as McClelland called them, worked extremely hard and constantly sought to improve their performances. Power seekers, conversely, were motivated by the prospect of controlling subordinates. Affiliators wanted pleasant relationships with colleagues and to help other individuals. McClelland used the term nAff to characterise an individual's need for friendly relations with others. People with a high nAff had strong desires for approval by peers and in consequence tended to adopt conformist attitudes when working in groups.

Arguably, individuals with high achievement needs often make good entrepreneurs running their own businesses, or managers of self-contained units within large companies. Note however that need achievers are not *necessarily* effective managers. They are concerned with their personal advancement, but may not be capable of encouraging others to succeed (a vital management skill). It could be that the best executives are those with a high need for affiliation.

6. Conflict of needs

A person may wish to satisfy two needs simultaneously, but find that they are mutually exclusive; if one is satisfied, the other cannot be satisfied. For example, if the individual wishes to retain his or her job, duties may have to be carried out in a way disliked by the worker, or the boss may expect the individual to stay late frequently although this has adverse effects on the person's family life. A situation of this kind, where an individual is pulled in two ways at once, is called a *conflict of needs*. Until it is resolved, it may show itself in anxiety and irritability, or sometimes in what appears to be physical disorders like headaches or stomach complaints.

At work, management should try to avoid putting employees into situations where conflict may occur; for instance, employees should not be promoted unless it is certain that they would welcome the promotion. A person promoted to take charge of a branch in a part of the country he or she dislikes would be torn between the wish to advance in the company and the wish to remain in a certain district. The resulting conflict might be difficult to resolve and its effects might not be beneficial to the company or the employee.

7. Achievement of goals

The assumptions regarding human behaviour set out in **2** may be shown in diagrammatic form as shown in Fig. 4.1.

The left-hand column shows the need-path-goal hypothesis in general terms. The other two columns show the ways in which actual needs might be satisfied.

The importance of *perception* should be noted. Although people are in many

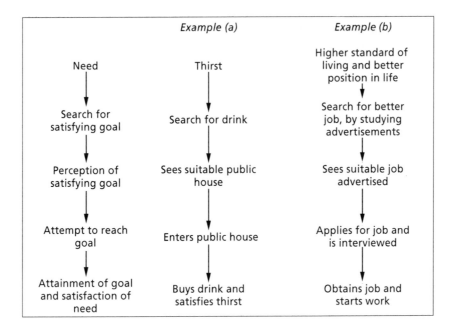

Figure 4.1

cases motivated by the same needs, their perceptions of need-satisfying goals are different. A teetotaller, for example, would not perceive a public house as a means of satisfying thirst, and job-seekers do not all apply for the same job. Need-satisfaction is usually complex; a new job, if well chosen, can satisfy needs ranging over the whole of Maslow's hierarchy.

8. Frustration

A goal which is attempted may not always be reached; the individual may be *frustrated* when attempting to reach it. The *positive reaction* to frustration is to try to solve the problem, perhaps by finding a way round the obstacle that prevents the person from reaching the goal, perhaps by perceiving an alternative goal which will satisfy the need – though probably not to the same extent. The perception and achievement of an alternative goal is sometimes called *deprivation*, because the individual is deprived of the extra satisfaction he or she would have gained if the original goal had been obtainable.

Frustration may also produce various forms of *negative reactions* – exceptions to the general rule that all behaviour is purposeful and goal-seeking. A negative reaction may occur for various reasons:

(a) The goal being attempted seems unique and there appears to be no practicable alternative, e.g. there is no other public house for miles, and this one has just closed.

(b) There is a strong emotional attachment to the goal, e.g. the candidate has boasted to everyone of being certain to get the job applied for, and then hears that he or she has been turned down.

(c) The individual is by nature prone to react negatively.

Negative reactions can take several forms; the four found most often are:

(a) *Aggression* – a physical or verbal attack on some person or object, e.g. abuse of the landlord of the public house.

(b) *Regression* – a reversion to childish behaviour, e.g. sulking or tears.

(c) *Resignation* – giving up, apathy, withdrawal, e.g. a person disappointed in promotion may come late, leave early and avoid making decisions.

(d) *Fixation* – persistence in useless behaviour, e.g. pushing on the public house door long after it is apparent that it is locked.

9. Frustration at work

Frustration may frequently occur among the employees of an organisation, for the following reasons:

(a) Their methods and speed of work may be closely controlled, and not what they themselves would choose.

(b) Their work may appear meaningless.

(c) Their grievances and problems may not be dealt with speedily or adequately by management.

(d) They may not be told, or cannot understand, the reasons for many management decisions which affect them.

When employees are frustrated at work they may react negatively, their behaviour taking the following forms:

- Lateness, absence or eventually leaving the company
- Poor-quality work
- Unwillingness to take responsibility
- Quarrels with colleagues, disputes with management
- Accidents, damage to equipment and products.

10. Reducing frustration

Because frustration can have such serious consequences, every effort should be made to reduce it. A case may be made that the work situation is inherently frustrating because it implies that, for monetary payment, one person is putting him or herself under the instructions of another; however, the possibility of frustration at work can be reduced in the following ways:

(a) Designing jobs to give them greater meaning.

(b) Improving selection and training; a person will be more satisfied in jobs for which they are suitable and for which they have been trained.

(c) Recognising effort and merit, thus providing satisfaction of higher needs.

(d) Improving communications, consultation and disputes procedures so that potential causes of frustration may be identified and removed as far as possible.

11. Alienation

This is the feeling that work is not a relevant or important part of one's life; that one does not really belong to the work community. It is associated with feelings of discontent, isolation and futility. Alienated workers perceive themselves as powerless and dominated. Work becomes simply a means to achieve material ends. Great unhappiness can result from alienation; indeed, the mental or physical health of the employee can suffer. Alienation may result from lack of contact with other workers and/or with management, from authoritarian or paternalistic management styles, or simply through the boredom of routine work. Its consequences are numerous: poor quality output, absenteeism, resistance to change, industrial disputes, deteriorating inter-personal relationships, etc.

EXPECTANCY THEORY

12. Vroom's expectancy theory

The motivational process may also be explained in another way. *Expectancy theory* states that effort to satisfy needs will depend on the person's perception that he or she can expect the effort to be followed by a certain outcome which will bring desirable rewards.

According to V. H. Vroom, an individual's behaviour is affected by:

(a) What the person wants to happen

(b) His or her estimate of the probability of the thing happening

(c) How strongly the person believes that the event will satisfy a need.

To illustrate this, suppose there are three employees who wish to obtain promotion in order to satisfy self-actualisation needs (Maslow) or growth needs (Alderfer). The first employee perceives prominence in the firm's social club as the best route and spends much spare time there, confident that he or she will be voted into honorary office. The second employee perceives a professional qualification as the best way and works hard in the evenings to achieve one. The third also perceives the professional qualification as the best way, but does not make the effort to study because the person does not believe he or she would be able to pass the examinations; neither does the individual try to become an honorary officer of the social club because, unlike the first employee, he or she does not perceive this as a way of getting promotion.

Individuals normally base their predictions of what will happen in the future on what has occurred in the past. In consequence, new situations that workers have not previously experienced (e.g. job changes, new working conditions and environments) cause uncertainty and thus may reduce employee motivation, because the individuals involved have no prior knowledge of the likely consequences of altered circumstances.

13. Implications of Vroom's theory

The following implications emerge from Vroom's theory:

(a) Management should make clear to employees what exactly it expects from new working practices.

(b) Workers should be able to see a connection between their efforts and the rewards these efforts generate.

(c) Rewards should satisfy workers' needs.

(d) Complicated reward schemes (complex bonus schemes, for example) are unlikely to increase employees' effort because workers cannot relate harder work to higher wages.

14. Effort and performance: Porter and Lawler

The relationship between effort, reward and performance was further investigated by L. W. Porter and E. E. Lawler, who state that two factors determine the amount of effort put into a job:

(a) The extent to which the psychological and monetary rewards obtained from doing the job fulfil the worker's needs for:

(*i*) security
(*ii*) esteem
(*iii*) independence
(*iv*) personal self-development.

(b) The worker's expectation that putting a great deal of effort into the job will lead to the achievement of satisfying rewards.

Thus, the more attractive an employee considers a particular reward, and the higher the probability that the exertion of effort will lead to that reward, then the more effort the individual will put into his or her work.

HYGIENE FACTORS

15. Herzberg's theory of motivational hygiene

The American psychologist Frederick Herzberg has propounded a theory of motivation at work which divides the factors of the work environment into two classes: motivators or satisfiers on the one hand; and hygiene factors or maintenance factors on the other.

Herzberg developed his theory by analysing the answers to two basic questions he and his collaborators put to engineers and accountants:

(a) What events at work have resulted in a marked increase in your job satisfaction?

(b) What events at work have resulted in a marked reduction in your job satisfaction?

The replies showed that, in general, the experiences which were regarded as exceptionally satisfying were not the opposite of those which were exceptionally dissatisfying. For example, someone might say that a job is disliked because of poor working conditions, but very rarely would that person say that a job is liked because of good working conditions.

From his analysis, Herzberg concluded that the elements in a job which produced *satisfaction* were:

- Achievement
- Recognition
- Responsibility

- Promotion prospects
- Work itself.

He called these the 'motivators' or 'satisfiers'.

The elements whose absence or inadequacy in a job produced *dissatisfaction* were:

- Pay
- Relations to others
- Type of supervision
- Company policy
- Physical working conditions
- Fringe benefits.

Herzberg called these hygiene factors (because, using the analogy of drains and refuse collection, they made the job environment fit to occupy), or maintenance factors (because they tended to maintain an employee in his or her job). He said that an employee might leave a firm because he or she disliked its working conditions or thought the pension scheme inadequate, but the employee would not be motivated to work harder or better if working conditions or the pension scheme were improved (provided they were already reasonably adequate).

On the other hand, the absence of achievement or responsibility, for example, would be unlikely to cause an employee to leave, but if these could be increased the employee would be more motivated at work. Herzberg recognised that individuals varied in the relative importance they attached to motivators or hygiene factors; some were very concerned to seek achievement, recognition, etc., in their jobs, while others were interested particularly in pay, personal relationships, etc.

16. Discussion of Herzberg's theory

When Herzberg's enquiries have been repeated using his methods, his findings have been confirmed to a large extent. However, when other methods have been used, for example questionnaires, different results have emerged. Very few enquiries appear to have been conducted with manual workers. Herzberg's method of investigation, which may be described as anecdotal self-report, is likely to produce answers of a certain type. People frequently describe good work experiences in terms which reflect credit on themselves – success, greater responsibility or recognition. Workers will always be tempted to attribute bad work experiences to things beyond their own control – uncongenial colleagues, an unpleasant boss or poor working conditions. Thus they will take the credit for the good experiences and blame others for the bad experiences.

The main application of the theory has been in the enlarging or enriching of the jobs of non-manual workers. It would be possible to find theoretical justification for this in the hierarchy of needs without postulating a two-factor theory. Herzberg does, however, emphasise that improving fringe benefits or other conditions of work will not motivate employees; again the hierarchy of needs would explain this because working conditions are relevant to the lower needs, which in modern industry and commerce are usually adequately satisfied.

17. Motivation and wages

Herzberg's proposition that money is a hygiene factor rather than a motivator has aroused much controversy. Arguments *in favour* of money being the dominant motivator are listed below:

(a) High wages provide access to physical goods, services and lifestyles greatly valued by the majority of employees.

(b) High incomes indicate occupational competence and are a mark of success. This itself constitutes an important motivating factor.

(c) Money can *simultaneously* satisfy many needs. Thus, for example, it could be used to purchase expensive luxury goods that meet esteem needs, or to finance a personal hobby thereby helping satisfy a need for self-actualisation. People may say they do not value monetary rewards *per se*, but they still want the things that can be purchased with money.

(d) Comparison of a person's wage with the wages of others enables the individual to relate his or her job to others within the organisation and within industry generally.

The arguments *against* wages being a primary motivator are:

(a) Workers may fear that once the high performance targets attached to large pay packets have been met, these targets will be regarded by management as the norm so that no further pay increases can then be expected. Accordingly, employees might prefer a less intensive pace of work, albeit on lower incomes.

(b) The definition of 'good pay' is itself subjective. A certain level of wage might be seen as excellent by one person, but as paltry by another.

(c) Workers might assume that an offer of higher pay implies job losses among the labour force, including perhaps their own jobs.

(d) Employees often wish to assert their independence from management and may do this through the formation of tightly-knit and socially coherent work groups which influence workers' behaviour more forcefully than the prospect of higher wages.

Whether it is a primary motivator or not, money is a convenient way of measuring the worth of a job and of indicating the standards expected of the worker (by way of bonus schemes, for example). Also, pay rises awarded for excellent performance can greatly increase a worker's commitment and general morale.

Money is perhaps a better motivator in the short term rather than in the longer term. Note in particular that increasing amounts of money might be needed to achieve equal increments in employee satisfaction (for example, an extremely large pay rise may be necessary to increase the motivation of someone who is already on a high salary).

18. Equity and control theories of motivation

The *Equity Theory* of motivation asserts that an employee's own assessment of whether he or she is being fairly treated is a major factor influencing motivation. Workers are assumed to compare their personal reward/effort situations with those of colleagues and to feel aggrieved if they believe they are *relatively* underrewarded. If returns are regarded as equal to those of other employees – proportionate to the effort expended by the individual – a state of 'distributive justice' is said to exist. Otherwise 'cognitive dissonance' occurs, whereby the individual perceives the reward/effort relationship as inconsistent and out of balance. Consequently, the worker feels uncomfortable and discontented, and his or her effort and motivation may diminish. Problems with Equity Theory include the subjectivity that employees typically apply to the assessment of their own and other workers' contributions to an organisation, the difficulty of accurately measuring inputs to and rewards from jobs, and the fact that group pressures can override equity considerations.

A development of this approach is the *Control Theory* of motivation which suggests that workers compare their current job/task situations with desired ('referent') standards and are then motivated to behave in ways that will reduce discrepancies. Thus the theory suggests that motivation derives ultimately from how employees *perceive* the attractiveness of their work and the opportunities that exist for achieving improvements.

19. Practical techniques of employee motivation

Among the numerous devices known to be useful for motivating employees, the following are particularly worthy of mention:

- Ensuring that employees feel they are valued
- Senior management setting a good example
- Two-way communications (*see* 6:8)
- Respecting, trusting and empowering employees (*see* 2:13)
- Treating people as responsible human beings rather than as resources to be exploited
- Creating an organisational culture wherein effort is seen to result in fair rewards
- Providing leadership training to managers and supervisors

- Making the work that employees complete as interesting as possible
- Setting challenging goals (through allocating to employees the resources necessary for the attainment of objectives)
- Providing rapid feedback on employees' performances
- Enabling employees to exercise their full range of abilities
- Telling people what exactly they need to do in order to achieve their career aspirations
- Making employees feel good about themselves
- Ensuring that managers *listen* to employees' opinions
- Organising work so that employees see the end results of their activities
- Wherever possible, giving workers security of employment
- Establishing fair employee complaints procedures
- Giving workers opportunities to acquire new skills, and offering promotion to suitably qualified people.

JOB ENLARGEMENT

20. Job enlargement and job enrichment – definitions

A job is enlarged when the employee carries out a wider range of tasks of approximately the same level of difficulty and responsibility as before.

A job is enriched (or vertically enlarged) when the employee is given greater responsibilities and scope to make decisions, and is expected to use skills not used before. Both are examples of *job extension*.

21. Effects of job enlargement and enrichment

Both are attempts to build opportunities into the employee's job for the satisfaction of ego and self-actualisation needs. A greater range of tasks or decisions will, it is thought, make the employee feel more important, give a sense of achievement and make more use of the person's abilities. The worker will therefore receive satisfaction from the job itself (intrinsic satisfaction) as well as money and fringe benefits (extrinsic satisfaction).

Many companies have introduced either job enlargement or job enrichment and increased the job satisfaction of their employees. In most cases it appears that non-manual workers (often managers) rather than manual workers are concerned. It is easier to extend the job of a non-manual worker, whose responsibilities and actions are very often not precisely described, than to change the job of a manual worker whose tasks may be highly specialised and precisely defined because they are part of a complex production process. There may be a conflict between specialisation and development of specific skills required for efficient operation of the process and the construction of a job sufficiently enlarged or enriched to give greater satisfaction to the employee. In order to make the job significant to the worker it may have to be extended so much that productivity is seriously affected. The result may be a compromise between efficiency and job satisfaction in which the worker, instead of doing one meaningless task, is now expected to do several meaningless tasks.

Extension of jobs may meet with trade union opposition because demarcation lines between skills are eroded. It will almost certainly necessitate increases in pay; wider or deeper responsibilities must be recognised by an increase in the monetary worth of the job, as measured by job evaluation. An employer might hesitate, therefore, before introducing job extension because the benefits to the employer would be somewhat uncertain, whereas the costs might be considerable.

22. Job rotation

Some of the difficulties the employee finds in job extension can be avoided if *job rotation* is used instead. Employees are trained in several minor skills and exchange jobs with each other at intervals. Greater satisfaction is obtained because the employee has a greater understanding of the work process through experiencing several jobs within it, and the increased versatility of the workers is useful to management when sickness absence is high. It is not necessary to redesign production methods, and rises in pay, if any, are small.

Not all individuals respond favourably to job enlargement, enrichment or rotation. Some do not appear to be motivated very strongly by the higher needs, or do not expect to satisfy them at work. Others resist any attempt to give them decision-making functions; they say that managers are there for that purpose.

23. The relationship between job satisfaction and productivity

Although common sense might lead us to expect that a worker who finds a job satisfying would produce more than one who is not satisfied, many investigations have shown that, generally speaking, productivity and job satisfaction are not related. It is possible for any degree of job satisfaction to be associated with any degree of productivity, i.e. a satisfied worker may have low productivity or a dissatisfied worker may have high productivity, or vice versa. Closer analysis may provide at least a partial explanation of this apparently irrational effect.

The expectation that a satisfied employee will work hard is basically a paternalistic attitude on the part of the employer. It implies either that the employee, grateful for being given a satisfying job, will show gratitude by complying with the employer's wishes, or that because the worker is satisfied he or she is inevitably enthusiastic, conscientious and persistent and therefore produces at a high rate. However, a more realistic assumption is that the employee may not have any feelings of gratitude towards the employer and that the worker's enthusiasm may either show itself in a form unwelcome to the employer, for example an overemphasis on accuracy, or may be tempered by other considerations, for example a wish to adhere to group norms of production. The interests of the employer and the employee do not always coincide.

From the employee's point of view, work brings many kinds of rewards: money, friendship, status and achievement among others. In some circumstances working harder may increase these rewards, in others it may reduce them. Status and achievement, which might be expected to favour higher productivity, are needs which have little appeal to some employees, or are needs which they do not expect to satisfy at work. It is quite possible for employees to work hard in jobs they dislike because they fear dismissal, are attracted by a high level of pay, or simply find hard work the best way of making the time go quickly. On the other hand, many employees, in particular professional and skilled workers and those who have a moral involvement in their jobs, combine high job satisfaction with high productivity, perhaps because they are motivated by loyalty towards a profession, craft or ideal rather than towards an employer. The relationship between productivity and the motivation of employees is extremely complex, and much research remains to be done.

24. Job satisfaction and costs

Although a manager who is successful in increasing the job satisfaction of employees may or may not benefit from an increase in their productivity, the manager will probably find that the costs of running his or her department are reduced. Labour turnover and absence can be extremely expensive to the company and may well be reduced if jobs are made more satisfying. The manager should, however, be sure that the cost of redesigning jobs (which may include less efficiency in working methods and higher pay rates) does not outweigh the expected saving.

25. The concept of total rewards

An employee may receive extrinsic rewards (pay and fringe benefits) or intrinsic rewards (friendship, status and self-fulfilment) from work. The total reward is the employee's *perception* of the total value of all these. For example, individuals differ in the value they attach to achievement as compared with pay, or promotion opportunities as compared with security. For their part, employers recognise that some rewards compensate for the absence of others; a job which requires a strong moral involvement, e.g. social work, is often accompanied by a low level of pay, and a company which traditionally offers its employees almost complete security of tenure may have lower wage rates than a company with a 'hire and fire' reputation.

Employers and employees may have different perceptions of the rewards to be obtained from various jobs. Changes in working conditions regarded by the employer as improvements may not appear to be such to the employees, for example a new open-plan office instead of small separate offices. Sometimes the way in which the decision is reached and the change introduced is more significant than the change itself.

26. Absence from work

Absenteeism is a major source of cost and disruption in British companies. Currently, UK industry is losing 200 million working days each year to deliberate non-attendance. The average worker takes eleven days per year off, and on any given day up to 7 per cent of the workforce of a typical large British company will be absent – four times more than the rate among UK industry's leading international competitors. Losses attributable to absenteeism include reduced production, sick pay, the need for additional overtime to cover for absent workers, hassles resulting from having to reschedule projects, failure to meet deadlines, additional clerical and supervision expenses (telephone calls, administering statutory sick pay, etc.) and so on. Factors contributing to non-attendance include:

(a) *The nature of the job*: physical conditions, boredom, inconvenient working hours, stress, unsatisfactory interpersonal relations, poor supervision.

(b) *Characteristics of the worker*: individual disinclination to work, age and sex (young people and females on average take more time off work than others), length of service (long-serving employees are less prone to absenteeism), a person's state of health, extent of family responsibilities, attitudes and perspectives concerning regular attendance, travelling difficulties.

(c) *Motivating factors*: incentive schemes (bonuses, special awards for consistent attendance), availability of sick pay, extent of piece rate working (*see* 14:2), effectiveness of managerial exhortations aimed at persuading employees to turn up for work, the firm's readiness to apply disciplinary actions (formal warnings, deductions from pay, and other penalties short of dismissal, etc.).

Note how some of these factors interconnect, e.g. the fact that on average women take more time off than men but that women are also known to predominate in many tedious and low status occupations.

Measures for controlling absenteeism include job design and job rotation intended to make work more interesting, increased employee participation in decision making, explicit consideration of job applicants' attitudes towards absenteeism during employee selection procedures, employee counselling, implementation of flexitime and job sharing arrangements, and careful record keeping to identify individuals and types of work with the highest absenteeism rates.

27. Grievances

Grievances can result from external circumstances – such as an employer imposing detrimental working conditions on employees, or from internal feelings of unhappiness and/or frustration. Externally created grievances may be remedied through altering the environmental circumstances that cause them: restoring a contractual right, improving conditions, increasing a benefit, or whatever. Grievances resulting from workers' hurt feelings might be best resolved through non-directive counselling (*see* 16:**16**).

Many grievances develop from misunderstandings rather than fundamental conflicts of interest, and a simple statement of facts may be all that is required to resolve the difficulty. Minor complaints can arise from breakdowns in communications, from petty jealousies, interpersonal rivalry, or from interdepartmental disputes. Such problems may usually be settled quite easily through increasing the flow of information within the organisation, by defining the authority and responsibilities of people and departments more carefully, and by generally promoting co-operation between sections.

No organisation is so well managed that its employees never need to complain, and even if a firm consciously seeks to be a good employer, staff may still *feel* that certain complaints are justified even if, objectively, they are not. Well-constructed grievance procedures enable firms to resolve complaints quickly, fairly, and without resort to industrial action on the part of employees. Formal procedures minimise the risk of inconsistent decisions: the employer is *seen* to be trying to be fair. And, of course, the absence of formal procedures will severely prejudice an employer's case if the grievance eventually results in legal proceedings.

A grievance 'procedure' is an established set of agreed rules for enabling management and the aggrieved employee to settle a complaint. Such rules restrain both sides from behaving irresponsibly, provided both are committed to their application and have confidence in their impartiality. Other advantages of formal procedures are:

(a) Both sides have a common understanding of how a grievance will be received and processed.

(b) The managers and union representatives who deal with grievances change periodically on account of promotions, resignations, retirements and staff transfers. However, the existence of written rules enables procedures to be applied consistently over time.

(c) Written rules clarify important matters such as who has authority to take decisions in settlement of disputes, the time-scale for registering a grievance, how an appeal should be lodged, etc.

(d) Formal records of grievance hearings avoid subsequent disputes about what was discussed and agreed in the hearing.

(e) Employees have the security of knowing that whenever major problems arise they can air their concerns to the highest levels of management within the firm.

There are, however, arguments in favour of *informal* procedures. Formalisation reduces flexibility, since precedents established through following formal rules must be adhered to in future cases. A mini legal system will build up around the policies, with its own protocol, norms, case law and rules of interpretation. It becomes impossible to 'turn a blind eye' to certain practices regardless of the circumstances in which they occur.

References

Alderfer, C.P. (1972), *Existence, Relatedness and Growth: Human Needs in Organisational Settings,* The Free Press.

Hersberg, F. (1966), *Work and the Nature of Man*, New York, World Publishing Co.

Hull, C.I. (1943), *Principles of Behaviour*, New York, Appleton-Century Croft.

McCelland, D.C. (1961), *The Achieving Society*, Van Nostrand Reinhold.

Maslow, A.H. (1954), *Motivation and Personality*, Harper and Row.

Porter, L.W. and Lawler, E.E. (1968), *Managerial Attitudes and Performance*, Irwin-Dorsey.

Vroom, V.H. (1964), *Work and Motivation*, Wiley.

Progress test 4

1. What are the three basic assumptions underlying the study of motivation?
2. What is the hierarchy of needs?
3. Define frustration, and illustrate how it may produce either positive or negative reactions.
4. Define the expectancy approach to motivation.
5. Define, and give examples of, job enlargement and job enrichment.
6. What are the major sources of employee grievances?
7. List the main factors that cause employees to be absent from work.
8. Job evaluation has recently been attacked as 'one of the major obstacles to significant organisational change in most large organisations', the argument being that people should be valued and rewarded according to their contribution, not on the job they do. How far do you agree with this critique of job evaluation?
9. One result of technology has been to increase the number of boring jobs. What factors would you consider essential when looking at job design?

5

LEARNING

INTRODUCTION

1. Definition

Learning is a relatively permanent change in the repertoire of behaviour occurring as a result of experience.

This definition implies that learning can only be said to occur when a person shows different behaviour, for example when he or she can prove the knowledge of new facts or do something the individual was not able to do before. Changes in behaviour due solely to ageing or injury would not be examples of learning. If, however, an injured person had found ways of adapting to a disability, this new behaviour would then have been learned.

2. Important terms in learning

In studying the psychology of learning it is necessary to understand the meanings of four important terms – drive, stimulus, response and reinforcement. In the following definitions the word organism will be used to denote either a human being or an animal:

(a) *Drive* – the necessary condition of arousal or readiness for action or behaviour to begin. It is a condition in which the organism wishes to satisfy a need.

(b) *Stimulus* – the cue or signal which initiates a response. It is usually conveyed by sight, hearing, smell or touch. For example, the ringing of the telephone is the stimulus to pick it up, or the change of colour of the material is the stimulus to alter the application of paint.

(c) *Response* – the behaviour which is the result of stimulation (even though it may not be possible to identify the stimulus). Often a particular response becomes associated with a particular stimulus so that one almost automatically follows the other, for example changing gear when approaching a corner. The object of much industrial training is to establish these associations.

(d) *Reinforcement* – any event or object which strengthens a response, either by causing it to continue or increase, by providing the organism with some kind of reward. A dog after performing a trick may be rewarded either with food or with a pat and a friendly word. A learner-driver when he or she changes gear smoothly may be rewarded with the instructor's approval.

3. Classical conditioning

Experiments with animals have shown two important learning processes: classical conditioning and operant (or instrumental) conditioning.

Classical conditioning is associated above all with the Russian psychologist Pavlov. A typical experiment in this field would proceed as follows.

(a) *First stage* – a dog which is hungry (drive) is shown some food (stimulus). Its mouth waters (response). Eventually it is allowed to eat the food (reinforcement).

(b) *Second stage* – as before, but when the food is shown a bell is also rung.

(c) *Third stage* – the food is not shown, only the bell being rung. The dog's mouth waters at the sound of the bell.

The dog has now been *conditioned* to respond to a new stimulus. Since this response (watering of the mouth) is a reflex action, i.e. not consciously controlled, it is called a *conditioned reflex*.

By elaboration of this procedure Pavlov was able to show that dogs were colour-blind and that they could distinguish between a circle and an ellipse.

It is possible that certain superstitions and fears in humans may be due to a classical conditioning process. For example, an American psychologist was able to produce in his infant son terror of a teddy bear by making a loud noise whenever the child was shown the bear. Later he deconditioned his son by associating the bear with a favourite fruit jelly. Although classical conditioning may contribute to the development of certain personality traits, it is of only minor importance in learning within commerce or industry.

4. Operant (or instrumental) conditioning

This process, which is much more relevant to human learning, is associated with the American psychologist B. F. Skinner. A typical experiment would proceed as follows:

(a) A special cage is constructed which contains a lever on one side and a food receptacle on the other. Whenever the lever is depressed a piece of food is released from a container into the receptacle.

(b) An animal (very often a pigeon) which is hungry (drive) is placed in the cage. Eventually, during the course of random behaviour, it touches the lever with some part of its body and depresses it. This releases the food, which the pigeon eats. After some accidental repetitions of this sequence, the pigeon learns the connection between the lever and the food. The sight of the lever (stimulus) leads to the response of pressing it. The food is then eaten (reinforcement). This is an example of learning, because through experience the pigeon now behaves in a new way.

(c) Once behaviour is established in this way, the occasional reinforcement gets better results than the reinforcement of every response (compare people who are told continually while they are learning that they are doing very well).

(d) Behaviour can be *shaped* by operant conditioning, that is gradually made more precise and less general. For example, pigeons have been trained to play table-tennis with each other, to play simple tunes on a toy piano, and even to reject misshapen tablets in a pharmaceutical factory by pressing levers with their beaks as the tablets go past on a moving belt.

Operant conditioning is *different* from classical conditioning in the following respects:

(a) The animal is not passive but active (hence operant).

(b) Its behaviour is *instrumental* in obtaining a reward or reinforcement; in classical conditioning the reward is not important.

(c) It learns new behaviour instead of providing an existing response to a new stimulus.

(d) Its behaviour is consciously controlled, not a reflex action.

There are, of course, a number of criticisms of operant conditioning theory, especially the assumption that probable human behaviour can be inferred from observing the behaviour of non-human animals. Experiments on animals may reveal much about the psychology of cats, dogs, rats and pigeons, but not be relevant to the psychology of human beings. Animals possess motivations which are possibly quite different from those of humans, and mute animals cannot be asked *why* they chose to act in a particular way. Also, the operant conditioning model says little about how insight and understanding develop, about how people 'learn how to learn', or about the best means for transmitting basic intellectual concepts of space, time, logic or fundamental philosophy. Moreover, it ignores the issue of *who* should devise training courses and which topics should be covered in a course.

HUMAN LEARNING

5. The application of animal experiments to human learning

Classical conditioning is not appropriate to learning in commerce and industry since it does not deal with consciously determined responses. Operant conditioning has had one very specific human application, programmed

81

learning (*see* 22:**11**), but it has been valuable above all in emphasising the patterns which must be followed if any human learning is to be successful, though it must be borne in mind that operant conditioning with animals as subjects is a form of trial-and-error learning, whereas most human learning occurs by copying and by receiving explanations in words or diagrams. Taking training in a manual skill as an example:

(a) The trainee must be motivated (cf. drive) to complete the course and must see some benefit from it, for example an increase in pay, a different job title, or the satisfaction of possessing a skill that few have.

(b) Individual motivation must be maintained during training by various methods:

(*i*) Intermediate goal-setting – dividing the whole task into self-contained units or elements, each with a given standard of performance the trainee tries to achieve

(*ii*) Competition – though it should not be carried too far, competition between trainees is frequently motivating

(*iii*) Indicating relevance – the purpose of any theoretical knowledge or exercises that are given should be explained

(*iv*) Maintaining the trainee's attention.

(c) In designing the programme, the stimulus and response must be made very clear. Recognition of the appropriate stimulus among many incoming sensations, or the appropriate response to a particular stimulus, can be very difficult for a trainee to learn unless the training programme is carefully designed.

(d) At frequent intervals during the training programme the trainee's responses should be reinforced, not of course by pieces of food but by much less tangible rewards.

(*i*) Knowledge of results is an extremely powerful reinforcement for humans. A trainee should very frequently receive reports of the progress he or she is making, either from the instructor or by feedback of a score against a target. The Cambridge psychologist, F. C. Bartlett, said: 'That practice makes perfect is not true. But it is true to say that it is practice, the results of which are known, which makes perfect.'

(*ii*) Praise by the instructor is strongly reinforcing. Strong criticism or penalties for incorrect responses should be avoided; they tend to emphasise wrong methods unduly, encourage unadventurous behaviour and may cause the trainee to dislike the instructor and the task.

The principles of operant conditioning, therefore, indicate how the best results can be obtained from training in industry and commerce. Other important factors in human learning, not derived from animal experiments, are described in the next paragraph.

6. Other factors in human learning

The principles described below are generalisations and tendencies rather than scientific laws; their truth varies according to the qualities of the learner and to the type of subject-matter which is being learned.

(a) *Whole v. part learning* – a task to be learned is usually taught in parts if it involves difficult perceptions or unusual stimulus-response associations. Motivation is stronger when the whole, rather than parts, is taught, particularly when the learners have relatively high intelligence. Whole methods are also preferable where the task loses much of its meaning unless it is dealt with as a complete unit. The teacher must therefore decide which method to follow by weighing difficulty against motivation. If a task is learned in parts (A, B, C, etc.), the following procedure has been found to give the best results:

> Learn A, then practise A.
> Learn B, then practise A + B.
> Learn C, then practise A + B + C, etc.

In this way the early parts are not forgotten when the later parts are learned, and the task has more meaning as it is gradually built up.

(b) *Distribution of practice* – continuous learning should be avoided; either rest periods should be given or practical training alternated with theoretical training. In general, training sessions should be shorter at the beginning of a training programme and longer towards the end. Another generalisation is that complex or difficult material requires shorter sessions than straightforward and simple material.

(c) *The learning plateau* – graphs showing the relationship between performance and training time are called *learning curves*. Figures 5.1 and 5.2 show learning curves for easy and difficult tasks respectively. The curves can, of course, be interpreted in terms of the learner's ability or motivation. Figure 5.3 shows that during weeks 2 and 3 the learner has apparently been at a standstill; from week four onward he or she again makes progress. The horizontal part of the curve (in weeks 2 and 3) is called the *learning plateau*; it can be found in many learning situations where the learner appears to mark time for a period after the programme has been started. The learning plateau has been explained as follows:

> (*i*) The trainee is temporarily discouraged by the increasing difficulty of the task; he or she has lost motivation.
> (*ii*) The trainee has acquired some incorrect responses during the first part of the learning programme which he or she must lose if further progress is to be made.
> (*iii*) The trainee wishes to look back over the material learned so far and discover its significance.
> (*iv*) In the case of manual training, the task may include some difficult

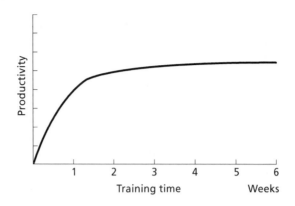

Figure 5.1   Learning curve – easy task

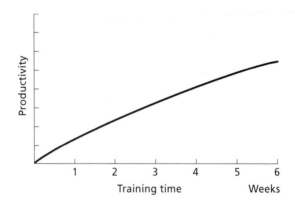

Figure 5.2   Learning curve – difficult task

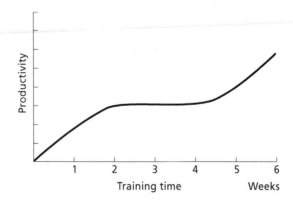

Figure 5.3   Learning curve showing plateau

perceptions or stimulus-response associations. Up to a point the trainee can make progress simply by copying, but beyond this point, he or she must understand and mentally organise these difficulties. The individual must see the significance of the various cues and responses and realise how one movement is co-ordinated with another. When this level of under-standing has been attained, then he or she is able to make progress once more.

The learning plateau can be shortened or removed altogether if the material to be learned is carefully analysed and a method devised which anticipates the learner's difficulties instead of leaving the individual to solve them. Skills analysis (*see* 21:**5**) is an example of this approach).

7. Other theories of learning

Not everything is known about learning, and the operant conditioning (behaviourist) model previously outlined is just one of several approaches to the subject. According to operant conditioning, learning is a *responsive* process with learners taking no part in deciding what should be learned or the methods of training to be applied. The usefulness of this model is contested by the *action learning* school, which regards learning as an essentially partici-pative process that actively connects individuals to their environments. Learning is regarded as a *manifestation* of general intellectual development that need not depend on stimulus-response factors. For example, people learn about time, space and logic through means not at all connected with operant conditioning.

Advocates of action learning assert that learning occurs as people adjust their attitudes and perceptions in consequence of their attempts to relate to the outside world. The mind is said to perform a function similar to that of the digestive system: constantly assimilating, interpreting and accommodat-ing new material.

Another approach to learning is the *social learning* model, which assumes that the individual possesses an intellect which from the very first day of life attempts to understand events and surroundings. The social learning approach has the following implications:

(a) Much human learning results from the observation of other people. At work, individuals learn to behave, feel and perceive the world in the same way as other employees occupying similar work roles and positions.

(b) Failure of trainees to learn typically results from mismanagement of the learning process rather than from trainees' personal inadequacies.

(c) Individuals interact with, and hence learn from, social as well as material environments.

The *cognitive* model of learning is a further alternative to operant condi-tioning. 'Cognition' is the mental process that governs the acquisition of knowledge. It involves intuition, perception, imagination and reasoning, and concerns how people acquire ideas and how perceptions are organised. Accordingly, the cognitive model regards learning as the process whereby individuals come to make sense of their experiences, which they constantly re-evaluate in order to understand better the environments in which they function. This has the following implications:

(a) For learning to occur, learners need to be continually and actively involved with learning materials, which they should perceive as valuable and directly relevant to their training requirements.

(b) Since cognitions derive from complex interactions of thoughts, emotions, observations and experiences, the learning process cannot be dismembered into simple stimulus-response components as suggested by the behaviourists.

8. Memory

For learning to occur the information that has been learned must be stored in some manner, i.e. it must be remembered. Note (importantly) that a trainee's failure to demonstrate knowledge of something that he or she should have learned could be the result not so much of the person's inability to learn, but rather of his or her not being able to retrieve what was learned. The latter could be due to:

(a) Decay of learned information, i.e. not using it for a long period so that less is remembered over time. Memories rarely disappear in their entirety, however, and may be recovered decades after a event even though the memories have lain dormant during the interim period.

(b) Interference with information about a certain topic stored in a person's memory by information concerning other matters, e.g. contradictions between material learned in earlier periods with that learned later on, or confusions among information relating to different topics. The latter might be experienced by a student who spends the day and evening before a chemistry examination revising (say) history. Thoughts relating to history may inhibit the student's recall of material relevant to chemistry during the chemistry examination.

(c) Memory 'blocks'. People sometimes know that they have the answer to a question but (frustratingly) cannot bring it to mind. The answer is 'on the tip of the tongue', yet remains elusive. Little is known about the physiological causes of this phenomenon.

(d) Repression, i.e. the stifling of painful memories in order to avoid the feelings of anxiety associated with them. Certain memories might be so deeply suppressed that psychotherapy and/or drugs are needed to facilitate their recovery.

Forgetfulness

A number of events and situations are known to encourage forgetfulness. These include:

- Inability to practise
- Lack of repetition of important points during the learning process
- An individual's refusal to recognise the validity of a point because it contradicts his or her internal value system, or is seen as distasteful in some way
- Conflicts between new information and what has been learned in the past
- Previously acquired bad habits where learning is concerned.

Information that is unusual or particularly interesting is less likely to be forgotten (even if it is unimportant) than information that is mundane. These highlighted items are said to have been 'sharpened' in the learner's mind, the remainder having been 'levelled', i.e. remembered only in very general terms.

Dual memory theory

This postulates that individuals can transfer large amounts of information from short-term memory to long-term memory through combining small units of information into larger blocs. This is only possible, however, if the learner *understands* each small unit and is thus able to place units into a meaningful context. Examples are remembering telephone numbers by splitting them into sub-units of three or four digits, or learning a song or poem 'line by line' (each line containing just a few words).

Memory is greatly assisted by understanding. Memorisation of information that is not understood is extremely difficult. This fact has many implications for learning, especially learning by parts (*see* **6**).

TRANSFER OF LEARNING

9. Transfer of learning

If someone learns task A and then task B, which is somewhat similar, to what extent will his or her learning of task B be affected? If it is made easier, then it is said that there is *positive transfer of learning*; if it is made more difficult there is *negative transfer*. There are two theories regarding transfer of learning – *identical elements* and *transfer through principles*.

(a) *Identical elements* – this theory states that if parts of task A are the same as parts of task B there will be positive transfer of learning for those parts of task B. For example, two office jobs may be different from each other except that they both include telephoning and alphabetical filing. A clerk who has been transferred from the first job to train for the second job will have an advantage over someone who has been transferred from a completely different job, because he or she will benefit from a carry-over of the learned skills in telephoning and filing.

Unfortunately this theory, although apparently attractive, has difficulties in practice. The elements may not in fact be as identical as they appear at first sight. There are, for example, differences between telephoning to collect debts and to give advice, and between alphabetical filing by company name and by name of town. The clerk may therefore not learn the job as quickly as was hoped, possibly even more slowly than someone whose previous job contained no identical elements. Quite possibly, perception is again important; an operation which outwardly looks the same within two jobs may be perceived differently by the worker because it occurs in different contexts.

(b) *Transfer through principles* – according to this theory, transfer of learning is facilitated not because identical elements are present but because the learner applies to the new task general principles derived from experience in the previous task. Thus a clerk is likely to learn a different clerical job more easily than, for example, a manual worker because he or she can bring to the new job experience of organising documents in an orderly manner.

There is some common ground between the two theories, especially at the point where an element becomes a principle. The second theory, however, encourages an approach to industrial training which is more in accordance with other trends in industrial psychology. It suggests that instead of a rigid training programme run authoritatively, training methods which enable the employee to understand the purpose of the task and its context will help the trainee to adapt in the future to new jobs more easily.

Negative transfer, that is increased difficulty in learning a new task because of knowledge of a previous task, is frequently found. Drivers often report difficulty when first driving a car with an automatic gearbox; quite possibly a novice driver would have much less trouble with it. A typist who has learned to type using two fingers finds a course in touch-typing more difficult than someone who has never used a word-processor before. On the other hand, a touch-typist who is used to copying from documents has little difficulty in learning to type from a dictating machine.

The general rule seems to be that negative transfer between tasks is particularly probable where the same stimulus occurring in both tasks is followed by a different response in each case, e.g. for the same driving conditions one action is required for a manual gearbox, another action for an automatic. Where the stimuli are different, but the responses are the same, there will probably be some degree of positive transfer, e.g. a driver who has learned to stop suddenly to avoid a pedestrian will just as easily be able to stop when confronted by a red light.

10. The importance of transfer of learning

The possibility of negative transfer makes it very important for new employees to be taught correct methods of work from the very beginning, rather than be allowed to pick up incorrect methods which they might find difficult to lose.

Positive or negative transfer may occur when an employee moves to another job, depending on the similarities and differences between the two jobs. Transfer may also be significant when an employee leaves a training environment and begins productive work. The ex-trainee often finds adjustment very difficult, in consequence of having been taught methods which are different from those which other workers are using, or the equipment the person has been trained on may not be similar. The social atmosphere and working conditions in a training school do not usually resemble those in a productive workshop or office, again giving the trainee problems of adjustment. For this reason on-the-job training is sometimes held to be preferable to off-the-job, but the difficulties can be reduced by continually reviewing training methods and equipment, emphasising principles as well as methods, and introducing the trainee gradually to the training environment instead of giving that person the sudden plunge.

LEARNING AND ORGANISATIONS

11. The learning organisation

The term 'learning organisation' is sometimes applied to companies operating in turbulent environments that require transformations in working methods and which – in order to facilitate the introduction of new systems – train and develop their employees on a continuous basis. Hence the very essence of the business – its products, markets, processes and orientations – is likely to alter totally from period to period. Learning organisations discover the key characteristics of their environments and are thus better able to plan ahead. The learning organisation will attempt to identify interactions between the firm's sub-systems that facilitate or inhibit the management of change and is better able to cope with environmental and other change because it can accommodate unpredictability. It is not encumbered with rigid and out-of-date plans and procedures.

Nature of organisational learning

To learn means to absorb knowledge, acquire skills and/or assume fresh attitudes. Learning results in permanent changes in ability or behaviour, as opposed to short-term changes which are soon reversed. Organisational learning means all the processes whereby freshly discovered solutions to administrative problems pass into the firm's 'managerial memory', hence becoming integral parts of the organisation's mechanism for reacting to future events. A consequence is that decision-making procedures are continuously modified and adapted in the light of experience.

12. Single-loop and double-loop learning

According to Chris Argyris, organisations can be extremely bad at learning, unless the learning is simple and routine. Hence an organisation quickly loses the benefits of experience and reverts to its old bad habits. 'Single-loop' learning, according to Argyris, is the learning necessary for an employee to be able to apply existing methods to the completion of a job. This is contrasted with 'double-loop' learning that challenges and redefines the basic require-ments of the job and how it should be undertaken. Single-loop learning typically involves the setting of standards and the investigation of deviations from targets. Double-loop learning means questioning whether the standards and objectives are appropriate in the first instance.

Implementing DLL

DLL inevitably occurs within organisations as they experience crises, fail to attain targets, and experience environmental change. Learning about mistakes in these situations however is costly and inefficient: decisions are taken too late to be effective, and all the benefits of forward planning are lost. Rather the organisation needs to:

(a) Educate its managers in the methods of learning by doing.

(b) Formulate its objectives and standards in such a way that they can be evaluated on a continuous basis and the basic assumptions that underlie them can be empirically tested.

(c) Seek to learn in advance of environmental turbulence or, if this is not possible, adapt its behaviour systematically through trial and error as situ-ations develop. The first loop in the double-loop system is the discovery of facts, acting upon them and evaluating the consequences. Knowledge gained is formal, systematic and explicit. The second loop involves the development of skills and 'know-how' resulting from the first loop and hence a change in fundamental perspectives on the matter under consideration. This feeds back into the interpretation of the facts embodied in the first loop and the actions taken thereafter. Hence, both behaviour and understanding of events and environments will change.

Training, employee relations and staff development

Companies operating in fast-changing environments require regular transfor-mations in working methods and (in order to facilitate the introduction of new systems) must train and develop their employees on a continuous basis. Note however that a learning organisation is far more than a firm which spends large amounts on training. Rather, it requires the unqualified accep-tance of change at all levels within the business, including basic grade operatives. Implications of the learning organisation for training, employee relations and staff development are as follows:

(a) Current policies should be open to question and challenged by all grades of employee. Indeed, management should welcome and actively support such questioning.

(b) Individuals should not necessarily be penalised for experimenting on their own initiative and making mistakes.

(c) There is a need for heavy emphasis on employee communication, with management diffusing information on current environmental trends throughout the organisation.

(d) Employee appraisal and reward systems need not be linked to the attainment of existing goals but rather to finding new and profitable fields of activity.

(e) Workers must possess an understanding of customer requirements.

(f) Employees need to 'learn how to learn'; taking their example from top management.

(g) Managers should encourage workers to manage themselves in relatively autonomous work groups.

(h) Two-way communication between bosses and their subordinates is essential.

(i) Managers (especially supervisors) need to develop coaching skills, and to see their role as being that of facilitator rather than simply issuing instructions.

Note how an organisation is, at base, a group of individuals, so that the manner whereby groups within it learn is affected by social, interpersonal and other intangible factors as well as information systems and other formal learning facilities.

Problems of implementation

Creating a learning organisation is difficult, for a number of reasons:

(a) Employees at all levels within the organisation must want to learn. Thus, the establishment of a learning organisation is a bottom-up process that may not fit in with the culture of a pre-existing bureaucratic and hierarchical system.

(b) Inadequate information gathering and internal communication systems.

(c) Organisational politics that might impede widespread acceptance of the idea.

(d) Top management might not be genuinely committed to the idea.

(e) Certain employees may be unable to learn. Replacement of such people can be troublesome and expensive.

(f) Implementation requires careful planning.

Progress test 5

1. What are the advantages and disadvantages of using experiments with animals as a guide to human behaviour?
2. Define and show the connection between drive, stimulus, response and reinforcement.
3. What are the differences between classical and operant conditioning?
4. Describe how the results of experiments in animal learning can be applied to human learning.
5. What is the learning plateau?
6. Define and give an example of transfer of learning.
7. What is a learning organisation?
8. Distinguish between single-loop learning and double-loop learning.

6

CHANGE AND COMMUNICATIONS

COMMUNICATIONS

1. Definition

Communications consist of all the processes by which information is transmitted and received. The subject matter may include facts, intentions, attitudes, etc., and the chief purpose of communications is to make the receiver of a communication understand what is in the mind of the sender. Therefore a communication is incomplete unless it is received and understood. As the usual result of the understanding is a change in behaviour, effective communications can be regarded as part of a learning process (*see* Chapter 5). A general model of the communication process is offered by Claude Shannon and Warren Weaver who characterise communication systems as relations between inputs and outputs of data. The Shannon and Weaver model is sketched in Fig. 6.1.

Within the system there will exist separate mechanisms for:

(a) Encoding messages (e.g. choosing an appropriate form of words prior to transmission); and

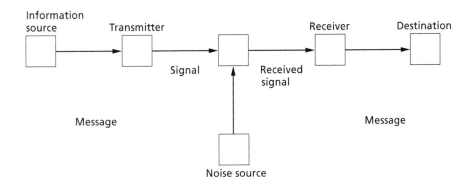

Figure 6.1 Shannon and Weaver's model of the communication process

(b) Decoding (interpreting) the information sent. The recipient may or may not provide feedback to the sender of a message. Noise is any form of interference with messages that has the effect of producing extra and distracting information. Examples of noise are technical jargon, unclear sentences and flowery language.

2. The importance of communications

An organisation may consist of management, employees, premises, equipment, materials, etc. but will not come to life unless communications effectively link all these parts together and co-ordinate their activities. The decisions of management must be made known to employees, and some kind of control system arranged to ensure that these decisions are acted on; the decisions themselves should be based on a flow of information reaching management from all parts of the organisation. Communications in a large, complex organisation with many departments and locations are obviously more difficult than those in a small single organisation; in a large company errors and inefficiency can easily occur because an individual or a department has not informed another of its actions, or has not been informed.

From the psychological point of view, communications have an importance which goes beyond the transmission and reception of information. The form which a communication takes (or, of course, whether communication takes place at all) can profoundly affect the attitudes of the employees and the degree to which they understand and support management policies. Many industrial disputes originate in a failure of communications – a misunderstanding by the employees of the intentions of management (or vice versa) or a misinterpretation of company policy.

3. Types of communications

It is useful to divide communications within an organisation into two kinds: *formal*, meaning arranged or approved by the management; and *informal*, meaning unofficial and unplanned methods of communication.

Another distinction that can be made is between *one-way* communication, in which the sender makes no provision for a reaction from the receiver, and *two-way* communication, which is framed in such a way that a response from the receiver is provided for and encouraged. One-way communication is quick and preserves management authority; two-way communication is much slower and indicates a more participative approach to decision making.

The written or spoken word dominates formal communications, but informal communications also include for example gestures, facial expressions, what is *not* said, or who is present or not present at a meeting. Many rumours begin because someone has drawn conclusions from several non-verbal indications. A glimpse of a senior manager studying a plan of the offices, accompanied by a stranger who holds a large tape-measure, would no doubt start a rumour that the office accommodation is to be changed.

Communications may be analysed yet again according to their *direction*. They may be:

(a) *Downwards* – from a higher level in the organisation to a lower

(b) *Upwards* – from a lower level to a higher

(c) *Lateral* or *sideways* – from one level to another of approximately the same level.

Most formal communications are downwards, while informal communications are mostly upwards or lateral. It seems that many organisations have communications problems because they do not make formal arrangements for communications to flow upwards or laterally, thus cutting management off from employees' ideas and opinions and making co-ordination between departments unnecessarily difficult.

4. Barriers to communication

Both vertical and horizontal communication systems sometimes experience obstacles that prevent information from flowing smoothly around the organisation. Examples of such barriers are:

(a) *Distortion of messages* as they are passed from one person to another through long channels of communication.

(b) *Communication overload* occurring when individuals receive so much information that most of it is disregarded.

(c) *Transmitting messages that are not suitable for the audience* for which they are intended (e.g. sending complex, closely argued memoranda containing long words and sentences to people who possess only a low level of literacy).

(d) *Using vague, meaningless words* and sentences that fail to convey the meaning of a message effectively.

(e) *Inability to listen.* Communication involves receiving as well as issuing information. Some managers are good talkers but poor listeners, hearing only what they want to hear and disregarding any critical comment.

5. Formal methods of communication

The various formal methods of communication may be summarised as follows:

(a) Written instructions and announcements by notices on boards, internal memoranda, notices in pay-packets, company magazines, letters to each employee. One-way, downwwards and permanent.

(b) Broadcast messages over a public address system. One-way, downwards and not permanent, i.e. misunderstandings cannot be checked.

(c) Large meetings of employees addressed by a senior manager. One-way (because response is inhibited in a large meeting), downwards, and not permanent unless the information given is confirmed later in writing.

(d) Small meetings of no more than about twenty employees. Two-way (because comments and questions are easy). Mainly downwards, but with some provision for upwards communication. Not permanent.

(e) Inter-departmental committees. Two-way and lateral. Not permanent in themselves, but usually followed by a written summary of the discussion and decisions reached.

(f) Interviews to give instructions or information or to review a subordinate's performance, i.e. appraisal (*see* Chapter 17). One-way or two-way according to the manner in which the interview is conducted. Downwards and not permanent. If this method is used to transmit instructions through several layers of the organisation by a series of interviews, distortion is possible because the original instructions may be reworded or misunderstood on their way down.

(g) Joint committees of management and employee representatives. Two-way, downwards, upwards and lateral, usually followed by published minutes of proceedings and therefore permanent. These committees may meet regularly, or meet only when required, e.g. to hear appeals against dismissal.

6. Briefing sessions

In a briefing session the manager is concerned not only with imparting information but also with inculcating in employees feelings of participation, security and involvement with the firm. Briefing sessions give managers the opportunity to explain their decisions and remind subordinates of current company procedures. Unfortunately, managers frequently err in calling these meetings only when crises arise. Rather, they should occur regularly (preferably at predetermined intervals) and not just as things go wrong. Sessions should be short and offer:

- Brief reviews of progress to date
- The manager's opinions on contemporary problems
- Outline proposals (with justifications) for future activities.

Suitable topics for briefing sessions include suggested changes in working arrangements, staff transfers and promotion, results of implementation of new methods, details of available welfare and recreational facilities, and examples of how efficiency has been improved in other departments. Briefing sessions, however, are not an appropriate medium for collective bargaining on significant issues such as pay or terms and conditions of employment. Their fundamental purpose is to transmit decisions that have already been taken. Decision making itself requires separate procedures.

7. Informal methods of communication

(a) The normal casual conversations which occur between employees at all levels. Two-way, multi-directional, not permanent.

(b) A private network of telephone or personal contacts in other parts of the organisation, to help in getting the work done more quickly than by using the official methods of communication. This network, often based on mutual favours or personal friendships, is extremely active in most organisations. It is two-way, multi-directional and not permanent.

(c) Surreptitious written material circulating within the organisation, e.g. caricatures, satirical poems. One-way, multi-directional, permanent.

(d) Secret signs and gestures, e.g. warning others of the approach of a manager. One-way, lateral, not permanent.

(e) Rumour, or the grapevine, spread by a combination of the four methods above, and based on miscellaneous sources of information and guesswork. It is rarely entirely false but concentrates on the more sensational aspects of a situation.

It is probably true to say that when the formal communication systems of an organisation are comparatively inefficient, the informal systems become more active.

8. One-way and two-way communication

The sender of a communication should always try to motivate the receiver to understand the message and put it into practice. People can become frustrated quite easily when they try to understand a difficult communication, especially when it is unexpected. When they hear an announcement about important matters concerning their personal welfare, or about topics on which they could express useful opinions, frustration is again likely to occur because it is obvious that decisions have been made without consultation. The conclusions that may be drawn are:

(a) *One-way communication*, which is easy and quick, is quite adequate for subjects which are straightforward, expected or urgent. Methods which can be used are notices, letters, public address announcements, and talks to large meetings.

(b) *Two-way communication*, which can be quite time-consuming and demands some patience and personal skill, should be used for subjects which are complicated, unexpected, of personal concern to the receivers or about which they could make a worthwhile contribution. A better decision may be reached, and it will be accepted more readily. Methods which can be used are small meetings, interviews and committees.

CHANGE

Change can be continuous or discontinuous. The former is generally predictable, smooth and incremental with an orderly transition from one situation to the next; while the latter is (usually) unforeseeable and the result of an external shock that breaks existing trends and patterns. Examples of causes of discontinuous change are new inventions, takeovers of companies, increases in the extent of competition within an industry, or sudden loss of major customers.

9. The effects of change

During recent years radical changes have been occurring in all parts of commerce, industry and the public services. A very rapid rate of technical innovation has produced new materials, new methods and new products. Some companies have ceased to exist, some have been taken over by larger and more successful competitors, while others have grown very quickly and changed their character completely.

The consequences of change include:

(a) Increased complexity of methods of production.

(b) Job changes or redundancy for many workers.

(c) The need for employees to acquire new skills or to modify existing competencies.

(d) Geographical relocation of industries and workers.

(e) Extensive reliance on computers, information technology and decision-support systems.

10. Resistance to change

Research and experience show that there is a widespread tendency among employees to resist change, even though it might appear to outside observers that working conditions would be improved. The resistance may, of course, disappear eventually, the employees then saying that they prefer the new arrangements to the old, but before this happens opposition from employees, accompanied sometimes by industrial action, can make the introduction of change very difficult.

The main reasons for resistance to change are:

(a) Important and permanent decisions about an employee's working life are made by people who are often unknown and remote.

(b) The employee may lose his or her job or be transferred to a lower-paid job.

(c) The skill and experience he or she has acquired over the years may suddenly become valueless.

(d) The worker's status in the firm may be lower.

(e) Cohesive social groups may be broken up, together with established relationships, roles, and customs.

(f) New relationships must be established, new customs learned.

(g) Familiar things represent security: unfamiliar things insecurity.

(h) Personal life may be upset by new working times or a move to a new district.

(i) Workers may feel personally inadequate *vis-à-vis* new technologies, fearing they will not be able to understand new methods and systems.

(j) An individual may resent not having been consulted about a proposed change.

There are individual differences in employees' attitudes to change. Some people welcome change, enjoying the excitement and the disturbance of familiar routine. Others dislike change of any kind, even in their private lives. The great majority lie between these two extremes, their reaction to change at work being influenced partly by the nature of the change and partly by the way it is handled. Again, some companies have a tradition of frequent change and tend to attract employees who like uncertainty and variety. In these companies changes are not likely to be resisted by the employees unless they are obviously unreasonable.

11. Reducing resistance to change

Investments in technological or organisational innovations will not bring the benefits that management expects if the employees show resistance to change. The costs of dealing with disputes and the low level of productivity that is often found can be so great that some managers, particularly in companies where industrial relations are poor, prefer to retain an out-of-date technology rather than face the turmoil that the introduction of new methods would bring. A manager should therefore realise that resistance to change is likely to occur, is not based on stupidity or obstinacy, and can be reduced, if not overcome, by some forethought.

Managements intending to introduce changes in working methods or company organisation should consider carefully the effects of the changes on the firm's human resources. The following should be taken into account when implementing change:

(a) Details of proposed changes and their effects on groups and individuals must be precisely defined. Current attitudes and perspectives on working methods must be identified, as must the attitudes and perspectives necessary for affected employees to adapt successfully to new environments.

(b) Where it is practicable, there should be some participation by the employees in decisions which affect their daily work. If the decision cannot be changed in principle then there should be participation about the way it is put into effect.

(c) The threat to security which many employees feel may be reduced by telling employees individually, and at the earliest possible moment, what their new jobs will be and their position in the new organisation structure.

(d) The loss of valuable skill and experience can be counter-balanced by a programme of retraining, emphasising that no one will be expected to do work he or she is unfitted for, and that an opportunity to learn a new skill is being offered.

(e) It is occasionally possible to preserve existing social groups, transferring them to new work as a unit instead of dispersing them.

(f) The employees who will suffer financially should be at least partially compensated, e.g. by removal and settling-in expenses if they are required to move house, by guaranteeing their previous income for a period if they are transferred to a lower-paid job, and by giving generous *ex gratia* payments if they are made redundant.

(g) Even when the change is comparatively small, perhaps affecting only a few people, resistance will be reduced if the top management of the company show that they know about the change and understand its effects on the employees.

(h) The change should be made known by a two-way communication process (*see* **8**), and two-way communication should be encouraged while the change is proceeding.

(i) Organisations can prepare 'skills inventories' listing all their employees' qualifications, work experiences and competencies. This information can assist management when assessing employees' suitabilities for alternative types of work and perhaps thereby avoid compulsory redundancies.

(j) Bonus schemes might be introduced to encourage the acceptance of new methods.

In some companies it must be admitted that the procedures described above would not be practicable. Employees in a company which has very bad industrial relations may not respond favourably to participation and may not believe statements made to them by management. In such cases, the advice often given is to plan the change in all its aspects very carefully, but secretly, and then implement it very suddenly and without warning. Drastic action of this kind is rarely justified, however, and managers usually have to make their own diagnosis of the situation and decide what position to take up between participation and two-way communication on the one hand and complete authoritarianism on the other.

12. New technology agreements

A new technology agreement is an accord whereby management and unions jointly consider, negotiate and agree procedures for the introduction of major technological innovations. Such an agreement will (hopefully) encourage acceptance of change, reduce uncertainty and involve unions directly at the time a significant change is contemplated. Bargaining then ensues over the amendments to job specifications, working practices and employee reward structures implied by new methods and systems.

Altering technologies by introducing new equipment, materials, etc., is one way of implementing change. Other possible measures are the alteration of *structures* (by changing authority and accountability systems, by centralisation or decentralisation of functions, etc.); the alteration of *tasks* through changing the contents of workers' duties; or the alteration of the *people* who do the work.

13. Re-engineering

This means the radical redesign of business processes, normally *via* the use of the latest information technology, in order to enhance their performance. Conventional approaches to efficiency improvement sometimes fail because they focus on automating and speeding up *existing* systems and processes, merely perpetuating old ways of performing operations rather than addressing fundamental deficiencies and replacing out-of-date systems as a whole. Further problems with orthodox restructuring are that:

(a) The revised structure is likely to become out-of-date very soon after it is implemented.

(b) Frequent alterations in company structure destabilises the organisation and demoralises workers.

(c) Existing employees are likely to be thrust into new and unfamiliar roles for which they lack experience and/or training.

(d) Significant time periods are needed for people to adjust to each restructuring.

Re-engineering, conversely, involves challenging underlying assumptions and changing the basic rules and structures of business management. Examples of re-engineering include:

(a) Abolition of job descriptions and departmental boundaries

(b) Widespread use of empowerment (*see* 2:**13**)

(c) Integration of operations

(d) Finding new ways of achieving specific outcomes

(e) Creating organisation structures based on desired *results* rather than on the functional duties needed to attain them, e.g. by having one person overseeing several types of task and assuming full responsibility for reaching a specific objective

(f) Involving users of the outputs to processes in the design and execution of those processes. For example, departments that work on raw materials could be made partially responsible for selecting and controlling suppliers of the raw materials.

(g) Centralisation of control procedures using computers

(h) Having decisions taken on the spot where work is performed. Note how this implies the removal of some layers in the management hierarchy and hence a 'flattening' of the organisation.

Typically, business process re-engineering attempts to simplify radically the basic low-level operations of a company (e.g. all the operations that go into satisfying a customer order). This could involve collapsing departmental boundaries, integrating computerised management systems, shortening lines of communication and removing marginally useful procedures. Outcomes are likely to affect jobs (employees typically have to become multi-functional), reward systems, and the total number of workers required. *Criticisms* of re-engineering are that:

(a) It is allegedly little more than a device for speeding up work *via* the application of the division of labour and close detailed supervision of employees, hence causing work to become mundane and boring to complete.

(b) Re-engineering is typically accompanied by redundancies within the existing workforce. This demotivates the employees who remain and reduces their commitment to the firm, particularly if they are poorly trained and unsure about their new roles.

(c) The use of technology to control employees' workplace activities represents a directive rather than participative management style.

(d) Human relations issues are trivialised.

(e) Re-engineering might lead to deskilling rather than to multi-skilling.

Downsizing

Downsizing may be completed in the short or long term. Short-term work-force reduction involves getting rid of people quickly, which itself can lead to significant costs consequent to the needs to offer incentives for early retirement, voluntary redundancy and so on. Outplacement expenditures (*see* 10:9) could also be substantial. Long-term downsizing might accompany the systematic implementation of new technologies or working methods which necessitate a gradual reduction in the size of the workforce. Retraining and redeployment are key features of the long-term approach.

Benefits anticipated from a downsizing exercise could include lower overheads, faster decision making, less bureaucracy, better internal communication and more adventurous executive behaviour.

Criticisms of downsizing are that:

(a) It might represent a naive short-term reaction to problems that really require long-term solutions.

(b) Changes implemented may be superficial and ineffective.

(c) Uncertainties surrounding downsizing exercises could encourage a company's best employees to resign, resulting in the loss of crucial skills.

(d) Increased workloads for remaining staff can lead to demotivation and low quality work.

(e) Disruptions caused by downsizing could result in major operational problems.

Morale within a downsized organisation is likely to collapse if the remaining employees feel that layoffs were unnecessary and/or not fairly handled. Also, 'survivors' need to be given a new sense of purpose and not just the belief that they will be expected to work harder to cover the jobs of people who were dismissed. Survivors may feel insecure and lack confidence in their abilities to assume extra responsibility. Pre-existing career ladders may now be blocked, and informal interpersonal communication and support systems will have been disrupted.

Victims of downsizing are likely to react to the loss of employment in disparate manners according to their personalities and how they perceived the importance of their jobs. Certain people are adaptable and deal with redundancy proactively, regarding it as an opportunity to do something different and to take a new direction in life. Typically such individuals possess high skill levels and can find alternative positions with ease. Others become angry and depressed. They feel betrayed by the organisation to which they devoted significant parts of their working lives. This leads to lack of energy, stress, irritability, inability to concentrate and loss of self-esteem.

Managers confronted with the need to downsize an organisation should:

- Implement honest open communication systems with employees (in order to prevent rumours sweeping through the organisation)
- Allow employees to express painful emotions
- Explain carefully the need for downsizing and the lack of any alternative
- Plan the downsizing operation in great detail, exploring all possible options and scenarios
- Recognise the strains imposed on managers who have to convey bad news to colleagues (training for this role might be necessary).

Delayering

This is a technique of downsizing and efficiency improvement that consciously seeks to increase senior managers' spans of control. It has been applied most commonly in tall managerial hierarchies containing several levels of middle management, each individual executive controlling the work of just a few immediate subordinates. A major justification for delayering an administrative system is the advent of computer-assisted management which sometimes enables managers simultaneously to oversee the work of up to 30–35 subordinates. This saves money and speeds up the flow of communications within the firm. Conditions for successful dalayering are:

(a) It needs to be completed as part of an overall strategy for restructuring an organisation; not as a panic measure during a financial crisis.

(b) Paperwork and administrative bureaucracy must be reduced and simplified so as to enable the remaining executives to perform effectively.

(c) The company's most talented people should not be delayered just because they happen to occupy a certain position in the management hierarchy.

(d) Delayering should be done in a single 'big bang'; otherwise uncertainties concerning the possibility of further delayering exercises can greatly demotivate the surviving workforce.

CHAOTIC CHANGE

14. Chaos

More than ever before, HRM specialists have to operate in turbulent environments, and need therefore to learn how to cope with 'chaotic' change. Chaos theory challenges the view that change can be managed in a systematic way. Arguably, disorder and confusion are endemic to business situations, so that management theory and practice should focus on the best means for responding to uncertainty and change. Scientists have been interested in the theory of chaos for generations, seeking to understand the effects on macro-systems of micro events (e.g. a butterfly flapping its wings in northern Siberia can generate a chain of events leading to a hurricane in the USA). The number of possible combinations of micro events and potential outcomes was so immense that new thinking on the nature of 'prediction' and 'uncertainty' was required, taking into account the fundamental instability of nature. These ideas have begun to influence management theory as the pace of organisational and environmental change has accelerated to unprecedented levels.

The 'chaos approach' challenges the conventional scientific emphasis on seeking to discover relationships between cause and effect, since the conventional approach assumes regular mechanistic 'laws of the universe'. Rather it is necessary to recognise that every event affects every other event in some way or other, so that there are no clear and direct chains of causality: the consequence of a change in one variable causes something else, which affects other things which themselves have implications for numerous further variables, including that which altered in the first instance. Thus, nature is a continuous feedback system with inputs and outputs mutually interacting. 'Laws of nature' exist, but are far too complex to be explained in terms of straightforward cause-and-effect relationships. Consider for example the determination of the shape of a snow-flake as it drifts towards the ground. The surrounding air quality, temperature and other environmental conditions affect the snowflake, which itself is simultaneously influencing the environment (by lowering its temperature, changing the humidity, etc.), which affects the form of the snowflake, and so on.

A state of equilibrium (balance) in a business situation can be upset by seemingly trivial events (staff transfers, personal disagreements, changes in procedures, etc.) that have knock-on effects which interact and multiply in an extremely complicated manner. Chaos theory has been offered as an explanation for unexpected turmoils on stock exchanges and foreign exchange markets, the instability of world oil and other commodity prices, and the sudden collapse of organisational structures. The chaos approach has many implications for management, including the following:

(a) Managements cannot control long-term future activities because future environments are totally unpredictable (in consequence of the complexity of cause/effect linkages).

(b) Stable environments can suddenly explode into unstable environments for no seemingly apparent reason, and vice-versa. Hence it is necessary to recognise that 'anything can happen' and plan accordingly.

(c) Organisations can appear to be stable and then suddenly become highly unstable.

(d) Unstable organisations need not be unsuccessful.

(e) Dynamic forces are constantly pulling a business in different directions. Examples of such forces are market conditions, regulatory frameworks, decentralisation of decision making, and human desires for excitement or for a quiet life. An organisation that moves towards stability is likely to ossify and lose its innovative edge. Equally, however, movements towards extreme instability can lead the organisation to collapse.

(f) Firms must be flexible and responsive to environmental change. They need to have effective information-gathering systems and to focus on short-term rather than long-term activities.

(g) Long-term planning is basically useless, as it is not possible to predict future environments.

(h) Mission statements should be regularly updated.

(i) Statistical forecasts will typically be wrong. Simulation and scenario building is preferable as a means for taking decisions.

(j) There can never be an end to the process of change.

To cope with chaotic situations firms need to be able to learn from past and current activities, systematically review the lessons learned from recent experience, and hence develop rapid and flexible responses to fast-changing environments.

NEW WORKING PRACTICES

15. Lean production

The term 'lean production' is used to describe manufacturing processes that minimise waste while maximising the quality of output. Lean production normally involves teamworking with teams themselves taking decisions and solving problems; quality circles (*see* 2:**12**); empowerment (*see* 2:**13**); and flexibility in working methods.

Flexible working practices require employees with attitudes and perspectives which make them willing to assume personal responsibility for workplace problem solving and quality control. Workers must be committed to the enterprise, capable of exercising initiative, and amenable to change. 'Lean production' can succeed only if:

(a) the firm has stable industrial relations (a handful of workers can disrupt the entire production process in, say, a just-in-time system)

(b) the workforce is multi-skilled

(c) managers are well-qualified and themselves adopt flexible approaches

(d) there is regular training of workers. Note how the use of robots (invariably found in lean production systems) can actually increase employees' skills requirements *via* multi-tasking, the need to undertake wider ranges of duties, greater workplace autonomy, etc.

(e) everyone in the enterprise is committed to high quality production and willing to accept change

(f) there are clear chains of command, well-publicised rules and procedures and the constant pursuit of increased efficiency. Critically, management's relations with its workforce must be *predictable*, with employees turning up for work on time and not engaging in voluntary absenteeism. Lunch and other breaks should not be extended and the working day should not finish early.

16. Total quality management and HRM

A firm's total quality management (TQM) system comprises all its policies, operational methods and organisational structures concerned with quality management and the continuous improvement of the quality of its output. TQM focuses on the totality of the system rather than its individual parts, seeking to identify the *causes* of failure rather than the simple fact that failures have occurred. TQM has implications for human resource management because it demands a management style that evokes full and committed co-operation from employees. It requires from *the company*:

(a) provision of training to enable employees to complete a multiplicity of tasks

(b) trust in workers' abilities to deal with quality issues

(c) day-to-day involvement and face-to-face communication with the work-force.

TQM requires from employees the acceptance of responsibility for the success of the business; willingness to contribute to problem solving; flexible attitudes and a preparedness to undertake a wide range of tasks. Further implications of TQM are that:

(a) Even the totally unskilled worker requires training, i.e. instruction in the need for quality and how the organisation is seeking to achieve it.

(b) Employees working in different departments need to know about each others' problems.

(c) Piece rate wage payment systems are to be avoided, as they encourage the production of substandard output.

Policy requirements for involving employees in TQM include the following:

(a) Management should consciously regard employees as if they were the firm's customers. Hence, management must attempt to discover employees' needs, perspectives and situations. Managers become mentors and facilitators rather than authority figures.

(b) Managers need to regard basic grade workers as having valuable contri-butions to make to the quality management process.

(c) Workers have to be educated to believe that they *should* seek continuously to improve working practices. This means convincing the workforce that employee suggestions and contributions are highly valued.

(d) Each worker needs to be shown how his or her actions affect the attainment of the firm's quality objectives.

Quality champions

One way to inculcate a commitment to TQM among the existing workforce is to identify among supervisors and within the workforce a handful of highly influential individuals and enlist their support in championing the cause of quality management. People who are known, liked and trusted by current employees are far more likely to be believed than any amount of management exhortation. Recruitment of quality champions will not be possible if management is not (a) itself totally committed to the new methods, (b) seen to be attempting to protect employees' interests, or (c) making available the information and resources necessary to effect change. Quality champions might be invited to participate in planning the implementation of intended systems and in solving problems as they arise.

17. HRM in the IT-driven firm

Use of computers and the latest information technology presents the employee with:

- New alternatives regarding how work can be completed
- More interesting tasks, challenges and responsibilities
- A wider range of duties to be completed
- The need to take an increased number of decisions
- Fresh possibilities for structuring the working day.

Traditional dividing lines between occupational categories break down, and the demarcation of jobs can become irrelevant: vertically as well as horizontally. Other important possible consequences of computerisation that have implications for human resource management include:

(a) Deskilling of tasks in certain parts of the enterprise, while new types of skill are required elsewhere, leading perhaps to resentments and conflicts between various categories of worker.

(b) Total integration of all phases of production, office administration and internal communications, causing more frequent and perhaps closer interactions among employees in different sections of the firm and between various levels in the managerial hierarchy.

The competencies needed to succeed within a computerised work environment are general in nature and not necessarily related to particular occupations. Hence there is much scope for job rotation, undermining thereby workers' specific control over what were previously highly specialised jobs that could not easily be given to other categories of employee.

18. HRM implications of end-user computing

End-user computing means the imaginative manipulation of computer packages and systems by employees who have no special qualifications or expertise in computing or IT, so that non-specialist package users have maximum discretion in determining the outputs of the system. The implications of end-user computing for human resource management include:

(a) There is a levelling out of the performance of the firm's best and worse employees, since the computer will do a lot of the employee's basic work. This makes it difficult to appraise workers' performances accurately and to determine a fair system for rewarding employees.

(b) Staff require a flexible approach to their work, must undertake tasks relating to a wider variety of business functions, and need to be able to assess the reliability of outputs from systems that contain information on topics with which they are not familiar.

(c) Workers' capacities to choose *how* they complete IT-related tasks should make their jobs more interesting and provide numerous possibilities for acquiring experience of higher-level work.

(d) There is less need for middle managers.

(e) Employees have open access to a wide range of the firm's databases. Note how this can create data security problems and possibilities for the deliberate disruption of systems.

Japanisation of working methods

The term 'Japanisation' is sometimes used to describe the alteration of group working arrangements and social relationships following the introduction of Japanese working methods and personnel practices. Japanese approaches typically involve close supervision of workers in conjunction with genuine attempts to overcome the boredom and alienation typically associated with automated production lines. This is (hopefully) achieved through single status (see 8:**23**), the removal of as many restrictions as possible on how workers do their jobs, and employee involvement in management decisions (via quality circles for example).

Problems arising from Japanisation have included:

(a) Naive attempts by western firms to copy Japanese production methods but *without* accompanying them with Japanese employment conditions (long-term job security, provision of training and welfare benefits, worker participation in decision making, etc.).

(b) Western workers' typical dislike of what they perceive as their employing firms' interference with their private lives.

(c) Hostility towards the imposition of the Japanese work ethic, with its emphasis on long hours, unquestioning loyalty and obedience to the company, intensive working, conformism, and so on.

(d) Disquiet over the Japanese practice of recruiting only young people to work in their foreign operations, generating much resentment in the local workforces in the areas around subsidiaries. Recruitment of young workers is justified by Japanese employers on the grounds that they have no inhibitions about flexible working practices, are more receptive to discipline, and are physically fit and energetic. They have hopes for the future and will willingly accept overtime and greater responsibility.

Single union deals, moreover, are still regarded with great suspicion by many people, and the provision of welfare benefits by employers may be viewed as disagreeable paternalism.

Reference

Shannon, C. and Weaver, W. (1949), *The Mathematical Theory of Communication*, University of Illinois Press.

Progress test 6

1. Why are communications important in an organisation?
2. What is the difference between these types of communication:
   (a) formal and informal
   (b) one-way and two-way
   (c) downwards, upwards and lateral?
3. Describe three methods of formal and three methods of informal communication.
4. When should two-way communication be used in preference to one-way?
5. Why do employees resist change?
6. How can resistance to change be reduced?
7. What is meant by re-engineering? Discuss the problems associated with re-engineering.
8. What is a quality champion?
9. List the implications of end-user computing for the management of human resources.

Part Two

INFLUENCES ON
EMPLOYEE BEHAVIOUR

7

INDIVIDUAL DIFFERENCES

INTRODUCTION

1. Fitting the person to the job

It is essential to achieve a good fit between worker and job; one of the aims of human resources management is to see that employees are working in jobs which are suitable for them and that their jobs are designed with due regard to the abilities and limitations of the employee.

The methods by which employers try to make the best use of their employees and satisfy their needs are mainly in the fields of training and development, transfer and promotion, and pay. A manager must have some understanding of the important differences that exist between individual employees. Managers must know how these differences can be identified, to what extent they can be measured, and how they can be related to job performance.

2. Heredity and environment

Variations in behaviour are due to differences between individuals, which in turn derive from differences in heredity and environment. Since there are countless possible combinations of these two factors, the differences between individuals are infinite in number and degree – a fact which makes life interesting, though sometimes difficult, and presents the manager with the opportunity to use the differences in a productive way. When they are thoughtfully used they can help to increase productivity and job satisfaction; badly used, or ignored, they can reduce efficiency and bring about unhappy relationships at work.

It is usual to deal with individual differences under three headings – physique, intelligence and personality.

3. Physique

This can be defined as the attributes of the body; its size and shape, its speed and strength of movement, the efficiency of its senses. Physical qualities are basically determined by heredity, though they can be developed or suppressed by upbringing or training. For example, there are inherited tendencies to be short or tall, fast or slow, but a poor diet will cause a person to be shorter than otherwise might have been the case, and appropriate training will enable an athlete to run longer and faster than before.

It is easy to measure most physical characteristics objectively, i.e. measurements of height, weight, eyesight, reaction speed, etc., can be quickly and simply made, independent observers producing identical results. Under modern conditions physical differences are not very important in placing individuals in appropriate jobs. The advance of technology has greatly reduced the number of jobs in which great physical endurance or strength is required, and instrumentation often decreases the need to rely on the senses of touch, hearing, etc.

Eyesight is the most important physical factor in the employment field; in some manual jobs it is necessary for employees to have above-average eyesight or perfect colour vision. In other jobs, co-ordination of limb movements or speed of reaction may be important. Tests are available to measure these qualities.

A small number of candidates for jobs have disabilities which exclude them from certain occupations or compel them to work only in sheltered conditions. The Disabled Persons (Employment) Acts 1944 and 1958 and the Disability Discrimination Act 1995 place obligations on employers in this respect (*see* 15:**12**).

INTELLIGENCE TESTING

4. Intelligence

Intelligence is the capacity to make effective use of the intellect, which is the sum total of the mental functions of understanding, thinking, learning, observing, problem-solving and perceptual relationships. It is sometimes called mental ability.

The structure of intelligence is still the subject of intense controversy among psychologists. It is not necessary to recount the various theories that have been put forward; in simple terms, most British psychologists believe that there is a general factor of intelligence which enters into all functioning of the intellect and influences the performance of all tasks. Subordinate to general intelligence are a number of specific mental abilities which enter into the performance of some tasks but not others, e.g. verbal fluency, spatial ability, mechanical aptitude, numerical ability.

5. Intelligence tests

If they are to be useful, intelligence tests must be *reliable* and *valid*.

(a) *Reliable* means that the test gives consistent results when repeated.

(b) *Valid* means that the test measures what it claims to measure, i.e. intelligence and not general knowledge.

Most intelligence tests used in commerce and industry are group written tests, i.e. they may be given, if necessary, to several candidates simultaneously, and consist of a number of printed questions to which the candidates must give a written reply. The test is then scored with the use of a key.

Publishers of tests usually restrict their sale to people who have been trained in their use. They must be given in precisely the manner described in the test manual, and the results interpreted by a qualified person. Critics of this practice allege, however, that in so doing publishers and psychologists conceal the foundations upon which tests are constructed and the validity of their assumptions, and thus exclude all possibilities for external scrutiny, criticism and academic debate. And people who take such tests but are then not happy with the scores they are awarded cannot challenge the marking criteria and propriety of the test.

6. Types of questions

Some intelligence tests contain questions of only one kind, e.g. verbal, numerical or spatial (i.e. diagrammatic) questions. Most tests used in industry contain a mixture of all three types, the candidate being asked questions along the following lines:

(a) Identify a word or phrase which has the same or opposite meaning as the one given.

(b) Solve anagrams or decode words.

(c) Perform addition, subtraction, multiplication and division.

(d) Identify one or more shapes which match or complete others.

(e) Write down a number in a series.

(f) Solve a problem in logic.

Intelligence tests have a time limit (usually between 20 and 60 minutes), and very few candidates indeed complete a test within the limit.

7. Intelligence quotient

The early work on intelligence testing conducted in the first half of this century was done with children, and it was found convenient to introduce the concept of *mental age*. If a child was able to accomplish tasks which were considered appropriate to a child of average intelligence aged x, he or she was said to have a mental age of x which could, of course, be higher or lower than the child's chronological age, or the same. An easy measure of intelligence was then possible by expressing a mathematical relationship between mental age and chronological age, as follows:

$$\frac{\text{Mental age}}{\text{Chronological age}} \times 100$$

This formula is known as the *intelligence quotient*, usually abbreviated to IQ. A person of average intelligence will obviously have an intelligence quotient of 100.

It is found that the mental age shown by intelligence test scores does not increase beyond a certain point; for some people the maximum mental age is as low as 13, for others as high as 20. Therefore, in order to avoid an apparent steady decrease in intelligence with age, chronological age in the IQ formula never exceeds 15. Although mental age may not increase, adults may perform many tasks better as they get older because they have learned from experience.

To compute intelligence quotients for adults, testers give a series of problems to a large number of people and compute the average score which then represents average intelligence, or IQ = 100. People scoring above or below level 100 in the tests are regarded respectively as above or below average intelligence.

Intelligence testing is a highly specialised skill for which extensive training is necessary. And trained psychologists themselves are the first to cast doubt on the usefulness of attempts to measure IQ. The questions asked need to be culturally neutral, independent of general knowledge and past training (otherwise people could learn to become intelligent), while answers given should not depend on environmental factors or be related to the circumstances of the test. In reality, however, results are often sensitive to how people feel at the time the test is attempted – whether they are tired, nervous, have the flu, or whatever; and quite often candidates do not take the exercise seriously. Intelligence tests should give consistent results when they are repeated and outcomes compared with other indicators of ability and records of actual performance.

Success in an intelligence test does not guarantee that a candidate will perform well in a job. The demands of a particular type of work could be much greater or less than the level of intelligence required by an IQ test. Also candidates who are told they scored highly might wrongly assume that they possess exceptional ability for their work.

Race and intelligence

In 1969 the US psychologist Arthur Jensen reported that on all known IQ scales black Americans scored an average 15 points lower than white Americans. According to Jensen, 80 per cent of all variation in IQ was due to hereditary factors. Hence he suggested that black people on average had an inherited and therefore uncorrectable lower level of intelligence than whites and thus should be encouraged to pursue only lower-level learning of specific skills, not higher-level learning that required abstract reasoning. Critics of Jensen were quick to point out that:

(a) The IQ tests applied were devised by American whites, for whites and preassumed that test candidates possessed educational backgrounds common only in white communities.

(b) There was much hard evidence demonstrating that improvements in socio-economic conditions in black areas soon led to huge increases in observed average IQ in those areas (Hunt 1969).

(c) Whites in poor areas were also observed to have a lower than average IQ.

(d) Studies of black children adopted by white (middle class) parents in the 1930s and 1940s reveal that these children had an average 20 point higher observed IQ than their natural mothers.

(e) Studies of the recorded IQs of identical twins separated at birth and reared apart showed large differences in the observed IQs of the twins in each pair (14 points on average with a range of 30 points) regardless of race. How could this happen if hereditary factors explained IQ more than environment?

PERSONALITY

8. Definition

Personality may be defined as the sum total of the various qualities that are shown in behaviour. Although this definition taken literally includes intelligence and physique, the term personality is usually taken to include above all emotions, motivation, interests and social qualities. It is incorrect to use the word personality as a synonym for charm or dominance; everyone has a personality, just as everyone has weight, height and intelligence.

9. Personality judgments

We assess the personality of someone we know well by recalling their behaviour in different circumstances, usually describing it in terms of traits, e.g. they are judged to be sociable, enterprising, tolerant, etc. As an individual passes through adolescence into adulthood, the personality becomes more consistent in the sense that behaviour in various circumstances becomes more predictable.

It is dangerous, however, to describe personality in terms of traits because they are affected so much by the situation at the time, as well as by personality. A person may be dominant when dealing with subordinates but submissive when speaking to his or her boss. Co-operation and honesty are other traits which are often highly dependent on the situation at the time.

10. Self-report personality tests

Most personality tests are written questionnaires of the self-report type, asking subjects for their views about their behaviour in various hypothetical situations or their opinions about other people. Although tests of this kind are used as one of the tools of personnel selection by a few consultants and large companies, the general opinion in this country is that personality questionnaires are unlikely to be useful and reliable in industry, for various reasons.

(a) Self-report is inherently unreliable when people answering the questions have a strong reason for presenting themselves in the best light. The prospective employer can never be sure which answers are genuine and which have been faked.

(b) Even when the candidate tries to answer the questions sincerely, a misleading impression might be given because the person's self-image and self-perceived personality may not correspond with his or her personality as seen by others.

(c) Experience has shown that personality questionnaires are not reliable predictors of success in a given job and that the scores are unstable – when a test is repeated with the same candidates, different scores are obtained.

11. Other tests of personality

These seek to identify individual traits such as introversion, extroversion, personal assertiveness, or ability to cope with stress and/or expected future patterns of behaviour (management style, potential for leadership, etc.). Personality covers very many aspects of individual identity – emotions, motivations, needs, interests, attitudes, social relationships, many of which are environmentally or culturally determined. A personality test tries to discover whether the candidate really wants to do certain things, rather than simply whether he or she is technically capable of doing them. Interpretation of results is of course highly subjective. Specific problems are that:

(a) Candidates, knowing their personalities are being examined, will attempt to present themselves in ways that create favourable impressions.

(b) Individual attitudes and behaviour can change drastically over time and according to circumstances.

(c) Assessments relate to observed behaviour and expressed opinions at a particular moment. These might be untypical, so average behaviour is largely ignored.

(d) Because of the subjectivity in interpreting results, candidates might be given very different personality descriptions by differing assessors.

Techniques for personality testing include **(a)** projective tests, where candidates supposedly project their personalities by describing what particular shapes or objects (ink blots, etc.) mean to them; **(b)** assessment of candidates' contributions to leaderless group discussion; and **(c)** self-analysis sessions where candidates state their own interpretations of their personal behaviour and motivation. All these are prone to the problem that subjects can (and do) behave abnormally when being observed, and they all rest on subjective, intuitive interpretations of candidates' performances.

12. Physical indications

Many people when selecting employees are influenced by intuitive first impressions, based perhaps on an interpretation of body-build, manner and speech and affected by prejudices about dress and hair style and by the mood of the moment. Some claim to be able to judge a person as soon as he or she enters a room. Occasionally, such judgments have turned out to be surprisingly accurate; usually they are not. In some jobs the first impression a person makes is very important, e.g. sales representative, but in most jobs it is irrelevant. In any case, training can often greatly improve the first impression a person makes.

13. Situational tests of personality

In tests of this type, the personality of the candidate is not judged indirectly from answers to questions or interpretation of appearance but more directly from the observation of actual behaviour under controlled conditions.

Usually, candidates are dealt with as a group (typically from five to ten in number), with the group being asked to discuss a topic of current interest for about 30 to 45 minutes without a chairperson; hence its title 'leaderless group discussion'. Several observers are able to watch and listen, but they do not intervene except to bring the discussion to an end or introduce a new subject.

Misleading results can, however, sometimes occur. Some candidates, normally quiet and retiring, can for the day of the test successfully act the part of the self-assertive leader; and frequently the performance of individuals is affected by the composition of the group – if it contains one or two uncongenial members the remainder may behave out of character.

14. Examples of psychometric tests

Tests of intelligence, personality, motivation and other aspects of an individual's psychological make-up are collectively known as 'psychometric tests'. Typically, test subjects complete a checklist questionnaire which asks them to express their preferences in relation to various issues and situations, e.g. by requiring candidates to state which outcome to a problem they find most desirable, or to select words and phrases (such as 'persuasive', 'gentle', 'innovative') which they regard as describing aspects of their personalities most and least accurately. Tests that require subjects to choose between several alternatives when answering each question are referred to as 'ipsative' tests.

Examples of psychometric tests commonly used by UK companies include:

(a) *The 16 PF test*, which assumes the existence within people of 16 clusters of behaviour ('factors') relating to such matters as a person's excitability, assertiveness, emotional stability, conscientiousness; whether he or she is extrovert or introvert, cheerful or depressive, etc.

(b) *The Myers–Briggs type indicator*, which seeks to categorise test subjects under four main headings: objective/intuitive, logical/emotional, decisive/ hesitant, introvert/extrovert.

(c) *The DISC test*, which aims to identify the extents of 'dominance', 'influence' (or 'inducement'), 'submission' (or 'steadiness') and 'compliance' in test-subjects' personalities. Test results are plotted onto star-shaped graphs which purport to show a person's self-image, actual personality, and ability to cope with pressure.

(d) *The Eysenck personality inventory*, which consists of a simple questionnaire involving yes–no answers to questions intended to measure candidates' introversion/extroversion and stability/neuroticism. Each of these dimensions is then broken down into sub-categories. For example, 'stability' segments into 'phlegmatic' and 'sanguine'. 'Phlegmatic' is then split into categories for passive, careful, thoughtful, peaceful, controlled, reliable, eventempered, and calm. The term 'inventory' (rather than 'test') is used here to indicate that there is no pass/fail cutoff. Rather, the exercise aims to isolate personal strengths and weaknesses in specified psychological dimensions.

15. Usefulness of psychometric tests

Advantages to using psychometric tests for employee selection include:

(a) Tests are cheap to administer. A single person can give a test to (say) 30 or 40 people at each sitting. This makes testing useful for situations where large numbers of employees have to be engaged within a short period.

(b) It enables distinctions to be made between candidates with exactly the same academic qualifications and work experience.

(c) Objective information about a candidate's psychological characteristics can be a valuable adjunct to other selection procedures. This additional information should help remove subjectivity in selection.

(d) There is little point in (expensively) training employees who are not mentally capable of absorbing relevant information. Psychometric testing, its advocates argue, can weed out such individuals.

(e) People of genuine intellectual ability who, nevertheless, have received minimal formal education may be identified.

Arguments against the use of psychometric tests are that:

(a) It may be unfair. People might be arbitrarily labelled as outstanding or mediocre on the basis of a (perhaps ill-conceived and poorly-validated) 20-minute test, while ignoring their overall achievements and educational backgrounds.

(b) Workers may be allocated to (inappropriate) roles and occupations in direct consequence of inaccurate information about their psychological characteristics.

(c) Practice at psychometric tests can lead to improved test performance; indeed, there exist publications on 'How to Pass Psychometric Tests'.

(d) A candidate's motivation and state of mind at the time a test is taken (e.g. if the person has just suffered a bereavement) can affect results significantly.

(e) The total worth of a person depends on so many factors that any selection of a sub-set of them is bound to be arbitrary.

(f) Requiring a job applicant to take a test can itself cause that person to feel nervous and to fear the humiliation of possibly doing badly. This can create a self-fulfilling prophecy; the individual loses self-confidence, which leads to poor performance in the test!

APTITUDE AND ACHIEVEMENT TESTS

16. APTITUDE TESTS

Quite frequently a candidate applies for a job in which he or she has had no previous experience. The employer accepts that training will be necessary, but wants to ensure as far as possible that the candidate is suitable for training. The employer wishes to know whether the candidate possesses an aptitude for the job, i.e. the basic mental and physical qualities which can be developed into the specific skill.

An aptitude seems to be made up of several components: general intelligence, one or more specific mental abilities, physical attributes (such as muscular co-ordination), experience in a related activity and possibly personality factors like interests and motivation.

Some aptitudes, e.g. managerial or selling aptitudes, are so complex and controversial that no satisfactory way of testing for them has yet been discovered.

Some of the simpler aptitudes, for which tests have been shown to give worthwhile results, are:

(a) *Verbal aptitude* – a good command of written or spoken English.

(b) *Arithmetical aptitude* – ability in addition, subtraction, multiplication and division.

121

(c) *Spatial aptitude* – facility in judging shapes and dimensions important in e.g. drawing, packing or driving.

(d) *Mechanical aptitude* – understanding of mechanical principles.

(e) *Manual dexterity* – more accurately called psychomotor dexterity.

Tests are available for these aptitudes, but their construction and interpretation is a skilled task, only to be carried out by psychologists or under their guidance.

17. Achievement tests

In contrast to aptitude tests (which measure potential ability after training), achievement tests measure the skill and knowledge that the candidate already has. They are the most common of all tests; every candidate during his or her interview is asked at least one question about previous experience.

Construction of achievement tests is usually quite simple; generally they are either *work-sample* or *symbolic*.

(a) *Work-sample tests* consist of a carefully-chosen part of the actual job. If the candidate fails to reach the required standard of performance in this part it is assumed that his or her performance in the whole job will be inadequate. Examples are the shorthand and keying tests frequently given to candidates applying for secretarial posts, the vehicle-handling test for road transport drivers, and the test piece of work for engineering craftsworkers.

(b) *Symbolic tests* are used when a work sample would be impracticable; they represent aspects of the job in symbolic, usually verbal, terms. They may consist of questions to probe the candidate's knowledge, circuit diagrams or technical specifications to be interpreted, or occasionally in-tray exercises in which the candidate is confronted with a batch of incoming letters and memoranda to be answered.

Advantages of achievement tests are that **(a)** they can expose candidates who claim to possess abilities (keying speeds, machine skill, etc.) they do not actually have, and **(b)** tests are directly relevant to the work the successful candidates will have to perform in the job. Note, however, that a test will necessarily cover only a part of the successful candidate's eventual duties. A candidate who fails the test might be assumed incapable of doing the entire job, which need not be true. A secretary, for example, might fail to achieve a predetermined minimum speed under test conditions, but this does not necessarily mean the candidate is an inadequate secretary overall.

Also, tests are undertaken in specific test conditions. Success in a driving test proves that the candidate did well over the test circuit, yet this person may not be a good driver elsewhere. Job applicants will feel nervous during a test, and this may cause them to do badly. It is a fact that people who have done a particular test previously do better on average than people attempting it for the first time. Thus, candidates who have already taken and failed a similar test will have an advantage, yet these might be precisely the sort of candidates the test was originally intended to weed out. Further problems are outlined below.

(a) Candidates who have passed a test might assume they possess knowledge or ability which in fact they do not have. Supervisors also might conclude that new entrants are fully competent simply because they did well in a single test, conducted in highly specific conditions.

(b) An internal candidate for promotion who is given and fails a test might lose self-confidence and hence underperform in a currently held job. That person will, moreover, be identified by colleagues as a failure and in consequence the worker's morale might collapse.

(c) Some ethnic and other minority groups consistently do badly in certain types of achievement test because they have not had access to educational and training programmes necessary to equip them with the basic skills expected of test candidates.

(d) High marks obtained in a test do not guarantee that the successful candidate will do well in the vacant post. In particular, high marks do not say why the candidate passed. Knowledge of the causes of success or failure might be as valuable to management as identification of individuals capable of obtaining high marks.

(e) Achievement tests do not evaluate the whole person; only a small sub-section of his or her characteristics. Note that a formal educational qualification awarded after perhaps several years' study should in principle offer much more information about a person overall.

VALIDATION OF TESTS

18. Methods of validation

All tests used to measure individual differences should be validated, i.e. an investigation made to see if the test measures what it is claimed to measure, or predicts what it is claimed to predict. During this investigation the text may also be standardised, i.e. a cut-off score decided, below which a candidate is to be rejected.

There are four types of validity, the last two being particularly relevant for personnel selection.

(a) *Content validity* – an inspection is made of the subject-matter of the test to see if it is relevant to the quality being measured.

(b) *Construct validity* – the results of the test are compared with the results obtained by the same group of candidates who have taken another test, the validity of which has already been established.

123

(c) *Predictive validity* – a group of candidates is given the test. They are all engaged, and their subsequent job performance compared with their test scores. If there is a reasonable relationship, the test is valid and it can be standardised, i.e. a score identified which will cut off the unsuitable and admit the suitable candidates. There are possible disadvantages with this method:

(*i*) Job performance may be difficult to assess objectively.
(*ii*) The process of validation may be lengthy; adequate assessment of performance may not be possible until a long time after the test has been given and a large number of results will be necessary before validation is complete.
(*iii*) In practice it is rarely possible to engage *all* candidates, but if the results of the test are compared with the performance of a selected group only it is not completely validated.

(d) *Concurrent validity* – the test is given to present employees in the job in question. If the test is valid, then the more proficient the employee, the higher the score. This method is quick, but has the following disadvantages:

(*i*) Standardisation is difficult.
(*ii*) The test is validated against a non-typical group, i.e. present employees rather than candidates for employment.
(*iii*) The employees may not behave normally when they do the test. They may be suspicious and deliberately give a poor performance, or they may be anxious to excel themselves and give an unusually good performance.

A common method of validation is to combine predictive with concurrent validity. The test is first tried out on present employees, after reassuring them that it is not in their interests to falsify their performance. Prima-facie validity can be established and standards approximately found. The test is then used on candidates for the job concerned, their subsequent progress being compared with their test scores. Validity can therefore be confirmed and the standard fixed more precisely. It is in any case good practice to make a continual review of test scores and proficiency because many jobs gradually change in character, thus reducing the validity of the test.

GENDER AND ETHNIC DIFFERENCES

19. Sex differences

Men and women are different on account of their chromosomatic makeup. Humans normally have a total of 46 chromosomes; 23 from each parent. Twenty-two of the 23 pairs concern the general development of the individual (shape, hair and eye colour, etc.), regardless of sex. The 23rd pair (comprising two *gonosomes*) determines sex. Women always carry the basic X gonosome. Men transmit X or Y. An XX combination at the moment of conception results in a female baby; an XY combination means a male. Thus a child cannot enter the world without a female X chromosome, but does not have to possess the male Y. Accordingly, there is no YY gender; the most that can occur is the XY composite. Male chromosomes *must* have female chromosomes, but not *vice versa*, implying that female is the core sex.

How different are men and women?

Is a man basically a woman with extra bits and pieces (caused by evolution and the biological division of labour); or are men and women *fundamentally* different beings, who happen circumstantially to mate? Medical science is not yet able to answer this question, and there are arguments in favour of either proposition. The issue is important for human resources management, however, because the belief that men and women are *quintessentially* different can contribute to sexual stereotyping (e.g. that men are tougher, more aggressive and competitive, rational, etc., whereas women are more emotional, interested in people rather than ideas, dependent, and so on), which can lead to discrimination and the absence of equal opportunities at work.

The case for regarding men and women as basically the same includes the following observations:

(a) Gender difference is only one (albeit important) element of human genetic make-up. Genetic messages for characteristics such as eye colour, facial features, hair texture, etc. are common to both sexes.

(b) Men have breasts that serve no useful purpose, implying a common biological ancestry and both sexes deriving from a single hermaphrodite source.

(c) It has been noted that the timings of the menstrual cycle of women forced to live together in close proximity for several years within isolated and self-contained groups (women serving long-term prison sentences, for example) sometimes converge, suggesting that the timing of the menstrual cycle might be partly determined by psycho-physiological factors and not therefore a purely physical phenomenon. Reproductive functions (such as the menstrual cycle), according to this argument, are nothing more than an evolutionary biological convenience enabling half the population to specialise in bearing children while the other half specialises in other fields of activity.

Arguments *against* men and women deriving from a single source are as follows:

(a) Males and females are constructed from different materials. The sex of an individual may be determined from virtually any part of the human body: a fragment of tissue, a piece of bone, a strand of hair, a drop of saliva, a fingernail, etc.

(b) Arguably, men and women have disparate instincts that are independent of upbringing, social experience, and so on. Examples might be a women's instinct to nurture and defend her children, or aggression in males.

125

20. Ethnic differences

All humans belong to a single species, *homo sapiens,* and share common inherited characteristics. Hereditary traits vary among individuals. However, when intermarriage occurs within a group which is isolated from others through geographic or other barriers, some of the characteristics become highly concentrated in the members of a local population. Separations of groups that last for many thousands of generations can result in the emergence of races. Racial differentiation, therefore, is *fluid* since races are changeable over the centuries as the pool of common human genes is redistributed and refocused in consequence of intermarriage. Also, individual variability of genetic make-up *within* racial groups often outweighs racial similarities. It follows that racial differences are a matter of degree rather than of kind.

Communities adapt to their physical environments, so that outsiders come to associate the physical characteristics of certain groups with behaviour relevant to certain environments (for example, Eskimos coping with the arctic climate). Such communities then come to be perceived by others as representing a distinct racial group. Clearly, therefore, there are no grounds for supposing that any particular ethnic group will perform better or worse as employees, because (i) the group itself will have emerged from many other groups, and (ii) the factors that created the racial characteristics of the group over thousands of generations have no relevance to the contemporary world of work. Hence the case for racial segregation and discrimination against certain ethnic groups in employment situations has no logical foundation.

References

Hunt, J. (1969), Has compensatory education failed? *Harvard Educational Review,* Series 2, 130–152.
Jensen, A.R. (1969), How much can we boost IQ and scholastic achievement? *Harvard Educational Review,* 31, 1–23.

Progress test 7

1. In what way is the measurement of physique different from the measurement of intelligence or personality?
2. Define 'intelligence'.
3. What does 'IQ' stand for? Define the term
4. Why is a high intelligence test score not a guarantee of success in a job?
5. Define 'personality'.
6. What are 'self-report' personality tests? What is their value in personnel selection?
7. Should personality be judged by first impressions?
8. What are the chromosomatic differences between men and women?

9. What is the difference between an aptitude test and an achievement test?

10. Describe one way in which a test may be validated.

11. Tests can, however, measure some attributes which are difficult to assess by interview. They can thus help to reduce the areas of subjective judgement and of possible human error in the selection process as a whole. (Plumbley – Recruitment and Selection).

(i) Explain the uses in employee selection of each of the following tests and attempt definitions of the italicised words:

   (a) General *intelligence* tests
   (b) Special *aptitude* tests
   (c) *Attainment* tests
   (d) *Personality* tests.

(ii) State and briefly discuss two objections to the use of psychological testing in personnel work.

8

PHYSICAL AND PSYCHOLOGICAL INFLUENCES ON WORK

FATIGUE

1. Definition

Because it is used rather loosely, the term fatigue is difficult to define. The most satisfactory definition appears to be 'a reduction in the energy available to perform a task'. Fatigue is used to explain physical changes occurring in the body as a result of effort, the subjective feeling of tiredness and the cause of an otherwise unexplained reduction of output during a working spell.

Towards the end of the nineteenth century the Italian scientist Mosso, using a device known as the ergograph, formulated some laws of physical fatigue, i.e. the fatigue occurring as the result of muscular effort. The most important of his laws are:

(a) Light loads lifted frequently cause less fatigue than heavy loads lifted infrequently.

(b) Rest pauses can give complete recovery from fatigue.

To illustrate the first law, moving a heap of sand by 100 movements of a large shovel will be more fatiguing than moving the same amount by 200 movements of a shovel half the size. Jobs which involve lifting should therefore be designed in such a way that heavy loads are avoided and lighter loads used instead.

The second law has been verified in industry many times. It seems that the output of employees engaged on manual work gradually rises at the beginning of an uninterrupted working spell until it reaches a steady amount; after a time output begins to decrease until the spell is over. The periods when output is increasing, stable or decreasing vary in their length according to the characteristics of the job and workers, but the pattern remains the same.

If a rest pause is introduced before production begins to fall, the period of stable production will usually continue after the pause, and the period of decreasing production will be shorter. The more physically taxing the job, the more frequent the rest pauses that are required.

Physical fatigue shows itself in ways other than reduced output and a feeling of tiredness. Evidence of an objective kind can be found in the changed chemical composition of body fluids and in the accumulation of waste products of muscular exertion, particularly lactic acid. The physiological effect of a rest pause is to allow the body fluids to return to their normal state and for the waste products to be removed from the vicinity of the muscles, but the recovery will take longer if the rest pause occurs after the physiological changes have started.

Experiments can be made to determine the number and timing of rest pauses which give the best results; it is not advisable to allow workers to rest when they feel tired, because by then fatigue will be well established and a comparatively long rest pause will be necessary before they feel refreshed and are able to put out their normal amount of energy. To obtain the greatest benefit, therefore, the rest pauses should be compulsory and occur before the worker begins to feel tired. Study of the rate of output will show a decrease or irregularity occurring before the feeling of tiredness arrives; the rest pause should be taken at the average time of this change in output.

STRESS

2. Stress at work

Stress has both positive and negative aspects. Some employees thrive on pressure; it helps them draw on physical and emotional resources and they actually enjoy tense and challenging situations. Stress triggers in these people the adrenalin needed to sustain intense effort and to be able to cope with several different problems all at the same time. Continued exposure to stress, however, can cause extreme tiredness, irritability, physical upsets such as headaches and rashes, insomnia and, possibly, aggression towards fellow employees.

Individuals react to stress physiologically. On encountering a threatening situation, a person experiences a release of hormones which drains blood from the skin and the digestive system; glucose and fat are released into the bloodstream, and breathing becomes more rapid. Whether this is harmful or beneficial depends on the background to the event and its duration – initial excitement can quickly develop into serious long-run distress. Causes of stress at work include:

(a) Not knowing which tasks should assume priority and thus trying (unsuccessfully) to complete all of them simultaneously.

(b) Unclear job descriptions and organisation charts/manuals leading to ambiguity about who should do what.

(c) Feelings of personal inadequacy and insecurity.

(d) Frustrations at not being able to get things done.

(e) Lack of communication with superiors, and conflicting demands placed on the individual by superiors who impose incompatible goals. For example, technical managers may demand high-quality output from a certain section, while the firm's accountant concurrently insists that the head of the section drastically reduce its operating costs.

(f) Bad personal relationships with other workers.

(g) Overwork, which may be quantitative (having too much work to do) or qualitative (finding work too difficult). Moreover, long working hours are frequently connected with a poor diet, lack of exercise and inadequate relaxation.

The symptoms of stress can be physical, psychological and/or behavioural. Physical manifestations include restlessness, hyperactivity, impatience, high blood pressure, headaches, weight loss and skin complaints. Stress might also cause other illnesses which result from its effects – excessive smoking, drinking, poor diet, and so on. Severe exhaustion, cramp and backache can occur in extreme cases.

Anxiety is perhaps the clearest indicator that someone is unable to cope. It affects the abilities to concentrate and relax, creates irritability and generates feelings of malaise and unease. Perceptions are affected – stress-ridden individuals can become irrational, emotionally volatile and excessively suspicious. Employees who experience stress-created fatigue will be dull, clumsy, unable to think clearly or perform work for long periods.

Work performance typically deteriorates when individuals experience protracted exposure to high levels of stress. Some individuals become antagonistic, others withdraw into themselves. Tension, tiredness and anxiety often lead to outbursts of hostility and aggression. Workers become oversensitive to criticism, and increasingly unable to relate to friends and working colleagues. Sleep patterns alter, daytime tiredness ensues. The general run-down in a person's health can lead to frequent colds, upset stomachs and other minor illnesses. Routine errors become more frequent. Stress-prone individuals have more accidents than others. Many people respond by taking tranquillisers (or anti-depressants), smoking heavily (with consequent health problems), or by drinking excessive amounts of alcohol. Marital and other family difficulties are common among stress-ridden people.

3. Coping with stress

The first step in coping with stress is to recognise its inevitability in certain types of work: repression of anxiety only makes the situation worse. Thereafter, the following techniques and strategies might be useful for accommodating stress:

(a) Delegation of duties to subordinates to avoid work overload.

(b) Deciding in advance when to withdraw from particularly stressful activities, e.g. making a conscious predetermined decision to leave a meeting if certain contentious issues are discussed, or specifying a maximum personal workload and never exceeding this.

(c) Keeping a *stress diary* to record all stressful occurrences and hence identify common causes.

(d) Conscious relaxation.

(e) Training in personal assertion and/or psychological self-awareness methods such as transactional analysis.

(f) Restructuring jobs in order to remove exceptionally stressful elements (which should then be redistributed equally among all the staff).

4. Bullying at work

Workplace bullying is increasingly recognised as a major cause of stress. It can result from personality characteristics within the bully, or from external factors which encourage managers to behave in bullying ways. Examples of such factors include:

- 'Macho' management cultures within an organisation
- Pressures to meet efficiency targets, reduce costs, etc.
- Perceptions that departmental objectives can be achieved more quickly through using threats and intimidation
- Implementation of downsizing exercises, restructuring, delayering, re-engineering, and so on.

Manifestations of bullying at work are shouting and swearing; physical intimidation; the use of threatening body language; sexual, racial or age-related harassment; and persistent public and/or private criticism or ridicule. Workplace bullying could also involve:

- Seeking complaints about the bullied individual from other members of staff
- Deriding the value of the victim's contributions to the organisation's work
- Giving a person jobs that he or she cannot reasonably be expected to complete satisfactorily, and then claiming that the individual is incompetent
- Removing responsibilities from the bullied worker while simultaneously allocating menial tasks
- Withholding information or deliberately supplying false information
- Sabotaging or impeding the victim's work performance
- Applying excessively tight supervision

- Increasing the victim's workload and/or setting impossible deadlines.

The mental effects of bullying can include depression; anxiety; loss of concentration, motivation and self-confidence; and feelings of anger and hostility towards colleagues and the employing firm. Physical consequences are similar to those arising from fear and extreme stress: insomnia, fatigue, headaches, skin rashes, ulcers, and so on. Absenteeism is likely to be high in organisations where extensive bullying occurs. And overall organisational efficiency will fall. Possible solutions to the problem are:

- Changes in the organisational culture of the enterprise
- Appointment of a company ombudsperson with whom victims may discuss their experiences in total confidence. The ombudsperson needs to have direct access to the firm's chief executive.
- Creation of formal grievance procedures specifically designed to deal with bullying
- Provision for rapid redeployment of victims to alternative jobs
- Counselling of bullies, followed by disciplinary proceedings if their behaviour does not improve.

Violence at work

The UK Health and Safety Executive describes violence at work as a miserable, dangerous and stressful experience that must not be considered an acceptable part of any job (except in special occupations, e.g. police officers) no matter what form the violence takes or the reasons behind an incident. Employees should not be expected to put up with violent or aggressive behaviour. According to the Executive, certain factors are likely to increase the likelihood of an employee encountering workplace violence, notably:

- Involvement with money
- Contact with the general public
- Working with unpredictable people, e.g. in healthcare or social welfare situations
- Guarding valuable property
- Working outside or in a mobile workplace such as a taxi or lorry
- Transporting or delivering goods or services
- Working alone or with a small number of colleagues
- Working late at night or out of normal working hours.

If threatened with violence, the Executive recommends, a person should try to appear calm; be aware of his or her tone of voice and speak slowly using short sentences; maintain physical distance from the potential aggressor and avoid prolonged eye contact; listen; attempt to change the subject; and try to negotiate a suitable compromise. In Britain it is a legal requirement under the Reporting of Injuries, Diseases and Dangerous Occurrences Regulations 1995 that all acts of 'non-consensual' violence inflicted on persons at work be notified to the Health and Safety Executive if they result in incapacitation for longer than three days. However the Executive recommends that employees report all injuries or mental distress arising from violence to their employer, and that if possible the firm provide training in how to diffuse and/or avoid violent situations, e.g. instruction on dealing with difficult customers, personal assertiveness, breakaway techniques, etc.

Sexual harassment

Sexual harassment in the workplace can involve unwelcome sexual advances, requests for sexual favours, improper physical contact, or other conduct of a sexual nature (sexist comments, jokes and so on) where such conduct unreasonably interferes with an individual's performance at work and/or creates an intimidating, hostile or offensive working environment. It is especially serious when someone's conditions of employment or benefits (promotions, pay rises, etc.) depend on submission to this form of behaviour. Psychological distress within the victim and his or her eventual resignation from a job is likely to result from the practice. Sexual harassment is an infringement of personal freedom because it restricts an individual's ability to act as he or she wishes. It represents a loss of *control* over one's personal affairs. Responses to sexual harassment can be confrontational or acquiescent. The latter involves feelings of helplessness about the situation and/or nervousness at the prospect of having to complain. Confrontational reactions (shouting, assertive complaints to supervisors, etc.) carry the risk of long-term embarrassment if management simply ignores the victim's plight.

Companies can deal with sexual harassment *via* the establishment and publication of complaints procedures for use by victims; by informing all members of a firm that sexual harassment will not be tolerated; and through the development of appropriate policies and codes of practice. Problems with sexual harassment policies are that:

(a) Sexual harassment in practice is extremely difficult to prove.

(b) Targets of sexual harassment are frequently reluctant to report the problem, fearing adverse consequences if a complaint is not upheld.

(c) Most accusations of harassment are made against men. It may be that males who engage in sexually harassing behaviour are more likely to be accused of impropriety than are women who act in exactly the same way! Consequently, sexual harassment might come to be regarded as an exclusively male-initiated activity, hence discouraging men from complaining about being harassed.

(d) Policies are useless if the people guilty of harassment are themselves top managers within the firm.

(e) It can be difficult to distinguish between sexual harassment and 'normal' male/female flirting behaviour.

133

ACCIDENTS AT WORK

5. Accident proneness

An accident at work is an unplanned event which occurs within a planned programme and is actually or potentially harmful to the worker. During the 1914–18 war, studies in munitions factories produced the concept of accident proneness – that certain employees are inherently likely to be involved in accidents to a greater degree than others, irrespective of the job or working environment. The original research showed that a large proportion of the accidents suffered by a group of workers happened in fact to a very small minority; the members of this small minority were then called accident prone.

Later research has not always confirmed the findings. It has often been found, for example, that workers who appear to be accident prone during one period are safe workers during another period, their places being taken by workers who previously had low accident records. As an illustration of this, it was found in a study of nearly 30,000 bus drivers in America that the unsafe drivers in a three-year period became the safe drivers over the next three years. Conversely, the safe drivers in the first period, i.e. those who had one accident or none, became unsafe in the second, causing no less than 96.4 per cent of all accidents occurring in the whole group.

The explanation of this kind of result seems to be that the liability to become involved in accidents is due more to chance factors and the behaviour of others than to an inherent quality in the worker. On the other hand, accident statistics have sometimes shown that even in different periods the same workers have an above-average proneness to accidents, but only when their jobs have not changed. The generally accepted view at present is that accident proneness in the sense of a disadvantage that certain workers always take with them wherever they go is very rare; we must think instead of accident proneness as a result of the interaction between the worker and his or her job situation. Thus, insofar as accident proneness exists at all, it is due to:

- Unsuitability for the job, or lack of training in it
- Temporary factors, e.g. frustration, worry or ill-health
- A very small number of inherently unsafe workers.

Other theoretical approaches to the explanation of differences in accident rates between organisations and workers are:

(a) *The domino theory* of accidents, which asserts that accidents typically occur following a predictable series of independent stages involving (*i*) an unsafe environment, (*ii*) individual fault, and (*iii*) a dangerous act.

(b) *The situational theory* of accidents, i.e. the hypothesis that accidents typically result from failures in working systems rather than individual behaviour or accident proneness.

ERGONOMICS

6. Definition

Ergonomics is concerned with the study of the mutual adjustment between people and their work. It draws contributions from both psychology and physiology in order to design equipment, the environment and working procedures which will promote both the well-being of employees and the effectiveness of work processes. It regards the worker not as an adjunct to the machine but as part of a human/machine production unit, behaving according to the following sequence:

(a) Stimulus, e.g. instruments, warning lights and buzzers, appearance, sound or smell of work in progress.

(b) Perception (through the appropriate senses) and decision making.

(c) Response, e.g. operating controls, using tools or hands, communicating with others.

(d) Result, i.e. a change in the work, which produces new stimuli, thus repeating the sequence.

The ergonomist tries to fit the process to the person, rather than expect the individual to do the best with equipment which has been designed with engineering, rather than human, considerations in mind. The following approaches are adopted:

(a) *Displays* – are the things the operator looks at and listens to providing information quickly, easily and unambiguously? Should dials, gauges, warning lights, etc., be redesigned? Is perception difficult?

(b) *Controls* – can the operator change the state of the machine and materials, quickly, easily and naturally? Are levers, wheels, switches, etc., in the most convenient position?

(c) *Working environment* – is the operator's place of work well lit, heated to an appropriate temperature and free from excessive noise or humidity?

THE WORKING ENVIRONMENT

7. Illumination

Research has established minimum standards of illumination necessary for many industrial tasks. Expert advice is available from illumination engineers, but some of the most important rules are:

(a) Task lighting should be focused on the task itself; focusing on an area adjacent to the task will cause fatigue and loss of attention.

(b) Too much contrast between the lighting of the task and the lighting of the environment causes eye fatigue, and may lead to accidents because the worker may find difficulty in adjusting his or her vision when moving from a bright to a relatively dark area.

(c) Glare can produce discomfort or poor vision. It can be minimised by ensuring that lights do not shine in workers' eyes and that working surfaces do not reflect light.

(d) Some variety in the visual environment should be provided by walls of different colours or the sight of some distant object, e.g. a view through a window.

(e) Even when workshops and offices appear to be well lit by daylight from windows and glass roofs, the illumination may have to be supplemented by artificial light because some areas may be in shadow. The colour of the supplementary lighting should then be a good match to daylight.

(f) Dirty windows, walls or light sources reduce the illumination available. They should be cleaned and maintained regularly.

8. Noise

There are four unfortunate effects of excessive noise in industry:

(a) *Deafness* – exposure to loud and prolonged noise will in most people produce deafness, beginning with inability to hear high notes. Deafness may occur so slowly that the worker may not notice it; an enlightened employer will test the hearing of the firm's employees to see if their hearing is deteriorating in noisy conditions.

(b) *Efficiency* – research shows that repetitive work which is not mentally demanding does not suffer when carried out in noisy conditions. On the other hand, work which requires accuracy, concentration and alertness will deteriorate. For example, inspection and calculation become less efficient under noise, and scrap or spoiled work becomes more frequent. It is also probable, though not definitely proved, that noise increases the number of accidents.

(c) *Annoyance* – employees seem able to become accustomed to practically any level of noise in time, but they will complain about it when the noise is:

(*i*) occasional (particularly when high pitched)
(*ii*) apparently unnecessary
(*iii*) unexpected
(*iv*) unexplained.

Therefore the annoyance caused by noise can often be reduced by explanations or warnings.

(d) *Interference with communication* – oral messages may be unheard or misunderstood in noisy conditions.

9. Heating and ventilation

In this field three factors are important: temperature, humidity and air movement. All three can affect performance and comfort at work.

(a) *Temperature* – in factories the optimum air temperature for light work is 10°C (65°F) and the range in which most people feel comfortable is 15° to 20°C (60° to 70°F). Heavy work in factories is best carried out within a range of 12° to 15°C (55° to 60°F). In offices the comfort zone is 19° to 23°C (67° to 73°F).

(b) *Humidity* – this is only important when conditions are extremely damp or extremely dry. In the first case employees complain of stuffiness and in the second they feel uncomfortable because of dryness of the nose and throat.

(c) *Air movement* – it is generally agreed that an air movement of about ten metres per minute should be aimed at; this level of movement is just perceptible. If temperatures are above or below the ideal, then air movement should be greater or less, respectively, than ten metres per minute. Air movement may be improved by the use of fans or by an air conditioning system.

The sick building syndrome

Deficiencies in some of the previously mentioned environmental factors can combine to create what has come to be known as the 'sick building syndrome' (a syndrome is a collection of several symptoms of a malaise). The term is commonly applied to certain types of recently constructed office premises that have air conditioning, sealed heating systems, sound-proofed rooms, uniform layout of sections, etc., which in unison tend to cause headaches, eye strain, lethargic depression, and other minor illnesses among the people who work in them.

SAFETY

10. Safety at work

The cost of accidents at work is enormous, both in human suffering and in lost production, and the management of every company should give special attention to improving safety. As the concept of accident proneness is now largely discredited (*see* **6**), safety programmes concentrate as far as possible on ensuring that the employee is suitable for the job and that work is conducted in a safe environment. The following are often included in a safety programme:

(a) *Thorough investigation of all accidents*, to try to prevent the same accident occurring again. Therefore a system of reporting all accidents is required; in some companies near misses as well as actual accidents have to be reported.

(b) *Continuous review of accident prevention measures*, bringing them up to date

137

particularly when there is a change in process or materials, and ensuring that machines are guarded, gangways kept clear, electrical equipment insulated, etc.

(c) *Careful selection of new employees* to eliminate those who are physically or mentally unsuitable.

(d) *Training which includes safety as an integral part* rather than as an after-thought.

(e) *Safety devices and clothing* which are acceptable to employees; if they hinder the performance of the job or make the wearer feel clumsy and conspicuous, they will not be worn.

(f) *Consideration of the possible effect of PBR schemes on safety.* If workers frequently remove safety guards or adopt dangerous practices in order to earn high bonuses it may be necessary to abandon PBR and pay time rates only if the company can find no way of making the process completely safe.

(g) *Propaganda campaigns,* e.g. posters, safety suggestion weeks, etc., are sometimes used, but there is general agreement that their effects are short-lived.

(h) *Provision of adequate first-aid and medical services* to mitigate the effects of any accidents which occur.

11. Law regarding safety

The Health and Safety at Work, etc. Act 1974 covers not only all people at work (except domestic workers in private employment) but also the general public who might be affected by the work of others. It is mainly an enabling measure, laying down general principles of safety and providing the power to make detailed safety regulations. For the time being the previously existing safety legislation continues in force, in particular the Factories Act 1961 and the Offices, Shops and Railway Premises Act 1963.

The most important general duties laid down by the 1964 Act are:

(a) Employers must maintain safe plant, safe systems of work and safe premises. They must also ensure adequate training and supervision in safety matters.

(b) A written company safety policy must be prepared and made known to all employees. Employers must let employees know the arrangements for putting that policy into effect.

(c) A company must be conducted in such a way that the health and safety of persons not in employment there are not affected.

(d) Manufacturers and suppliers of articles for use at work must ensure that they are safe when properly used.

(e) Employees have a duty to take responsible care to avoid injury to themselves or to others, and they must co-operate with employers in meeting statutory requirements.

(f) Safety representatives from among the employees may be appointed by recognised trade unions. They must be consulted by the employer on health and safety matters, they may inspect the employer's premises, and they have the right to be informed by the safety inspectors of any matters found to affect health and safety. If at least two safety representatives require it, the employer must set up a safety committee.

> *Note*: The Health and Safety Commission recommend that in companies where trade unions are not recognised, a safety committee should nevertheless be set up consisting of members drawn from management and employees. The employee representatives on such a committee would not have the rights of inspection and information described above.

12. Management of health and safety

A number of EU Regulations on the management of health and safety at work came into force in 1993 requiring employers to undertake 'risk assessment exercises' intended to identify potential dangers to the health and safety of employees or anyone else likely to be affected by the firm's operations. The Management of Health and Safety at Work Regulations 1992 in particular required that the risk assessment be completed by competent people (who may be outside consultants) and, that, for firms with five or more workers, a permanent record of the exercise be maintained. In addition the firm is obliged to:

(a) Devise and implement specific procedures for dealing with emergencies.

(b) Draw up a plan for putting into effect preventative and protective measures.

(c) Train employees in safety matters and ensure that workers are capable of avoiding risks. Employees (including temporary workers) must be informed of risks in *language they can understand.*

(d) Take into account working conditions and local workplace hazards when selecting equipment.

(e) Identify unavoidable risks in relation to handling operations, having regard to the shape, size and weight of the load and the ergonomic characteristics of the workplace (humidity, space available, etc.).

Other major Regulations in the 1993 package were:

(a) *The Provision and Use of Work Equipment Regulations 1992*. Under these regulations 'work equipment' is defined to include everything from hand tools to complete factories or refineries, while 'use' means *every* aspect of equipment operation, servicing and cleaning. Employers are obliged to make sure that equipment is suitable for its intended use and that it is only used for appropriate purposes. When selecting equipment, employers must take into account working conditions and the hazards of the workplace. Proper training and information relating to the equipment must be given to workers.

(b) *The Manual Handling Operations Regulations 1992.* These require employers to identify unavoidable handling risks in terms of the shape, size and weight of the load, the handler's posture while performing operations, and the ergonomic characteristics of the workplace (space available, humidity, etc.). By law, hazardous manual handling operations must be avoided wherever possible.

(c) *The Workplace (Health, Safety and Welfare) Regulations 1992*, and *Personal Protective Equipment at Work Regulations 1992.* The purpose of these two sets of Regulations is to tidy up and consolidate a large number of existing pieces of legislation currently spread over several different statutes. They concern such matters as the working environment (lighting, ventilation, room space per worker and so on), facilities (toilets, rest areas, drinking water, etc.), removal of waste materials, cleaning and maintenance of protective clothing and equipment, and the design and approval of new personal protective equipment.

13. Accident reports

There are government regulations which compel employers to report all serious accidents (and other accidents involving more than three days' absence from work) within seven days. Approved report forms may be purchased from commercial stationers or from HMSO (form F 2508). Records of accidents, dangerous occurrences and outbreaks of certain specified industrial diseases have to be kept for at least three years.

Accident reports are useful for identifying and preventing the recurrence of dangerous activities. Also, formal records are needed to investigate subsequent claims for compensation from injured employees. Every firm employing more than nine persons, or less than nine if the firm is covered by the Factories Act, is legally obliged to keep an accident book. Reports should be completed as quickly as possible after the incident (before memories fade) and give full details of the victim (age, sex, occupation, etc.) and of the accident (time, date, circumstances). It should list witnesses, describe the injuries sustained, first aid administered and note whether (and if so when) an ambulance was called and when it arrived and departed. The cause of the accident should be stated, with details of whether safety rules were followed, whether protective clothing was actually worn, machinery properly guarded, etc.

Copies of the report should be circulated to the worker and his or her union, to safety representatives and to the personnel department. Collectively, accident reports should be analysed to identify recurring causes and the effects of changes in machinery, working methods, paces of production, shift work pattern, etc. on the frequency of accidents.

14. The Health and Safety Commission

This was set up under the Act to develop health and safety policies. It consists of representatives of employers, employees, local government and appropriate professional bodies. The Commission's policies are operated by the Health and Safety Executive, which enforces the relevant legislation and inspects premises. The separate inspectorates, which previously existed under various safety Acts, are now combined in one body under the Executive.

15. Enforcement

If an inspector discovers a contravention of the Act, one of the previous Acts or a safety regulation he or she may do one of the following:

(a) *Issue a prohibition notice*, requiring the employer to stop a process which carries the risk of serious personal injury until remedial action has been taken.

(b) *Issue an improvement notice*, requiring the employer who contravenes a statutory provision to remedy matters within a certain time. Appeals against an improvement notice or a prohibition notice may be made to an industrial tribunal.

(c) *Seize, render harmless or destroy* any substance or article that is considered a cause of imminent danger or serious personal injury.

(d) *Prosecute* any person contravening a relevant statutory provision, in addition to or instead of serving a notice as in **(a)** and **(b)** above. For most offences a fine is levied, but serious cases may be prosecuted on indictment in the Crown Court, with the possibility of an unlimited fine or imprisonment for up to two years. The powers given under the Act to prosecute a person rather than a company apply not only to a director or manager but also to any employee who does not co-operate in safety matters for his or her own or for colleagues' protection.

16. Compensation for accidents at work

An injured employee who considers his or her injury to be due to the negligence of the employer may bring an action for damages against that person under common law. The employer is also held liable for accidents caused to employees by the action of other employees, provided that this behaviour was in the course of their employment. If the employee's action is successful he or she will be awarded a lump sum depending mainly on the severity of the injury. The Employers' Liability (Compulsory Insurance) Act 1969 requires employers to take out insurance against such claims.

Legal claims of this kind are independent of any action a health and safety inspector may bring against the employer, though of course if the inspector has taken action as in **8**, the claimant's case will be greatly strengthened.

WORKING CONDITIONS

17. Hours of work

Manual workers in most companies work longer hours than non-manual workers, partly because they are expected by custom to start earlier in the morning and partly because they do more overtime. Statistics published by the Department of Employment show that on average, male manual employees work about seven hours a week longer than male non-manual, and female manual employees about three hours a week more than female non-manual.

Overtime

A company asks its employees to work overtime for the following reasons:

(a) to maintain production when there is a shortage of labour

(b) to increase production temporarily or seasonally without increasing the number of employees

(c) to enable maintenance to be carried out on plant and equipment while its users are not working.

Therefore, when properly managed, overtime can add considerably to the efficiency of the company. Research shows, however, that much overtime is worked not in response to one of the above needs but as a means of supplementing employees' incomes. It then becomes an inefficient practice because factory services have to be maintained beyond normal working hours for no gain in production.

Some companies have reduced or abolished overtime by negotiating with their employees a higher basic rate of pay so that earnings without overtime become approximately the same as total earnings were previously. A salaried worker is often not paid for overtime; when this is the case, the rate is usually plain time or a very low premium rate.

18. Shift work

During the last 30 years, no doubt because expensive capital equipment now being used must be continuously operated to cover its costs, there has been a steady increase in shift work, i.e. an arrangement in which one set of workers takes over from another to enable the production process to continue operating without a break.

It takes the form either of 'double day shifts' in which there are two successive shifts but no night shift, or three-shift working, in which the process continues for the 24 hours without a break.

Three-shift working can bring the following problems:

(a) Supervisors require special training because management is not there to support them outside normal working hours.

(b) An incoming shift frequently blames an outgoing shift for bad work, an untidy workplace, etc.

(c) Canteens, first aid and security services must be provided.

(d) Machinery may break down more frequently because it is in constant use.

(e) Travelling to and from work by public transport is often difficult at shift change-over times.

Shift work, moreover, can cause significant problems to the individual employee, including:

(a) Disruption of biological rhythms (adrenalin secretions, sleep/waking patterns, body temperature, etc.)

(b) Reductions in the quantity and quality of sleep, accompanied by constant tiredness

(c) Digestion problems and possible loss of appetite

(d) Disruptions of family life, anxieties about child care, social isolation and worsening social relationships.

Shift workers, on average, have more severe accidents than others, and the quality of their outputs is sometimes poor.

19. Flexible working hours

A comparatively new development, sometimes called flextime or flexitime, allows employees to choose within limits what hours they work. Schemes differ in detail, but they frequently contain the following features:

(a) Employers must all be present during a certain part of the day, usually called *coretime*, e.g. from 10.00 to 12.00 and from 14.00 to 16.00.

(b) They may choose when they arrive or leave within limits set by the company, e.g. not before 8.00 or after 19.00.

(c) They may vary the length of the lunch break.

(d) Hours worked in excess of the standard total for the accounting period (usually a month) may be taken as whole or half-day holidays.

The advantages claimed for the system are that it improves employee

143

satisfaction by giving considerable freedom for individuals to arrange their hours to suit their own circumstances, that it reduces absenteeism and that it enables the place of work to be staffed outside the usual hours. On the other hand, lighting and heating will cost more, and those employees who attend early or late may not be able to work normally because other people on whom they depend are not there.

20. The Working Time Directive 1994

This entitles employees to a daily rest of eleven consecutive hours in any 24-hour period; to rest breaks during any working day longer than six consecutive hours, and a weekly rest period of 24 consecutive hours. The maximum working week is restricted to 48 hours, although member states have the right to opt out from this provision until the year 2006 *provided* employees are legally permitted to refuse to work more than 48 hours without jeopardising their employment. Full-time employees can take three weeks' paid leave annually (four weeks after 1999). Under the Directive, night workers may not work more than eight hours in any 24-hour period. They can also demand a free initial health assessment plus regular medical checkups thereafter. If night working causes an employee to experience health problems then he or she should (wherever possible) be transferred to day work.

Objections to the Directive have included:

(a) Rest breaks within a shift might be unworkable in continuous process operations where plant cannot be left unattended.

(b) Opportunities for overtime could be an important incentive necessary to induce employees to accept night-shift working.

(c) Overtime night-shift working is a convenient means whereby firms facing labour shortages can satisfy short-term increases in the demands for their products.

The Directive on the Protection of Young People 1996

This establishes a minimum working age of 15 years (except in special circumstances) and requires that working conditions for employees aged between 15 and 18 be adapted to protect their physical, moral and social development. Persons under 18 are prohibited from undertaking certain types of work, and risk assessments (*see* 8:13) must be completed before young people commence employment. Also they must not work for more than eight hours a day or 40 hours weekly: night work is heavily restricted. 'Working children' (i.e. school students under 15 years of age who are undergoing work experience or training) must be given 14 hours continuous rest in any 24-hour period. Other young workers under 18 must have at least 12 hours continuous rest daily. All young people are entitled to two consecutive days' rest each week. A half hour break must be given after four and a half hours' work. The

UK has secured an opt-out from the Directive's provisions on the length of the maximum working week until the year 2000.

21. Employee welfare

Workers' morale and feelings of attachment to an employing organisation may be greatly enhanced through the provision of welfare services. Examples of such services are:

(a) Payment by the employer of subscriptions for employees' membership of private medical schemes

(b) Provision of a welfare officer able to counsel employees in relation to their private problems (including bereavement and retirement counselling)

(c) Occupational health screening

(d) Social and recreational facilities

(e) Having a company lawyer provide free legal advice to employees in approved circumstances

(f) Rehabilitation schemes for injured workers

(g) Availability of company loans to workers, benevolent funds and the provision of financial help with housing or transport costs.

SINGLE STATUS

22. Equalising status

An increasing number of firms apply 'single status' to all grades of employee, who share the same canteen, use the same car park, have equal access to company superannuation schemes, etc. The most important effects on manual workers' conditions are:

(a) Fringe benefits, particularly pensions and sick pay, are improved.

(b) Hours of work are shortened.

(c) Control becomes less strict; for example, manual workers are no longer required to clock on.

(d) A salary is paid instead of a wage, though often the employees prefer it to be paid weekly rather than monthly.

Benefits and drawbacks to single status

The following reasons are often given for equalising status:

(a) In many companies improvements in work methods have made the boundary between manual and non-manual employees much less distinct.

(b) Today there are law guaranteeing men and women equal pay for work of equal value.

(c) It is necessary to recognise the importance of the production operative's role and of the need to motivate production workers (via teamwork, quality circles, etc.).

(d) European Union Directives on aspects of employee protection (health and safety for example) that apply to *all* categories of employee.

(e) Staff status will reduce labour turnover among manual workers.

(f) Jealousies between manual and non-manual workers will be reduced.

(g) Industrial relations within the company will be improved.

The last three reasons are hopes rather than certainties because deep-rooted attitudes cannot change rapidly. A much more important reason is the belief that it is morally wrong and logically indefensible to treat manual workers in an inferior way.

Other factors encouraging the adoption of single status are:

(a) A century of public education has created a labour force that, for the most part, is literate and capable of communicating meaningfully with people from other backgrounds and in higher level occupations.

(b) Nowadays, skills shortages are just as likely in manual as in non-manual occupations so that it is no longer necessary to offer higher status to non-manual workers as a recruitment incentive.

(c) Many manual jobs that (normally) do not carry 'staff' status (with superannuation and so on) in fact require more skill and longer periods of training than certain non-manual jobs which automatically attract 'staff' benefits.

(d) The values to the firm of manual and non-manual occupations have narrowed in many areas.

(e) The terms 'white' and 'blue' collar workers are themselves not *literally* applicable today because (compared to the past) relatively few contemporary manual jobs need to be physically dirty. There is no reason in principle why operatives and managers in most modern firms should not dress in a similar manner.

Specific advantages to single status are that it might:

(a) cause individual employees to identify with the company *as a whole* rather than with a particular grade within its status hierarchy

(b) increase the firm's ability to deploy workers. (The existence of numerous status differentials makes it difficult to move people into jobs that do not carry the same status privileges as previously.) Thus, single status necessarily encourages the acceptance of change.

146

(c) encourage workers to adopt a responsible approach to their jobs, willingly participate in workplace group problem-solving and decision making, exercise initiative, etc.

(d) improve the organisational climate of an enterprise through underpinning management's concern to be fair to all employees.

Problems with introducing single status include:

(a) The potentially high cost of applying common terms and conditions throughout the organisation, especially in view of the tendency to 'harmonise upwards' in borderline situations.

(b) The pride that some workers feel in being recognised as undertaking a certain occupation.

(c) Interest groups (white collar employees or skilled workers for example) seeking to maintain their existing privileges.

SUGGESTIONS

23. Procedure

Many companies have formal arrangements to encourage their employees to submit suggestions regarding efficiency, safety or welfare. It is usual to have a committee consisting of representatives of managers and employees to assess the suggestions and recommend whether they should be adopted, perhaps after taking expert advice. The originator of a successful suggestion receives an award. The benefits of suggestion schemes are that:

(a) The company may be able to use more efficient methods.

(b) There may be fewer accidents.

(c) New uses may be found for scrap.

(d) Two-way communication is encouraged.

(e) Use is made of the employees' ingenuity and creativity.

(f) The recognition of these qualities will give the employees greater job satisfaction.

However, interest in a suggestion scheme will flag unless the management actively encourages it. Steps which may be taken are:

(a) Publicity for every successful suggestion, perhaps with a circulated description and photograph of the formal presentation of the award

(b) Occasional suggestion campaigns asking for ideas to solve specific problems

(c) Generous awards, e.g. 25 per cent of annual savings

(d) Careful treatment of unsuccessful suggestors, i.e. full explanations of the reasons for rejection

(e) A scrupulously fair procedure for assessing suggestions

(f) A convenient channel through which suggestions can be submitted, e.g. a suggestions box.

JUSTICE

24. The importance of justice

Personnel policies and procedures designed to utilise, motivate and protect the human resources of a company will fail unless they are perceived by the employees to be just and fair in themselves and applied in a just and fair way. Justice in this context will provide:

(a) similar treatment to employees in similar circumstances

(b) greater rewards to those who merit them or are particularly deserving

(c) the opportunities to express an opinion which management will consider and possibly act on.

Job satisfaction is reduced and industrial relations deteriorate when employees perceive injustice and unfairness in company personnel policies and the way in which they are applied. Injustice will be minimised if the following conditions are observed:

(a) Job and personnel specifications are accurate and unbiased; performance standards, if set, are reasonable.

(b) New employees are not engaged at rates of pay higher than those received by present employees doing the same work, or offered exceptional privileges.

(c) Promotion, transfer, demotion and retirement policies are open and uniformly applied.

(d) Dismissal procedures (including those for redundancy) are clearly defined and if possible negotiated with employee representatives.

(e) Appraisal schemes give employees the opportunity to discuss their progress with their manager.

(f) Selection for training is regarded as a reward rather than a punishment.

(g) Rates of pay are appropriate to the job and to the individual employee, i.e. they are based on job evaluation, with recognition to the individual by means of a well-maintained payment-by-results scheme, merit rating or length of service increments.

(h) Fringe benefits and working conditions are applied uniformly.

(i) Communications are two-way in all appropriate circumstances and participation is used where practicable.

(j) Disciplinary procedures are carefully applied. There should be warnings and provisions for appeal, and penalties must not be disproportionate to the offence or capriciously applied. The Code of Practice published by the Advisory, Conciliation and Arbitration Service gives useful guidance here.

Disparities between departments in the treatment of e.g. time-keeping, pay increases or leave of absence cause great resentment. Departmental managers have the difficult task of dealing with their subordinates in ways consistent with those elsewhere in the company yet responsive to the circumstances of individuals.

Attitude surveys can be used to measure the extents to which employees feel that a company's personnel policies are fair (especially those concerned with appraisal, promotion, salary determination and the processing of grievances); the effectiveness of management–worker communications; how closely workers perceive themselves to be participating in management decisions; the quality of training and staff development programmes, and so on.

Progress test 8

1. What are the two most important laws of physical fatigue?
2. What are the major causes of stress at work?
3. Is there such a thing as accident proneness?
4. Explain why heating and ventilation can be a more difficult problem than illumination or noise.
5. What duties regarding safety does an employer have under the Health and Safety at Work, etc. Act?
6. Name the benefits of overtime working to an employer.
7. What problems are found in three-shift working?
8. What benefits does a company hope to obtain from giving staff status to its manual workers?
9. What are the benefits of suggestion schemes?
10. Give some examples of the importance of justice in personnel procedures.
11. Health and safety is sometimes regarded as a luxury by senior management. What action could be taken, on the initiative of the personnel department, to change this view? How would you go about formulating health and safety policies and procedures which have genuine importance in an organisation?

12. Your firm is considering the introduction of a flexible working hours scheme for all staff below management level. What are the advantages and disadvantages of such a scheme from a management point of view.

13. (a) Identify, with brief examples, *four* organisational causes of individual stress.

    (b) Make recommendations for the management of stress in the work situation.

9

OTHER INFLUENCES ON EMPLOYEE BEHAVIOUR

FLEXIBILITY

1. Fluctuations in work

Most companies experience variable demands for work. When demand is high the usual response is overtime working, sometimes augmented by the recruitment of temporary employees. When it is low the employees are under-employed and some may eventually be made redundant. In either case the traditional remedies are expensive.

Alternative methods, believed to be more cost-effective, are as follows:

(a) Defining the period of work by reference to a year instead of to a week. This allows extra hours worked in a busy time to be compensated during a slack time either by a shorter working day or by whole days off. The main advantage to the employer of annualised hours arrangements is that more staff can be deployed when demand is at its greatest, and *vice versa*. Nevertheless, employees receive their full annual salary (normally as a standard monthly amount). Problems with annualised hours systems are:

- Supervisors need to spend more time planning workloads and advising staff about when to turn up for duty (rather than employees being 'on hand' all the time).
- Employees may find it difficult to plan their family arrangements and social lives.
- Individuals may be overworked in certain periods.
- A worker who is sick during a month when he or she is expected to work just a few hours causes little disruption to the company, but someone absent through sickness within a peak working hours period creates many difficulties (and costs) for the firm. Accordingly some annualised hours systems require workers who take sick leave during busy periods to work additional hours later in the year.

(b) Removing the distinctions between jobs, so that, for example, during a slack time a production operative can overhaul his or her machine instead of calling in a maintenance worker.

(c) Reducing the permanent employees of the company to a core group who have secure employment, supported by peripheral groups who may be temporary employees (sometimes part-time) or workers supplied by sub-contractors. The number and type of the peripheral groups will vary according to the current demand for work.

Key time working

Workers on 'key time' contracts are called-in as required at the busiest times of the week, month or year. Such arrangements are convenient for firms with highly cyclical business characterised by large peaks and troughs, e.g. on Saturday mornings or during the New Year sales. Advantages to the employing company of hiring labour on key time working contracts include flexibility of staffing levels, the ability to cope with an increased volume of business during certain periods, reductions in customer waiting/queuing times, and greater customer satisfaction. Employees, however, receive lower incomes and are uncertain as to when and how intensively they will be working. Key time staff differ from part timers in that they have no set working hours. Indeed, the employer has no commitment to employ them in any period; rather they are called-in when needed, working alongside full time staff and conventional part-timers. Key timers themselves are under no contractual obligation to accept work as it is offered.

This form of employment is said to be suitable for people taking early retirement and for those with variable family commitments. Key time contracts might be offered to workers made redundant from full time jobs. Problems with using key time staff include:

- Administrative difficulties associated with calling-in the appropriate number of people at short notice
- Possible resentments among full timers at having to work alongside key time staff, whom they might perceive a threat to their security of employment
- Additional staff management problems (training, appraisal, etc.)
- Erratic earnings for key time workers
- The need to pay key time employees on a weekly basis.

2. Flexibility

The demand for flexible working derives from firms' desires to cut costs in order to obtain competitive advantage; from the need to adapt quickly to changes in market demand and production technologies; and from alterations in organisation structures.

Flexibility has three aspects: *task* flexibility which involves multiskilling to enable workers to be redeployed quickly between various activities; *numerical* flexibility whereby the size of the workforce can be expanded or decreased at will; and *pay* flexibility which means that reward levels are set by the forces of supply and demand for labour rather than by collective bargaining between trade unions and the managements of firms. The following problems might apply to a business which operates in a 'flexible' manner:

(a) The firm's ability to recruit workers who are prepared to work on a casual basis depends substantially on the existence of high unemployment in the wider economy. As economic conditions improve, employees demand more stable conditions and long-term contracts. Hence a 'flexible firm' could quickly find itself without enough workers.

(b) The organisation becomes highly dependent on unskilled labour.

(c) Bad industrial relations arising from the imposition of flexibility might outweigh the benefits of potential cost-savings.

3. Multiskilling

Multiskilling involves:

(a) Undertaking a wider range of tasks, from manual unskilled to skilled/technician level.

(b) Crossing traditional boundaries between skills; for example, a mechanical craft worker also carrying out electrical work.

(c) Willingness to work an irregular pattern of hours.

(d) Accepting throughout working life retraining in new skills.

(e) Workers being involved in the implementation of production processes and new work practices.

(f) Accepting that all decisions concerning labour deployment shall be made by management.

(g) Employees being prepared to help train other workers.

The advantages of multiskill flexible working are that:

(a) New equipment and working methods can be introduced quickly.

(b) Workers 'learn by doing' and hence improve their overall levels of skill.

(c) It ensures the fullest possible use of plant, equipment, people and machines.

(d) Individuals are able to contribute to the firm's work to their fullest potential.

There are however a number of problems attached to multiskill flexible working, including:

(a) To the extent that flexible working helps workers develop their levels of skill it becomes easier for workers to find jobs in other companies.

(b) It involves heavy training costs.

(c) Labour shortages in one work group can require their being covered by workers from another, thus detracting from team-working.

(d) In principle, total flexibility should apply to management as well as operatives. However, managers may use their authority to avoid performing anything other than a narrowly defined range of tasks.

(e) Some workers will have an aptitude for certain kinds of tasks; so why force them to undertake jobs at which they will be less efficient?

4. Effects on employees

Flexibility requires employees to accept drastic changes affecting their personal lives, security and status. They will therefore expect its introduction to be handled with the utmost care. Employee participation and frequent two-way communication are extremely important. Some of the changes affecting the employee are:

(a) Flexibility of task is difficult to reconcile with strict supervision; employees will work with a loose control only. Fewer supervisors may be needed, and they will behave more as co-ordinators and advisors than as disciplinarians. Job satisfaction will almost certainly be increased.

(b) Some changes in trade union organisation will be necessary to accommodate the multi-skilled worker.

(c) The employee's leisure time might be affected by irregular hours.

(d) Those employees who are engaged temporarily or as members of a sub-contracting firm must accept insecurity of employment. They will be difficult to organise in trade unions and there is a danger that hostility will grow between them and the permanent unionised employees who will seem to be in a privileged position and members of closely-knit working groups.

5. Effects on management

The flexibility which is advocated for manual and clerical workers is necessary also for managers. They too will find it necessary to work irregular hours, accept retraining and cross traditional job boundaries. They may need to devise new methods of management and work out their implications. For example, the following changes in management practices might be required:

(a) The multiskilled worker will require very careful selection.

(b) Job specifications can no longer be detailed.

(c) Job evaluation systems must be changed in order to cope with flexibility.

(d) Pay structures based on output may be impossible and systems based on merit difficult to operate.

(e) The training function of the company will become very important and probably expensive.

(f) New working arrangements will be resisted unless through some kind of consultative machinery they are discussed and possibly amended before they become effective.

(g) Contracts of employment must be revised on the one hand to encourage stability among the core group of workers and on the other to provide fair conditions for those who work temporarily.

6. The influence of occupations on behaviour

The changes described in this chapter so far affect only a minority of employees; in most companies job structures and occupations continue in their well-established ways and produce typical behaviour as follows:

(a) *Professional workers*, e.g. lawyers, teachers and doctors, who have undergone a long course of training carefully controlled by a professional body which usually has statutory recognition. There is a strict code of ethics, and often some restriction on the numbers entering the profession. Most professional workers seem to have high job satisfaction, their working life often extending into their leisure time. When they are employed by a company their loyalties appear to be divided between their profession and their employer.

(b) *Craftspeople*, e.g. skilled manual workers in engineering, building, printing, etc., who have served an apprenticeship. They enjoy high status among other manual workers, have an independent outlook because they can use their skills fairly easily with another employer, and become more valuable as they get older because of their increased experience and skill. There are many similarities between the craftsperson and the professional.

(c) *Machine minders and assembly workers*, who apply a moderate level of skill to a very restricted range of operations. Training is short, the work has little interest or variety and generally is part of a tightly controlled process. These workers often become less valuable as they get older because their stamina and speed of reaction decrease. When they change employers they frequently change their occupation also. They tend to have a detached attitude to the job and company.

(d) *Process workers*, who monitor processes which are almost entirely automatic, e.g. chemical manufacture and oil refining. They have to be intelligent enough to understand the science and technology on which the process is based so that they may deal with emergencies and breakdowns. A fairly long

155

training period is necessary, emphasising theory and procedures rather than physical skills. Their job satisfaction is often high because of the responsibility they feel for the safety of the process, the lack of human pressures to increase production and the special training they have received. On the other hand, the need to do shift work to keep the process continuously operating may cause some job dissatisfaction.

(e) *White collar workers*, who traditionally are expected by employers to share management attitudes rather than associate themselves with manual workers. They sometimes enjoy greater fringe benefits, shorter hours and less control than manual workers, and are on progressive salaries. They are usually treated by managers as individuals rather than as categories; differences in salaries usually reflect this. Their job satisfaction can be quite high when they are able to control their own work and see its results, but low when they do routine and apparently meaningless clerical operations. Their experience is often valuable to one employer only, and is difficult to transfer.

There appears to be a trend towards the merging of types (b), (c) and (d) as processes become more automatic and computer controlled.

USE OF CASUAL AND PART-TIME EMPLOYEES

7. Changes in the workforce

A large increase in casual and/or part-time work has occurred in the UK during recent decades, creating several new problems of human resources planning, control, and the appraisal of employees. In many firms there now exists an important distinction between 'core' workers (who are permanent and full time) and 'peripherals' engaged part time or casually and laid on or off as market conditions change. Core workers plan, take decisions and supervise peripherals. Typically, they are superannuated, receive training and staff development, and qualify for a variety of fringe benefits. Peripherals, conversely, exercise little discretion over their work and undertake routine duties organised by core workers. This arrangement enables the size of the workforce to be changed quickly and with few legal consequences (frequently, casuals and part-timers are not covered by employment protection legislation). Also the wage cost of a casual/part-time workforce may be lower than for full-time workers (who might not be fully occupied throughout the year).

The special problems attached to the management of this type of workforce include:

(a) Possible low morale among peripherals (who are denied permanent status and benefits) possibly resulting in high labour turnover.

(b) Communication difficulties including communication overload on core workers (each of whom must deal with very many peripherals) and the need to arrange peripheral employees' representation on health and safety and other important employee relations committees.

(c) Control problems attached to day-to-day operations (peripherals are not normally capable of handling crises without the help of core staff), perform-ance appraisal (*see* Chapter 17), and ensuring the quality of recruitment of fresh peripheral employees (which by definition occurs on a regular basis).

(d) Interpersonal relations difficulties emerging from permanent employees possibly regarding low-cost peripherals as a threat to their jobs, and from peripherals' resentments against higher-paid full-time workers.

Some of these problems might be overcome through job extension (*see* 4:**20**) among peripheral workers, through explicit recognition of peripherals' contributions to the firm (*via* the provision of fringe benefits, guarantees of re-employment following breaks in continuity of service, etc.), and through incorporating grievance procedures, right of appeal against dismissal and so on into peripherals' contracts of employment. Other possibilities are the introduction of job-sharing arrangements (although the 'two Monday morn-ings' syndrome might result from this); making peripherals responsible for the quality of their work; homeworking (*see* **9**); and having peripherals attend training and staff development courses.

8. The EU Draft Directive on part-time employees

The Commission is anxious to improve the employment rights and terms and conditions of employment of part-time workers. Accordingly, the Draft Directive on this matter provides for:

(a) Wages for part-timers that are strictly proportional to wage levels paid to full-time workers doing the same work

(b) Equal access to vocational training

(c) Making it unlawful to discriminate unfairly against part-timers when selecting employees for promotion

(d) Equal access to occupational pension schemes

(e) Equal rights in relation to health and safety at work

(f) Proportional entitlement to paid holidays, sick pay, redundancy and retirement benefits

(g) The right of part-timers to claim unfair dismissal (*see* 19:**5**) on the same basis as full-time workers.

The proposal applies to all part-timers working at least eight hours a week. An employer intending to use part-time (or temporary) workers would have to inform employee representatives about this in good time. Employers would also be required to advise part-time (and temporary) workers of any permanent full-time vacancies that arose.

Similar provisions apply to a Draft Directive on temporary and fixed-contract workers, who would become entitled to social security benefits identical to those of permanent employees. Individuals engaged under temporary contracts would have to be informed of the reasons for their being on temporary rather than permanent contracts. Additionally, the client companies of employment agencies would be made liable for the pay and national insurance contributions of temporary agency workers following an employment agency's collapse. All EU health and safety legislation would apply equally to full-time, part-time and temporary workers.

Objections to these Draft Directives have included:

(a) Many part-timers work this way through preference rather than inability to find full-time jobs. Extension of employment protections to part-time workers will reduce the number of firms willing to engage such employees, thus lessening the availability of part-time work.

(b) The cost of employing part-timers will increase dramatically if the proposal becomes law; leading to lower international competitiveness of UK firms. In particular, the Directive would oblige employers to pay national insurance for *all* workers employed more than eight hours a week, including those earning less than the current NI threshold. Up to two million UK workers could be affected by this change.

9. Homeworkers

The rapid development of computerised networking systems has made it possible for many employees to work from home, communicating with head office through a computer terminal, telephone calls, and occasional face-to-face meetings. Homeworkers save much (productive) time through not having to travel to and from work (which can be fitted around the transportation of children to and from school); there are fewer interruptions to the working day; the individual may complete duties when he or she wishes; and the completion of work in a relaxed environment might lead to a higher output, increased effort and greater job satisfaction. Also there are savings on premises costs for the employing organisation. However, a number of significant problems attach to the management of home-based workers, including:

(a) Control problems and the need to employ head office staff to liaise with outside employees, provide them with input materials and information, etc. Such difficulties are especially severe when project completion depends on several outworkers meeting deadlines simultaneously. Note, moreover, that homeworkers who are constantly on the phone or meeting supervisors and colleagues would be more conveniently employed in a central head office.

(b) Appraisal problems. Management needs to know how energetically each

158

outworker is working, how much time is actually spent on particular assignments, whether certain jobs might be deskilled and completed elsewhere at lower cost, how efficiency can be improved, and so on.

(c) Security problems. Ambiguities could arise over the ownership of intellectual property (patents, designs, computer programmes and other copyright materials) developed by outworkers. Also, head office will want to ensure that a homeworker is not simultaneously working for competitors using equipment and knowledge provided by the parent organisation.

(d) Morale problems possibly caused by homeworkers feeling isolated and not really part of the firm. Usually, homeworkers are not able to progress through the career ladder available to head office staff.

To deal with these problems head office will set targets, conduct inspections, possibly pay homeworkers through a piecework system (*see* 14:2) or perhaps treat outworkers as self-employed sub-contract labour paid *ad hoc* sums for specific assignments. In the latter case, the head office cannot directly control the homeworker's working methods (otherwise the Inland Revenue will not allow the homeworker self-employed status) and the homeworker is free to work for other employers.

10. Culture of the workplace

A firm's culture evolves gradually, and employees may not even be aware that it exists. Organisational culture is important, however, because it helps define how workers feel about their jobs. Culture involves common assumptions about how work should be performed and about appropriate objectives for the organisation, for departments within it and for individual employees. It consists of the organisation's customary ways of doing things and its members' shared perceptions of issues affecting the organisation's work. Culture helps define how workers *feel* about their jobs and about what is and is not correct. It affects individual perceptions of colleagues and situations, and the leadership style (*see* Chapter 2) applied within the organisation.

Determinants of a firm's culture include senior management's core values and goals, employee selection methods, induction systems, training techniques applied, and procedures for bonding the worker to the firm (e.g. company uniforms, housing loans, superannuation schemes, provision of fringe benefits, etc.).

Charles Handy distinguishes four types of culture: power, role, task and person. One of these might dominate the entire organisation, or different cultures may exist in various parts of the firm. The *power culture* stems from a single central source, as in a small business that has begun to expand. Here, there are few rules and procedures, and few committees. All important decisions are taken by a handful of people, and precedents are followed.

A *role culture*, in contrast, is highly bureaucratic. It operates through formal roles and procedures, and there are clearly defined rules for settling disputes.

Organisations dominated by role culture offer security and predictability but, since they are rigidly structured, cannot adapt quickly to accommodate change (as can a power culture organisation). The *task culture* is job or project orientated. There is no single dominant leader; all group members concentrate on completing the collective task. A task culture will encourage flexibility in approach, and is ideal for an environment of change. Job satisfaction is high and there is much group cohesion. However, relationships are complex and control is difficult. A *person culture* might arise in an organisation which exists only to serve the people within it. Examples are partnerships, consultancy firms and professional organisations.

According to Handy, none of these cultures is 'better' than the others. A culture arises, he argues, from historical circumstances, the existing environment, technology, and the human needs of people within the organisation. The problem, of course, is that whereas an organisation's needs will alter over time, its culture may remain constant. Alteration of a culture might require extensive external recruitment of new staff, the implementation of incentive schemes designed to alter workers' attitudes, or the conspicuous promotion of individuals who display flexible and appropriate cultural values.

Culture management

The term 'culture management' is used to describe conscious managerial attempts to develop within employees attitudes, values and beliefs congruent with an organisation's goals and strategies. Primary aims of culture management include the creation of working environments which facilitate the implementation of company policies, the provision of information to workers about what is expected of them, and the promotion of employee commitment to the firm. Hence culture management might require the systematic management of change, the reinforcement of those elements of an organisation's existing culture that support management's cultural aims, and the removal of dysfunctional elements. In practice, culture management involves:

- Senior managers setting a good example to the workforce
- Creation of reward systems that encourage appropriate attitudes and modes of behaviour
- Recruitment, selection and promotion policies relevant to the desired organisational culture.

Progress test 9

1. What do you understand by flexibility?
2. Define the difference between core workers and peripheral workers.
3. What are the advantages of flexibility?
4. Define the differences between task culture and role culture.
5. What are the main provisions of the Draft Directive on part-time employees?
6. Examine the problems associated with the management of homeworkers.

Part Three

PRACTICAL ASPECTS OF HUMAN RESOURCES MANAGEMENT

10

HUMAN RESOURCES PLANNING

NATURE OF HUMAN RESOURCES PLANNING

1. Definition

Human resources planning (HRP) may be defined as an attempt to forecast how many and what kind of employees will be required in the future, and to what extent this demand is likely to be met. It involves the comparison of an organisation's current human resources with likely future needs and, consequently, the establishment of programmes for hiring, training, redeploying and possibly discarding employees. Effective HRP should result in the right people doing the right things in the right place at precisely the right time.

2. Purpose

Human resources planning can help management in making decisions in the following areas:

- Recruitment
- Avoidance of redundancies
- Training – numbers and categories
- Management development
- Estimates of labour costs
- Productivity bargaining
- Accommodation requirements.

Company HRP needs continuous readjustment because the goals of an organisation are unstable and its environment uncertain. It is also complex because it involves so many independent variables – invention, population changes, resistance to change, consumer demand, government intervention, foreign competition and above all domestic competition. It must include feedback because if the plan cannot be fulfilled the objectives of the company may have to be modified so that they are feasible in human resources terms.

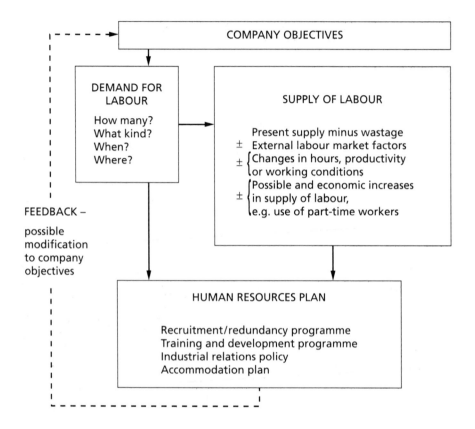

Figure 10.1 The human resources planning process

3. The importance of company objectives

Figure 10.1 shows that the essential first step in company HRP is a statement of company objectives which covers products, methods, markets, etc. From this is derived the demand for labour, which is then related to the supply of labour to produce the human resources plan.

The implications of the human resources plan must then be considered by the top management of the company in case company objectives need amendment – for example, it may not be possible to increase production by the planned amount because labour of the kind required is either impossible to train in the time available, or does not exist in the quantity needed.

4. Steps in long-term company HRP

A long-term company human resources plan is usually regarded as one which attempts to forecast for about five years ahead.

As shown in Fig. 10.1, the company must consider the demand for labour, its potential supply (with corrections for its present misuse, over-use or under-use) and the external environment. By studying the interaction of all these factors it can then produce a plan showing how many and what kind of employees are expected to be required in the future. The main points to be considered are:

(a) *The creation of a company HRP group*, including the managers in charge of the main functions within the company.

(b) *The statement of human resources objectives* in the light of company objectives by considering:

(*i*) capital equipment plans
(*ii*) reorganisation, e.g. centralisation or decentralisation
(*iii*) changes in products or in output
(*iv*) marketing plans
(*v*) financial limitations.

(c) *The present utilisation of human resources*, in particular:

(*i*) numbers of employees in various categories
(*ii*) estimation of labour turnover for each grade of employee and the analysis of the effects of high or low turnover rates on the organisation's performance
(*iii*) amount of overtime worked
(*iv*) amount of short time
(*v*) appraisal of performance and potential of present employees
(*vi*) general level of payment compared with that in other firms.

Note that for all the above, accurate and complete personnel records are essential.

(d) *The external environment of the company:*

(*i*) recruitment position
(*ii*) population trends
(*iii*) local housing and transport plans
(*iv*) national agreements dealing with conditions of work
(*v*) government policies in education, retirement, regional subsidies, etc.

(e) *The potential supply of labour, in particular:*

(*i*) effects of local emigration and immigration
(*ii*) effects of recruitment or redundancy by local firms
(*iii*) possibility of employing categories not now employed, e.g. part-time workers
(*iv*) changes in productivity, working hours and/or practices.

165

5. The final company HRP

After considering and co-ordinating these factors a human resources plan may then be made, showing in detail, by function, occupation and locations, how many employees it is *practicable* to employ at various stages in the future. The following should appear in it:

- Jobs which will appear, disappear, or change
- To what extent redeployment or retraining is possible
- Necessary changes at supervisory and management levels
- Training needs
- Recruitment, redundancy or retirement programmes
- Industrial relations implications
- Arrangements for feedback in case modifications in the plan or company objectives are necessary
- Details of arrangements for handling any human problems arising from labour deficits or surpluses (e.g. early retirement or other natural wastage procedures).

The advantages of HRP include:

(a) The organisation should be better equipped to cope with the human resourcing consequences of changed circumstances.

(b) Careful consideration of likely future human resource requirements could lead the firm to discover new and improved ways of managing human resources.

(c) Labour shortfalls and surpluses might be avoided.

(d) It helps the firm create and develop employee training and management succession programmes.

(e) Some of the problems of managing change may be foreseen and their consequences mitigated. Consultations with affected groups and individuals can occur at an early stage in the change process: decisions can be taken unhurriedly and by considering all relevant options, rather than being taken in crisis situations.

(f) Management is compelled to assess critically the strengths and weaknesses of its labour force and personnel policies.

(g) Duplication of effort among employees can be avoided; co-ordination and integration of workers' efforts is improved.

When agreed, the plan must be communicated to all levels of employees, but particularly to managers and unions or employee representatives; it is often necessary and advisable to negotiate with the trade unions on the detailed implementation of the plan.

6. Short-term company HRP

This type of plan, which usually covers a period of up to one year ahead, is much more common than a long-term plan. Many firms do not have the quality of management to forecast long-term objectives, or they feel that the nature of their business makes it impossible to look ahead for more than one year.

A short-term manpower plan is comparatively easy because a firm will usually make a production or marketing plan for a year ahead involving budgets, orders for new materials and components, and sales quotas. From this can be derived the amount of *direct labour* in terms of labour-hours required in future, and then, by dividing into this figure the number of available working hours, the number of workers can be obtained. Overtime and the average level of sickness absence and machine breakdowns must be taken into account when available working hours are calculated.

The amount of *indirect labour* may be estimated partly by fixed commitments and partly as a rule of thumb percentage of indirect to direct labour. From the total labour requirements a recruitment or redundancy plan can be derived, but the period is usually too short for any worthwhile training plan to be made.

An advantage of the short-term plan is the ease with which the forecast can be compared with the labour that was actually required, and any discrepancies analysed.

7. Limiting factors

In practice, human resources planning can be difficult and often inaccurate. The chief reasons are:

(a) The type of industry: some depend on new product development in an extremely competitive environment; others may depend on political decisions which are impossible to forecast; while others work on a tendering basis, so that plans can only be short term because it is never known whether a tender will be accepted.

(b) Opposition or scepticism among members of management; all must be convinced of the value of human resources planning if it is to be a success.

(c) Resistance to the changes expressed in the plan. The forecasts of labour structure, with their effects on skills and status, may be regarded as a threat.

(d) The difficulty of forecasting social and economic changes accurately, particularly in an era of high unemployment.

(e) The need to have very complete and accurate employee records, maintained for at least the last five years, which it is hoped can be used to detect trends in employee movements. These trends may, however, be very unreliable in times of high unemployment.

167

(f) The rapid growth of new technologies.

(g) The plan may indicate recruitment and training programmes which, although desirable, may be impossible to put into practice because the money to pay for them may not be available now. Because of its financial position the company may find long-term plans useless.

In general, the longer the period over which the plan is made, the greater the effect of these limiting factors. Nevertheless, long-term HRP is a growing practice, particularly in large companies which have to plan their expenditure on capital equipment several years ahead in any case. Even when unemployment is high, the difficulties of recruiting, selecting and training some types of employee are so great and the cost of redundancy so expensive that HRP is amply justified, even though its results may be somewhat inaccurate. Plans may be made more easily when the personnel records are held on a computer. It is possible to purchase ready-made HRP programmes for use with computers.

8. Relocation

The physical relocation of a business's premises creates a number of human resource management problems, including the needs:

(a) for staff and union consultation

(b) possibly, for redundancy planning and the application of outplacement procedures (*see* below)

(c) to assist relocated employees find suitable accommodation, schools for children, new jobs for spouses, etc

(d) to recruit fresh workers locally.

There exist personnel management consultants who specialise in relocation. As well as handling the human aspects of the situation they will also locate suitable premises, liaise with local authorities, arrange for the transport of files and equipment, etc. Their objective is to ensure the business runs smoothly immediately before the move, during it and in the subsequent settling-in period.

9. Outplacement

Outplacement is the practice of employers actively helping workers threatened with redundancy to obtain other jobs. Examples of outplacement procedures include:

(a) Counselling to assist affected employees cope with the psychological effects of being declared redundant

(b) Psychometric testing to discover employees' aptitudes for alternative types of work

168

(c) Providing retraining facilities within the firm

(d) Contacting supplying and client companies to ascertain whether they have any vacancies

(e) Circularising local firms advising on the availability of labour in the company in question and inviting them to conduct recruitment interviews on its premises

(f) Helping employees draft and wordprocess their CVs

(g) Giving workers time off to look for other jobs over and above minimum statutory requirements.

LABOUR TURNOVER

Labour turnover is the movement of people into and out of the firm. It is usually convenient to measure it by recording movements out of the firm on the assumption that a leaver is eventually replaced by a new employee. The term separation is used to denote an employee who leaves for any reason.

10. Measurement of labour turnover

Two formulae are in common use for measuring labour turnover:

(a) The separation or wastage rate, which expresses the number of separations during the period (usually one year) as a percentage of the average number employed during that period. It is therefore:

$$\frac{\text{Number of separations during period}}{\text{Average number employed during period}} \times 100$$

(b) The labour stability index, which shows the percentage of the employees who have had at least one year's service. It is usually expressed as follows:

$$\frac{\text{Employees with at least one year's service}}{\text{Number of employees employed one year ago}} \times 100$$

A variation on the labour stability index is the 'fringe turnover index':

$$\frac{\text{Number of employees who joined and left within one year}}{\text{Average number employed during the year}} \times 100$$

This shows the percentage turnover of short-term workers.

Another method of measuring labour turnover is to study a group of employees recruited during a certain period (usually three months) and record the rate at which they leave the company. An example is shown in Table 10.1 based on the assumption that the company engaged 500 new employees during the period.

Table 10.1

	Quarterly periods of service	Number of leavers	% leaving	% remaining
First	(1–13 weeks)	200	40	60
Second	(14–26 weeks)	100	20	40
Third	(27–39 weeks)	50	10	30
Fourth	(40–52 weeks)	25	5	25
Fifth	(53–65 weeks)	15	3	22
Sixth	(66–78 weeks)	10	2	20
Seventh	(79–91 weeks)	5	1	19
Eighth	(92–104 weeks)	5	1	18

These figures are sometimes presented graphically by plotting the percentage leaving against quarterly periods of service. The result is called a *survival curve*.

A useful application of survival curve computations is the determination of the 'half-life' survival rates of workers in various employment categories. A half-life survival rate is the time that elapses before 50 per cent of a particular cohort of workers who all began work at the same time have left the organisation. Half-life survival rates may then be compared for different departments, age groups, etc. in order to ascertain the 'staying power' of each cohort.

11. Use of turnover measurements

The separation rate is easy to calculate and is widely used. It also has the great advantage of indicating costs because separations and replacements can involve the company in considerable expense. It can be somewhat misleading, however, for two reasons.

(a) Recently engaged employees are more likely to leave than long service employees (*see* Table 10.1), and therefore an increase in the separation rate may simply be due to some increased recruitment a few weeks previously rather than to a sudden deterioration in worker satisfaction.

(b) Some jobs in the company may be vacated and filled several times during the year. Suppose, for example, that in a company employing 1,000 workers 250 leave during the year, giving a separation rate of 25 per cent. The true position might be as follows:

150 jobs vacated and filled once	=	150 leavers
25 jobs vacated and filled twice	=	50 leavers
10 jobs vacated and filled three times	=	30 leaver
5 jobs vacated and filled four times	=	20 leavers
Total: 190 jobs vacated during year	Total:	250 leavers

In such a case the separation index can give a false impression because 100 of the 250 leavers are short-service employees (though the cost of replacing them can still be considerable).

The stability index is best used in conjunction with the separation rate, showing the extent to which the company is retaining its experienced employees. On the figures shown above, the stability index would be

$$\frac{1,000 - 190}{1,000} \times 100 = 81\%$$

Survival rates always show that the tendency for employees to leave is greatest during their early weeks with the company; they are useful in showing if the company is losing a particularly large number of employees early in their service compared with a previous period. It is often instructive to compare survival rates in different departments or different employee categories, e.g. by age groups or occupations.

12. Cost of labour turnover

Separations and their consequent replacements can be surprisingly expensive. The cost of labour turnover increases when employees are more specialised, more difficult to find and require more training. It is made up of some or all of the following components:

- Lower production during learning period
- Lost production while the employee is being replaced
- Payment to other employees at overtime rates while waiting for a replacement
- Possible diversion of efforts of more highly skilled employees while waiting for a replacement
- Cost of scrap and spoiled work while job is being learned
- Cost of recruitment, selection and medical examination
- Training cost
- Administrative cost of removing from and adding to payroll.

Therefore, when the separation rate is high the employer can incur considerable costs which are not always immediately obvious.

Reducing labour turnover

All employers expect to have a certain degree of labour turnover; without it the company would stagnate. The average age of employees would increase (meaning also that a large number of employees might retire simultaneously); and there could be insufficient new blood coming into the organisation. No doubt many companies would be content if their separation rates lay between 10 and 15 per cent, though few rates in the private sector of industry and commerce are as low as this. If an employing firm wishes to reduce its labour turnover because it considers it is excessive for the district and the industry, it may take the following action:

(a) *Recalculate* the separation rate for various categories of the firm's employees, e.g. departments, age groups, occupations, to see if turnover in any of these categories is particularly high; if so it can be specially investigated.

(b) *Ensure* that selection procedures are adequate; suitable employees are more likely to stay than unsuitable.

(c) *Ensure* that the immediate supervisor, by being involved in selection, feels some responsibility towards a new employee.

(d) *Check* that employees are being fully utilised – some may be leaving because of boredom or job dissatisfaction.

(e) *Overhaul* pay structure perhaps using job evaluation (*see* Chapter 13).

(f) *Introduce or improve* an induction course.

(g) Give new employees appropriate *training*

(h) *Show that prospects* in the company are good by promoting from within wherever possible.

(i) *Ensure that physical working conditions are adequate.*

In general, an increase in job satisfaction and in the cohesiveness of working groups will decrease the rate of labour turnover.

Progress test 10

1. State two formulae by which labour turnover may be measured.
2. Which labour turnover formula indicates costs?
3. State some ways in which labour turnover may be reduced.
4. Define human resources planning. What is its purpose?
5. What are the main points to be considered in formulating a long-term human resources plan?
6. What is a short-term human resources plan, and what are its advantages?
7. What factors reduce the accuracy or the benefits of human resources planning?
8. Define outplacement and explain how it operates.

11

PERSONNEL RECORDS AND STATISTICS

PERSONNEL RECORDS

1. Purposes

Personnel records provide the following:

(a) A store of up-to-date and accurate information about the company's employees.

(b) A guide to the action to be taken regarding an employee, particularly by comparing the worker with other employees.

(c) A guide when recruiting a new employee, e.g. by showing the rates of pay received by comparable employees.

(d) A historical record of previous action taken regarding employees.

(e) The raw materials for statistics which check and guide personnel policies.

(f) The means to comply with certain statutory requirements.

Specific information about individual employees (i.e. their biographical details, training, educational qualifications, disciplinary records, etc.) is called *item* information. Summaries of item information on groups of employees which enable the company to define the general characteristics of various types of workers (e.g. age and sex distributions in certain departments, differences in educational levels between workers in various grades, etc.) is known as *profile* information.

2. Documents

An employee's personnel record begins with the application form which he or she completes when applying for a job. To this is added the copy of the letter formally offering the job and the employee's acceptance. These papers are usually put into an envelope or folder which becomes the *personal file*.

From time to time other documents are put into the personal file, e.g. appraisal reports, applications for promotion, sickness certificates, etc.

A summary of the information in the personal file is made on an *employee record*, which is set out in such a way that it is easily read and compared with other employee records. It is usually filed departmentally, unlike personal files, which are filed alphabetically.

3. The employee record

The essential details to be included in the employee record are as follows:

(a) Personal data:

(*i*) name, address and telephone number
(*ii*) company number (if any)
(*iii*) sex
(*iv*) date of birth
(*v*) marital status
(*vi*) disablement registration number (if any).

(b) Company data:

(*i*) date of joining company
(*ii*) past and present departments and dates
(*iii*) past and present job titles
(*iv*) past and present wage or salary
(*v*) reasons for changes
(*vi*) absence record
(*vii*) accident record
(*viii*) hours of work
(*ix*) holiday entitlement
(*x*) retirement date and pension scheme membership
(*xi*) disciplinary warnings.

(c) Qualifications and skills:

(*i*) formal education
(*ii*) qualifications
(*iii*) training record
(*iv*) appraisals.

(d) On leaving the company:

(*i*) date of leaving and reason
(*ii*) name of new employer (if known)
(*iii*) suitability for re-employment.

Once included in the employee record, any information must be kept up to date, which in many cases is a considerable clerical task. Therefore, before adding new items, it is important to consider how often the information would be used, whether it could be obtained quickly from some other source, how easy it is to keep up to date and whether there is room to show it.

4. Manual employee records

In many companies employee records are kept in card indexes or loose-leaf binders. Many proprietary systems are available which provide quick identification of particular types of employees, e.g. the registered disabled, by attaching coloured signals to their records and are successful in showing all the information listed in **3** in quite a small space. Particularly in small companies manual records are quite satisfactory, being flexible, quickly amended, convenient and comparatively cheap.

5. Computer records

A computer can store many times more information than a card index system. It has the following advantages:

(a) In a modern system, information is immediately available either on a visual display unit or a printer.

(b) Lists of employees can be quickly produced according to a desired category, e.g. all over age 60 or disabled persons.

(c) Summaries, e.g. the number of employees in each category, and employee statistics can be easily produced.

(d) Ready-made programs may be purchased and personnel staff can easily be trained to interrogate the computer or insert new and changed information.

DATA PROTECTION ACT 1984

6. Summary of the Act

It protects the individual against the misuse of personal details held on a computer or word processor and gives a remedy if the details are inaccurate. It covers almost the whole field of automatic data processing but is especially relevant to personnel records. All data users (i.e. persons or organisations which hold personal details on a computer) must register with the Data Protection Registrar, informing the Registrar of what kind of personal information is held, the use made of it, to whom it may be disclosed and how it is obtained. The Registrar must try to ensure that the user observes the eight Data Principles which are based on a Council of Europe Convention. They may be summarised as follows:

1. The information must be obtained and processed fairly.
2. Data shall be held only for specified and lawful purposes.

3. Data shall be used and disclosed only in the manner described in the Register.
4. Data must be adequate and relevant.
5. Data must be accurate and up to date.
6. Data must not be kept longer than is necessary.
7. An individual may be entitled to be told what information is held about him or her and to have it corrected or erased, if appropriate.
8. Data must be held securely.

The data user has 40 days in which to comply with any request for disclosure. A court may order data users to pay compensation for damage caused by lost, destroyed or inaccurate data or by unauthorised disclosure, i.e. to a person or organisation not named in the registration.

Inaccuracy will be excused if the data user can show either that the information was obtained with reasonable care, or that it was obtained from the person concerned (the 'data subject') or a third party. Other exemptions which are of interest to personnel departments are:

(a) Although data which expresses an *opinion* about an individual is covered by the Act, indications of the user's *intentions* for the individual are not.

(b) The Act does not apply to data held only for the purpose of calculating payroll or pensions.

(c) Individuals have no right of access to data held solely for research or statistical purposes, providing the results cannot identify any person.

7. Application to personnel records

A company of any size should appoint a co-ordinator to ensure that the Act is observed and to deal with requests for disclosure from employees. It should be noted that data subjects will include unsuccessful job applicants and former employees, if information regarding them is held on the computer.

(a) *Communication.* Employees should be told about their rights under the Act and the limitations on those rights. An explanatory section could be included in the employee handbook, if one exists, or made easily available on the same lines as the detailed conditions of employment. When an employer comes under the provisions of the Act for the first time its effects should be explained and discussed with employee representatives. It is important to establish a simple procedure for employees to use, involving either the co-ordinator or a named person of senior status in the company.

(b) *Review of data.* The information held on the computer must be checked to see if it complies with the Data Principles. It should be noted that information not held on the computer, for example on handwritten record cards, is not subject to the Act. The important steps to be taken as regards computer-held data are as follows:

(*i*) An opinion about an employee should be clearly distinguished from a statement of intention about his or her future. 'Fit for early promotion' could be both, and its disclosure might be embarrassing if because of unforeseen circumstances early promotion proved to be impossible. If the results of appraisal are fed into the computer rather than recorded manually the wording or coding must show clearly whether a statement is an opinion or an intention.

(*ii*) The source of the data supplied by the data subject or a third party should be indicated; this indication is known as the 'received status marker'. An example is information extracted from an application form (*see* 15:7). This safeguard ensures that data subjects cannot claim compensation for damage caused by inaccurate information they supplied themselves. Employees should be given the opportunity to check the accuracy of information supplied about them by third parties, for example former employees.

(*iii*) It is important to keep data up to date, in order to comply with the fifth Data Principle.

(*iv*) Data held on the computer for research and planning should not contain clues to individual employees – for example, job title, age, length of service – so that it may be exempt from disclosure.

(*v*) If the results of appraisal are held on the computer, i.e. data which expresses opinions, employees will be entitled to ask for disclosure. Appraisal schemes which have previously been secret or partly secret will now become open, and managers will be obliged to discuss the computer-held ratings with their staff. Training in the appraisal interview may perhaps be necessary.

STATISTICS

8. Essential statistics

The following are the statistics which are essential:

(a) Statistics required by official bodies, e.g. Department of Employment and the Department of Health and Social Security.

(b) Total number of employees, subdivided as far as possible into departments, geographical location, age groups, male or female, etc. and showing the gain or loss over the previous period.

(c) Number of accidents reported to the health and safety inspector, analysed by department and cause.

(d) Labour turnover and stability rates.

(e) Days lost through absence (expressed as a percentage of the total number of working days during the period) and the number of spells of sickness, both analysed departmentally.

These statistics are usually compiled at monthly intervals.

9. Optional statistics

The following provide useful information for management, but are not so necessary as those listed above:

(a) Numbers of employees in various wage or salary grades. It is not essential to compile these at monthly intervals but it is common practice to do so annually when remuneration is reviewed. Pay statistics are sometimes needed for a special purpose, e.g. if a trade union makes a claim for a wage increase.

(b) Labour turnover (*see* Chapter 10).

(c) For human resources planning purposes, an analysis of employees by skill, training, place of residence, etc. If redundancy is expected, an analysis by length of service.

All personnel statistics carry much more weight if they are accompanied by a report which describes and explains them, and perhaps suggests future action.

Progress test 11

1. What is contained in the personnel file?
2. List the information which should appear in the employee record.
3. What are the advantages of keeping employee records on a computer?
4. What is the main purpose of the Data Protection Act?
5. What defence might a data user have against a claim for damages due to the use of inaccurate data?
6. Why is it important to distinguish between opinion and intention in computer-held data?
7. Name the most important statistics relevant to personnel work.

12

JOB ANALYSIS AND JOB SPECIFICATIONS

JOB ANALYSIS

1. Methods of job analysis

In personnel management it is very often necessary to obtain and record a description of a job (*see* **2**). The description must then be kept up to date to take account of changes in organisation or technology. Job analysis is the process by which a description of a job is compiled. There are many difficulties in job analysis, some practical, some concerned with the attitudes of employees. The following are the most important methods which may be used:

(a) *Direct observation* – this is always necessary but has several drawbacks:

(*i*) a skilled worker can make a job look easy
(*ii*) an experienced worker can make a job look difficult
(*iii*) mental processes are not revealed
(*iv*) some manual work is too fast or intricate to be observed accurately, unless film or video is used.

(b) *Interview with the job-holder* – this is nearly always necessary but difficulties often occur, largely because the worker may be suspicious of the job analysis. The employee may decide to exaggerate the importance of the job or occasionally try to make it seem unimportant. The main problems with these interviews are:

(*i*) the worker's attitude may influence his or her account of the job
(*ii*) the employee may, even if co-operative, forget some details of the job, and emphasise the most recent events
(*iii*) the employee may not be able to express him or herself clearly.

(c) *Interview with the supervisor* – this again is an inevitable occurrence, though its value varies for the following reasons:

(*i*) supervisors are surprisingly often out of touch with the details of the job

(*ii*) they frequently have never done the job themselves

(*iii*) they sometimes allow their description of the job to be influenced by their opinion of the job-holder

(*iv*) they may exaggerate the duties and responsibilities of the job in order to increase their own importance.

(d) *Materials of work* – a study of the tools, working materials, machines, documents, communication media, etc., frequently provides a useful check on information obtained in other ways, and may suggest questions to be asked.

(e) *Previous studies*, e.g. work study records, training manuals and accident reports, are sometimes available and can be brought up to date or added to other information.

(f) *Do-it-yourself* – in some jobs it is feasible for the analyst to spend some time actually performing the work personally. The analyst should then be careful not to form too subjective an impression, e.g. if he or she is not good at figures the analyst may tend to over-estimate the difficulty of an accounting job.

(g) *Questionnaires* are sometimes used, but are highly unreliable. The job-holder is asked to fill in answers to written questions about the job, but may be suspicious of the questionnaire (*see* **(b)** above), may not understand questions, and feel unduly restricted by them.

(h) *Work diaries* are sometimes used, chiefly for managers and clerical workers. The job-holder records his or her activities in detail throughout the day over a period of about a month. The diary is then analysed to obtain a list of duties and their frequency. If kept conscientiously and accurately, a work diary can be very helpful, but often the job-holder forgets to complete it until the end of the afternoon when recollection of the day's work may not be reliable.

In order to analyse a job with some degree of accuracy it is obviously necessary to use a combination of several of the above methods, each checking the other.

JOB SPECIFICATIONS

2. Definitions

The Department of Employment has published a glossary of training terms from which the following definitions have been taken:

(a) Job description – a broad statement of the purpose, scope, duties and responsibilities of a particular job.

(b) Job specification – a detailed statement of the physical and mental activities involved in the job and, when relevant, of social and physical environmental matters. The specification is usually expressed in terms of behaviour, i.e. what the worker does, what knowledge he or she uses in doing it, the judgments he or she makes and the factors taken into account when making them.

For general discussions of jobs, a broad description is all that is necessary. For example, when examining the staffing of a department for human resources planning purposes a detailed statement of activities is not required.

A job description can be written under these headings:

- Title of job
- Scope of job (in broad terms)
- Reporting to . . .
- Responsible for. . . .

3. Use of job specifications

For several personnel functions a detailed account of the job is necessary. The most important of these are:

- Selection
- Promotion
- Appraisal
- Setting performance standards
- Job evaluation
- Training.

The job specification is therefore of fundamental importance in personnel management, though it should be used with discretion. When relations are poor between manager and subordinates, the latter may use their job specifications (if they have been issued) as self-defensive weapons, refusing tasks or responsibilities because they do not appear in the specifications.

There are few companies where job specifications can genuinely remain unchanged for any length of time, since they are partly the result of the organisational needs (which frequently change) and partly the result of the way in which successive employees have carried out the job. Many companies therefore prefer to keep job specifications confidential, giving employees copies of their job descriptions only.

4. Drawing up a job specification

There is no standard layout or set of headings for a job specification; it is found that variations are necessary according to the type of work, e.g. manual or non-manual, and to the organisation.

The statement in the definition (*see* **2**) that a job specification should emphasise activities and behaviour is most important. A specification written in terms of responsibilities, for example, can be very misleading. To say that someone is responsible for obtaining and collating information from the company's branches may sound very important but in fact that person may simply receive straightforward sales statistics on standard forms and copy them onto an analysis sheet.

Whenever possible the job specification should show *what* the person does, and by *what means*. It is also desirable to indicate approximately what proportion of working time is spent on each activity, or group of activities, and how frequently any occasional duties occur.

The job specification should begin with the job description (*see* **2**) and then continue with a more detailed account of the job, perhaps using these headings:

- Major responsibilities and results expected
- Routine duties under those headings
- Non-routine or infrequent duties under the same headings
- Working conditions
- Equipment and materials used
- Personal contacts.

For appraisal and training purposes, performance standards should also be included; these are dealt with below. An example of a job specification for a manual job appears in Appendix 1.

PERFORMANCE STANDARDS

5. Purpose

It is sometimes necessary to specify the quantity or quality of work which should be attained by the holder of a certain job. As stated above, the most frequent use of performance standards is found in appraisal and training; to assess an employee either in his or her normal work or after training it is essential to have a criterion against which to compare actual performance. Performance standards are also used in some wage systems.

Competence standards

Standards of competence are benchmarks indicating what people should be capable of doing in specific workplace situations. Competencies typically involve the ability and willingness to perform particular tasks and to transfer knowledge and skills from the performance of one type of work to others. Personal competencies are the individual characteristics that people bring to their duties, e.g. leadership ability or good communication skills. Occupational competencies are the outputs and performance levels that individuals are expected to attain.

6. Setting standards

Performance standards are most easy to set when some kind of physical activity takes place. They can state how many articles should be produced, how many documents completed or how many selling calls made in a day. When the task becomes varied, e.g. when articles of several different types are made during a working day or the calls are scattered over a large area, standards expressed in such simple terms become misleading. A performance standard should also contain some reference to the quality of work.

In many cases, therefore, they are less easy to set than may appear at first sight; the standard of output may have to refer to a period considerably longer than one day in order to include a typical range of tasks, or subjective judgements introduced, e.g. 'performs work satisfactorily'. To reduce these difficulties it may sometimes be possible to select from the range of tasks the employee performs a very small number which must be done satisfactorily if the complete job is to be accomplished well. Careful analysis of the job may reveal these key points or critical incidents for which it may be possible to set performance standards expressed in measurable behaviour.

7. Standards for managers and supervisors

It is a very difficult problem to set performance standards for managers and supervisors because their work is extremely varied and emphasises mental rather than physical activity.

In some cases there may be obvious targets, e.g. a sales manager may be expected to maintain sales at a certain minimum level, or a supervisor to keep waiting time in his or her section below a certain level. Criteria such as these, which are similar to the key points or critical incidents mentioned in 6, are particularly valuable when they can be measured objectively and are within the control of the person concerned. A target for a supervisor to 'maintain satisfactory industrial relations within the section' would be valueless, first because of the subjective interpretation of the word satisfactory and secondly because the quality of industrial relations would depend on many factors outside the supervisor's control.

It is often claimed that careful analysis aided by ingenuity will show that any job contains elements for which performance standards can be expressed in terms of measurable behaviour, and some approaches to appraisal and training are based on this assumption.

PERSONNEL SPECIFICATIONS

8. Definition

According to the Department of Employment's glossary of training terms a personnel specification (sometimes called a person specification) is an interpretation of the job specification in terms of the kind of person suitable for the job. A personnel specification is used above all in recruitment, selection and promotion as part of the process of utilisation, i.e. finding the most suitable person to fill a job. It contains a series of desired attributes against which candidates for a job are judged; in some cases it may be possible to set an achievement or aptitude test to obtain a more exact measure of their suitability.

For convenience, and to ensure that no important points are overlooked, it is common practice to use a standard set of headings in a personnel specification. These headings often correspond with those used in recording the interview (*see* 16:6), e.g. the seven-point plan or the five-fold grading, so that the candidate can be matched more easily against the requirements of the job.

The personnel specification must always be based on the job specification; every statement in it must be justified by evidence obtained from the analysis of the job. Phrases like 'possessing outstanding initiative', which are sometimes found in personnel specifications, are not only vague but often have no relation to the actual demands of the job. The specification is intended to describe the person who is capable of doing the job adequately, not an impossible ideal.

9. Adapting the job to the employee

It is unrealistic and somewhat inhuman to suppose that a candidate will be found who fits the personnel specification exactly or can be precisely moulded into it by training. Quite often the job is changed after it has been analysed, sometimes deliberately, sometimes gradually and unconsciously by the jobholder to suit his or her abilities, personality and experience. In any case job analysis can never produce a completely reliable result (*see* 1) and job and personnel specifications based on it must always be interpreted flexibly.

Progress test 12

1. Describe, with comments, the chief methods of analysing a job.
2. What is the difference between a job description, a job specification and a personnel specification?
3. For what purposes is a job specification used?
4. Define performance standards.
5. For what purposes is a personnel specification used?
6. 'Job descriptions are of little benefit. They are out of date as soon as they have been written and agreed.'
   Discuss the value of job descriptions in a changing business environment.

13

JOB EVALUATION

THE BASIS OF JOB EVALUATION

1. Definition

Job evaluation is the process of placing jobs in order of their relative worth so that employees may be paid fairly. It is concerned with the demands and conditions of the job and not with the personal qualities of the individual who is occupying the job. Since jobs differ in so many respects, numerous problems arise in assessing their relative importance. A 'job' consists of a whole series of tasks, responsibilities and obligations, including the skills, knowledge and mental agility required, qualities of initiative, reliability, ability to withstand stress; capacities for planning, controlling others, co-ordinating the nature of the environment in which the work is completed, and so on. Ideally, jobs should be ranked according to objective criteria – known and understood by all who work in the organisation. The first stage in job evaluation is usually to establish a rank-order for jobs and the second is to apply money values to it.

2. Importance of job evaluation

Payment for work can fulfil many functions, from the provision of food and shelter to the recognition that an employee's job has a certain status and value, i.e. it can satisfy both lower and higher needs. Because pay is significant not only for what it will purchase but also for what it symbolises, a company's pay structure is very important to its employees, who will strongly resent what they perceive to be unfairness or injustice. In some companies, for example, pay anomalies have appeared perhaps because of inconsistency of treatment in the past, a merger with another company, or high rates being offered to meet a temporary shortage of a certain type of employee. Sometimes no one can explain the anomalies. The purposes of job evaluation are therefore:

(a) to make pay administration easier by reducing the number of separate rates of pay

(b) to harmonise internal rates of pay with those found in other companies

(c) to provide a means by which a reasonable rate of pay can be fixed for new or changed jobs within the company

(d) to protect the employee from arbitrary decisions by management

(e) to justify wage differentials and hence avoid frequent invocations of grievance procedures

(f) to facilitate fair promotion systems based on rationally determined job grading structures (each grade should specify all the qualifications and personal attributes needed to occupy a job within that grade).

In a small company these purposes can obviously be fulfilled without a formal system; no doubt some kind of intuitive evaluation takes place. Large companies, however, with their much more complex organisation and greater variety of occupations will find job evaluation almost essential unless their job structure is completely static, with pay relativities firmly established by tradition. Such firms are rare.

3. Factors determining pay

A wage or salary is influenced by many different factors. Some of these affect the basic pay for the job and others the pay that individual employees receive.

(a) *Supply and demand* – eventually, when the supply of a particular type of labour is scarce, its price, i.e. its wage or salary, will rise, and vice versa. The operation of this economic law is, however, affected by the following:

(*i*) people are often unwilling to move to another district
(*ii*) pay is not the only reward gained from employment
(*iii*) knowledge of the various rates of pay offered is not widespread
(*iv*) training for a new occupation may take some years.

(b) *Difficulty of the job* – it is generally agreed that jobs which require a high level of intelligence, experience, knowledge or skill deserve a high rate of pay.

(c) *Unpleasant working conditions.*

(d) *Cost of living.*

(e) *Government intervention.*

(f) *Productivity, merit or length of service* – often determining the pay received by an individual over and above the basic rate.

4. Introducing job evaluation

A new or altered job evaluation system is a change which must be very carefully introduced by management because it affects the vital subject of pay.

The method of evaluation must be clearly explained to employees and their representatives, some modifications perhaps being made at the employees' request. It is usual to guarantee that no employee at present employed by the company will receive a reduction in pay, though if the job is found to be overpaid his or her successors in it may be given a lower wage.

Some companies have found that the fairness of the scheme in the employees' eyes is increased if an appeals committee is set up to listen to complaints that jobs have not been given the value they deserve. Employee representatives, e.g. shop stewards, often sit on these committees.

5. Essential requirements

Any method of job evaluation requires two things:

(a) Job specifications for all jobs which are to be valued (*see* 12:**4**).

(b) A committee to consider the job specifications and apply to them the particular technique of evaluation which it has been decided shall be used. The committee usually contains a few permanent members, e.g. the personnel officer, the work study officer, the organisation and methods officer together with other members drawn from a panel of managers who have all had training in the technique. Job evaluations carried out by an individual are not likely to be well received; using a committee will reduce the effects of bias and prejudice.

METHODS

6. Job evaluation methods

Three methods of job evaluation are in common use:

(a) *Ranking*, a non-analytical method because the job is valued as a whole, an impressionistic view being taken.

(b) *Grading*, a semi-analytical method in which the job specification is examined fairly closely but not exhaustively.

(c) *Points rating*, an analytical method which requires a very detailed examination of the job specification.

7. Ranking

In this method the committee judges each job as a whole and places the set of jobs in order of their worth. Sometimes this process is aided by using as points of reference one or two jobs whose place in the hierarchy is generally accepted.

(a) Advantages:

(*i*) It is quick and requires no complicated administration.

(*ii*) It is easily understood.

(*iii*) It is particularly suitable for fairly homogeneous jobs, e.g. all clerical, or where it is known that the pay structure is already reasonably satisfactory.

(b) Disadvantages:

(*i*) Although the method is easy to understand, its results are difficult to defend as they are based on impressionistic, almost intuitive judgments.

(*ii*) It is impracticable in large companies or in smaller companies in which jobs are very varied.

(*iii*) It does not indicate the spaces between positions in the rank order, i.e. job A may be judged to be worth more than job B, but the method will not show how much more.

(*iv*) This type of system (often referred to as 'felt-fair' evaluation) may provoke industrial tribunal actions initiated under the 1984 revisions to the Equal Pay Act by aggrieved workers who claim they are unfairly paid less than members of the opposite sex who do work of equivalent value to their own. Recent test cases have established unambiguously that the results of felt-fair job evaluation systems will be ignored by courts and tribunals when determining equal pay cases (*see* **14**).

A refinement of ranking is the *paired comparison* method, in which each job is ranked against every other job, taking a pair of jobs at a time. If N jobs are dealt with in this way then $N(N - 1)/2$ comparisons have to be made, i.e. to rank 20 jobs will require 190 comparisons. It is usual to distribute the pairs of jobs among several judges and collate the results on a computer. By showing how many times a job has been given first preference, not only may a rank order be prepared but spacing along the rank order will also be shown. The paired comparison method also enables jobs of different types to be evaluated.

The subjectivity of ranking is obvious, though experienced judges using this method very often achieve remarkable agreement.

8. Grading

This method provides a framework into which jobs can be fitted. It is decided in advance how many grades or classes of pay shall be created, and the jobs which should fall into each grade are defined. The lowest grade, for example, will be defined as containing those jobs which require little skill and are closely supervised. With each successive grade skills, knowledge and responsibilities increase. The committee then reads the specification for each job, matching it against the various grade definitions until an appropriate grade is found. Eventually every job in the company has been allotted to a grade.

(a) Advantages:

(*i*) It is relatively simple, quick and inexpensive.
(*ii*) The decisions of the committee can be supported by the definitions of the job grades.

(b) Disadvantages:

(*i*) Complex jobs are often difficult to fit into the system; a job may seem to have the characteristics of two or more grades; like ranking, the method is at its best when a fairly homogeneous family of jobs is being evaluated.
(*ii*) Because of the difficulty in (*i*) the original grades tend to be sub-divided into smaller grades, making the scheme more difficult to operate.
(*iii*) The method is less objective than appears at first sight. To a large extent jobs are valued before the specifications are examined because arbitrary decisions have been made that certain features of a job belong to certain grades. For example, an unscrupulous employer could attempt to depress the remuneration of employees by defining the grades in such a way that the majority of jobs fell into the lower grades. On the other hand, this will not occur if the grade definitions have been prepared and published by an independent body, such as the Institute of Administrative Management, part of whose system of clerical workers' job grading is shown in Appendix 3.
(*iv*) Semi-analytical schemes have been adjudged inadequate by courts hearing equal pay cases. Courts now insist that firms adopt fully analytical techniques when comparing the value of work done by men and women.

9. Points rating

This is the most widely used method. A number of factors are first agreed against which jobs can be analysed. A very simple set of factors for manual jobs might be:

Skill
Effort
Responsibility
Working conditions.

However, it is usual to sub-divide each of the main factors into about three sub-factors, making about twelve altogether. For example, 'skill' might be divided into education, experience and dexterity. Sometimes non-manual jobs are provided for by extending the factors to include, for example, complexity of duties, contacts with others or requirement to handle confidential information, or sometimes a special set of factors is used for a particular family of jobs.

Each factor carries a range of points; the committee analyses each job specification to decide how many points shall be awarded to the job for each factor. The total of points when set against other totals indicates the position of the job in the hierarchy. An example of a job evaluation scheme for manual workers is shown in Appendix 3.

10. Weighting

The factors chosen for job evaluation may not all have equal importance; skill, for example, may contain the three sub-factors training, experience and dexterity of which experience is thought to make the greatest contribution to the value of a job.

Weighting is the name given to the process by which some factors can be given greater emphasis than others. It can be carried out in two ways:

(a) A multiplier is introduced so that the points value given to a factor can be doubled, trebled, etc. Each factor carries the same range of points, e.g. 1 to 10, but the value given to, say, experience might be multiplied by 4 and that for training by 2.

(b) Factors judged to be more important have a wider range of points attached to them. This is the practice followed in the scheme shown in Appendix 3.

11. The choice of factors and weights

The choice of factors and weights is intuitive rather than objective. A company with no experience of job evaluation will probably begin by using a scheme borrowed from another company, or one which has appeared in a book. If the results of evaluating a few well-known jobs do not agree with commonsense or tradition the company will change the factors or weights until an acceptable set of relationships is obtained.

Different jobs require different factors; it is very unusual for a company to be able to evaluate all its jobs by the use of one scheme only. For example, factors for evaluating management jobs would be quite different from those shown in Appendix 3, consisting perhaps of:

Judgment
Qualifications and experience
Extent of decision-making
Control of staff
Contacts with others.

These factors would probably be subdivided.

12. The subjectivity of points rating

The justification for the points rating system of job evaluation is that it works, not that it is objective or scientific. There are several subjective elements in the method, some of course being found in any job evaluation system.

(a) The job specification may reflect the bias of the job analyst.

(b) The members of the job evaluation committee, although guided by detailed job specifications and carefully-described factors, still make subjective judgments about the worth of a job.

190

(c) The selection of factors is based originally on imitation or conjecture and confirmed by intuition.

(d) Weights are selected according to the same principles.

In spite of its subjective elements points rating usually provides acceptable and consistent results if job specifications are well prepared and the committee is thoroughly familiar with the system.

13. Criticisms of job evaluation

The problem of subjectivity in the allocation of points to factors during job evaluation exercises has been referred to in **11**. Other criticisms of job evaluation are that:

(a) The forces of supply and demand for labour could cause the pay relativities established *via* a job evaluation exercise quickly to become out of date. Labour shortages in a particular category may force the market wage for that type of job to exceed the upper limit of the grade established by the exercise.

(b) By determining and writing down a list of the precise duties, activities, responsibilities and other characteristics of each job within a company, management might encourage inflexible attitudes and working practices. Rigid job definitions could lead to the strict demarcation of functions and tasks and hence to workers' declining to complete tasks not strictly within their job descriptions.

(c) Unscrupulous managements might introduce pseudo-scientific job evaluation exercises merely to confuse simple issues, deliberately mystify the procedures whereby wage levels are determined, and thus undermine management/union collective bargaining.

(d) Since it necessarily involves value judgements, it can never be truly scientific, hence causing many disagreements and conflicts within the firm.

(e) It ignores traditions that for many years may have helped set wage differentials within companies, quite independent of job content. These traditional disparities may not be objectively justified, but their removal can cause cultural shock waves that actually damage the company.

14. Legal considerations

Under the 1984 amendments to the Equal Pay Act any person is entitled to the same remuneration and conditions of service as a member of the opposite sex who is doing similar work, or *work which is of a similar value*, as judged under a *job evaluation* exercise. If a job evaluation has not already been undertaken within the organisation, the employee has the legal right (regardless of length of service, current grade or whether part-time or full-time) to apply to an industrial tribunal for an order (which is legally enforceable) that a job evaluation be carried out by an independent expert appointed by and reporting to the tribunal. This evaluation will consider the effort, skills and responsibility needed to take decisions and so on attached to the post, and the demands made on the individual worker in this job compared to jobs done by the firm's other workers.

Apart from the report submitted by the independent expert appointed by the tribunal, other reports may be submitted to the tribunal by each side based on the job evaluation studies undertaken by their own (paid) experts. These are presented as evidence in support of each party's case. The tribunal's decision is legally binding: wages *must* be increased and jobs regraded if the tribunal orders that this should occur. Moreover, Article 119 of the Treaty of Rome (which overrides UK domestic law) explicitly demands 'the application of the principle that men and women should receive equal pay for equal work'.

The revised Equal Pay Act clearly states that job evaluations must use *analytical methods*, i.e. they must examine 'in terms of the demands made on the worker under various headings (for instance, effort, skill, decision) the jobs to be done by all or any of the employees in an undertaking'. In other words, overall ranking or felt-fair classification will not be regarded as satisfactory. This is a point of great significance for employers, since it means that any non-analytical study is open to challenge in the courts.

The law as it stands requires the complainant whose job has been rated as *unequal* by an analytical study to demonstrate that there was a fundamental flaw in the analytical techniques adopted. But if the job evaluation was non-analytical, there is no need to demonstrate a flaw in the method. It is automatically assumed that the study was inadequate and that it did not meet the requirements of the Act. In consequence, it cannot be used as a barrier against a claim in an industrial tribunal – the aggrieved party may simply ignore the fact that the evaluation occurred and can proceed directly to the tribunal without having to prove the study was faulty. Moreover, recent test cases have upheld complaints that certain analytical evaluation exercises which resulted in pay differentials between jobs were not in fact analytical enough. The details and methodology of job evaluations are today increasingly questioned by the courts.

15. Measuring equal value

Even if an analytical job evaluation fairly demonstrates that two jobs done by members of the opposite sex differ in content, a claim can still be made if the jobs have equal value in terms of the effort, skill, decision making, etc. required to undertake them but they are not equally paid. The amended Equal Pay Act emphasises that the relevant yardstick in determining equal value is whether the jobs are equivalent with respect to the *demands made on the employee* when doing the job rather than the perceived value of the work to the employer. In other words, it is the *nature* of the work actually done that matters.

The Equal Opportunities Commission's own guide to the amended Equal Pay Act offers examples of possible similar and dissimilar demands made on the workers undertaking two hypothetical jobs. These are reproduced below.

Examples of similar demands

Job A	Job B
Responsible for contact with public	Responsible for staff
Lifts heavy weights occasionally	Lifts small weights continuously
Diagnoses machine faults	Analyses written reports
Checks stocks and orders replacements	Checks work done by subordinates and allocates tasks
Uses drilling machine	Uses typewriter
On feet most of day	Has to concentrate on numbers

Examples of dissimilar demands

Job A	Job B
Drives a van	Examines customer complaints
Sweeps up	Chooses fabric for new designs
Decides shift rosters	Responsible for packing and despatch

Cases that go before tribunals are judged on their individual merits, though all rely heavily on the results of independent analytical job evaluation studies. Already, such studies have determined that the work of a factory nurse was of equal value to that of a skilled fitter, that a secretary's work had equal value to a scientific assistant's, that an administrator's job was equal to a data analyst's, and that the demands made on a seamstress were of equal value to those made on a fork-lift truck driver. Other pairings have involved quality controllers and technical trainers, and the comparison of catering assistants with drivers. There are no limits on the jobs that can be compared, and every organisation must be fully cognisant of this when devising job evaluation procedures.

16. Job evaluation and pay

After evaluation has been completed by the ranking or points rating method the jobs appear in an order of value. They are then divided into groups or grades, the object being to allot to each grade a particular basic pay rate or pay-range. If the grading system of job evaluation is used this division will have been done already.

In very many cases it is found that most jobs contained in any grade are already paid at about the same rate; the few jobs for which pay is inconsistent are then brought into line. Occasionally however a job appears to be in one grade by job evaluation but in a considerably higher grade according to its present pay. If after checking the job specification and evaluation this difference remains it is usual to regard the discrepancy as being due to temporary abnormal market conditions; employees in that job are shown in the company's pay records as receiving pay for their grade plus a special allowance to bring their total remuneration to the market rate.

Pay surveys

Some companies regularly make comparisons between their own rates of pay and those paid by other companies for similar jobs, e.g. rates are compared for the copy-typists, forepersons or accountants employed in those companies. These rates are then applied to pay grades. This procedure can be misleading because:

(a) Pay is not the only reward from a job – some companies may have low rates of pay but a high reputation for security.

(b) The jobs compared may in fact be similar only in title; the duties and responsibilities may be different.

(c) It is not logical for a company to evaluate its jobs systematically and then base its pay structure on the wages or salaries paid by a company which may have made no attempt to bring order into its remuneration system.

Progress test 13

1. What are the purposes of job evaluation?
2. Name the most important factors determining levels of pay.
3. What do all methods of job evaluation require?
4. Describe briefly the ranking and grading methods of job evaluation.
5. How are factors and weights chosen in the points rating method?
6. In what circumstances might an industrial tribunal regard a job evaluation as sexually discriminatory?
7. How are the results of job evaluation expressed in monetary terms?

14

WAGES AND SALARIES

WAGE STRUCTURES

1. Definition

A wage is the payment made to manual workers. It is nearly always expressed as a rate per hour. In addition to the basic rate the worker will often receive other payments, the most common examples of which are:

(a) *Overtime pay* for any work done beyond normal hours. It is usually paid at premium rates, at time and a quarter, time and a half, double time, etc., the rate varying according to the time of the day on which the overtime is worked.

(b) *Shift pay* for employees who work unusual or changing hours, to compensate them for inconvenience and hardship. The amount of shift pay varies in different industries, but seems to range from about 10 to 20 per cent of the basic rate.

(c) *Special additions*, e.g. danger money, dirt money or wet money which are paid to the employee during abnormal working conditions. Since the circumstances which justify these additions are hard to define, many employers find it preferable to allow for these contingencies in the job-evaluated basic rate rather than give special extra payments which are often difficult to take away again.

(d) *Merit or length of service additions* to employees either on the results of appraisal or on completion of a certain period of service. Merit payments are not very popular with wage-earners, who feel they are influenced by prejudice and subjective judgments. Length of service payments have an approximate relationship with merit, encourage employees to stay with the company, and can be precisely defined.

(e) *Cost of living allowances* are given quite commonly in response to a rise in the general price level or to employees who work in high-cost areas, e.g. London. In many cases they are eventually consolidated into the basic wage.

(f) *Policy allowances* cover miscellaneous extra payments, like the addition to the job-evaluated rate for temporarily scarce employees.

(g) *Payments by results bonus*, i.e. an extra payment based on the output of the worker or of the group to which he or she belongs (*see* **3**).

PAYMENT BY RESULTS

2. Principles of PBR

In nearly all methods of payment by results the employee receives a basic rate to which is added a variable payment based on output. For each job a standard is set expressed either as a quantity produced per unit of time or as the time taken to do the job; bonus becomes payable when the employee exceeds this standard.

If a company installs a PBR system for the first time it therefore needs to take the following steps:

(a) The scheme is communicated to the employees with perhaps some modifications after consultation with representatives. Supervisors and managers are trained in its use.

(b) A standard rate of output is set for each job by measuring the reasonable time taken to do it and making allowances for rest periods and personal needs. There are various methods of setting standards, from intuitive judgment to detailed analysis of bodily movements.

(c) Administrative arrangements are made to record each employee's output, calculate his or her bonus, and add it to the worker's basic wage.

The cost of running a PBR scheme, including work study, clerical work and dealing with disputes arising out of it, can be considerable. Some schemes are also rather complicated to compute and difficult to understand because the bonus does not increase proportionately with output but at a faster or slower rate.

3. Advantages of PBR

A well-designed and well-maintained scheme will increase productivity from the same number of employees and the same equipment and thus reduce unit costs. The work study which it requires may well show more efficient methods of production, and the supervisor need not control subordinates so closely because the monetary incentive makes human control unnecessary.

The popularity of PBR is shown by the fact that about 40 per cent of manual workers are paid by this method. To operate at its best, however, it requires a steady flow of measurable work, the pace of which is within the control of the worker.

4. Disadvantages of PBR

There has been a reaction against PBR in recent years because the advantages described above are sometimes outweighed by the following disadvantages:

(a) A PBR system is exceptionally liable to decay; new methods and materials, introduced gradually, may slowly cause a standard to become loose so that workers can earn high bonuses very easily.

(b) It is a constant source of shopfloor conflict, both when a new rate is being fixed and when a worker is asked to move from a job where the rate is loose to another where the rate is tight.

(c) Supervisors are tempted to show favouritism in allocating jobs when it is easy to earn bonus in some but difficult in others.

(d) It is difficult to reward fairly the labourers and skilled setters or maintenance workers whose output cannot be measured although their work influences the output of others. Such workers are usually paid a lieu bonus, based on the average bonus earned by the PBR workers.

(e) Salaried supervisors sometimes earn less than their subordinates who are paid by PBR.

(f) Output norms are frequently found. A group of employees decides that no one shall exceed a certain level of output, on penalty of unofficial sanctions, e.g. ostracism, hiding or spoiling tools, damage to clothing. Output is restricted because:

(*i*) loose rates are not so obvious
(*ii*) employment is safeguarded
(*iii*) by reducing discrepancies in performance, the unity of the group is maintained.

(g) Earnings can fluctuate because an employee is not given a steady supply of work; at certain times therefore he or she is not able to earn bonus.

(h) Quality and safety may be adversely affected.

5. Group bonus schemes

In some forms of PBR the standard is based on the performance of a group rather than an individual. The bonus earned by the group is shared among its members sometimes equally, sometimes in proportion to basic pay. The advantages of group bonus schemes are:

(a) They can include indirect workers, e.g. labourers or maintenance workers.

(b) They improve team spirit.

(c) They encourage flexibility, because individuals are more willing to move to other jobs within the group.

(d) They simplify clerical work.

(e) They are particularly suitable for jobs which are carried out by a team of workers of various levels of skill, e.g. electric cable jointing.

Group bonuses tend to be unsatisfactory when the group becomes large, when its members constantly change or when it contains a mixture of very fast and very slow workers. Some companies have PBR schemes which are virtually group bonus schemes extended to cover a whole plant, bonus being payable according to the extent by which factory output exceeds a given standard.

6. Stepped pay systems

Productivity levels achieved under measured day work have often been disappointing, as there is no incentive for the employee to work to a level above the contracted rate. To overcome this problem some companies have introduced a more complicated system, often called the 'stepped pay band', which defines several levels of performance with a rate of pay for each. Employees may choose the level they work on and are checked from time to time to ensure that this performance is being maintained. They may ask to move up to a higher level if they feel they are capable of working at that rate. This method combines regular levels of pay with individual incentives.

WAGES LAW

7. Payment of wages

Rules determining how wages may be paid are specified in the Wages Act 1986. This removed all previous restrictions on employers paying their workers by means other than cash (or cheque or credit transfer in appropriate circumstances), although the actual method of payment is a matter for negotiation. Under the Act it is generally illegal to deduct money from an employee's pay or for the firm to require the employee to pay back money received in wages except in the following circumstances:

(a) Deductions for income tax and national insurance; or if a court has ordered that part of a person's wages be paid to a third party (e.g. to settle a fine or money owing under a court judgment).

(b) Payments requested in writing by the employee, such as trade union or sports clubs subscriptions.

(c) Agreed deductions for lateness or poor work, provided the agreement is incorporated into the employee's contract of employment.

(d) Accidental overpayment of previous wages or expenses.

(e) For *retail employees only*, deductions to make good cash shortages (e.g. money missing from the cash till) or stock deficiencies. 'Retail employment' means anyone involved in the sale and supply of goods or services. Hence, the Act covers not just shop assistants, but any employee handling cash transactions with customers – bus conductors, milk deliverers, booking office clerks, bank counter staff, etc. Deductions must not exceed more than 10 per cent of the wages due on any one pay day (except the last pay day before the employee leaves the firm) and the deduction must be made within twelve months of the detection of the shortage or deficiency.

The Wages Act covers self-employed contractors as well as employees. If an employer makes an unauthorised deduction, the worker or sub-contractor may apply to an industrial tribunal for recompense.

SALARY STRUCTURES

8. Definition

A salary is a fixed periodical payment to a non-manual employee. It is usually expressed in annual terms, implying a relatively permanent employment relationship, though normally paid at monthly intervals. In many ways, it resembles a retaining fee. Salaried workers are usually termed staff.

9. Characteristics of salaries

A salary differs from a wage in many respects, reflecting the different attitudes traditionally held by an employer towards the firm's non-manual compared with manual employees.

(a) A salary is usually all-inclusive; there are no additional payments of danger money or productivity bonus, for example.

(b) A salary is progressive, in most cases increasing annually, whereas a wage-earner reaches the standard rate for the job early in adult life and does not receive annual increases.

(c) A salary is often regarded as personal to the individual, but a wage is the sum paid to all workers at a particular job.

(d) A salary is often confidential, but there is no secret about a wage.

(e) In the private sector of employment, salaries are less likely than wages to be the subject of trade union negotiations.

10. Salary administration

This comprises a set of processes for determining, controlling and monitoring the salaries paid to employees. It is particularly concerned with the design and operation of salary structures (including the choice of criteria for salary grade), with determining relations between fringe benefits and basic salary, the timing of salary reviews, and the administration of salary progression systems. The objectives of salary administration are:

(a) To enable the organisation to forecast accurately its future salary bills and to control these effectively.

(b) To establish fair differentials between various grades of staff.

(c) To provide incentives to employees through offering them a career ladder through which they may progress.

(d) To relate salaries to employees' contributions to the organisation.

(e) To attract, retain and motivate employees of the appropriate calibre.

An effective salary system will keep the organisation's salary levels in line with market levels; will adjust salaries as the cost of living changes; will be consistent yet sufficiently flexible to allow for additional salary increases for employees of exceptional merit; and will be easy to operate and clearly understood by all salaried staff.

11. Salary administration methods

Implementation of a salary system requires the following:

(a) A survey of the salary levels offered by comparable firms.

(b) Determination of salary budgets for various employee categories.

(c) Job analysis and evaluation (*see* Chapter 13).

(d) Decisions concerning salary ranges and overlaps.

(e) Policies regarding merit and performance-related pay increases.

There are a number of ways in which a company can administer its salaries:

(a) *Ad hoc*, in which there is no attempt at any kind of job evaluation to assess a fair level of salary for a job. Increases in salary are given erratically, often at the demand of the employee rather than at the initiative of the company. In a small company this method is workable, but in a large company it can produce an illogical and unfair salary structure which will cause discontent and jealousy. For obvious reasons salaries paid by this system are intended to be confidential.

(b) *Merit review*, usually found in medium and large companies in the private sector. After job evaluation, a salary range is attached to every staff job. Employees are appraised and given personal merit increases each year which will move their salaries at varying speeds through the range. In this way individual effort and merit are rewarded. However a large amount of administrative work might be needed to assess the merit increases of all employees in the organisation, and if this task is delegated to heads of department substantial discrepancies in the amounts awarded to equally worthy individuals might emerge. Also, if very many employees simultaneously receive high merit increases the organisation is presented with a large unexpected salary bill. It is customary for salaries under this system to be kept confidential; in most cases the employees do not know the maximum salary it is possible to earn in their jobs.

(c) *Incremental scale*, found above all in the public sector, e.g. the civil service, local government and nationalised firms, though its use appears to be increasing in the private sector. All staff jobs are evaluated and graded, the salary range appearing as, for example, £18,000 × £500 – £23,500 indicating that there is a standard increment of salary each year of £500. Most schemes permit a manager to award double increments for exceptional merit or withhold an increment for unsatisfactory work or conduct, but as a rule the standard increment is given automatically. In this system long service and loyalty are encouraged by regular salary increases and merit by the speed of promotion to a higher grade. Sometimes grades overlap, creating the opportunity to reward long-serving workers whose ability levels make them unsuitable for promotion. It is customary for salaries in the incremental system to be non-confidential.

(d) *Rate for age*. This is an incremental scheme frequently applied to young workers, who receive pay rises of a predetermined amount on each of their birthdays up to a certain age (usually 21 years). Thus it assumes that the employee's contributions to the firm increase according to his or her experience and maturity. Provision for merit increases may be incorporated into the system.

Control over the firm's aggregate salary expenditures might be exercised through the following devices:

(a) Setting overall salary budgets for various sections, departments, functions or activities.

(b) Restricting the total amount available for salary increases to the amount generated by improvements in employee productivity.

(c) Careful forecasting and the statistical analysis of relationships (referred to as 'maturity' or 'salary progression' curves) between employees' ages and salaries (hence enabling the firm to predict future salary costs as the average age of its workforce alters).

(d) Deliberate salary attrition. Here the firm imposes a rule that resigning employees shall not be replaced until the expiry of a minimum period (six months, for example) during which colleagues are expected to cover the ex-worker's duties. This creates additional resources for the payment of merit increases to remaining staff. Note, moreover, that new starters are normally appointed in the bottom part of a grade whereas leavers will often be at a higher end of the scale.

A common procedure for monitoring trends in aggregate salary movements is the use of the 'compa-ratio' (short for comparative ratio). The mid-point of each salary grade is taken as the target salary for that grade. Then, the extent to which average salaries in a grade deviate from the mid-point is measured using the following formula:

$$\frac{\text{Average of all salaries in the grade}}{\text{Mid–point of the salary range}} \times 100$$

Thus, a compa-ratio of 100 would mean that the average salary within a grade is exactly equal to the mid-point. A high value indicates the presence of a large number of long-serving employees in a particular grade, and/or too many new appointments in the top end of the grade category. Low compa-ratio values could mean that the firm is paying salaries that are no longer competitive, or that there are too many recently recruited (and thus inexperienced) workers.

Rewards for senior executives

The reward levels of senior executives relative to other employees have increased sharply in many countries during recent years, a fact that has created much controversy. Senior managers are sometimes criticised for paying themselves very high salaries, whilst severely restricting the remunerations of lower ranking employees. Directors may be able to set their own pay levels with little regard for market forces in the short term, and minimal accountability to shareholders (perks and fringe benefits are frequently not revealed to outsiders). Criticism is markedly severe in situations where there are few clear relationships between organisational performance and executive pay. The case for providing extremely high salaries to senior managers rests on the following propositions:

(a) They are necessary in order to motivate individual executives (e.g. through performance-related pay).

(b) High renumeration implies high status and recognition of individual worth.

(c) Competent top-level managers are in great demand and likely to be head-hunted, so that high wages are needed to secure their loyalty and long-term commitment to the organisation.

(d) Senior management involves taking risky decisions which, if wrong, have serious adverse consequences both for the organisation and for the individual executive. A high salary is needed to compensate for the assumption of such a high level of risk.

(e) Only a small number of executives possess the management skills, knowledge and contacts necessary to succeed in competitive situations, and market forces of supply and demand naturally raise the renumeration levels of these people.

(f) Failure to attract the best managerial talent available will damage the firm in the longer period.

(g) Senior management is at the top of the managerial pyramid, so that high salaries are needed to maintain differentials while enabling lower levels to earn a reasonable reward.

(h) High salaries generate a culture of effort and achievement within the firm.

Some companies have 'remuneration committees' comprising non-executive (i.e. part-time advisory) directors of the business in question and/or people from outside the firm. This practice has been criticised on the grounds that, very often, virtually all the members of a remuneration committee are friends or acquaintances of the individuals whose pay they are determining, so that an 'old pal's system' develops which supports far higher pay increases for senior managers than otherwise would be the case. Criticism has been particularly severe in situations where large pay rises have been awarded to directors of loss-making companies.

Pay review bodies

In the public sector there exist 'pay review bodies' which determine the pay of workers in certain fields. A pay review body is nominally independent, comprises outsiders with no direct interest in outcomes, and prepares a report for consideration by the government (which need not accept the body's recommendations). Key considerations in formulating a pay review body's proposals include changes in the cost of living, pay trends in comparable industries, skill levels of relevant groups of workers, and the number of employees leaving the public sector to work for private firms in related fields.

OTHER PAY LEGISLATION

12. Equal Pay Act 1970

This Act requires employers to give equal treatment regarding terms and conditions of employment to men and women if:

(a) they are employed on like work; or

(b) they are employed on work of equal value (*see* 13:**14**).

In 1996 the Equal Opportunities Commission published a Code of Practice on Equal Pay containing practical guidance to businesses concerning the elimination of pay discrimination between men and women. The Code has sections covering, *inter alia*, the meaning of pay, implications of the law for employers, pay systems, the identification of discrimination, job evaluation and grading, plus a model equal pay policy. The Code is admissible in evidence before an industrial tribunal in any proceedings under the Sex Discrimination Act 1975 and the Equal Pay Act 1970.

13. Maternity pay

Under the Trade Union Reform and Employment Rights Act 1993 all pregnant employees are entitled to 14 weeks' maternity leave irrespective of length of service. This may not begin until eleven weeks prior to the expected week of childbirth, at the earliest. The woman has the legal right to return to her original job at the end of the period. Twenty-one days notice of intention to take maternity leave must be given, in writing if the employer so wishes. If the employee decides to return to work before the end of the 14 week period she has to give seven days' notice. A woman with more than six months' but less than two years' service with the employer is entitled to remuneration from her employer at the rate of 90 per cent of her normal wage for six weeks, plus statutory maternity pay for a further 12 weeks. Pregnant employees with less than six months' service are not entitled to remuneration from their employers, although they will receive the appropriate amount of state benefit. It is (automatically) unlawful for an employer to dismiss an employee for being pregnant, having a child or taking maternity leave, even if the pregnancy makes her incapable of doing her job. In the latter case the worker must be found alternative work or, if none is available, be 'suspended' on full pay.

A woman with more than two years' continuous service has extra rights, conferred by the Employment Protection (Consolidation) Act 1978. Such an employee will receive maternity pay at the standard rate for a period not exceeding eighteen weeks, but if she has continued to work up to the eleventh week before the baby is due and has given her employer at least three weeks' written notice of absence, she will receive for the first six weeks of absence maternity pay at a higher rate, i.e. nine-tenths of her normal pay. After six weeks she will receive (for not more than twelve weeks) maternity pay at the standard rate.

14. Guarantee payments

The Employment Protection (Consolidation) Act 1978 also gives employees, who have been laid off or put on short time because of a shortage of work, the right to continue to receive pay for a limited period, i.e. for up to five days in any period of three months. Many employers have made agreements with their employees which provide for guarantee payments more favourable than this.

15. Suspension on medical grounds

Employees who are suspended under certain health and safety regulations because their health is endangered are entitled under the Employment

Protection (Consolidation) Act 1978 to receive a normal week's pay for every week they are suspended up to a maximum of 26 weeks. An employee will lose the right to this pay if he or she unreasonably refuses to do any suitable alternative work that the employer offers.

Progress test 14

1. Name possible extra payments a manual worker may receive in addition to a basic wage.
2. What must a company do when it introduces a payment by results scheme for the first time?
3. What are the main advantages and disadvantages of PBR?
4. For what kinds of job is a group bonus scheme particularly suitable?
5. State the main provisions of the Wages Act 1986.
6. How does a salary differ from a wage?
7. What is an incremental salary scale?
8. Summarise the Equal Pay Act 1970.
9. What is a remuneration committee and what is its role?

15

RECRUITMENT AND SELECTION

RECRUITMENT

1. Definitions

It is useful to make a distinction between recruitment and selection:

(a) *Recruitment* is the first part of the process of filling a vacancy; it includes the examination of the vacancy, the consideration of sources of suitable candidates, making contact with those candidates and attracting applications from them.

(b) *Selection* is the next stage, i.e. assessing the candidates by various means, and making a choice followed by an offer of employment.

If the vacancy is additional to the present workforce, i.e. it has occurred because of some new or increased activity, then in all probability the need for the new employee has been established and a job specification compiled. The majority of vacancies, however, occur as replacements for people who have left the company or as the final event in a chain of transfers and promotions following on a reorganisation. In these cases consideration may be given to the following points:

(a) It may be possible to fill the vacancy from within the company.

(b) It may be filled by a different kind of employee, e.g. a school-leaver or a part-timer.

(c) The job and personnel specifications may need to be revised.

2. Internal sources

The advantages of filling the vacancy internally rather than externally are:

(a) Better motivation of employees because their capabilities are considered and opportunities offered for promotion.

(b) Better utilisation of employees, because the company can often make better use of their abilities in a different job.

(c) It is more reliable than external recruitment because a present employee is known more thoroughly than an external candidate.

(d) A present employee is more likely to stay with the company than an external candidate.

(e) Internal recruitment is quicker and cheaper than external.

3. External sources

Very many vacancies are filled from external sources; even when an internal candidate is transferred or promoted the final result is usually a vacancy elsewhere in the company which has to be filled from outside. External recruitment can be time-consuming, expensive and uncertain, though it is possible to reduce these disadvantages to some extent by forethought and planning.

External sources may be divided into two classes: those which are comparatively inexpensive but offer a limited choice, e.g. unsolicited applications, jobcentres, direct links with schools and colleges, and those which are comparatively expensive but give the employer access to a wider range of candidates, such as advertising and the use of private agencies.

Even when unemployment is high certain categories of employee who possess scarce skills are difficult to find and the employer may have to use the more expensive means of recruitment. Other types, for example unskilled workers, can be found very easily using inexpensive means; the problem then lies in selecting the suitable candidate from among a very large number of applicants.

4. Colleges and agencies

Many employers maintain connections with universities, colleges and schools. Candidates are usually available from these sources only at one time of the year, but this difficulty can often be overcome if companies begin their internal training courses in the autumn, or fill junior vacancies with temporary staff until school-leavers are available.

Government agencies

The Careers Service and the various services of the Department of Employment provide a means of recruitment which is either free of charge or costs very little. The choice offered by these services is limited, however, because many types of employee prefer to seek jobs by other methods and do not register with the appropriate government agency.

Private agencies

Organisations which are run as commercial enterprises for supplying employers with candidates for jobs are of two main types:

(a) *Office staff employment agencies*, which mainly deal with clerical, typing and office machine operator vacancies. The employer informs the agency of the vacancy, and the agency submits any suitable candidates on its register. When a candidate is engaged the employer pays a fee to the agency, part of which is usually refunded if the employee leaves within a specified time. There is no charge to the candidate, who of course is at liberty to register with several agencies if he or she likes. Unless the agency takes care to submit only reasonable candidates for the vacancy its services can be expensive because of the time taken up in interviewing, testing and processing applications.

(b) *Selection agencies for senior staff*, which usually undertake the complete recruitment process and the first stages of selection for managerial and professional vacancies. The agency analyses the job, prepares job and personnel specifications, advertises, sends out application forms and interviews selected candidates, sometimes testing them also. The employer is then presented with a shortlist of candidates, the career and qualifications of each being described, so that the employer may make the final choice. This method of recruitment is expensive because it is usual for the employer to pay a substantial fee whether or not a suitable candidate is found. Agencies have two disadvantages:

(*i*) In many cases it is impossible for an outside body to understand in a short time what kind of a person will fit in with the present management of the company.

(*ii*) It is very difficult for the agency to follow up and validate its recommendation.

5. Headhunting

Very senior managers are sometimes recruited by a process known as 'executive search' or 'headhunting'. Its advocates believe that the best candidates are not those who reply to advertisements or look for new jobs in other ways, but those who are successful in their present jobs and are not thinking of moving elsewhere.

On receipt of a commission from a client the headhunter will search for potential candidates (*i*) in competing businesses (possibly obtaining their names from company reports, brochures, etc.), (*ii*) in the membership lists of professional bodies, trade association yearbooks, newspaper and magazine reports that mention successful managers in the relevant industry, and (*iii*) through confidential headhunting networks. Selected individuals are then approached discreetly and, following a discussion regarding the job and its remuneration, one or two of them are introduced to the client firm. Advantages to headhunting are:

(a) Headhunters should possess expert knowledge of the salary levels and fringe benefits necessary to attract good calibre candidates. Also, they will analyse the vacancy and offer an opinion about the type of person required, will conduct initial screening, administer psychometric tests (*see* Chapter 7), etc. This saves the client many administrative costs and advertising expenses.

(b) Possibly, top managers already in employment will not bother to read job advertisements, newspapers and other conventional media and hence cannot be reached by these means.

(c) Senior managers prepared to consider a move sometimes make this known to leading headhunters, even though they would not openly apply to competing companies.

(d) If a targeted candidate does not want the job, he or she may suggest someone else who is equally suitable and who may in fact be interested.

(e) Recruiting firms are assured that candidates presented to them will almost certainly be well equipped for the vacant position.

(f) The anonymity of the recruiting organisation is preserved until the final stages in the procedure.

Criticisms of executive search include:

(a) Headhunting is highly disruptive to successful businesses, which stand to lose expensively-trained senior managers.

(b) It can be used to avoid equal opportunities laws on recruitment and selection.

(c) A headhunted individual might subsequently be enticed by other headhunters to leave his or her new firm after a short period. To avoid this some companies attach 'golden handcuffs' to senior management positions, i.e. they pay large cash bonuses which are only available to executives who stay with the firm a certain number of years.

(d) Arguably, headhunters rely too heavily on existing networks and trade contacts, creating thereby a glorified 'old boy system' which ignores good people from other sources.

(e) Headhunters' fees are far higher than for conventional employment agencies (up to 50 per cent of the recruited individual's initial salary in some instances).

(f) An unsuitable candidate might bribe the headhunter to recommend that person for the vacant job.

(g) The headhunter might acquire confidential information about the client company which could then be passed on to competing firms.

(h) Headhunters are not subject to the same long-term accountability as personnel managers employed within the business. Also they lack detailed knowledge of the client organisation's culture (*see* Chapter 9) and operations.

(i) A headhunter might misleadingly suggest to potential candidates that a job carries a high level of salary when this is not actually the case. The salary quoted may in fact depend on meeting unrealistic targets. Equally, a recruiting firm might expect a headhunter to find a candidate capable of solving all its difficulties, when in reality the business is so weak it is bound to fail.

6. Advertising

The most popular method of recruitment is to advertise the vacancy and invite candidates to apply to the company. It has been estimated that about 10 per cent of all press advertising expenditure is devoted to situations vacant advertising; there is no doubt that much of this huge sum is wasted, chiefly because so little research has been carried out compared with research in the field of product advertising.

Many employers have been able to reduce their job advertising costs with no adverse effect on the quality or quantity of candidate response by experimenting with styles of advertisements, media and wording, and keeping careful records of the number of replies received to each advertisement and the candidate who was eventually selected. The only reliable guidance about advertising comes from the person who receives and analyses the replies, i.e. the employer. Newspapers and advertising agencies, which often claim to advise on the style and size of advertisements, are not usually in a position to know and evaluate the response.

Job advertisements should aim at procuring a small number of well-qualified candidates quickly and as cheaply as possible. Note the high cost of placing job advertisements in newspapers. A single advertisement covering 140 mm × 2 columns (approximately one-eighth of a page) in one issue of a quality daily newspaper will cost between £1,750 and £3,100, depending on the newspaper's circulation and the page position of the advertisement. Even a small advertisement in a regional newspaper can cost in excess of £350. An advertisement which produces hundreds of replies is bad; the employer will then be faced with the lengthy and expensive task of sorting out a few candidates for interview. The advertisement can become the first stage in selection by describing the job and qualifications required so comprehensively that borderline candidates will be deterred from applying and good candidates encouraged.

The small amount of research that has been done in this field shows that information about the job contributes much more to the effectiveness of an advertisement than its style or size. There is also general agreement that including the word training in an advertisement increases the response.

Advertising may be made more effective and less expensive if the following principles are observed:

(a) The advertisement should contain a job specification and a personnel specification in miniature, including the following:

(*i*) job title
(*ii*) description of job and employer (including location)
(*iii*) experience, skills and qualifications required
(*iv*) age range
(*v*) working conditions, e.g. wage or salary, fringe benefits
(*vi*) training given (if relevant)
(*vii*) what action the candidate should take, e.g. write a letter, telephone for an application form, etc.

(b) It should appear in the appropriate publication, e.g. local press for manual and routine clerical jobs, national press for senior jobs, professional journals for specialists.

(c) Experiments should be made to test the response for different sizes, headings, wording, page position, day of the week, etc.

(d) Careful records should be kept showing:

(*i*) which publication was used
(*ii*) which date and day of the week
(*iii*) which position on the page
(*iv*) which style and size, e.g. display, semi-display, run-on
(*v*) names of the candidates replying to each advertisement
(*vi*) names of the candidates who are selected for interview
(*vii*) name of the candidate who is successful.

(e) The response should be analysed so that advertising expenditure can be directed towards the publication and the style of advertisement which give the best result for a particular type of vacancy.

(f) Rejected candidates should be sent a prompt and courteous letter; inconsiderate treatment will eventually detract from a company's reputation and adversely affect the response to future advertisements.

Sometimes other considerations besides cost and response must be kept in mind. For example, suppose that evidence has been collected which shows that small advertisements are just as effective as large, providing the information given is the same (a not uncommon finding). The company may decide that small advertisements are not consistent with its prestige and that large advertisements must be used even though they can be shown to be wasteful. In this case part of the cost of the advertisement should logically be paid out of the company's general advertising account as it is concerned as much with public relations as with recruitment.

On the other hand, the prestige of the company can sometimes be made use of; a recruitment campaign is very often more successful if it follows a national advertising campaign for a new product which has brought the company into the public eye.

211

SELECTION

7. The application form

Whatever method of recruitment is used, the candidate should be asked to fill in an application form, firstly to ensure that no important details are omitted and secondly to provide information about the candidate in a logical and uniform order.

The layout of application forms varies, but most of them contain the following headings, usually in this order:

(a) Job applied for

(b) Name, address, telephone number

(c) Date and place of birth, nationality

(d) Education

(e) Training and qualifications

(f) Medical history, e.g. any serious illnesses, whether disabled

(g) Employment history (names of previous employers, description of jobs held, dates of employments, reasons for leaving)

(h) Any other information the candidate wishes to provide

(i) A signature under the words 'This information is correct to the best of my knowledge'

(j) Date.

The application form is not only the basis of selection, but is the fundamental document in an employee's personnel record and has legal importance in the contract of employment.

Application forms are also useful for:

- projecting a favourable image of the recruiting organisation
- obtaining names and addresses of people to contact when future vacancies arise
- researching the effectiveness of various recruitment advertising media
- monitoring the effectiveness of equal opportunities policies.

8. Selection method

The manager's next step is to compare the application form with the personnel specification, looking for attributes which show the candidate to be apparently suitable for the job and shortcomings which may either rule out the candidate from consideration or necessitate special training if he or she were engaged. From this comparison the manager can make a list of candidates for interview and a list of those to be rejected. The latter should be written to at once regretting their lack of success.

When, because of high unemployment, a large number of applications is received the task of compiling a list of candidates to be interviewed becomes very difficult and time-consuming. Various suggestions have been made for dealing with this problem. When managerial, supervisory or specialist vacancies are being dealt with an enlarged application form can be used asking for precise details of past employment. Candidates are then rejected or not following a ruthless comparison of their experience with the demands of the post as shown by job analysis. A few companies ask candidates to complete a biographical questionnaire which has been carefully designed in respect of the job to be filled, though the process of compiling and validating the questionnaire is itself a lengthy and expensive undertaking. The majority of vacancies, however, are not suitable for such additional procedures, which assume that candidates have above-average powers of self-expression and are willing to complete complicated forms. Perhaps the usual method in such cases is first to reject some candidates on the application form and then give quick interviews to the remainder (often a very large number) concentrating on relevant experience. This will produce a shortlist who will go through a more searching selection procedure.

After the shortlist has been drawn up the manager will decide what type of interview should be given – individual, successive or panel, and what tests should be used, e.g. an intelligence test, an aptitude test or an achievement test. The interview, which is the main and indispensable part of the selection process, is described in Chapter 16. Notes are made, and filed for a reasonable period, of each candidate's performance in the interview and tests in case an unsuccessful candidate questions the decision, e.g. under the Race Relations Act or the Sex Discrimination Act.

9. Offer of the job

Assuming that a suitable candidate has emerged from the selection process, he or she must now receive an offer. It is usual for the person to be made an oral offer, and if he or she accepts it (perhaps after an interval for consideration) the individual is given a written offer. The initial offer of a job needs special care, particularly as regards the following points:

(a) The wage or salary offered must not only be appropriate to the job and attractive to the candidate but consistent with the earnings of present employees.

(b) The job must be named and any special conditions stated, e.g. 'for the first six months you would be under training at our Birmingham branch'.

(c) The candidate must know the essential conditions of employment, e.g. hours, holidays, bonuses and fringe benefits.

(d) Any provisos must be clearly stated, e.g. 'subject to satisfactory references and medical examination'.

(e) The next stage must be clearly defined; if the candidate asks for time for consideration, it must be agreed when he or she will get in touch. If the candidate accepts the oral offer, that manager must say what will happen next, and when.

10. References

A clear, unbiased and comprehensive description of a candidate's abilities and behaviour by his or her previous employer would be of enormous value in selection, particularly if the employer also supplied a job specification. Unfortunately this ideal is never realised, for several reasons:

(a) Most candidates are employed at the time of their application, and do not wish their employers to know they are looking elsewhere.

(b) Because of **(a)** a prospective employer would be breaking a confidence if he or she asked for a reference before an offer of a job had been made and accepted.

(c) By the time an offer has been accepted, selection is over and the reference is too late to affect it.

(d) An offer may be made 'subject to satisfactory references', but as most references are received after the candidate has started work they can only be used to warn managers of possible faults in the candidate which in serious cases may eventually lead to warnings followed by dismissal.

(e) Employers giving references are usually extremely cautious; many references merely state the job title, the dates of employment, and the reason for leaving.

(f) References are occasionally biased, giving a good reference to hasten an employee's departure or a poor one because of a grudge.

Most references do not give rise to second thoughts about the selection of a candidate, but in a few cases information is given (usually by telephone call) which shows the request for a reference to have been worthwhile.

There is no legal obligation for employers to provide references, though failure to do so can be extremely damaging to the employee concerned because failure to give a reference is likely to be construed as a condemnation of the current work of that person. Conventionally, therefore, firms provide at least very basic information on workers (dates of employment, job title, starting and present salary levels and so on) regardless of their assessment of an individual's worth. In order to extract more than this elementary information, many recruiting organisations send to referees a matrix style form asking them to assess the candidate against certain prespecified criteria. Legal issues arise if a reference is defamatory, or contains knowingly false information that causes a recruiting firm to hire an unsuitable person whose incompetence then causes financial losses to the new employer. Hence, referees:

- should not comment on subjective matters (e.g. a person's potential to perform a new role in another organisation) unless the referee has full knowledge of those matters (the demands of the job for instance) prior to expressing an opinion
- ought to be able to back up their comments with supporting factual information.

11. Applicants with criminal records

A person with a criminal conviction is not necessarily obliged to disclose this to a recruiting company, provided the conviction has been 'spent', i.e. a certain period has elapsed since the time of the offence. The Rehabilitation of Offenders Act 1974 contains a table of the time intervals that must pass by before a conviction becomes spent. For example, sentences of imprisonment are spent after seven years if the sentence was for less than six months, or ten years for sentences of between six and 30 months. Fines become spent after various periods according to the level of fine imposed. A probation order is spent after 12 months. The periods are halved if the person involved was under 17 years of age when he or she was convicted. However, some sentences can never be spent, notably life imprisonment (which in practice can mean that only a short period is actually spent in jail) and other periods of imprisonment for more than 30 months. Also there are exceptions to the Act whereby candidates for certain jobs do have to reveal past convictions, namely any form of work with young people under the age of 18, lawyers, chartered accountants, nurses, vets, dentists, medical practitioners, social and health workers, firearms dealers and prison officers.

Under the Act it is unlawful for an employer to deny someone a job solely on the grounds that the applicant has a spent conviction and, if the person is asked to declare on an application form whether he or she has a criminal record or is questioned about this during an interview, the applicant is legally entitled to 'forget' about ever having been convicted. If an employee is dismissed in consequence of a spent conviction being discovered the dismissal is unfair (*see* Chapter 19). Indeed, the employer may not reveal that the employee possesses a spent conviction to third parties (when writing references for example). The justification for the Act is twofold:

1. That in the absence of legislation the possession of a criminal record would effectively debar the vast majority of petty criminals from obtaining employment, hence encouraging them to commit further offences.
2. That criminal records are held only by people who have *already* been punished for their crimes, so that it is improper for such individuals to be punished again through not being able to get a job.

12. Employment of disabled persons

Attitudes towards the disabled in the workplace can be extremely negative, with disability being perceived as the source of poor performance, low levels of skill, absence of work ethic, accident-proneness, and taking long periods off work. None of these beliefs stand up to proper scientific scrutiny, yet they continue to distort non-disabled observers' perceptions of the person concerned. Many employers believe they have a social duty to employ disabled people, where possible adapting production lines or telephone exchanges, for example, to allow this. There is also statutory backing for the employment of the disabled in the Disabled Persons (Employment) Acts 1944 and 1958, which provide for:

(a) A register of disabled persons, open to all who are substantially handicapped in getting or keeping suitable employment.

(b) A requirement that every employer with 20 or more workers should employ at least 3 per cent registered disabled workers.

(c) An employer may not dismiss a registered disabled person without reasonable cause if the firm is below its quota or if the dismissal would bring its numbers below it.

(d) The designation of two jobs, passenger lift attendant and car park attendant, which may only be filled by registered disabled persons.

The Acts have helped many disabled persons to find work, but in some areas employers find the quota difficult to fulfil, although they employ a reasonable number of disabled people. The reason for the difficulty is that although there is a legal requirement for employers to maintain a three per cent quota there is no legal requirement for disabled persons to register. Indeed, many disabled people maintain that being registered may be a drawback in their careers and that they prefer not to indicate that they regard themselves as in a different category from other people. Employers who are not able to meet the quota of registered disabled persons must approach their local Job-centre to explain their difficulties.

The 'designated employments' in the Acts are another problem, because both the occupations (*see* **(d)**) can be quite arduous and require regular attendance. It is often difficult to find candidates who are registered as disabled but yet are fit enough to meet the physical requirements of these jobs.

The Disability Discrimination Act 1995

This legislation introduced new rights for disabled people in the areas of employment; education; public transport; and access to goods, facilities and services. A National Disability Council was established to advise the government on eliminating discrimination against disabled people, and a Code of Practice was published containing a wide range of examples to illustrate how employers and others can comply with the Act. The Code is not legally binding *of itself*, but is admissible as evidence in courts and industrial tribunals in order to establish whether discrimination has occurred. 'Disability' is defined as 'a physical or mental impairment which has a substantial and long-term adverse effect on a person's ability to carry out normal day-to-day activities'. Hence a severe disfigurement represents a 'disability' (though not if it results from tatooing or body piercing), as does anything likely to restrict an individual's mobility, manual dexterity, physical co-ordination, speech, hearing or eyesight, perception of danger; or his or her capacities to learn or understand or to lift or carry everyday objects. However, addictions and anti-social behaviour do not entitle people to protection under the Act. Hay fever is also excluded (unless it aggravates another condition), together with behavioural tendencies towards theft, setting fires, or exhibitionism. Specific provisions of the legislation are as follows:

(a) It is unlawful for an employer with 20 or more workers to treat disabled people less favourably than others unless there are justifiable reasons. Employers have to make 'reasonable adjustments' to working arrangements or environments where that would overcome the practical problems created by an individual's disability.

(b) No service-providing firm of any size may discriminate against the disabled, who have a legal *right* to be served. Thus for example an hotelier who pretends that all rooms are fully booked in order to refuse a booking from a mentally ill person is breaking the law.

(c) People letting or selling land or property must not discriminate against disabled persons.

(d) Colleges of Further Education are required to publish Disability Statements to inform students about the arrangements they have made to help them to gain access to college facilities.

(e) A disabled person who feels that he or she has been unfairly discriminated against in employment or when applying for a job has a right of redress through an industrial tribunal.

(f) New buses, taxis, trains and trams must satisfy minimum standards for access by disabled people.

13. The written offer of employment

Assuming that the oral offer has been accepted the employer must now confirm in writing. The employer will repeat in this letter the conditions already stated, taking great care that they are accurate because they will be on permanent record as the basis of the contract of employment. In many companies it is the rule that written offers may only be sent by the personnel manager or company secretary to ensure their accuracy.

The Trade Union Reform and Employment Rights Act 1993 requires that employees working at least eight hours a week must be given a statement of their conditions of service within the first eight weeks of employment. Some employers combine the written offer of employment with the statutory statement which must contain:

(a) Names of employer and employee

(b) Date when employment began and the date when continuous employment began

(c) Pay, or method of calculating pay

(d) Intervals at which payment is made, i.e. weekly, monthly, etc.

(e) Terms and conditions relating to:

(*i*) hours of work
(*ii*) holiday pay, including the pay due on termination of employment
(*iii*) sick pay
(*iv*) pension scheme

(f) The length of notice of termination the employee is obliged to give and entitled to receive

(g) A note indicating the employee's right to join, or not to join a trade union

(h) A description of the manner in which an employee can seek redress of any grievance relating to his or her employment

(i) The title of the job

(j) A note showing whether any period of employment with another employer counts as part of the period of employment for notice purposes

(k) For firms employing more than 20 persons, reference to a document stating the disciplinary rules, and naming a person to whom the employee can apply (and by what method) if he or she is dissatisfied with a disciplinary decision

(l) Any collective agreements which directly affect terms and conditions

(m) Place(s) of work

(n) For temporary jobs, how long the employment is expected to last

(o) For employees working abroad, the period to be spent outside the UK, the currency of payment, any additional benefits payable in consequence of working abroad, and the terms and conditions relating to the employee's return to the UK.

It is not necessary for the written statement to cover all these points in detail; the employee may be directed to documents which are easily accessible for the full particulars. These documents could include, for example, pension scheme handbooks or copies of the works rules.

Employees must be informed in writing of any changes in conditions not more than one month after the change has been made.

14. Induction

The process of receiving employees when they begin work, introducing them to the company and to their colleagues, and informing them of the activities, customs and traditions of the company is called induction. It may be regarded as the beginning of training or the final stage of the selection process. It has also been shown to have a close relationship with labour turnover.

Induction may be divided into two stages:

(a) Introduction to the working group is important psychologically and best done by the employee's immediate supervisor, who should introduce the recruit to colleagues and show him or her round the department.

(b) Company background (in a large company), which may be described by lectures, films or visits. Probably this should not be done in the first day or week of employment because the employee is at that time more concerned with his or her immediate surroundings and his or her own job. The worker will become interested in the wider scene two or three months after joining the company and can then take part in a second-stage induction course at some central point in the firm, if the company is a large one, or a supervisor may talk to the worker informally if the company is small.

15. Follow-up

All selection should be validated by follow-up. The employee is asked how he or she feels about progress to date and the worker's immediate superior is asked for comments, which are compared with the notes taken at the selection interview. If a follow-up is unfavourable it is probable that selection has been at fault; the whole process from job specification to interview is then reviewed to see if a better choice can be made next time.

An employee can be followed-up about three months after starting if the job is fairly straightforward, and after a longer period if the job is more complex and responsible.

DISCRIMINATION IN EMPLOYMENT

16. Equal opportunity in employment

An equal opportunity employment situation exists when there is no unfair discrimination against either of the sexes or against any ethnic or legally constituted social group in terms of access to jobs, terms and conditions of employment, promotion, training, remuneration, or termination of employment. Today, many organisations have 'equal opportunities policies' in which they formally state their commitment to equal opportunity ideals. The advantages to having such a policy are that:

(a) Top management is seen to endorse equal opportunity measures creating an example to be followed at lower levels.

(b) As part of its policy the firm might critically examine the sex and ethnic compositions of all its departments, divisions, occupational categories and levels of worker, exposing any unfair employment practices currently operating.

(c) The best candidates for jobs will (or should) be recruited or promoted regardless of their sex or ethnic origin.

(d) Discontent among existing minority group employees may be avoided.

Problems attached to equal opportunity policies are:

(a) Organisations sometimes publish extensive equal opportunity policy documents in order to placate existing minority group workers and/or external bodies (local authorities, government purchasing agencies, the EOC or CRE (*see* **20**), etc.) but in fact have no commitment to equal opportunities whatsoever. They have no procedures for *implementing* their equal opportunity policy documents. This creates disillusion and cynicism among all concerned.

(b) Recruitment costs increase substantially. Job advertisements have to be placed (expensively) in magazines and newspapers read by each of the sexes and by various ethnic minorities. All applications have to be examined carefully from an equal-opportunities viewpoint, interview panels need to be larger, more candidates must be interviewed and more time has to be spent in interviewing.

(c) An organisation might apply an equal opportunities policy to operatives and low-grade managers, but not to middle managers or senior executives. Hence the representation of minority groups collapses at higher levels, so that corporate strategy cannot be influenced by individuals from minority groups.

Implementation of equal opportunity policies can proceed through the following devices:

(a) Strict adherence to the terms and recommendations of government Codes of Practice on equal opportunities.

(b) Active encouragement of *both* sexes and people from minority groups to apply for jobs and for promotion at all levels within the organisation.

(c) For gender equal opportunities, application of flexitime and job sharing arrangements.

(d) Provision of special training for disadvantaged groups.

(e) Fast tracking, i.e. putting individuals from an underrepresented sex or ethnic group on to separate training and promotion systems where advancement occurs automatically – as of right – provided certain training and other targets are attained. A series of 'milestones of progress' towards senior management positions are identified and the precise requirements for reaching them are laid down. Any trainee satisfying these requirements is routinely promoted to the next level of the hierarchy.

17. Legal provisions

Three Acts, the Sex Discrimination Acts of 1975 and 1986 and the Race Relations Act 1976, make it illegal to discriminate in all aspects of employment, e.g. job advertising, selection, terms of employment, promotion, training, dismissal and retirement. Discrimination means the less favourable treatment of a person by reason of sex, colour, race or ethnic or national origins.

Employers are liable if their subordinates discriminate unlawfully. Indirect discrimination is also unlawful, i.e. applying a condition or requirement which, although applied to both sexes or to all racial groups, is such that a considerably smaller proportion of one sex or of one racial group can comply with it, unless the employer can show the condition to be justified. An example would be a requirement for applicants for a senior clerical post to be at least six feet tall. The Sex Discrimination Act also covers unfair discrimination against people who are married.

18. Exceptions

Employers may lawfully discriminate in the following cases:

(a) *For sex discrimination:*

(*i*) where the job requires a person of a particular sex for reasons of physiology, e.g. modelling, authenticity (e.g. acting), or decency (e.g. lavatory attendant)

(*ii*) jobs in a single-sex establishment

(*iii*) jobs which provide individuals with personal welfare or education services and those services can be most effectively provided by a person of a particular sex, e.g. a female counsellor for female offenders

(*iv*) jobs where there are legal restrictions on the employment of one sex

(*v*) employment in a private household, where the degree of physical or social contact or knowledge of intimate details might reasonably cause objection to the employment of a particular sex

(*vi*) employment carried out wholly or mainly outside the UK.

(b) *For racial discrimination:*

(*i*) where the job requires a person of a particular race for reasons of physiology, authenticity or the provision of food or drink for consumption by the public in a special ambience, e.g. a Chinese restaurant

(*ii*) jobs which provide persons of a certain racial group with personal services promoting their welfare and those services can most effectively be provided by a person of that racial group

(*iii*) employment in a private household (note, however, that this exemption probably falls foul of EU law and is unlikely to survive much longer)
(*iv*) employment carried out wholly or mainly outside the UK.

All these provisions apply to contract labour, employment agencies, partnerships, trade unions and to professional and training associations. Note, however, that it is lawful to recruit predominantly one sex or race on to a training scheme that seeks to redress an imbalance in employment of the races or sexes in a department or organisation where the imbalance has existed during the previous twelve months. People who give orders to discriminate are covered by the Acts as well as those who implement the unfair discrimination.

19. Complaints by individuals

A complaint of sex or racial discrimination in employment is made to an industrial tribunal within three months of the Act complained of. A conciliation officer may be asked by both parties at this stage to settle the matter without a tribunal hearing, or may intervene on his or her own initiative. If a settlement cannot be reached in this way a tribunal will hear the case and if it decides in favour of the complainant it may award:

(a) an order declaring the rights of both parties

(b) an order requiring the respondent, i.e. the employer, to pay the complainant damages

(c) a recommendation that the respondent should take a particular course of action within a specified time.

20. Enforcement through statutory bodies

The two Acts set up the Equal Opportunities Commission and the Commission for Racial Equality respectively. These bodies have a general duty to work towards the elimination of discrimination and promote equal opportunity between sexes and between racial groups. They may also investigate relevant matters, institute legal proceedings in cases of persistent discrimination and in exceptional cases help individual complainants.

If they find that an employer has contravened one of the legal provisions they may serve discrimination notices requiring the employer not to commit further unlawful acts. An employer may appeal against such notices to an industrial tribunal.

Codes of Practice

Both the EOC and CRE publish Codes of Practice setting out the steps to be taken to eliminate unfair discrimination in recruitment and other employment matters. The Codes offer practical guidance on how personnel policies and procedures should be constructed in order to avoid discrimination, and how existing employees must be instructed about preventing contravention of the Act when interviewing, dealing with subordinates, selecting staff for promotion, etc.

21. Implications for personnel management

Although discrimination in many areas of personnel management takes place constantly on the basis of personal qualities, experience, age and length of service, a company should be able to show that there has been no intention to discriminate unlawfully and that such discrimination has not taken place.

Job advertisements must not therefore state or imply that applicants of a particular race or sex will be favoured, and communications within a company regarding promotion, training or dismissal should obey the same rule. An employer should be able to show that the criteria for selection, promotion, etc., are fair, appropriate and without bias, and that candidates or employees are judged fairly against these criteria. As far as possible objective rather than subjective assessments should be made. Documentary evidence should be kept in case a candidate or employee makes a complaint.

EFFICIENCY IN RECRUITMENT AND SELECTION

22. Costs

As in other management processes, careful control should be exercised over recruitment and selection to ensure that money is not being spent unnecessarily. The recording of advertisements and response is one control that may be used. Others include:

(a) Can new sources of candidates be found which are less expensive?

(b) Could a less expensive selection procedure be used?

(c) Is the application form too complicated, containing unnecessary information, or is it too simple, omitting important information?

(d) Are internal candidates being considered sufficiently?

(e) Are selection standards too high or too low?

23. Efficiency ratios

A manager who recruits and selects on a large scale can check the efficiency of recruiting procedures by calculating some of the following ratios:

(a) Average time during which a vacancy remains unfilled.

(b) $\dfrac{\textit{Number of candidates replying to an advertisement}}{\textit{Number of candidates called for interview}}$

223

(c) $\dfrac{Number\ of\ interviews}{Number\ of\ offers\ made}$

(d) $\dfrac{Number\ of\ offers\ made}{Number\ accepted}$

(e) $\dfrac{Number\ starting\ work}{Number\ judged\ satisfactory\ in\ follow-up}$

(f) $\dfrac{Number\ starting\ work}{Number\ still\ employed\ after\ one\ year}$

(g) $\dfrac{Cost\ of\ recruitment\ and\ selection}{Number\ starting\ work}$

(h) $\dfrac{Number\ of\ vacancies}{Number\ filled\ internally}$

(i) $\dfrac{Total\ value\ of\ wages\ and\ salaries\ offered}{Cost\ of\ recruitment\ and\ selection\ for\ those\ vacancies}$

A downward trend in any of these ratios, except **(i)**, will show that an improvement is taking place in the efficiency of recruitment and selection.

Progress test 15

1. What is the difference between recruitment and selection?
2. What are the advantages of filling a vacancy internally?
3. Describe, with comments, three inexpensive external sources of recruitment.
4. What are the advantages of using a headhunter?
5. Outline the steps in selection which occur before the candidate is called for interview.
6. What should the initial job offer contain?
7. What is a spent conviction?
8. What information must be given in writing to an employee?
9. In what circumstances is racial discrimination in the recruitment of employees lawful?

16

INTERVIEWING

THE SELECTION INTERVIEW

1. Description

A selection interview is an extension and development of the inevitable meeting which takes place between an employer and a prospective employee. It includes questions designed to test achievement or aptitude, and is at present the most commonly used method of personality assessment. There is much conflicting evidence concerning the reliability and validity of selection interviews. Some studies have shown how easily interviewers can disagree about a candidate, and how predictions made on the basis of an interview are often not fulfilled. Other studies, however, provide evidence of agreement between interviewers, and of predictions coming true. The majority opinion is that the selection interview is in any case unavoidable, so the best possible use should be made of it. Reliability and validity can be greatly improved if the following conditions are observed:

(a) Interviewers are not rigid or authoritarian in their views and are reasonably sensitive to other people.

(b) The job is thoroughly studied and described.

(c) Interviewers plan their questions in advance.

(d) They are trained in interviewing.

2. The philosophy of the selection interview

There are two schools of thought regarding the way a selection interview should be conducted.

The first makes the assumption that an individual's general behaviour has become stable by the time he or she has reached adulthood, i.e. that the individual's personality has now become established. At the interview, therefore, questions should be asked about the candidate's past behaviour, in particular his or her motivation, how he or she dealt with crises and about the person's social adjustment. The pattern that emerges from the candidate's answers will be a reliable guide to his or her future behaviour, after making allowances for a different environment. In order to obtain this information the interviewer must establish a good personal relationship with the candidate (establish rapport, as it is sometimes called) and encourage the candidate to speak freely and frankly. This is the approach favoured by most employers.

The second view is that candidates attending a selection interview will intentionally or unintentionally distort their answers, exaggerating points in their favour and minimising others. Since none of the information they give about their past lives can be relied on, the interviewer must draw conclusions based on candidates' present behaviour only, i.e. the way they react to situations contrived and controlled by the interviewer. Testing is, of course, a special example of this attitude with which no one would quarrel; a test taken away by the candidate to be done at home and unsupervised would be valueless. Leaderless group discussion is another example where candidates are observed in a controlled social setting. When this philosophy is applied to the interview its outcome is usually a situation where mental stress is applied; for example, the candidate may not be invited to sit down, his or her answers may be ridiculed or the interviewer may remain silent and expressionless for long periods.

The stress-interview is intended to provoke the candidate into displaying his or her true personality rather than the facade the candidate is trying to maintain to impress the prospective employer. Though superficially attractive, this approach is rarely used by reputable employers for the following reasons:

(a) Behaviour under the created stress conditions will probably not be typical of the candidate's behaviour under genuine stress. All the interviewer will learn is how the candidate behaves when he or she encounters some rather foolish and annoying events at a selection interview. The candidate's responses will largely depend on how badly the person wants the job.

(b) The employer's good name will suffer and candidates may withdraw their applications.

(c) A stress interview, by concentrating entirely on personality, is incomplete. It makes the candidate unwilling to talk freely about his or her experience.

3. Purposes of the selection interview

A well-conducted selection interview fulfils three functions:

(a) To elicit information about the candidate's motives and behaviour in order to assess personality.

(b) To check the factual information the candidate has already given about him or herself and to examine the value and relevance of experience and qualifications.

(c) To give information to the candidate about the job and company. This part of the interview is very often omitted or skimped, but it is quite essential. Selection is mutual; the employer selects the candidate, and the candidate must be given the information needed to select the employer.

4. Preparing for the interview

It is impossible for an interview to be done well unless thorough preparations have been made.

(a) The job is analysed and described (*see* Chapter 12). If a job specification already exists, it should be brought up to date. It is impossible to say if a candidate is suitable for a job unless the job is thoroughly known.

(b) Written information about the candidate is obtained in the form of references.

(c) The candidate's written statement is compared with the job specification so that the interviewer can decide where clarification or further information is needed. The interviewer makes a note of the key questions to be asked.

(d) The interviewer makes sure that the interview will not be interrupted by visitors or telephone calls.

(e) Interviewing across a desk which is cluttered up with filing trays, telephones, ornaments and other objects is avoided, because a physical barrier between two people seems to create a psychological barrier. The candidate is placed at the side of the desk, or better still the interview takes places away from a desk, using perhaps two chairs with a low table between them.

5. Conduct of the interview

Most experienced interviewers begin the interview with a few remarks and questions designed to welcome and set the candidate at ease. For example, a question about the candidate's journey to the place of the interview not only breaks the ice but provides the interviewer with useful information.

It is often easier to get the candidate to talk freely if the early questions are about that person's present job rather than about his or her schooldays followed by a laborious plod in strict chronological order. The order in which topics are dealt with is not important as long as they are all covered. Maintaining an easy conversational tone should have precedence over a rigid programme of questions.

The object of the questions is to get candidates to talk about their experience and reveal their motivations, social adjustment and the ways in which they have dealt with any difficult episodes in their private or working lives. These rules should be followed when framing questions:

(a) *Questions should not suggest their own answers* (e.g. 'I'm sure you have had experience in stocktaking, haven't you?') or be answerable in a very few words (e.g. 'I see from your form that you've passed GCSE in four subjects'). Open-ended questions are best; they suggest no particular answer and encourage the candidate to talk at some length. Examples are: 'Tell me about any stocktaking experience you have had', or 'What were your best subjects at school?'

(b) *The meaning of questions should be clear* and they should be expressed in a way appropriate to the candidate's experience and education. The interviewer must try to adapt his or her manner and choice of words to suit the candidate, though not to a ludicrous degree.

(c) *Probing questions should be used*. If a candidate says he or she was responsible for a certain activity, this must not be taken at its face value – further questioning may show that the responsibility was confined to keeping records about it. Similarly a candidate's impressive list of hobbies and interests may be merely things the person has done once or watched others do.

(d) *The interviewer should unobtrusively guide* the course and subject-matter of the interview by questions which introduce new topics, linking them to what has been dealt with before. The candidate should do most of the talking, but on subjects which have been chosen and introduced by the interviewer.

(e) *A very large number of questions* should begin with the words how or why. The reasons behind the candidate's actions and the way he or she goes about getting things done are invaluable clues to personality.

(f) *Rude, insensitive and irrelevant questions* should not be asked. Critical remarks that might upset and fluster the candidate (thus causing the interviewee to 'clam up' and not reveal important information) should not be made during the interview.

(g) *Interviewers should not compare candidates with themselves*, since interviewers may hold overinflated opinions about their own abilities, and might wrongly assume that candidates most like themselves are necessarily best suited for *any* vacant position.

(h) *Inappropriate selection criteria must be avoided*, particularly the *'halo effect'*, whereby interviewers assume that one desirable characteristic in an applicant necessarily means the candidate is equally worthy in other respects. For example, an attractive physical appearance does not imply that an applicant for a secretary's job will be a good typist. Note how this phenomenon can work in reverse: an interviewer may conclude incorrectly that weakness in one area means low calibre overall.

During the interview the job, company and working conditions, e.g. hours, holidays, pension scheme, etc., should be briefly described, and the candidate if possible be shown the place of work. The candidate should be given plenty of opportunity to ask questions.

The interviewer should indicate clearly to the candidate when the interview is at an end, and what the next step will be, e.g. the candidate will receive a letter or should telephone the company on a certain day.

ASSESSMENT

6. Recording the interview

Note-taking during the interview should be avoided because it seems to inhibit the candidate from speaking freely; exceptions may be made, however, for information which must be recorded exactly, such as a change of address or the candidate's present salary. A full note should be taken *immediately after* the interview and certainly before the next candidate is seen.

It is essential for the record to be made in a systematic way to be sure that comments have been made on all important points and to enable comparisons with other candidates to be made more easily. There are many systems for describing candidates, two of which are as follows:

(a) *The seven-point plan of the National Institute of Industrial Psychology*, which suggests that the candidate should be assessed under the following headings:

(*i*) physical make-up
(*ii*) attainments
(*iii*) general intelligence
(*iv*) special aptitudes
(*v*) interests
(*vi*) disposition
(*vii*) circumstances.

(b) *The five-fold grading*, devised by John Munro Fraser, which uses the following classification:

(*i*) first impressions and physical make-up
(*ii*) qualifications
(*iii*) brains and abilities
(*iv*) motivation
(*v*) adjustment.

The second scheme is perhaps more realistic for adult candidates, particularly as it draws attention to the main fields an interview should cover. It is usually advisable to add a sixth heading, circumstances, since a candidate's domestic life, travelling problems, etc., are sometimes relevant to his or her suitability.

Two problems arise when applying these systems:

(a) Subjective and incorrect allocation of people to categories, e.g. what seems a pleasant disposition to one person may appear as surly and aggressive to someone else.

229

(b) Applying the same categories to candidates of widely varying background, experience and educational qualifications.

To illustrate the latter problem, consider the comparison of an older female applicant (who possesses certificates and diplomas with titles quite different to those obtained by younger people) with a male applicant who recently left college. The woman may have been out of employment for several years in order to raise children, and then may have worked in an industry quite different to that in which the recruiting firm operates. Interviewers will, of course, have to deal with this situation increasingly frequently as more and more women return to work through the 1990s in consequence of social trends and, in particular, of the projected shortage of skilled and qualified young people. This phenomenon may alter fundamentally the ways in which employers structure the interviewing process, competing with each other to obtain the best female returners available.

Comparing candidates with widely differing backgrounds

It is usual in these circumstances to look for common factors among candidates. For example, has the applicant a good record of passing examinations first time, or were several attempts required? Are there any observable gaps in particular subject areas (mathematics or English, for example)? Did the candidate drop out of particular courses? How much responsibility did the candidate carry in his or her previous post? Is there evidence of the candidate's willingness to attend courses and update skills? Did the applicant remain long with any one employer without being promoted? The fact that any of these are true does not necessarily mean the candidate is unsuitable, only that the issue should be further explored during the interview.

Many experienced interviewers evolve their own systems, often because they deal almost exclusively with a particular type of candidate, e.g. university graduates or manual workers, and wish to give attention to some points rather than others. Either of the two systems described above may be used as the basis of one's own scheme.

7. Assessing the candidate

The information given by a candidate and recorded by the interviewer must now be interpreted so that suitability for the job can be assessed. It is now comparatively easy to make an objective judgment about the candidate's experience and qualifications, particularly if questions on these subjects have been carefully thought out in advance. It is often possible, in addition, to give an achievement test.

Assessment of personality is much less reliable. The candidate's replies are interpreted by the interviewer, who has his or her own prejudices and preferences, and will be guided by perceptions unique to that individual. It is impossible to eliminate the effects of bias on the part of the interviewer, but they may be reduced by the following means:

(a) The interviewer should keep an open mind until the end of the interview; first impressions, though important in some jobs, can be extremely misleading.

(b) The interviewer must try to become aware of his or her prejudices, and allow for them.

(c) The candidate's statements are analysed to look for recurring patterns of behaviour, e.g. constant rebelliousness against authority or a tendency to avoid decision making. Any conclusions reached about personality are justified by reference to incidents the candidate has described, so that no personality assessment is made without evidence.

(d) Doubts about a candidate's personality can often be resolved by deferring a decision for 24 hours or by asking the candidate to return for a second interview.

(e) Several experienced interviewers are more likely to make a reliable assessment than one alone.

(f) The interview is validated by following up the successful candidate's progress and behaviour after he or she has been working in the job for some time. Unfortunately it is not possible to follow up the candidates who are judged unsuitable, so that interview validation will always be incomplete.

MULTIPLE INTERVIEWS

8. The use of several interviewers

In most organisations it is unusual for employees to be engaged on the authority of one person, e.g. a personnel manager, a departmental manager and his or her deputy might wish to be involved. The use of several interviewers enables a wider and more expert range of questions to be asked, and reduces the effects of personal bias. On the other hand, a single interviewer is more likely to establish rapport and develop a connected line of questioning to explore motivation and social adjustment.

There are three ways of arranging for a candidate to be seen by several selectors: successive interviews; panel interviews; and board interviews.

9. Successive interviews

In this method the candidate is seen by one interviewer, then by a second and then by a third (rarely more). This method preserves the one-to-one relationship but has disadvantages:

(a) The candidate often finds the procedure very tedious, particularly when asked the same question by all the interviewers.

(b) An inexpert interviewer can cause damage.

(c) The candidate's responses may change as he or she goes from one interview to the next because the person learns to expect certain questions and becomes more adept at giving acceptable answers to them.

10. Panel interviews

These are interviews in which the candidate is seen by a comparatively small number of people simultaneously. The usual membership of a panel is three or four; anything larger than this would best be described as a board.

A panel interview has the following *advantages*:

(a) The candidate's time is saved as compared with successive interviews.

(b) Each interviewer can specialise in asking questions in which he or she is expert.

(c) There is time for each interviewer to ask several questions.

(d) All the interviewers are able to take part in the joint assessment of the candidate and express their own views.

(e) Inexperienced interviewers can be trained by including them in panels.

The *disadvantages* of the panel interview are:

(a) It is less easy to establish rapport with the candidate than it is in a one-to-one interview.

(b) The questioning may be disorganised and repetitive.

(c) Occasionally, the interviewers transact company business during the interview.

(d) Certain panel members might not be genuinely interested in the proceedings, attending simply to fill out their time and/or appear important and influential.

These disadvantages can be overcome with some forethought. The interviewers should agree among themselves which one of them is to carry out the main part of the interview – the biography, the exploration of motivation, etc. The other interviewers arrange to join in later with prepared questions in their particular fields. The principal interviewer acts as chairperson, controlling and directing the proceedings. It is preferable to have the interviewers and the candidate sitting round a table rather than the common arrangement in which the interviewers sit on one side of a table and the candidate on the other.

For a panel interview to be effective it is necessary that:

(a) Each member has something definite to contribute.

(b) The panel establish an interview plan and definite criteria for assessing candidates.

(c) The majority of panel members be trained, skilled or experienced in interviewing methods.

(d) Each member has a predetermined role in the proceedings.

11. Board interview

In this method the candidate is seen by a comparatively large number of selectors simultaneously, i.e. five or more. The board interview is used above all in the public sector of employment, where boards of 30 or more members are not unknown.

Advantages
(a) It enables many people to see the candidate on one occasion.

(b) It shows the candidate's behaviour under stress.

Disadvantages
(a) Rapport between the board and the candidate is impossible.

(b) The candidate's behaviour may not be typical of his or her conduct under more normal kinds of stress.

(c) When so many wish to ask questions, any connected line of enquiry is impossible.

(d) The interviewers are seldom expert.

(e) With such large numbers, it is very difficult for the chairperson to agree and control an interviewing plan.

(f) Rivalries and disagreements among members of the board often appear, putting the candidate in an awkward position.

(g) It is difficult for a board to have adequate knowledge of the requirements of the job.

(h) The final assessment of candidates is very difficult.

As a means of selection there is very little to commend in the board interview. It has been suggested that if a large group wishes to be involved in selection it should delegate the actual interviewing to a panel drawn from the group, the rest observing the interview by a closed circuit television. This would be an improvement, but it would still not avoid the difficulties caused by lack of knowledge of the job and by the large number from whom agreement must be reached.

12. Other approaches to selection

Critics of the interview method of employee selection allege that so many biases creep into the interview process that it can never be a truly objective selection technique. They suggest that in too many cases it is a candidate's *demeanour* during an interview that actually leads to his or her selection. Managers who conduct interviews often have inappropriate and/or unrealistic expectations of what candidates should be like; assumptions based on their *own* life experiences, social backgrounds, outlooks, etc. These and other anxieties have created interest in alternative approaches to recruitment and selection, notably the application of psychometric testing, assessment centres, board interviews, and in-tray and other work-related selection methods. Further possibilities include the following.

(a) *Use of biodata*. Here, biographical data is assembled (usually *via* a multiple choice form) on each candidate's family background, upbringing, and lifetime experiences. Examples of questions asked are the number of brothers and sisters a candidate has, whether he or she is the oldest or youngest child, the person's social activities and outside interests, domestic circumstances, etc. The backgrounds of a sample of existing 'successful' employees currently undertaking work similar to that involved in the vacant position are then analysed, and the candidate whose biodata most closely matches that of existing successful workers is offered the job. This assumes that a person's characteristics are the consequence of certain lifetime experiences (being the youngest of a large family, for example). Advocates of the biodata method assert that it uses objective information, that the same questions are asked of all candidates, and that answers are scored in an identical manner. It is a cheap method of recruitment: anyone can undertake the scoring. There are, however, a number of problems with the technique, as follows:

(*i*) It rests on unproven psychological foundations.
(*ii*) There is no obvious way of choosing the criteria for evaluating candidates (i.e. for identifying the *particular* lifetime experiences that caused current employees to succeed).
(*iii*) The possibility of candidates not telling the truth about their personal details.
(*iv*) Selection *via* biodata might be used to circumvent equal opportunities legislation.
(*v*) Collecting biodata from large samples of existing employees is time consuming and administratively inconvenient.
(*vi*) Lifetime experiences such as type of school attended (state or private), area of residence, nature (and hence the cost) of childhood hobbies pursued, etc., typically depend on the economic status of a person's parents. Hence, the use of biodata for selection might unfairly discriminate against candidates from poor families.

(b) *Open-door recruitment*. This means appointing the first applicant who presents him or herself and who possesses all the attributes necessary to complete the job. It has been used by large department stores needing to appoint many staff simultaneously (immediately prior to Christmas, for instance) and for hiring production operatives. There is no interviewing or testing. Rather, the firm drafts detailed and extremely precise person specifications containing definitive listings of all the personal and other qualities needed to perform the vacant job. The first candidate to satisfy the specified criteria is automatically accepted. If the appointee subsequently fails, then the listing of necessary personal attributes is deemed unsatisfactory and amended prior to the next appointment.

Advantages to the open-door method are its low cost, its avoidance of tedious administrative routines, the removal of many sources of unfair discrimination, and the fact that management is forced to predetermine clearly and exactly the criteria to be applied when filling a vacancy. Equally, however, the appointed person might not fit in with the prevailing culture of the organisation, or be able to get on socially with colleagues.

13. Unconventional approaches

Interesting research has been conducted into the use of astrology and graphology as devices for employee selection. While the results are inconclusive, they do provide fresh insights into the fundamental nature and problems of the recruitment process.

Graphology

This is the study of the shape, size and manner of a person's handwriting, including closure of letters, positioning of words on paper and slope of lines, pressure exerted, etc., in order to predict personality characteristics such as attention to detail, persistence, etc. Advocates of graphology argue that it provides an objective base for assessing candidates (a person's handwriting does not change much over time) and that different graphologists typically give similar analyses of the same person's handwriting. However, there is little hard scientific evidence to support the method, and people can change their style of handwriting (making it neater and more consistent) in order to create a good impression if they know their handwriting is to be analysed.

Astrology

Although there are no known scientific links between star sign and individual behaviour and personality, popular interest in astrology is extremely high. Horoscopes are published in numerous magazines and newspapers and are known to be read avidly by large numbers of people. Arguably, the publication of so much material on astrology *itself* creates self-fulfilling prophecies, since most people know their own star sign and what this is supposed to mean in relation to their personalities. Consequently, individuals might describe

235

themselves in these terms when asked about their thoughts, feelings and behaviour. Indeed they might even answer questions in psychometric tests according to how they believe someone of their star sign *ought* to respond. This could create fallacious observed relationships between test results and the signs of the zodiac.

THE COUNSELLING INTERVIEW

14. When counselling is used

In general, counselling interviews are used for present employees of the company rather than candidates for employment. They are not primarily intended to obtain information, like the selection interview, but instead they are used to give advice and information and to discuss problems. Compared with a selection interview a counselling interview is unstructured, little preparatory work being necessary or possible because the interviewer's role is mainly to react to the interviewee.

Sometimes, particularly in appraisal or grievance interviews, the manager who conducts the interview makes up his or her mind to some extent to follow a particular line before he or she has seen the employee and then conducts a telling interview, rather than a problem-solving interview, in which the interviewer listens and responds to the employee's statements and attitudes. When the manager is highly respected and very knowledgeable, a telling interview may be successful because the employee learns clearly what the manager thinks of the employee and what is now expected, but in this type of interview the telling is one-sided; the manager is told very little about subordinates.

15. What counselling is

Counselling is the process of helping people recognise their feelings about problems, define those problems accurately, find solutions, or learn to live with a situation. Counselling situations arise when managers listen to griev-ances, handle disputes, deal with employees accused of improper behaviour, or assist people undergoing excessive work-related stress. A counselling session might involve:

- Giving advice
- Encouraging a change in behaviour
- Discussion of a problem not previously recognised or accepted by the counsellee
- Helping someone take a difficult decision
- Gaining acceptance of a situation that cannot be changed
- Altering someone's perceptions of an issue.

The aim is not to impose solutions but rather to induce people independently to learn how to overcome difficulties and take appropriate decisions. Counselling should always occur in private, and without interruption from ringing telephones, secretaries with messages, etc.

16. Counselling methods

There are two approaches to counselling: directive and non-directive. With *non-directive* counselling, the manager conducting the interview will make the following assumptions:

(a) Only the counsellee is capable of defining accurately his or her own problems.

(b) The most effective way of getting to the heart of a problem is to encourage the other party to talk about what he or she wishes to discuss.

(c) Solutions to problems will not be implemented unless counsellees wholeheartedly agree with solutions that emerge from the interview.

(d) Managers must accept situations as they are rather than as they would like them to be. Thus the aim is to understand and explain events rather than seek immediate change or remedy.

Directive counselling, conversely, requires the counsellor to take the initiative and suggest ways of solving a problem. This involves:

(a) Outlining the implications and possible consequences of various courses of action

(b) Suggesting a range of solutions to be considered

(c) Charting a path towards the correct decision.

The counsellee is encouraged to rely on the expert knowledge and experience of the other party, while gradually responding to the latter's conversation and advice. Ultimately, however, it is the counsellee who makes the final decision.

17. Problem-solving interviews

Although many managers find such an approach inconsistent with their usual management style, the problem-solving method is much more likely than any other to increase an employee's job satisfaction. Whether the purpose of the interview is to appraise the employee or to deal with a complaint, an approach which encourages the employee to state his or her own point of view and, with the manager's prompting, work out a plan of action is more likely to have a satisfactory sequel than an interview where the manager attempts to dictate to the employee a course of action based on insufficient information.

Problem-solving interviews are often difficult because the normal manager–subordinate relationship may inhibit frank speaking. The best way to overcome this is to remove the physical signs of this relationship, e.g. to conduct the interview in chairs side by side rather than across the manager's imposing desk.

The manager should try not to express his or her own point of view during the early part of the discussion; if this happens, the subordinate will tend to say things which conform with this point of view instead of what is really in his or her mind. In extreme cases the grunting technique may be used; in order to encourage the subordinate to talk the manager merely grunts or murmurs to show he or she is listening, with occasional remarks encouraging the subordinate to continue or summing up what has already been said.

THE DISCIPLINARY INTERVIEW

18. Definition

A disciplinary interview enquires into a complaint made about the work or conduct of an employee in order to see if the person should be reproved, warned or threatened. The dividing line between a disciplinary and a counselling interview is not always clear; an investigation into a complaint may end with the employee being given advice rather than a warning. Some counselling interviews may contain a veiled threat from the manager that he or she does not want the problem in question to occur again.

19. Conduct of the disciplinary interview

This is best illustrated by assuming that a manager has learned that an employee's work has become unsatisfactory. The manager should not automatically take disciplinary action but follow this procedure:

(a) Check the facts; on what basis and by whose judgment is it said that the employee's work has deteriorated?

(b) When interviewing the subordinate state the accusations clearly and the source of the manager's information.

(c) Give the employee every opportunity to reply; in some firms it is customary for a union representative to assist the employee in stating his or her case.

(d) At this point it may be apparent that the information is not as reliable as appeared at first, or that there are extenuating circumstances. The manager may then in the first case promise to investigate further, or in the second case continue the interview on a counselling basis.

(e) If the manager considers the employee has been at fault, this is communicated to the worker, giving reasons (if possible) in objective, quantitative terms, e.g. 'Your output is x per cent below the average for the department.'

(f) The manager then tells the employee what he or she proposes to do, e.g. give a warning that an improvement must occur within one month. This warning is recorded in writing.

(g) After a month the employee is seen again, whether or not his or her work has improved.

This procedure may seem cumbersome but it follows the rules of justice and obviates the awkward situation in which disciplinary action has to be withdrawn because the employee's case has not been properly heard. It should also improve industrial relations within the organisation.

Note that for serious cases of indiscipline and/or underperformance (i.e. cases where if a warning is unheeded the worker could be dismissed) it is necessary to follow up the interview with a letter formally advising the employee of the need to improve and of the possible consequences of ignoring the warning. This letter (which is required under the ACAS Code of Practice on disciplinary proceedings, *see* 19:8) should specify details of alleged inadequacies and of what the employee must do to overcome them.

References

Frazer, J.M. (1954), *A Handbook of Employment Interviewing*, MacDonald and Evans.
Rodger, A. (1952), *The Seven-Point Plan*, London, NIIP.

Progress test 16

1. How can the reliability and validity of the selection interview be improved?
2. What is a stress interview?
3. What are the purposes of a selection interview?
4. What kinds of questions should be avoided in a selection interview?
5. How should an interviewer assess personality?
6. What are the advantages and disadvantages of panel interviews?
7. Define biodata. How might biodata be used?
8. What is a problem-solving interview, and what is it used for?
9. To help individual members of staff resolve their problems, supervisors can make use of counselling interviews. How should such interviews be conducted in order to be effective?
10. One of your staff continues to be late for work despite being warned by you. This is now causing friction with other staff. Explain how you would resolve the matter.

17

APPRAISAL

TRADITIONAL APPRAISAL METHODS

1. Definition

Appraisal is the judgment of an employee's performance in a job, based on considerations other than productivity alone. It is sometimes called merit rating, more frequently when its sole object is to discriminate between employees in granting increases in wages or salaries.

All managers are constantly forming judgments of their subordinates and are in that sense continuously making appraisals; the term is, however, applied in personnel management to a formal and systematic assessment made in a prescribed and uniform manner at a certain time.

2. Purpose of appraisal

The principal uses of appraisal are:

(a) to help a manager decide what increases of pay shall be given on grounds of merit

(b) to determine the future use of an employee, e.g. whether the employee shall remain in his or her present job or be transferred, promoted, demoted or dismissed

(c) to indicate training needs, i.e. areas of performance where improvements would occur if appropriate training could be given

(d) to motivate the employee to do better in his or her present job by giving the worker knowledge of results, recognition of merits and the opportunity to discuss work with his or her manager.

3. Types of appraisal

Appraisal reviews are usually categorised into three types:

(a) *Performance reviews*, which analyse employees' past successes and failures with a view to improving future performance.

(b) *Potential reviews*, which assess subordinates' suitability for promotion and/or further training.

(c) *Reward reviews*, for determining pay rises. It is a well-established principle that salary assessments should occur well after performance and potential reviews have been completed, for two reasons:

(*i*) Performance reviews examine personal strengths and weaknesses in order to improve efficiency. If salary matters are discussed during these meetings, they might dominate the conversation.

(*ii*) Ultimately, salary levels are determined by market forces of supply and demand for labour. Staff shortages could cause the firm to pay high wages quite independent of the objective worth of particular workers.

4. Appraisal methods

There are many kinds of appraisal schemes, though usually they are elaborations or variations on one of the following:

(a) *Ranking*, which requires the manager to rank subordinates in order of merit, usually on their total ability in the job but sometimes according to a few separate characteristics.

It is quite easy for a manager to use this method for a small number of subordinates, and usually quite close agreement about the rank order is found among various judges who know the subordinates well. It can be used to decide pay, and to some extent to determine future use, but not to identify training needs or provide motivation. However, although it puts subordinates in order of merit it does not show how much better the first is than the last.

(b) *Grading*, which allots employees into a predetermined series of merit categories – usually five – on the basis of their total performance.

It works reasonably well for a homogeneous group of subordinates, and a fair agreement among raters is usually obtained. There is, however, a strong tendency for extremes to be avoided (the central tendency), i.e. very few subordinates are rated poor or exceptional. To overcome this, a forced distribution is sometimes used; managers are instructed to ensure that subordinates are put into the five categories in the following proportions, ensuring that the assessment of merit is distributed normally:

Poor	Below Average	Average	Above Average	Exceptional
10%	20%	40%	20%	10%

The forced distribution is, however, an unsound method to use if the number of subordinates is below about 40. Grading has the same uses and limitations as ranking.

(c) *The rating scale* is by far the most common method of appraisal. It consists of a list of personal characteristics or factors against each of which is a scale, usually of five points, for the manager to mark his or her assessment of the subordinate. An example is shown in Appendix 2. Instead of entitling the points of the scale 'poor', 'below average', etc., they are frequently defined (as shown in Appendix 2) to encourage consistency of judgment among the raters. The factors are also defined, and there are sections at the end of the form for general remarks and suggestions for future action.

This method can be used for deciding pay, determining future use and indicating training needs. It is rather difficult to use for motivating an employee, who may well be inclined to argue about the details of the ratings rather than discuss the job constructively.

The rating scale method is in some ways rather dangerous because it gives a false impression of analysis and exactitude. If it is to be successful the managers who use it must be trained, and the factors included in it carefully considered. Some of the faults often found, and ways by which they can be reduced, are described in **5**.

(d) *The open-ended method* is a comparatively recent innovation, introduced because of dissatisfaction with rating scales. Instead of requiring a manager to assess a number of personal characteristics, not all equally relevant, the method emphasises the way the job is performed and expects the manager to write a few sentences about the subordinate rather than put ticks in columns. The method has many varieties, a common one being to ask the manager four questions about the subordinate:

(*i*) What are the employee's strong points in relation to the job?
(*ii*) What are the employee's weak points in relation to the job?
(*iii*) What is the employee's promotion potential?
(*iv*) What are the employee's training needs?

Another approach is simply to ask the manager to write a general account of the subordinate's work over the past year and suggest any action that might be taken to improve his or her performance. In some companies subordinates simultaneously write their own versions of the year's work and suggest transfers or training that might help their career. The two documents are exchanged before the appraisal interview (*see* **7**) takes place.

The open-ended method cannot be used directly to decide pay but it fulfils the other purposes of appraisal very well. It is more intellectually demanding than the other methods and is perhaps at its best when the subordinates' jobs are relatively unstructured, allowing differences in performance to be clearly shown. In contrast, the rating scale can be completed with much less thought and seems to be suitable for subordinates who have similar and rather routine jobs.

(e) *Behaviour expectation scales* are an interesting development in appraisal methods. This approach – sometimes referred to as the 'Behaviourally Anchored Rating Scale' technique (BARS for short) – requires the assessor to select some aspect of a subordinate's behaviour considered by the appraiser to be typical of the appraisee's performance in a certain aspect of a job. For example, the superior of an employee being assessed under the heading 'ability to cope with stress' would be asked to complete a form which begins with the words, 'I would expect this employee to behave in the following way', followed by a list of statements from which the appraiser must choose. Among the statements might be:

remain calm and collected	5
become frustrated	4
show irritability	3
act erratically	2
fly off the handle	1

Alongside each statement is a certain number of points indicating the relative desirability of the behaviour. In the example given, 'becoming frustrated' under stress scores 4 points compared with only 1 point for 'flying off the handle', which is much worse. These scale values are said to be 'anchored' against the typical employee behaviour that each statement represents.

BARS systems are complex, time-consuming and difficult to administer. Specific problems include the following:

(*i*) how to select the categories of behaviour (called 'performance dimensions') that warrant assessment

(*ii*) specification of examples of good and bad behaviour within a category

(*iii*) deciding how many points to allocate to each example of behaviour (i.e. 'anchoring' scale points against appropriate descriptions of expected behaviour).

All methods of appraisal require employees to be matched against the demands of their jobs; therefore it is necessary to have job specifications which include performance standards expressed as precisely as possible.

5. Rating scale problems

Unreliable judgments may be made when using the rating scale method:

(a) Managers are often unwilling to use the extreme ratings (known as the central tendency).

(b) They have different standards of judgment, sometimes influenced by strong prejudices.

(c) They do not all attach the same meaning to the names of the factors, e.g. co-operation and initiative, unless these are carefully defined.

(d) They are strongly influenced by a subordinate's recent behaviour rather than by his or her work throughout the appraisal period.

(e) Their judgment is influenced by any particularly strong or weak characteristic of the subordinate, causing them to take a generally favourable or unfavourable view of the subordinate's other qualities (the halo effect).

(f) It is difficult to design a rating scale which is suitable for all types of employee. The scale shown in Appendix 2 would not, for example, be appropriate for managers.

These problems may be reduced by defining the factors and ratings and by training managers in the use of the rating scale.

6. Need for appraisals

There has been in recent years a reaction against formal appraisals, largely because of their tendency to decay into routine form-filling, managers sometimes copying what they wrote the previous year.

It has been said that a manager should, as a normal part of the managerial process, continually assess the merits of his or her subordinates and consider what training they need to improve their performance or meet new demands. The manager should take action, e.g. initiate a transfer, if his or her assessment indicates it is necessary and be ready to give a written appraisal whenever it is specifically required, e.g. if a subordinate has applied for promotion. There is general agreement, however, that an annual meeting between the manager and subordinate to review the latter's work during the year is useful because it gives formal recognition of the subordinate's efforts.

7. The appraisal interview

In many companies appraisal is one-way and secret; it can therefore only fulfil the first three purposes of appraisal in 2 and cannot be used to motivate the employee by reviewing his or her job performance.

A two-way and open appraisal requires that an interview takes place between manager and subordinate based on the techniques described in Chapter 16. A problem-solving approach is usually recommended, encouraging the subordinate to talk freely about his or her successes and failures over the period. The self-criticism that may occur in this process is much more likely to lead to action by the subordinate to remedy faults than criticism by the manager.

On the other hand, it is said that in many companies relations between manager and subordinate are not good enough to permit a problem-solving interview to take place. The subordinate will try to hide shortcomings rather than discuss them. Managers who have the time, patience and social skills to conduct problem-solving interviews are also rather rare. Moreover one of the functions of a manager is to assess subordinates and tell them if their work is unsatisfactory; subordinates expect the manager to do this and will not respect that person if he or she appears to avoid the task.

When conducting an appraisal interview a manager should adhere to the following guidelines:

(a) Begin the interview with an outline of its purpose, the assessment criteria the company has chosen to apply, and state that the object of the exercise is to improve performance, not to bully or harass the employee.

(b) Put the subordinate at ease, emphasising the positive aspects of his or her work during the review period.

(c) Offer an opinion of the subordinate's performance and ask whether the subordinate has any thoughts on how it could be improved. This request may bring to the surface any major difficulties experienced; if it does not, the topic of poor performance should be raised circumspectly, concentrating on *issues* rather than personal failings.

(d) Diagnose the causes of problems and root out the histories of specific failures.

(e) Ensure that all relevant information is available during the interview (appraisers should be well-prepared and fully briefed on the details of incidents of poor performance).

(f) Apply identical criteria when assessing subordinates of the same grade, avoiding favouritism, bias and subjectivity when interpreting information.

MANAGEMENT BY OBJECTIVES

8. Introduction

Management by objectives (MBO) is a system which attempts to improve the performance of the company and motivate, assess and train its employees by integrating their personal goals with the objectives of the company. The employee agrees with the manager what his or her performance objectives should be over a set period. The objectives are ideally expressed quantitatively and are taken from key areas of the job, i.e. tasks which if done well will cause the whole job to be done well. At the end of the period the employee and manager review jointly the achievement or non-achievement of the objectives.

9. Advantages

MBO is intended to encourage employee participation and increase job satisfaction by giving the employee a sense of achievement and involvement with his or her work. The manager can appraise the employee by referring to specific performances rather than by making subjective judgments. Training needs may also emerge during the discussion at the beginning and end of the review period. Other advantages are that:

(a) Employees are forced to think hard about their roles and objectives, about why tasks are necessary and how best to get things done.

(b) Targets are clarified and the crucial elements in each job identified.

(c) Superiors and subordinates are obliged to communicate with each other, and there is forced co-ordination of activities between various levels of management, departments and between short- and long-term goals.

10. Disadvantages

Many managers and employees find the joint objective setting and performance review interviews difficult and sometimes inconsistent with the general management style of the company. The system may then degenerate into a routine in which the manager simply instructs the employee which objectives to pursue. Quite often it is difficult to find new objectives which offer a challenge, and the system may encourage individual, selfish effort to the detriment of the working group. Further possible problems include:

(a) Attempts to quantify performance in activities that are not really quantifiable (advisory duties or the work of a receptionist, for example).

(b) Concentration on short-term measurable goals while neglecting important but less-precise long-term objectives.

(c) Difficulties arising from subordinates being given objectives; but not the resources, information and authority needed to achieve them.

11. Effects of MBO

Few companies now practise MBO in its entirety but it has left a beneficial legacy to the appraisal schemes which succeeded it, achievement of objectives being emphasised much more than the rather indefinable qualities of energy, co-operation, initiative, etc. It has encouraged the use of open-ended appraisal methods (*see* **3(d)**) and the appraisal interview (*see* **7**). Salaries or bonuses of senior managers are sometimes influenced by their performance against objectives set for them each year.

12. Performance management

This means the integration of employee development with results-based assessment. It encompasses performance appraisal, objective setting for individuals and departments, appropriate training programmes, and performance-related pay. Appraisal of managers by their subordinates, peers and people in other departments (perhaps even customers) might also be included in the scheme.

ASSESSMENT CENTRES

13. Assessment centres

A special form of appraisal intended to identify potential for promotion is the assessment centre. It consists of a series of exercises such as leaderless group discussions, role-playing, business games and ten-minute speeches. A group of candidates is brought together at a fairly isolated spot (for example, a country hotel) where they go through the exercises over a period of one to three days. They are judged by assessors who are usually managers of the company who have received appropriate training. Assessment centres are sometimes used for initial selection of supervisors, managers and sales staff.

The advantages of assessment centres are that:

(a) They offer assessors far more information about candidates than is available from conventional interviews.

(b) They present suitable environments for the evaluation of candidates' interpersonal skills, e.g. persuasiveness, assertiveness, ability to cope with stress, communication skills, etc.

(c) Candidates have time to settle into the assessment process and thus (hopefully) will not be as nervous as otherwise might be the case.

(d) Attendance at an assessment centre can itself be a useful and interesting learning experience for candidates.

(e) There should in principle be a higher *probability* of selecting the correct candidates than with any other selection method.

Problems with assessment centres include:

(a) They are expensive because they must be carefully designed to suit the company's special requirements and because staffing them takes up a considerable amount of management time.

(b) Arguably, the personal characteristics examined *via* assessment centre exercises (many of which have a psychological base) cannot be measured accurately, even over a period of three or four days.

(c) Assessors might not be fully familiar with the details of the work that successful candidates will have to undertake. Hence the wrong qualities may be assessed.

(d) Assessment of a candidate's personality and other characteristics must inevitably depend to some degree on the assessors' subjective value judgments.

Progress test 17

1. What are the purposes of appraisal?
2. Describe the rating scale method of appraisal.
3. Describe the BARS system of performance appraisal.
4. What are the difficulties in conducting appraisal interviews?
5. What are the main advantages and disadvantages of Management by Objectives?
6. What are assessment centres?
7. Why are performance appraisal procedures often criticised by both appraisers and appraisees? What practical and cost-effective steps could be taken to ensure that such criticisms are minimised?
8. (a) What are the essential features of effective staff appraisal systems?
   (b) Discuss any disadvantages of appraisal systems.

18

PROMOTION, TRANSFER, DEMOTION AND RETIREMENT

PROMOTION

1. Definition

A promotion is a move of an employee to a job within the company which has greater importance and, usually, higher pay. Frequently the job has higher status and carries improved fringe benefits and more privileges. Its purpose is to improve both the utilisation and motivation of employees. There are two main ways in which a company may promote its employees:

(a) *By management decision*, in which an employee is selected for promotion on the basis of information already known to the management. This method is quick and inexpensive and obviously suitable for a small company or for jobs for which the field of possible candidates is small and well known. In large companies it may cause discontent because the decision is arrived at in secret, possible candidates not having the opportunity to state their qualifications for the post. In all cases, this method depends for its success on complete and up-to-date employee records which can be used to identify all possible candidates for any job.

(b) *By internal advertisement*; employees are told by notices or circulars that a post is vacant and they are then invited to apply. Some or all of the candidates are interviewed and one finally selected. It is a comparatively expensive and time-consuming method, but is particularly suitable to a large organisation in which management cannot be expected to have personal knowledge of possible candidates. It does not rely on accurate employee records, and, being open rather than secret, appears fairer to the candidates than the management decision method. In the public sector promotions are made almost entirely through internal advertisements.

2. Promotion and motivation

Normally, employees derive satisfaction from a company policy of promotion from within, but badly handled promotions can cause dissatisfaction. The important points to note are:

(a) The criteria for promotion must be fair – usually a combination of ability, relevant experience and length of service.

(b) The method must be fair.

(c) Selection for promotion must be based on appraisals by present and past managers (*see* Chapter 17).

(d) The wage or salary offered to the promoted employee must be what the job deserves rather than what the management thinks he or she will accept.

(e) Unsuccessful candidates must be sympathetically treated.

(f) There must be no discrimination.

TRANSFER

3. Definition

A transfer is a move to a job within the company which has approximately equal importance, status and pay.

Selection for transfer

To manage human resources in a constructive way it is sometimes necessary to transfer employees to other jobs, sometimes because of changed work requirements and sometimes because an employee is unhappy or dissatisfied in his or her present job.

In some companies it is the custom for the least satisfactory employees to be transferred from one department to another with the result that a transfer is regarded as discreditable, particularly if it occurs at short notice and without explanation. An unhappy employee may therefore prefer to leave the company rather than seek a transfer.

In other companies transfers are used as a means of developing promising employees by giving them experience in several departments. A few companies advertise all vacancies internally and consider applicants for whom the new job would be a transfer rather than a promotion.

4. Transfer policy

Transfers can increase job satisfaction and improve utilisation under the following circumstances:

(a) A transfer is regarded as a re-selection.

(b) The need for a transfer is explained.

(c) Unsatisfactory employees are not dealt with by transferring them to other departments.

(d) Requests by employees for transfers are fully investigated.

(e) No employee is transferred to another district against his or her will.

(f) An employee transferred to another district is given financial assistance from the company to cover removal costs, legal fees, re-furnishing, etc.

DEMOTION

5. Definition

A demotion is a move to a job within the company which is lower in importance. It is usually, though not always, accompanied by a reduction in pay. An employee may be demoted for these reasons:

(a) His or her job may disappear or become less important through a company reorganisation.

(b) The worker may no longer be thought capable of carrying out his or her present responsibilities efficiently.

Unless the employee has requested it, demotion will probably have adverse effects.

(a) The employee may feel humiliated.

(b) He or she may become a centre of discontent in the company.

(c) Other employees may lose confidence in the company.

An employee who resigns in consequence of a demotion may complain of unfair dismissal under a special category known as 'constructive dismissal' (*see* 19:**5**).

RETIREMENT

6. Age of retirement

State retirement pensions are at present paid at age 65 for men and age 60 for women, providing retirement from work takes place. In the past, retirement policies were usually based on those ages, though in some kinds of public employment men normally retired at 60. Under the Sex Discrimination Act 1986 it is now unlawful for an employer to stipulate different retirement ages for men and women.

There are two schools of thought about the age of retirement; one maintains that the age is a minimum only and suitable and fit employees should be allowed to work on after this age. The other believes in a fixed retirement age.

Flexible retirement

(a) *Advantages*:

(*i*) Many employees are fit and active well beyond the official retirement age. By working on, they benefit financially and the employer profits from their knowledge and experience.
(*ii*) The financial burden on the pension scheme may be relieved.

(b) *Disadvantages*:

(*i*) Eventually the employer must decide that an employee is no longer fit to work; the decision may not be accepted by the employee, who may make accusations of favouritism if others older than him or her are still working.
(*ii*) Promotion may be held up if a senior employee does not retire, causing promising employees to leave the company.
(*iii*) The employee, not knowing when he or she will be asked to leave, cannot easily plan for retirement.
(*iv*) The company cannot prepare human resources plans (*see* Chapter 10) when retirement ages are uncertain.

Fixed retirement

A company which adopts a fixed retirement age policy insists on all its employees retiring from their present jobs at a certain age, although sometimes they are offered re-employment in a junior capacity for a limited period.

(a) *Advantages*:

(*i*) Employees can plan for retirement more easily.
(*ii*) No invidious judgments about efficiency have to be made.
(*iii*) The company can plan ahead more precisely.
(*iv*) Promotion is not held up.

(b) *Disadvantages*:

(*i*) The services of experienced and fit employees may be lost, though sometimes retired employees are used as consultants.
(*ii*) It is unfair to employees with a small company pension, e.g. those with short service.

Progress test 18

1. Describe two methods which a company may use to promote its employees.
2. What is the connection between promotion and motivation?
3. In what ways can transfers increase job satisfaction?
4. Summarise the relative merits of a flexible or fixed age of retirement policy.

19

RESIGNATION AND DISMISSAL

THE CONTRACT OF EMPLOYMENT

1. Legal aspects

A contract of employment exists when, in return for a wage or salary, an employee undertakes to put him or herself at the disposal of an employer during the agreed hours of work. The employer has the legal right to supervise the employee's actions and decide the manner in which the work should be done, and the employee has the duty to put the employer's interests before those of him or herself. The employee also guarantees, by statements, written or spoken at the time of engagement, that he or she is competent to do the work in question.

Under the Trade Union Reform and Employment Rights Act 1993 the employer must state certain of the terms of employment in writing (*see* 15:**13**); other terms may be either written, spoken or the consequence of customary practice in that particular occupation or industry.

Contracts of employment contain *express* terms that precisely determine pay, hours of work, etc., *implied* terms that arise from the nature of the relationship, custom and practice in a certain industry, and so on; and terms required by statute, e.g. the requirement that the employer provide safe and healthy working conditions. Implied terms cannot override statutory or express terms. A contract may be embodied in a letter of appointment, a written statement of terms, or in other documents (staff handbooks for instance). Contracts of employment can be struck orally but have to be confirmed in writing within eight weeks of starting work.

2. Termination of the contract

The contract of employment may be terminated by either side, i.e. employer or employee, giving notice making clear the date on which the contract will end. If the contract does not expressly state what period of notice must be given, the period can be deduced by reference either to accepted custom in the occupation or to previous case law. In many instances it has been held that the interval at which wage or salary is paid should be the notice period, e.g. an employee who is paid monthly is entitled to one month's notice.

The many difficulties which occur when the period of notice has not been clearly stated are removed to a large extent by the Employment Protection (Consolidation) Act 1978. This Act lays down minimum periods of notice which apply after an employee has completed four weeks' continuous service with the employer. Until that time has elapsed the period of notice, if not expressly stated, depends on custom or case law. The Act states that after four week's continuous employment an employee must give the employer at least one week's notice. The employer must give the employee minimum notice which increases with length of service as follows:

> After one month's service – one week
> After two years' service – two weeks
> After three years' service – three weeks

and so on, up to a maximum of:

> After twelve years' service – twelve weeks

These are only minimum periods of notice, and if the contract clearly or by custom provides for longer periods then the latter will prevail. The Act does not affect the right of the employer to dismiss an employee without notice under certain circumstances (*see* **6**) or for the employer and employee to terminate the contract without notice if they both agree to do so.

RESIGNATION

3. Definition

A resignation occurs when an employee gives his or her employer notice to terminate the contract of employment. The minimum period of notice may be whatever is customary, the period laid down in the Employment Protection (Consolidation) Act 1978, i.e. one week, or the period expressly stated in the contract. There is no legal requirement that a resigning employee should tell the employer why he or she is leaving. During the period of notice the employee remains, as before, under the control of the employer.

4. Treatment of resignations

Some resignations are disguised dismissals, the employee being allowed to resign as a face-saving measure. There is no objection to this if the employee has another job to go to, but if this is not the case, the employee may find difficulty in obtaining unemployment benefit. The worker should be warned of this possibility before agreeing to resign.

When an employee resigns it is not only courteous but necessary for a manager to interview him or her to find out the reason for leaving – the exit interview. Here, the employee is asked to explain fully why he or she has decided to quit, problems with working methods and with colleagues, the working atmosphere, etc. Although many employees are not entirely frank about their reasons for leaving they may give information which throws light on employee attitudes and may thus lead to a reduction in labour turnover (*see* Chapter 10).

DISMISSAL

5. Definition

Dismissal is the termination of employment by **(a)** the employer, with or without notice, **(b)** the employee's resignation, with or without notice, when the employer behaves in a manner that demonstrates refusal to be bound by the contract of employment (this is termed 'constructive dismissal', meaning that the employer is behaving so unreasonably that the worker has no alternative but to quit), and **(c)** the failure of the employer to renew a fixed-term contract.

6. Dismissal without notice

This is termed 'summary dismissal'. In most circumstances the employer must give the employee the notice due under the contract (*see* 2), but in rare cases the conduct of the employee is such that the employer is legally entitled to dismiss the employee without notice. Examples of misconduct which justify instant dismissal are as follows:

(a) Refusal to obey a reasonable instruction, providing the refusal is serious enough to indicate that the employee is repudiating the contract; a refusal in a fit of temper would not justify instant dismissal unless it was maintained afterwards.

(b) Serious neglect of duties.

(c) Absence from work without permission or good cause.

(d) Activities in private life which might adversely affect the employer's business, e.g. running a business in competition with the employer or discreditable behaviour which might drive customers or clients away from the company.

(e) Dishonesty towards the employer.

(f) Violence towards the employer or other employees.

It will be seen from these examples that there is considerable room for argument about the degree of misconduct in any particular case and whether

255

it is sufficient to justify dismissal without notice. Unless the employer is sure that the necessary degree of misconduct has occurred, the employer will often prefer to dismiss with notice, or with money in lieu of notice.

7. Dismissal with notice

The Employment Protection (Consolidation) Act 1978 requires that one week's notice of dismissal be given to workers employed for one month or more; two weeks' notice to workers employed for two years, plus an additional week's notice for each further year of service up to a maximum of twelve weeks' notice. Employees with at least two years' service are legally entitled to a written statement of the reasons for their dismissal, which must be supplied within 14 days of the employee's request. Any woman dismissed during pregnancy or while on maternity leave is entitled to a written reason for dismissal, irrespective of length of service or how long elapses before she asks for it.

Because dismissal is such a serious matter, the employer must be careful to ensure not only that it is done for good reason but that the manner in which the employee is dismissed is fair. Capricious dismissals carried out in an unjust way adversely affect the motivation of employees, lower the reputation of the company, create an industrial relations problem and expose the employer to legal action (*see* **9**).

8. Model disciplinary procedure

The Code of Practice prepared by the Advisory, Conciliation and Arbitration Service contains a model disciplinary procedure which may be summarised as follows:

(a) A disciplinary procedure which is fair, full and quick should be agreed between management and employee representatives.

(b) Each employee should know what the procedure consists of, its rules and the offences which can lead to dismissal.

(c) The procedure should state who has power to dismiss, provide that senior management should be consulted, give the employee an opportunity to state his or her case and be accompanied by an employee representative, and provide for a right of appeal.

(d) Before dismissal takes place two written warnings should have been issued, setting out details of the alleged offence and the consequences of continued errant behaviour.

The Code of Practice is not legally binding but it may be taken into account in any proceedings before an industrial tribunal or the Employment Appeals Tribunal. The procedure it suggests is in any case good personnel management practice.

9. Unfair dismissal

Wrongful dismissal occurs when insufficient notice is given; *unfair* dismissal, in contrast, is defined under the Employment Protection (Consolidation) Act 1978 as dismissal which has occurred for reasons other than **(a)** genuine redundancy, **(b)** gross misconduct, **(c)** inadequate performance, or **(d)** some other *substantial* reason. The term 'misconduct' has no legal definition – each case must be considered on its merits. Gross misconduct (theft, violence, etc.) justifies summary dismissal in certain circumstances; but the law insists that the employer 'act reasonably' at all times. The employer must be able to specify where and when the misconduct took place, how it affected the worker's job and/or workmates, and how in consequence the organisation was harmed. And the firm has to demonstrate that any extenuating circumstances and the worker's past record were taken into account prior to the decision to dismiss.

The dismissed person must not have been selected unfairly from others who were equally guilty, and the firm must be able to show that **(a)** dismissal rather than some lesser action was required, **(b)** formal warnings were issued, **(c)** proper investigations were carried out, and **(d)** that a fair dismissal procedure was followed, which included the right of appeal.

Inadequate performance (incapability) means that the employee cannot satisfactorily complete his or her work, or does not have the qualifications for the job. Note that a sick employee may be 'fairly' dismissed on these grounds although tribunals expect the employer to discuss the position with the worker concerned to ensure that the illness will in fact prevent effective performance, and also to seek less demanding work for the sick worker. Nevertheless, employers are entitled to dismiss any worker whose skill, aptitude, health or physical or mental qualities are not up to the demands of the job (though the employing firm must show that it acted reasonably at all times).

Other reasons for fair dismissal include disruption of staff relations, 'organisational efficiency' (the meaning of this must be established in each individual case), or a temporary job coming to an end provided the impermanent nature of the work was fully explained to the worker when the employment started. A business may also dismiss a worker if the continuation of that person's employment would cause the firm to break a law (for instance, if a driver lost his or her driving licence); and any worker who goes on strike may be 'fairly' dismissed. Note, however, that *all* striking workers must be sacked and not just some of them unless there are extenuating circumstances (e.g. certain strikers have been convicted for violence on picket lines).

Tribunals will hold that some dismissals are automatically unfair, and the victims of these sackings do not always have to satisfy the same eligibility criteria in order to be able to claim unfair dismissal in a tribunal. Four circumstances give rise to unquestionably unfair dismissal:

(a) Sacking a pregnant woman simply because she is pregnant.

257

(b) Dismissal for union membership or activity, or for refusing to join a union.

(c) Dismissal of workers when a business changes hands – unless significant technical, economic or organisational changes warranting the dismissal of staff also occur simultaneously.

(d) Sacking a worker because he or she has initiated proceedings against the employer to enforce a statutory right or has alleged a violation of a statutory right.

Certain categories of employee are excluded from the unfair dismissal provisions, the most important being those with less than two years' service and those over normal retirement age. However, provision **(d)** above applies regardless of the length of service or age of the worker.

An employee who considers he or she has been unfairly dismissed may, not later than three months afterwards, present a complaint to an industrial tribunal. The employer will then be required to state the reason for dismissal and justify it as being fair in accordance with the Act. An attempt is then made to settle the dispute by conciliation, but if this is unsuccessful the tribunal will hear the case, when the employer will try to show not only that the dismissal was fair but that it was reasonable in all the circumstances, for example that warnings had been given and that the employee had been given the opportunity to present a defence.

If the tribunal finds that the dismissal was unfair it will first, if the employee agrees, make an order for the worker to be reinstated, i.e. restore that person in the job as though the dismissal had never happened, or re-engaged, i.e. return to his or her previous employer but in a different job. If the employee does not wish to return to the former employer, if reinstatement or re-engagement is judged by the tribunal to be impracticable or if the employer refuses to comply with an order for reinstatement or re-engagement, then monetary compensation must be paid by the employer. It consists of:

(a) A basic award calculated in the same way as redundancy pay (*see* **10**)

(b) A compensatory award assessed by the tribunal as being just in the circumstances, taking into account what the employee has suffered in hardship or in company benefits lost

(c) A special additional award which is given when the employer refuses to comply with an order for reinstatement or re-engagement.

Under the Employment Act 1980, if an employing firm claims that it was induced to dismiss an employee who was not a union member because of pressure from a union or person, an industrial tribunal, if it agrees, may require the union or person to pay part of the compensation. There is no upper limit on the compensation payable for cases involving sex or race discrimination, since to impose such a limit would violate EU law.

Management action

In addition to complying with the Code of Practice summarised in **8**, a company should take the following steps to ensure that no one is dismissed unfairly and that there is a defence if a dismissed employee complains to a tribunal:

(a) Managers and supervisors must know whether or not they have the powers to dismiss.

(b) Records of performance, attendance, timekeeping, etc., must be maintained and preserved.

(c) Job specifications must wherever possible include performance standards.

REDUNDANCY

10. Legal definition

Under the Employment Protection (Consolidation) Act 1978 a dismissed employee is redundant when the whole or main reason for his or her dismissal is that the employer's needs for employees to do work of a particular kind in the place where he or she was employed have diminished or ceased. If an employee is no longer required in one section but instead of being made redundant is transferred to another section of the firm and displaces another employee who is dismissed, that employee is then redundant.

The Trade Union Reform and Employment Rights Act 1993 widened the definition of redundancy, but *only* for the purposes of statutory consultation with trade unions. This new definition of redundancy is 'dismissal for a reason not related to the individual concerned or for a number of reasons all of which are not related'.

Acceptance by an employee of another job in the firm will prevent the employee from claiming he or she is redundant, even if that job has inferior conditions, prospects and pay to the previous job. If the worker refuses the offer of another job in the firm, that person will only be regarded as redundant if the alternative job is inferior to the previous job, unsuitable to his or her skill and training, or an unreasonable distance from his or her home.

An industrial tribunal hears disputed cases of redundancy; it requires the employer to prove that the employee was not redundant or that the alternative job that may have been offered was reasonable. The working of the Act is described in diagrammatic form in Fig. 19.1.

A redundant employee, providing he or she has had at least two years' service, is entitled to redundancy pay at the following rates:

(a) For each year of employment between ages 18 and 21, half a week's pay

(b) For each year of employment between ages 22 and 40, one week's pay

259

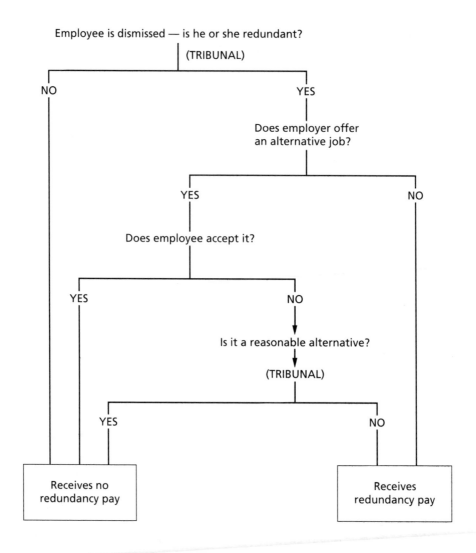

Figure 19.1 The redundancy process

(c) For each year of employment between ages 41 and 65 one-and-a-half weeks' pay.

11. Dealing with redundancy

The legal provisions for redundancy payments are reasonably clear and simple and are often supplemented by *ex-gratia* payments from the employer. The human problems of redundancy are much more difficult and if badly handled can have most unfortunate effects. A perfect human resources plan would avoid redundancy completely because all changes in a company's activities would have been foreseen and their effects on employees provided for. Even a rudimentary plan can reduce redundancy or give some warning of it.

A company may try to avoid redundancy by encouraging early retirements and by ceasing to recruit until the number of its employees has fallen to the desired level. This method is often slow, but it avoids the personal disasters that redundancy can bring. The recruitment 'freeze', if continued for too long, creates a gap in the age structure of the work-force which can be very serious in later years. To some extent the employer loses control over the situation because the firm is never sure which employees will leave and at what rate. Doubts about their future may cause many of the most valuable employees to resign, lowering the general quality of the staff.

If redundancy is going to occur the company must also observe the relevant provisions of the Employment Protection Act 1975.

(a) The employer must consult the appropriate independent trade union so that discussions may be held with a view to reducing the number of redundancies or mitigating their effect. Note the special definition of 'redundancy' (*see* **10**) applied for this purpose. The consultation must take place at the earliest opportunity, but not later than the following times:

> (*i*) if 10–99 employees are to be dismissed over a period of 30 days or less at one establishment, at least 30 days before the first dismissal
> (*ii*) if 100 or more employees are to be dismissed over a period of 90 days or less, at least 90 days before the first dismissal.

The trade unions must be told in writing the reasons for the redundancy, the numbers and descriptions of the employees affected, the present number of employees of those descriptions, the proposed method of selection for redundancy and the proposed method of carrying out the dismissals. The employer must reply to any representations made by the unions, giving reasons if any of them are rejected. Employers are legally obliged to consult with a view to *reaching agreement* with union representatives.

(b) If a union believes any of these requirements have not been met it may complain to an industrial tribunal. A conciliation officer of the Advisory, Conciliation and Arbitration Service will then be given the opportunity to try to bring about a settlement, but if this is not possible the tribunal will hear the complaint. The employer may offer the defence that consultation as required by the Act did in fact take place or that in the circumstances it was not reasonably practicable. If the tribunal finds the union's complaint justified it may either require the employer to postpone dismissal to enable consultation to take place or it may take a 'protective award', i.e. an award of pay to employees for a period regarded by the tribunal as 'just and equitable'. The length of the protected period will be determined by the tribunal but will not be more than:

(*i*) 90 days where 100 or more employees are to be made redundant over a period of 90 days or less

(*ii*) 30 days where 10 or more employees are to be made redundant over a period of 30 days or less

(*iii*) 28 days in any other case, e.g. for fewer than 10 employees.

(c) The employer must inform the Secretary of State, not later than the times shown in **(a)**, in order that the Department of Employment may assist in redeployment or retraining or possibly avoid or minimise the effects of the redundancy. If the Secretary of State is not informed the employer may be prosecuted and fined.

(d) An employee who accepts an offer of a different job in the same company may have a trial period of four weeks (or longer by agreement) in the new job, without loss of the right to redundancy pay (*see* **10**).

Finally, under the Employment Protection (Consolidation) Act 1978, an employee may complain of unfair dismissal if it is believed that he or she has been unfairly selected for redundancy, for example if the employer has not followed the agreed procedure or has not considered the possibility of offering alternative employment. In selecting workers for redundancy, employers are expected to take into account each worker's:

age
length of service
capabilities
qualifications
experience
past conduct
suitability for alternative employment within the firm.

Progress test 19

1. What period of notice should be given to a dismissed employee?
2. What are the main reasons why a dismissal may be unfair?
3. Define redundancy.
4. How can a company try to avoid making its employees redundant?
5. What is the difference between express and implied terms in contracts of employment?
6. **(a)** Why is it desirable to have a redundancy procedure?
   (b) How can human resources planning contribute to the avoidance of redundancy?

20

EMPLOYEE RELATIONS

1. Nature of employee relations

'Employee relations' is a subject that covers 'industrial' relations, employee participation in management decisions, communications, plus policies for improving co-operation between management and workers, the control of employee grievances and the minimisation of conflict.

Industrial relations

Industrial relations (IR) may be regarded as all the rules, practices and conventions governing interactions between managements and their work-forces, normally involving collective employee representation and bargaining. The rules of IR define procedures for settling wages and conditions of work, for resolving disputes and dealing with conflicts, and for implementing a wide range of grievance and disciplinary processes. Rules may be written or verbally agreed; internally formulated or externally imposed, e.g. through government legislation.

2. Employee relations strategies

Strategic management decisions concerning employee relations are necessary in the following areas:

(a) Whether to recognise trade unions

(b) The methods to be used for communicating with employees

(c) The basic formulae to be applied to the division of the firm's profit between the owners of the business and workers

(d) The roles and functions of workplace representatives

(e) The organisation, structure and scope of collective bargaining (*see* 7)

(f) The degree to which employee representatives are to be involved in management decision-making (through works councils for example)

(g) Whether management is prepared to use external bodies to arbitrate and help resolve disputes.

UNIONS AND EMPLOYERS

3. Trade unions

A trade union is an association of workers formed to protect their interests in employment situations. Unions have very specific objectives: they seek better wages and working conditions for their members, greater job security, and improved welfare benefits. Hence unions wish to negotiate with managements on many issues, and may also have wider social aims: higher social security provisions, employment protection legislation, more employee participation in management, and so on.

In a typical union a member is attached to a branch, usually in the nearest large town, which elects representatives to a district or regional committee. A national committee is elected to implement the policy of the union. There are permanent employees at district or regional level (called organisers or officers) and at headquarters (the general secretary and administrative, statistical and legal staff). The policy of the union is intended to be an expression of the views of its members rather than the decisions of its national committee or general secretary; it is a democratic rather than an authoritarian organisation, in contrast to a company.

Employees join a union for the following reasons:

(a) To try to improve their working conditions.

(b) To gain some control over working environments.

(c) In some cases, because of pressure from present union members. An employee is less likely to join a union if he or she is an isolated worker, feels his or her status is high, or has a conscientious or religious objection.

When a substantial number of its employers are members of trade unions the effects on the management of a company are that:

(a) Decisions and policies are subject to challenge and negotiation.

(b) Management powers are limited, and they may be used more cautiously.

(c) Decision-making may become centralised so that a unified company industrial relations policy can be formulated and practised.

(d) The management may be required to give certain information about the company to union representatives (*see* **25**).

Check-off agreements

Under a 'check-off agreement', the employer deducts trade union members' subscriptions 'at source' direct from workers' wages, thus saving the union the expense and trouble of collecting union dues. Since 1993, UK union members have had to give their explicit individual written permission for this to occur and to review the mandate every three years. This had a serious adverse effect on the financial situations of many British trade unions, as check-off arrangements greatly facilitate the collection of subscriptions. Also there is some wastage of membership at every round of mandate renewal. Not surprisingly, therefore, unions increasingly encourage members to pay their dues by direct debit, possibly offering sizeable discounts for doing so. Employers agree to implement check-off systems in the interests of good industrial relations, and because the threat of withdrawal can be used as a weapon during collective bargaining. The extent of trade union membership can be monitored, and contacts between union members and workplace union representatives may be reduced (as there is no need for the latter to approach the former to request payment).

4. Trades Union Congress

The TUC is a voluntary association of over 100 unions. Its policy is decided by its constituent unions at the annual congress, usually lasting a week, when debates on industrial relations matters take place and the general council of 38 members is elected. The TUC has very few powers over its constituent unions, its chief functions being:

(a) to agree and express a policy for the trade union movement

(b) to promote legislation to protect and benefit its members

(c) to be consulted by the government

(d) to deal with inter-union disputes.

5. Employers' associations

Employers within a certain industry usually form an association, partly for trade and information purposes and partly to negotiate on industrial relations matters for the industry. Some large companies prefer to remain outside the association for their industry while others, like the gas and electricity boards, cover the whole of their respective industries. In Britain the Confederation of British Industry (CBI) is the main combination of employers' associations and is in many ways the counterpart of the TUC. It was formed in 1965 by an amalgamation of some existing employers' federations. Unlike the TUC it deals with other matters besides industrial relations as its general purpose is to promote the prosperity of British industry.

6. Staff associations

Managements that do not wish to deal with trade unions sometimes set up company 'staff associations'. There are, however, difficulties associated with this strategy from management's point of view.

(a) Staff association representatives acquire experience of negotiation, disputes procedures, etc. (ideal training for future trade union officers) at the firm's expense.

(b) Formation of a staff association itself draws attention to the *need* for collective staff representation, and in so doing may strengthen the demand for a *bona-fide* trade union. It could even provoke a union into attempting to enter an organisation it had previously ignored.

(c) If they are to be effective, staff associations will inevitably begin to behave 'as if' they were trade unions. Demands increase, and the representatives making these demands may enjoy wider grass-roots support than would a union, simply because the association was established and sponsored by the firm's management in the first place.

Nevertheless, staff associations have proliferated over the last 20 years, particularly in white-collar service trades. There are perhaps two sets of reasons for this. First, managements often greatly prefer to deal with a staff association than with a union – even if the association behaves aggressively towards management at times. Management perceive staff associations as representing 'their' people rather than interest groups beyond the firm. Recognition of a union raises the possibility of third-party intervention in what management regards as its private internal affairs: unions are seen as obstructive and unhelpful; staff associations as reasonable, moderate, and easy to appease. Second, employees themselves might oppose a union's attempts to enter a firm. Staff feel they ought to be represented, but *not* by a trade union. Staff associations offer an attractive solution to this dilemma.

7. Collective bargaining

The system whereby an employee's terms of employment are settled, not by individual negotiation, but by agreements reached between representatives which apply equally to many employees, is called *collective bargaining*. In this country it is generally carried out at two levels, national and workplace, and results in 'substantive' agreements covering pay, hours of work, etc. and in 'procedural' agreements to regulate the methods applied to resolving disputes and conflicts (the negotiation of a grievance procedure, for example).

At national level, an employers' association negotiates with the trade unions which have members in the industry, sometimes forming a permanent body, meeting regularly, called a national joint industrial council. An agreement is made for the industry, typically involving minimum rates of pay for various categories of employee, maximum length of the standard working week, overtime premium rates, and minimum lengths of paid holiday. The typical national agreement is expressed in outline terms only and is intended to be supplemented by a further stage of bargaining at the workplace to determine the detailed application of the agreement to the particular company. The main functions of national agreements are to guarantee the employee minimum standards and to protect employers from competitors who might otherwise cut prices because they paid low wages.

Long-term pay deals

Most negotiated pay agreements are for a 12-month period. Sometimes however pay deals extend to longer durations (two years for example). Long-term agreements are said to stabilise industrial relations, reduce the time spent conducting negotiations, and enable the firm to implement long-run strategies and to prepare meaningful labour cost budgets. The problem from the employees' point of view is that a sudden rise in the rate of inflation can drastically reduce their living standards. Hence, long-term awards may include measures to deal with upswings in inflation, e.g. *via* automatic cost of living pay increases or through provision for *ad hoc* second-stage wage increases.

8. Local workplace bargaining

Agreements negotiated at the workplace have the advantage that they are immediately and directly relevant to existing circumstances and may be altered at short notice. Agreements negotiated by local union officials should enjoy the backing of local employees who, after all, elected local officials to office. However, the informality of local agreements might encourage negotiating parties to break agreements soon after they have been reached. Further problems with local bargaining are that:

(a) It is usually disjointed and disorderly, lacking the formal rules of procedure applied at national or industry level.

(b) There is leapfrogging of settlements among enterprises in the same industry sector or geographical area.

(c) Productivity and pay are not linked at the national level, possibly leading to inflation.

9. Advantages and disadvantages of collective bargaining

Collective bargaining enables industrial relations to be handled in an orderly and systematic manner. It encourages compromise; opposing viewpoints are openly discussed. Also negotiation with unions is an effective way of determining pay and working conditions and for settling disputes. If each employee were to negotiate his or her own pay individually, the firm's personnel authorities would need to spend enormous amounts of time in individual negotiations. Since every worker could earn a wage different to those of other employees, numerous petty differences would arise causing frictions and resentments among employees. Agreements negotiated with recognised, official trade unions will normally be accepted by all union members and can be expected to stick until the next round of negotiation.

Another argument for collective rather than individual bargaining is that the latter is not in keeping with modern approaches to team working (essential for the operation of certain new technologies) at the workplace level. Group cohesion may suffer badly if each employee has to negotiate his or her own wage independent of other members of the team.

Disadvantages of collective bargaining (from management's viewpoint) are that management's freedom to take decisions is affected and that labour costs will probably increase. Further problems are that:

(a) Management/labour relations become highly formal and bureaucratic, with a loss of personal communication between managers and the people who work for them.

(b) Collective bargaining might encourage 'them and us' attitudes.

(c) Arguably, collective bargaining helps promote the interests only of those who are a party to it, at the expense of the welfare of the general community.

(d) Certain individuals who could command higher wages if they negotiated their own pay are prevented from doing this, hence possibly reducing their motivation and productivity.

Personal contracts

A personal contract is the result of an individual bargain between the firm and the employee. It will specify a wage and terms and conditions of employment for that *particular* worker. Often the pay and conditions stated will differ from those pertaining to other employees. Personal contracts are more common for managers than for basic grade workers, although the practice of issuing personal contracts to manual workers is increasing throughout the industrialised world. Reasons for putting employees onto personal contracts include:

- The ability to pay higher wages to workers in occupational categories where there are skills shortages, and *vice-versa*
- Moves towards short-term contracts
- Facilitation of the introduction of performance-related pay
- Removal of certain grades of labour from the process of collective bargaining
- Partial or complete derecognition of trade unions

Problems with personal contracts are that in aggregate they might be no cheaper for the employing firm than the outcomes to collective bargaining and that:

- Workers could still join unions and collectively fight for improved pay and conditions.
- The administrative costs and time involved in negotiating individual contracts may be very substantial.

- As employees discover they are earning less than colleagues doing comparable work they become demotivated and agitate for improved terms and conditions.

10. Decentralised bargaining within the same firm

This occurs when there is a shift in the level at which collective agreements are concluded from the level of the overall company to individual divisions or other sections within it. Reasons for single-employer decentralisation of collective bargaining include management's desire to relate employee remuneration to productivity levels achieved in *local* operations, and the general trend toward overall decentralisation and diversification of activities in large companies, with quasi-autonomous profit centres, budgetary control by local managers, decisions on industrial relations management being taken at the establishment level, etc. Another advantage of decentralised bargaining from management's point of view is that unions find it more difficult to organise industrial action at the enterprise level because of the need to arrange ballots at each place of work, and the fact that workers in at least some decentralised units are likely to vote against and hence not become involved in strikes, etc. With centralised bargaining, conversely, a union need gain only an overall majority of votes in favour of industrial action at the *company* rather than individual workplace level. For more information on decentralised bargaining see *Employee Relations*, Chapter 9, in this series.

11. Single table bargaining (STB)

This means that the pay and conditions of *all* groups of workers employed by an establishment are determined around a single table in a single set of negotiations. It could involve a single union representing both manual and non-manual employees, although it is more common for single table bargaining to mean several unions negotiating at a single table in order to bargain as a single unit.

Advantages of STB are:

(a) Demarcations in working practices encouraged by fragmented bargaining can be avoided.

(b) Less time and other resources need be spent on the negotiating process.

(c) STB is an excellent medium for introducing major changes in working practices.

(d) All the company's collective bargaining activities are completed at the same time of year.

(e) Unions are induced to adopt a common position and resolve inter-union conflicts *before* negotiations open.

Problems with STB are:

(a) The system can become overloaded with work as diverse employee groups raise more and more issues for discussion at the single table. Yet if separate procedures are established to deal with matters that are specific to particular groups then the entire STB arrangement might lack credibility.

(b) STB requires higher levels of skill and maturity among negotiators than does separate bargaining, particularly where strategic matters concerning training, human resources planning, and the overall direction of the business are concerned. Management and union representatives might not be competent to undertake this work.

(c) Management loses the ability to change the conditions and working practices of specific groups of employees independent of the remainder of the workforce – management cannot easily reward those whose skills, motivation and commitment make their contributions to the firm especially valuable.

(d) Rivalries between manual and non-manual unions can still occur at single table negotiations.

(e) Arguably, STB undermines union power through restricting a union's ability to improve its members' conditions via separate negotiations.

12. Single-union agreements

Multi-unionism within companies has been criticised for encouraging demarcation ('who does what') disputes, for increasing the cost and complexity of collective bargaining, and for the leapfrogging of pay claims by various unions. A further difficulty is that as technologies change, so too do the skills requirements of workers – meaning that a previous trade union affiliation may no longer be appropriate. Firms confronting such problems may seek to de-recognise certain unions in favour of others (a somewhat drastic policy that may provoke adverse reactions) or, more commonly, may seek to negotiate a single-union agreement, i.e. a deal whereby an employer will only recognise one union for the purpose of collective bargaining. Workers who wish to belong to a trade union must join this single union.

Advantages to a firm having a single company union include:

(a) A more adaptable workforce capable of undertaking a wider variety of tasks

(b) Greater acceptance of change by the workforce

(c) Administrative convenience and cost effectiveness

(d) Indentification of the firm's employees with the overall activities of the company.

Problems with single-union deals are that:

(a) Union ability to impose serious sanctions to defend members' interests is weakened.

(b) Arguably, a union that represents manual workers is not necessarily the best union also to represent managers, supervisors and engineers.

(c) They are only relevant where the firm offers its workers long-term security of employment.

(d) The union recognised will not be genuinely independent and will inevitably become subject to management control.

13. Pendulum arbitration

Pendulum arbitration is a method for fixing the level of pay increase to be awarded to a group of workers. Management and (usually) a trade union each submit to an independent arbitrator figures they believe to be reasonable. The arbitrator selects one figure or the other: the parties are not allowed to haggle. The settlement is binding on both sides. The *advantage* claimed for pendulum arbitration is that it forces the parties to be realistic in their demands; there is no 'splitting the difference' as commonly occurs with conventional collective bargaining. Thus, a union which claims a ridiculously high pay increase (as an opening gambit prior to accepting something less) is bound to lose under this system provided management does not submit a proposal that is equally absurd.

Disadvantages to pendulum arbitration are that there is no *guarantee* that the disadvantaged party will actually accept the arbitrator's decision, and that it might encourage one of the parties not to negotiate as sincerely as otherwise might be the case, and not to offer concessions. The arbitrator may not understand the complex circumstances surrounding demands and offers, especially where the negotiations involve a package of pay rises, holiday entitlements, working hours, pension benefits, etc. Hence 'all or nothing' awards could be unfair in relation to certain elements of the package.

DISPUTES PROCEDURES

14. National procedures

Besides making agreements about conditions of employment (*see* **9**) employers' associations and trade unions also negotiate a programme or procedure to be followed in an industry for settling a dispute at a place of work without resort to industrial action such as a strike. Procedures differ in detail, but the following is fairly typical:

(a) The aggrieved employee asks his or her union representative or district officer to take up the case with the middle management of the company.

(b) Meeting between the district officer and senior management.

(c) Meeting between union officials and the regional committee of the employers' association.

(d) Meeting between national officials of the trade union and of the employers' association.

(e) In some industries, an independent arbitrator gives a final decision which both sides have agreed in advance to accept, although it is not legally binding.

The procedural agreement will state that no industrial action shall take place until all stages have been used.

15. Industrial action

Disputes that are not resolved via collective action may result in industrial action. The union workplace representative is prominent in these matters, and sometimes an informal procedure for dealing locally with disputes is evolved between the management and workplace representatives. If in these negotiations the union side wishes to put pressure on management it has the following sanctions at its disposal:

(a) *Withdrawal of co-operation,* for example the union will no longer help in solving disciplinary problems or interpreting national agreements.

(b) *Insistence on formal rights,* for example the union representative may insist on raising with management grievances that he or she would normally consider too trivial to mention.

(c) *Restrictions on output or overtime working.* The union will organise a go-slow in which employees without breaking any terms of the employment contract reduce output by time-wasting methods, unnecessary journeys to stores, etc. They may also refuse to work overtime, or work it only on their own terms, a particularly useful tactic if the company relies on overtime working to meet its production and delivery commitments.

(d) *Withdrawal of labour,* quite frequently only for a few hours as a demonstration of solidarity or as a sign of impatience with the slow pace of negotiations. A strike called by a workplace representative on his or her own authority is an unofficial strike because it has not been considered and authorised by the union. It is very unusual for a union to call an official strike unless a dispute remains unresolved after going through the complete agreed procedure or an employer is considered to have broken an agreement.

The sanctions at the disposal of a union representative have their counterparts in possible action by the employer, who can also withdraw co-operation, insist on formal procedures being observed, refuse to allow employees to work overtime when they need it to augment their basic pay, or lock them out. These sanctions are seldom used by an employer, who relies instead on the firm's power to refuse all or part of the demands made by the employees.

Employers' responses to strikes

The worst strike-related scenario that an employer might face is to have a major stoppage occur suddenly and unexpectedly and hence not permit management to devise a plan for dealing with the situation. Normally, a management will wish to develop action plans before a strike takes place, to assess its likely extent and consequences, and to list the options available for resolving the dispute and the financial costs of various contingencies. Communications with the workforce will be extended in an effort to avert the strike, e.g. *via* leaflets attached to payslips, letters sent to employees' home addresses, etc. A publicity campaign involving local (and perhaps national) press and radio or television will be mounted. Further possible measures include:

- Physical protection of the employer's property (keys, vehicles, computer terminals, etc.) during the period of the stoppage
- Rescheduling of maintenance programmes so that plant and equipment can be serviced and repaired while employees are on strike
- In appropriate circumstances invocation of legal action against the union(s) calling the strike
- Reallocation of tasks among workers not involved in strike action. Note the administrative difficulties associated with identifying which people are on strike and which are still working. It is important only to stop the pay of strikers.
- Establishment of a small team of senior managers to co-ordinate the firm's responses to the strike
- Issue of formal warnings to strikers advising them that they are in breach of contract and of the consequences that might result from this fact.

Plans need to be flexible and to have a wide range of options available, as the situation could quickly improve or worsen. Also the management needs to be aware that the dispute will be settled sooner or later and that improvident behaviour today could have adverse effects on the firm's industrial relations for years to come, especially if legal action is taken against the union.

STATUTORY BODIES

16. Industrial tribunals

These bodies were originally set up to deal with disputes arising from the Industrial Training Act 1964, but they now deal with an extremely wide variety of employment matters such as unfair dismissal, redundancy, discrimination, equal pay and safety.

They consist of an independent legally qualified chairperson, an employers' representative and a trade union representative. Their proceedings are informal and it is not necessary for the parties in a case to be legally represented. Their purpose is to decide what is reasonable in all circumstances of the case, and appeals from their decisions, which are heard by the Employment Appeals Tribunal (*see* below), can only be on points of law.

If doubt exists concerning a tribunal's ability to hear a case (e.g. if an employer claims a dismissed worker has not completed two years' continuous service), then a 'preliminary hearing' may be convened to consider this matter. Also, if following a brief examination of a case a tribunal feels that one of the disputants has no chance of winning, it may order a 'pre-hearing assessment' to establish agreed facts and, if appropriate, warn the erring party that its case is bound to fail. The party receiving the warning is entitled to proceed before a different tribunal, but if it loses could be made to pay the costs of the hearing (normally each side pays its own costs). Under the Employment Act 1990, tribunals are empowered to require an applicant to pay a deposit of up to £150 if a pre-hearing review considers a case to have been brought frivolously, vexatiously or to be entirely unreasonable.

Appeals from industrial tribunals are heard by the Employment Appeals Tribunal (which is a court rather than a tribunal) consisting of a judge and lay members representing both sides of industry. It was set up by the Employment Protection Act 1975 in place of the National Industrial Relations Court and hears appeals on points of law from industrial tribunals and on decisions made by the Certification Officer (*see* **20**). Unlike the decisions of industrial tribunals, the decisions of the Employment Appeals Tribunal establish precedents.

17. Central Arbitration Committee

This body, also set up under the Employment Protection Act, comprises people experienced in industrial relations. It will arbitrate in disputes referred to it by the Advisory, Conciliation and Arbitration Service, ACAS (*see* below), and also adjudicate on claims that an employer has not disclosed to union representatives information requested for collective bargaining purposes (*see* **25**).

18. Advisory, Conciliation and Arbitration Service

This is an independent body governed by a Council which consists of members appointed after consultation with workers' and employers' organisations. It has the following powers and duties:

(a) The general duty of promoting the improvement of industrial relations.

(b) Employers and trade unions can request its help in a possible or actual trade dispute.

(c) It may on its own initiative enquire into any industrial relations matter and publish its findings.

(d) It may enquire into a complaint by a recognised trade union that adequate information for collective bargaining purposes has not been disclosed (*see* **25**).

(e) It prepares and publishes Codes of Practice giving guidance for improving industrial relations.

An important duty of ACAS is to seek out-of-court settlements for unfair dismissal cases due to be heard before industrial tribunals. All applications to industrial tribunals are copied to ACAS officers who, if they believe the exercise will be worthwhile, will contact both parties to the dispute – separately and confidentially – to ascertain each side's minimum terms for an out-of-court settlement and/or whether grounds for reconciliation exist.

INDUSTRIAL RELATIONS LAW

19. Definitions

The following are shortened versions of the definitions appearing in the Trade Union and Labour Relations Act 1974, as amended by the Employment Act 1982:

(a) *A trade dispute* means a dispute between workers and their own employer concerning terms and conditions of employment, engagement, non-engagement or dismissal of workers, allocation of work, a procedural agreement or trade union membership.

(b) *A trade union* is an organisation consisting wholly or mainly of workers, whose principal purposes include the regulation of relations between workers and employers or employers' associations. It is not a corporate body but has the power to make contracts and to sue or be sued in its own name.

(c) *An employers' association* is an organisation consisting wholly or mainly of employers or proprietors whose principal purposes include the regulation of relations between employers and workers or unions. It may be either a corporate body or an unincorporated association, in the latter case having the same powers as a trade union.

In all the definitions 'worker' means any employee, manual or non-manual.

20. Independence and recognition

The Trade Union and Labour Relations Act 1974 defined an independent trade union as one which was not dominated by an employer because of the provision or withdrawal of financial or other support. A union is not independent, therefore, unless it is autonomous and financially self-supporting.

A Certification Officer was appointed under the Employment Protection Act 1975 to consider applications by trade unions for certificates of independence. A union certified as independent receives certain benefits under that Act.

A recognised union is one with which an employer negotiates with the object of reaching agreements. Very many companies have voluntarily recognised a union, or several unions, for a considerable time, but others have refused recognition. There are no statutory provisions for obtaining or enforcing recognition.

21. The closed shop

A closed shop is a place of work where membership of a particular trade union is necessary in order to obtain or retain a job. Closed shops are unlawful in Britain and most other countries. They originated from pressures exerted by trade unions as a means of increasing their bargaining power within a company, and sometimes voluntarily by managements because of the efficiency and convenience of dealing with one or just a few recognised unions.

However closed shops were criticised for interfering with individual liberty, constraining management's rights to manage in a company's best interests, and causing industrial inefficiency through encouraging over-staffing and the propensity of local union officials to initiate strikes.

The Employment Act of 1988 makes the dismissal of a worker for non-union membership *automatically* unfair. This means the dismissed worker will automatically win a claim for unfair dismissal in an industrial tribunal and, because the case concerns a closed-shop agreement, will be entitled under the Employment Act 1982 to a level of compensation considerably higher than is available in most other unfair dismissal cases. The 1988 Act (*see* **26**) states, moreover, that industrial action to enforce or maintain any kind of closed shop is unlawful. In consequence, a union is now liable to be sued by an employer for damages arising from acts undertaken by the union against the employer for:

(a) employing a non-union member

(b) considering employing a non-union member

(c) employing or considering employing someone who is not a member of a *particular* union

(d) failing to discriminate (under union pressure) against an employee in categories **(a)** or **(c)**.

Pre-entry closed shops, i.e. situations where job applications have to be members of a union in order even to be considered for a vacancy, were declared unlawful by the Employment Act 1990.

22. Legal immunities

When a lawful strike, as defined in **19(a)**, takes place, the trade union, its officials or any workers concerned in the dispute are immune from legal action for:

(a) Inducing or threatening a breach of contract, including a commercial contract or employment contract

(b) Interfering with, or threatening interference with, the performance of a contract

(c) Civil conspiracy, where two or more persons support non-tortious actions.

These immunities are contained in the Employment Act 1982 but the Trade Union Act 1984 removes them in cases where the trade union did not hold a ballot before authorising or endorsing the strike. The ballot must be held not more than four weeks before the strike begins.

The Employment Acts of 1980 and 1982 make unlawful 'secondary action' to bring about a breach of a commercial contract. 'Secondary action', defined as an inducement or threat to break a contract of employment with an employer outside the trade dispute, is only lawful when it is directed against a supplier or customer of the original employer with the aim of disrupting the flow of goods and services between them and is likely to achieve that purpose.

The 1980 Act also reduces the immunities hitherto given for picketing. Picketing a place of work in order to persuade someone to work or not to work carries legal immunity for actions in tort only if the pickets consist of:

(a) Employees who normally work there

(b) Former employees, if the trade dispute concerns their dismissal, redundancy or resignation

(c) Employees who have no fixed place of work, or who cannot picket their own place of work – they may in these cases picket their employer's premises or the premises from which their work is administered

(d) A trade union official accompanying a member of a union involved in the dispute.

The picketing must be in contemplation of furtherance of a trade dispute.

It should be noted that picketing solely to obtain or communicate information does not involve possible breach of contract and is therefore free from the restrictions stated above. However, picketing can sometimes become a criminal offence if, for example, it is violent or causes obstruction of a public highway.

23. Other legal rights of employees

Under the Employment Protection (Consolidation) Act 1978 it is unfair to dismiss an employee for trade union activity or for refusing to join a non-independent trade union.

If the employee is unfairly dismissed for refusing to join a union in a closed shop he or she is eligible for compensation at a higher rate than normal. The worker may make the union party to the dismissal proceedings where it is claimed that the union put pressure on the employer to dismiss that person.

The Employment Protection Act 1975 also gives an employee the right not to have any action short of dismissal taken against him or her:

(a) to prevent or deter the worker from joining or being active in an independent trade union

(b) to compel the worker to join a trade union.

The activities mentioned in **(a)** must take place either when the employee is not required to be working, e.g. lunch breaks, or at other times with the employer's permission. This protection is designed to help employees to organise where there is at present no recognised union or no union at all. However, once a union has been recognised its members must be given reasonable time off during working hours to take part in union activities.

Complaints that these rights have been infringed are made to an industrial tribunal, and a copy of the complaint sent to a conciliation officer in case the matter can be settled without a tribunal hearing. If the case is heard by a tribunal the onus will be on the employer to show that the firm has not infringed the employee's rights. If the decision is against the employing firm it may have to pay compensation to the employee, and the tribunal may make a 'declaration' which will form the basis of the employer's future policy towards trade union activity.

The Trade Union and Labour Relations Act 1974 states that a collective agreement is to be presumed not legally enforceable unless it clearly and in writing states otherwise. Voluntary rather than legally enforceable agreements have always been preferred in this country, though the Industrial Relations Act 1971 tried unsuccessfully to change this attitude.

24. No-strike clauses

The 1974 Act also states that a 'no-strike' clause in an agreement can only be part of individual contracts of employment when the agreement:

(a) is in writing

(b) expressly provides for the inclusion of the clause in individual contracts

(c) is reasonably accessible to the employee at the place of work

(d) is made with independent unions only.

The individual workers' contracts should include the no-strike clause either expressly or by implication.

No-strike clauses are increasingly attached to single-union agreements (*see* **12**)

25. Disclosure of information

The Employment Protection Act 1975 obliges an employer to disclose to representatives of an independent *recognised* trade union ('recognised' means that the employer has already negotiated with the union on *any* matter, not necessarily concerned with pay and conditions of employment), on request, certain information for the purposes of collective bargaining. It includes information which should be disclosed in accordance with good industrial practice or which, if withheld, would impede the union representatives in bargaining. Union representatives are not, however, entitled to information which:

- would be against the interests of national security
- would be illegal to disclose
- had been obtained in confidence
- relates to an individual (unless consent has been given)
- had been obtained for the purpose of legal proceedings
- would be likely to cause substantial injury to the employer's undertaking.

The Code of Practice on this subject prepared by the Advisory, Conciliation and Arbitration Service recommends that the employer should disclose information on pay and benefits, conditions of service, human resources, performance, e.g. productivity, sales and orders, and financial matters. It suggests that unions should identify and request the information before negotiations begin, stating why they consider it relevant. Employers are advised to be as open as possible and to present the information promptly and clearly.

A union which believes it has not received adequate information may complain to the Central Arbitration Committee, which may then refer the matter to the Advisory, Conciliation and Arbitration Service. If conciliation fails, the Committee will hear the case and make a declaration on whether or not the complaint is well-founded.

The Committee in making its decision will consider to what extent the Code of Practice has been followed, although the recommendations in the Code impose no legal obligations. If an employer refuses to comply with a declaration that certain information should be disclosed, the Committee may at the request of the trade union make an enforceable award of terms and conditions on behalf of the employees concerned.

It should be noted that the law affects national and workplace agreements equally, provided that recognised unions are involved.

26. The Employment Act 1988

Apart from removing a union's immunity from civil actions in closed-shop disputes (plus the measures outlined in **22**) this Act established the following rights for trade union members:

(a) A member who claims the union has called a strike without holding a ballot may apply for a court order which, if granted, will compel the union to withdraw its strike action.

(b) Members are given the legal right not to be unjustifiably disciplined by their union should they:

(*i*) not participate in or support a strike (e.g. by crossing a picket line)
(*ii*) fail to go-slow on union orders if this would contravene a contract of employment
(*iii*) initiate legal actions against the union or encourage others to do so. Union 'discipline' is defined as expulsion, fines, withdrawal of benefits or services; telling other unions not to accept an individual as a member, or 'other detriment'. The aggrieved person must complain to an industrial tribunal within three months of the incident, and the tribunal may award compensation of up to 30 weeks' average pay (though a ceiling is imposed on the value of a week's pay) plus an extra award to compensate for future loss of earnings, mental distress, etc. An upper ceiling also applies to the latter figure.

(c) All members can now inspect the union's accounting records.

(d) Employees have the right to insist that their employers stop deducting union subscriptions from their wage packets. If deductions continue, the employer is deemed to be in contravention of the Wages Act 1986 (*see* **14:7**).

Under the Act it is unlawful for a union to use its funds to compensate a member for the consequences of his or her unlawful conduct during a dispute, e.g. by paying a member's fine, or even to promise to do so. And the statutory procedures for electing members to important union committees (known as 'principal executive committees') are generally tightened. In particular:

(a) Every candidate must be able to prepare an address and have this delivered to all members – by post if necessary.

(b) Postal ballots, under the supervision of an independent scrutineer, must be used wherever 'reasonably practicable'.

(c) A strike scheduled to cover several different places of work *must* be sanctioned by a postal ballot.

The Act creates the position of *Commissioner for the Rights of Trade Union Members*, whose task is to assist individual trade unionists to claim their legal rights. Accordingly, the Commissioner is empowered to pay all the expenses and legal costs (including the fees of a solicitor and barrister) incurred in bringing a case that, in the view of the Commissioner:

(a) involves a major point of principle; *or*

(b) is so complex that it would be unreasonable to expect the individual to handle it personally; *or*

(c) concerns a matter of substantial public interest.

27. The Employment Acts of 1989 and 1990

The Employment Act 1989 removed a variety of restrictions on the employment of women in certain industries (e.g. coal mining) and on the hours of work (including night work) of young people between 16 and 18 years of age. The Employment Act 1990 outlawed the pre-entry closed shop by making it unlawful to refuse employment to an individual simply because he or she is not a member of a trade union. Additionally, the Act removed immunity from civil actions against workers engaged in secondary actions other than *lawful* and peaceful picketing, and unions became liable for the torts of *all* their officials (including shop stewards) unless they formally repudiate the erring officials' actions in a prescribed manner. Moreover, the Act rescinded the rule that striking workers may be 'fairly' dismissed (*see* 19:**19**) only if *all* strikers are sacked and not just some of them (e.g. if the employer wishes to make an example of a few individuals), although the new regulation only applies in circumstances of 'unofficial' industrial action. Persons subsequently striking in support of someone dismissed on these grounds are now liable to be sued for damages by employers and other interested parties. Unofficial action means industrial action not approved by the striker's trade union or, if the striker does not belong to a union, not approved by the union of fellow strikers. Note how this aspect of the 1990 Act cannot apply if *none* of the strikers is a member of a union.

28. The Trade Union Reform and Employment Rights Act 1993

This legislation extended the definition of 'automatic unfair dismissal' (*see* 19:**19**) and abolished all previous statutory involvement in fixing minimum wage rates in particular industries. Further provisions were that:

(a) 'Check-off' arrangements whereby union subscriptions are deducted at source from a worker's wages be confirmed by the employee in writing and renewed every three years.

(b) Seven days' notice be given to an employer of a union's intention to take industrial action or to ballot its members on industrial action. Union immunity from civil action is lost if this is not observed.

(c) Members of the public be given the right to apply for a court order restraining a union from taking *unlawful* industrial action.

(d) Any employee working more than eight hours a week be entitled to a written statement of his or her main terms and conditions of employment within two months of starting a job.

(e) Employees be free to join *any* trade union of their choice (i.e. unions will not be able to decide among themselves which workers shall belong to which union).

(f) Pregnant employees be entitled to 14 weeks' maternity leave irrespective of length of service.

Progress test 20

1. Describe the nature of employee relations.
2. What are the effects on management of the existence of active trade unions in the company?
3. Outline the problems of local bargaining.
4. What is meant by 'single table bargaining'?
5. What are the advantages of collective bargaining?
6. What are the main functions of an industrial tribunal, the Employment Appeals Tribunal and the Central Arbitration Committee?
7. Define an independent trade union.
8. In what respects is a union immune from legal action?
9. Under what conditions must an employer give information to a trade union?
10. There are three main trends in industrial relations in the 1980s in the United Kingdom: the gaining of managerial initiative; a broadened bargaining agenda (concerned not just with pay issues); and reductions in union membership. Examine the factors contributing to these trends and indicate your views about the possible direction for industrial relations in the next decade.

21

TRAINING PRINCIPLES AND ADMINISTRATION

THE SYSTEMATIC APPROACH

1. Purpose of training

Under favourable circumstances, training has the important dual function of utilisation and motivation. By improving employees' ability to perform the tasks required by the company, training allows better use to be made of human resources; by giving employees a feeling of mastery over their work and of recognition by management their job satisfaction is increased. When circumstances are unfavourable, these results may not be obtained, for example when the trainee sees no purpose in the training, when it is regarded as a punishment or a sign of displeasure or when the training seems irrelevant to the trainee's needs.

In detail, the gains which it is hoped training will bring are:

- Greater productivity and quality
- Less scrap or spoiled work
- Greater versatility and adaptability to new methods
- Less need for close supervision
- Fewer accidents
- Greater job satisfaction showing itself in lower labour turnover and less absence.

It is always desirable to attempt to validate a training course to see if any of these results have been achieved (*see* **10**).

Arguments against training are that it is expensive (often, trainees are not producing while they are being trained, and they might leave the company as soon as their training ends) and that individual firms can sometimes recruit competent employees at low cost from outside. Also, workers' job expectations typically increase in consequence of training, so that if trained employees are not immediately put on to work that requires them to exercise their recently acquired competencies they might become disaffected and look for other jobs where they can use their new skills.

2. Reasons for training

Sometimes training is a routine, e.g. all new employees in certain jobs automatically go through a training course. More often training is given as a response to some event, for example:

(a) The installation of new equipment or techniques which require new or improved skills

(b) A change in working methods

(c) A change in product, which may necessitate training not only in production methods but also in the marketing functions of the company

(d) A realisation that performance is inadequate

(e) Labour shortage, necessitating the upgrading of some employees

(f) A desire to reduce the amount of scrap and to improve quality

(g) An increase in the number of accidents

(h) Promotion or transfer of individual employees.

Training which is routine and traditional sometimes becomes out of date, irrelevant or inadequate. A review may show that the purposes, methods and standards of the training should be changed.

3. The systematic approach to training

Like any other business process, training can be very wasteful it if is not carefully planned and supervised. Without a logical systematic approach some training may be given which is not necessary, and vice versa, or the extent of the training may be too small or too great. When the training is complete, *validation* will show whether it has been successful in achieving its aims and *evaluation* will attempt to measure its cost-benefit.

The systematic approach to training follows this programme:

(a) The job is analysed and defined.

(b) Reasonable standards of performance are established, perhaps by reference to experienced employees.

(c) The employees being considered for training are studied to see if the required performance standards are being attained.

(d) The difference (if any) between **(b)** and **(c)** is considered. It is often called the 'training gap', though it may be partly due to faults in the organisation, poor materials or defective equipment.

(e) Training programmes are devised to meet the training needs revealed in **(d)**.

(f) Training is given and appropriate records kept.

(g) The performance achieved after training is measured; if the training programme has been successful the performance standards set in **(b)** should now be achieved (validation).

(h) An attempt is made to calculate the cost of the training and compare it with the financial benefit gained by the improved performance of the employees. The training programme may be revised if a method can be seen of achieving the same result at lower cost (evaluation).

The following mnemonic may be useful:

Analyse job
Performance standards
Performance attained
Requirements of training
Originate training programme
Administer training
Check results
How can training be improved next time?

4. The assessment of individual training needs

The systematic approach to training will show the training needs of an individual employee or a group of employees engaged on the same work.

Careful analysis of the job including the setting of performance standards is the first step. The performance now being attained by employees can sometimes be measured, but more often it is assessed through an appraisal scheme. Management by objectives again shows a different technique by reviewing measurable performance in previously agreed key areas of the job. Any disparities between standards and performance levels show possible training needs.

Often, of course, the assessment is done almost by intuition, particularly when an individual employee's performance could obviously be improved by clearcut training action, e.g. giving the worker more knowledge of the product or showing that person how to use an office machine. Validation of the training may be equally straightforward in such cases.

5. The assessment of long-term training needs

Many training programmes are necessarily lengthy, and can therefore be wasteful unless plans are made well in advance. A sudden need for skilled engineering crafts workers will not be met by increasing the number of apprentices entering a four-year scheme; on the other hand it is possible for a company to have jobs only for a small proportion of its apprentices when they complete their training because it is reducing or giving up some of its manufacturing activities.

The assessment of long-term training needs, usually carried out for a whole company, is therefore part of human resources planning (*see* Chapter 10). By estimating the expansion or contraction of the labour force, what categories will be affected, the probable number leaving the company and the present utilisation of employees, it is possible to plan what kind of training will be required in the future, when it should begin and how many present or new employees need to be trained. If financial or material resources are limited the analysis may also help to decide which training activities should be given priority.

TRAINING DESIGN

6. Training principles

The first step in designing a training course is to consider the training requirements under three headings:

Attitudes
Skills
Knowledge

For example a shop assistant in a men's outfitters would require a certain *attitude* towards customers, *skill* in selling, measuring, wrapping and display-ing, and *knowledge* of stock, sales procedures, current fashions and the company's general policy. Methods of training in these three aspects of a job will be described in the next chapter.

7. On- or off-job training

The methods of training will to a large extent dictate whether the training shall take place on or off the job.

(a) *On-job* training is given in the normal work situation, the trainee using the actual tools, equipment, documents or materials that he or she will use when fully trained. The trainee is regarded as a partly productive worker from the time training begins.

(b) *Off-job* training takes place away from the normal work situation, usually employing specially simplified tools and equipment. The trainee is not re-garded as a productive worker from the beginning, the initial work often consisting of exercises. Off-job training may take place on the employer's premises, at a training centre attended by trainees from several employers, or at a college.

8. Advantages and disadvantages of on-job training

(a) Advantages:

(*i*) It is less costly than off-job training because it uses normal equipment in normal surroundings.

(*ii*) Learning will take place on the equipment which will be actually used when the trainee is proficient; there are no transfer of learning problems (*see* 5:**9**).

(*iii*) The trainee is in the production environment from the beginning; he or she does not have to adjust to it after the rather sheltered conditions of off-job training.

(b) Disadvantages:

(*i*) The instructor (usually a supervisor or a nearby worker) may be a poor teacher and may not have enough time to give proper training.

(*ii*) If there is a payment-by-results scheme it may discourage the instructor from training and the trainee from learning properly.

(*iii*) The trainee may be exposed to bad methods and learn these instead of more efficient methods.

(*iv*) A large amount of spoiled work and scrap material may be produced.

(*v*) Valuable equipment may be damaged.

(*vi*) Training takes place under production conditions which are stressful, i.e. noisy, busy, confusing and exposing the trainee to comments by other workers. Stress usually inhibits learning.

(*vii*) Some forms of training can only take place on-job, e.g. job rotation, coaching, and those skills which are so uncommon that it is not worthwhile to set up off-job training facilities for these. Conversely, theoretical training can hardly ever take place on-job; the trainee must attend a college, which is off-job training.

9. Advantages and disadvantages of off-job training

(a) Advantages:

(*i*) As the training is given by a special instructor, it should be of higher quality.

(*ii*) Special equipment, simplified if necessary, can be used.

(*iii*) The trainee can learn the job in planned stages, using special exercises to enable the trainee to master particularly difficult aspects.

(*iv*) In the long-term off-job training may be less costly because it enables workers to reach higher standards of speed and quality.

(*v*) It is free from the pressures of payment-by-results schemes, noise, danger or publicity.

(*vi*) The trainee will learn correct methods from the onset.

(*vii*) The trainee does not damage valuable equipment or produce spoiled work or scrap.

(*viii*) It is easier to calculate the cost of off-job training because it is more self-contained than on-job.

(b) Disadvantages:

(*i*) The higher costs of separate premises, equipment and instructors can only be justified if there is a regular, fairly large intake of trainees (though this may be overcome by participation in group training schemes in which several employers co-operate).

(*ii*) Sometimes there are transfer of learning difficulties when a trainee changes from training equipment to production equipment and from a training school environment to a production environment.

(*iii*) No training can be entirely off-job; some aspects of the task can only be learned by doing them in the normal production setting, with its own customs and network of personal relationships. To illustrate this point, training in driving might be given to a very high standard on a private track, but the driver will not be truly expert until he or she has experienced driving on public roads; only then can a learner driver learn to react to the behaviour of other drivers.

(*iv*) Some methods of training which have become important in recent years can only be off-job, for example programmed learning, skills analysis and discovery learning (*see* Chapter 22); even here the final stages of training must be on-job.

VALIDATION AND EVALUATION

10. Validation of training

The systematic approach to training (*see* **3**) provides a means of validating a training programme. The trainee may be given a test to see if he or she is now able to reach the performance standards that have been set, or the quantity and quality of the trainee's production may be measured for the same purpose.

Unfortunately, training programmes are often extremely difficult to validate. Many jobs are not measurable in any significant way and therefore validation of training for them can only be subjective. For example, the performance of a manager who has attended a management training course may be assessed by his or her superiors before and after the course. They may well agree that an improvement has occurred, but could this not be due to the fact that the manager is now older? Perhaps the assessors, having sent the manager on a course, will simply assume that he or she must have benefited from it. Another possibility is that since the course began events have occurred which help the manager in the job.

The more specific the training, the easier validation becomes. If the management course referred to above had contained a course in accountancy, a test would show clearly whether this had been effective, in contrast with the more general parts of the course dealing with management principles, etc., which would be impossible to validate objectively.

11. Evaluation of training

By calculating the cost of training and comparing it with the financial benefits to the company from the improved performance of the trainees, validation may be extended to become evaluation. The ease and accuracy of evaluation vary a great deal.

(a) The cost of off-job training is much easier to ascertain than that of on-job training.

(b) The financial benefits of training are easier to estimate for manual than for non-manual workers.

(c) The costs of inadequate training can often be fairly easily measured, e.g. scrap material, spoiled work, customer complaints, overtime working to remedy mistakes.

(d) The benefits of training often go beyond an improvement in job performance (*see* 1). It is, however, difficult to estimate to what extent relaxation of supervision and reductions in accidents and labour turnover are due to improved training. Expressing these benefits in financial terms is even more difficult.

TRAINING ADMINISTRATION

12. Paying for training

Prior to 1989 there existed in many industries Training Boards that were legally empowered to maintain lists of all employers in those industries and to impose training levies on firms. Monies received from levies were then used for employee training in the relevant industry. Appeals by employers against being included in a levied 'industry' were heard by industrial tribunals. The philosophy behind Training Boards was that since firms can poach trained labour from each other, there is little incentive for the individual business to devote resources to training. Yet trained labour is essential for an industry to survive. Thus, *every* firm in the industry should contribute to the aggregate cost of training its labour; contributions being proportional to the number of workers each company employs.

Advocates of training levies allege that free market systems cannot deliver a nation's skill requirements. A low-skill workforce, they assert, leads to poor productivity and hence to business failures and, in consequence, a reduced level of demand for skilled workers (which in turn reduces the incentives to train). Hence a low-skill low-productivity cycle emerges which reduces the competitive strength of the entire nation. The only way the country can then compete internationally is on the basis of cost. Thus wages are driven down and the community impoverished. Specific benefits of a national training levy are said to include:

(a) A central body rather than individual firms takes key decisions concerning training priorities, the skills to be transmitted, and what constitutes an 'adequate' level of training. The state authorities can take a long-term view of the nation's overall training requirements.

(b) Firms are not able to avoid spending money on training (relying instead on poaching skilled labour from other businesses). Note how firms that do not incur the costs of training can afford to offer higher wages to new (trained) recruits in order to induce them to quit their jobs with the firms in which they were trained. Also, the more firms that refuse to engage in training the lower the number of skilled employees and hence the greater the vulnerability of companies that do train to the poaching of their staff by other businesses.

Arguments against a training levy are its interference with individual freedom of choice and that:

- The benefits might in practice accrue mainly to young males, at the expense of female workers, ethnic minorities and older people.
- Policing the system to ensure that all firms properly contribute can be difficult and expensive.
- Certain companies may get out more than they pay in to the scheme.
- Small businesses are unlikely to benefit.

In 1989, all Training Boards and levies were abolished except for the construction industry. Boards were replaced by 'non-statutory training organisations' (NSTOs), which were voluntary bodies responsible for predicting future skill requirements and for co-ordinating training activities within a specific industrial sector. Currently there are over 100 NSTOs in the UK. They have no legal authority and are funded entirely through voluntary contributions. Some NSTOs provide direct training, others simply monitor and comment upon the quality of training provided by external suppliers. Note that training levies are imposed in a number of continental EU countries.

13. Training schemes

In recent years the government has introduced various schemes intended to provide training for unemployed persons. They are usually engaged by employers to work on an organised training programme which includes a period of off-job training. Trainees receive an allowance to which the government and the employers each contribute. It is hoped that on completion of the programme they will be better qualified to obtain permanent employment.

Responsibility for administering such schemes lies with 'training agents', i.e. government-approved organisations which place individuals with local firms, which do not have to pay wages to trainees or even any national insurance contributions on their behalf. However, firms are expected to contribute a small amount to overall costs. This amount is subject to negotiation with the trainee's training manager, as is the period the trainee will spend with the firm and how long in other training locations. The maximum total training period is twelve months.

In 1990, responsibility for co-ordinating industrial training in various geographical areas passed to *Training and Enterprise Councils* (TECs), which consist of local company managing directors and other senior business executives (who participate on a voluntary basis) plus a salaried civil servant. There are about 80 TECs in the UK. Their task is to provide the country with a skilled workforce. To achieve this they contract training providers (e.g. local colleges or training agents – *see* above) to deliver courses and other training that correspond to specifications laid down by the area TEC. The aim is to match the training provided to the needs of local businesses. TECs do not themselves run training courses.

14. The National Council for Vocational Qualifications (NCVQ)

This is a governmental body established in 1986 to implement a national system for vocational qualifications and to determine standards of occupational competence on a national level. Examining bodies desiring NCVQ accreditation must develop courses that satisfy NCVQ criteria, which are laid down by *'lead bodies'* for various industries or occupations. A lead body is a committee comprising representatives of professional bodies, government departments and major businesses connected with the industry or occupation concerned. Its role is to devise criteria for measuring the competence of employees in a particular field. Currently there are about 140 lead bodies in the UK.

The NCVQ does not itself award certificates or diplomas. Rather, it 'hallmarks' approved qualifications, indicating thereby that the holder has attained a certain prespecified level of knowledge, skill and understanding of a certain subject. NCVQ-approved qualifications have to be competence-based, i.e. the training undertaken must contribute directly to a person's ability to complete a job. Thus, courses need to cover all the 'elements of competence' associated with a specific type of work. Elements of competence are descriptions of actions, behaviours, outcomes, or knowledge of what should be done in a workplace situation. These elements are then collected into 'units of competence' that form the basis for an NCVQ-recognised award. Each unit of competence is accompanied by 'performance criteria', i.e. definitions of what trainees should be able to do on completion of the training.

Critics of NVQs have alleged that there are no 'proper' syllabuses for particular subject areas, so that teachers do not know which topics to cover in depth (syllabuses have to be inferred from the lists of competencies that students need to demonstrate); that assessment methods vary from institution to institution; and that 'core' subjects such as mathematics, science and languages receive insufficient attention.

15. Responsibility for company training

Because training is so important in the utilisation and motivation of human resources it deserves the special attention of the senior management of the company. One of the advantages claimed for training levies (*see* 12) was that they 'brought training into the board room', the large amounts being paid to the training board forcing consideration at director level of possible ways of recovering the money.

Some companies have training officers or departments which advise on policies and methods and may administer some of the training. Consultants are sometimes called in, particularly to give advice about unusual training problems, or to overhaul methods which are obviously inefficient. These various roles in training may be summed up as follows:

(a) Senior management determines a general training policy which is consistent with the objectives of the company. It may be derived from the company human resources plan or based on an assessment of training needs to which junior levels of management have contributed.

(b) Line managers have a responsibility for training their subordinates and are often personally involved in giving it because training is always wholly or partly on-job (see 8). In some cases they may design and supervise training programmes, while in others the training of their subordinates may be largely off-job, line managers being expected to provide the finishing touches when the employees begin productive work. In all cases it is the responsibility of line managers to ensure that the training which is given, by whatever means, is relevant to the needs of the department and is effective in its results.

(c) Training officers advise senior management on policy by applying their expert knowledge of training to the needs of the company. They frequently conduct surveys or are consulted when changes are proposed which will necessitate training or retraining. They design courses, administering them if they are off-job. They are expected to advise on external education and training facilities, maintaining contact with the ITB (where it exists), colleges, and various training organisations.

(d) Instructors are in direct contact with trainees, and in most cases are concerned with off-job training. They are not responsible for designing the course but they are expected to report any deficiencies it seems to contain. They are usually proficient workers who have taken a short course in training methods.

(e) Consultants tend to be called in when a company is facing unusual training problems, for example poor productivity or the consequences of reorganisation or technical change. They study needs, advise on appropriate methods and set up training procedures which the management of the company can then continue.

Progress test 21

1. What benefits does a company hope to obtain when it trains its employees?
2. Outline the systematic approach to training.
3. Under what three headings should training requirements be considered?
4. Define and distinguish between validation and evaluation of training.

5. **(a)** In relation to administrators review the respective merits and demerits of training: (i) on the job; (ii) off the job.
(b) Describe in each case, two techniques of "off" and "on the job" training applicable to management development.
6. (i) Distinguish between training policy and training procedures.
(ii) For what purposes may organisations develop and publish training policies?
(iii) State, with reasons, whether you agree or disagree with the statement that training policies are more often determined by prevailing interest rather than principle.
7. **(a)** What methods exist for identifying the training requirements of an organisation?
(b) Why is it important to identify training needs?
8. Sending someone on a course is often the last resort of a guilty manager. Discuss:
(a) the reasons why courses may not be the best form of management development and training; and
(b) what other approaches could be more fruitful.

22

TRAINING METHODS

TRAINING IN ATTITUDES

1. The importance of attitudes

The definition of an 'attitude' is as follows: 'An individual's characteristic way of responding to an object or situation. It is based on experience and leads to certain behaviour or the expression of certain opinions.'

Attitudes determine the general approach of an employee to work; for example, the care that is taken to avoid mistakes, the way customers, clients or patients are dealt with or the degree of persistence shown in achieving work objectives. In some cases the appropriate attitude is already present when the employee enters the occupation in question – a nurse has probably chosen that particular career in consequence of possessing attitudes favouring the care of the sick. In other cases the employee has not felt a vocation towards the job but has perhaps taken it up because it is convenient or respectable. A shop assistant, for example, may have an attitude towards customers which does not produce sales and may injure the reputation of the shop. Unless this attitude can be changed the person will never be a successful employee. The importance of attitudes obviously varies according to the type of job; they are not particularly important when the work is highly structured because so long as the employee is at a work station he or she has little choice about the way the work is undertaken. On the other hand, unstructured work, with its freedom of choice and its opportunity for self-regulation, cannot be carried out successfully unless the employee's attitudes are consistent with the purposes of the job.

2. Attitude training

Attitude training is difficult because many attitudes are deep-rooted and cannot easily be changed in a short time. The usual methods employed are as follows:

(a) *On-job experience within a group of employees* whose attitudes are thought to be appropriate. There is often no practical alternative to this method, but it is slow to produce an effect and will fail if the attitudes of the other employees are unsuitable. It is therefore unwise to put a new employee in a group of disgruntled workers.

(b) *On-job training by attaching the trainee to a senior employee* who has appropriate attitudes and the personal qualities likely to influence their acceptance. Coaching or a period as a personal assistant are examples of this method.

(c) *Off-job training* in which a group of employees discuss case studies designed to emphasise the relevant attitudes. Usually the group is divided into sub-groups or syndicates, each reporting back to the whole group through a spokesperson. A discussion in a small group is thus reinforced by a discussion in a larger group. This method is useful because the case studies can be written with the particular background and needs of the trainees in mind. However, sometimes discussion of imaginary incidents involving imaginary people fails to produce an emotional response. It is also possible for lazy trainees to make no contribution to the discussion and be completely detached from it.

(d) *Off-job role-playing exercises* in which a situation is described up to a certain point of crisis. Participants in the exercise are then asked to act out the parts of the people involved in the situation, extemporising the dialogue and behaving in the way they think is characteristic not of themselves but of the individuals whose roles they are playing. The group might act out situations concerning dismissal, a difficult customer or negotiations with trade unions. This method is usually enjoyed by the trainees, who show emotional involvement, sometimes intense. The training officer can make sure that lazy trainees are included by giving them roles to play, and can use audio or video tapes to record the role-playing so that the participants may discuss their performance afterwards. Non-participant critics may be asked to attempt roles themselves in a repetition of the exercise. It seems that attitudes are often modified by this method, though a great deal depends on the support which is given when the trainee returns to his or her normal job.

(e) *T-groups* are an off-job training method (the T stands for training) which has been in vogue in recent decades. The group of trainees (not more than twelve in number) is told that its sole task is to examine and discuss its own behaviour. After a slow and awkward beginning, the group's discussion generally becomes somewhat emotional, even heated, with members criticising each other's attitudes or indulging in frank self-criticism. Group sessions often continue for several days, and are regarded by some as enjoyable and by others as unpleasant. The purpose of T-group training is partly to bring about a change in attitudes by showing individuals what others think of them, partly to demonstrate the importance of personal behaviour in group processes and partly to improve the social skills of the trainees. This form of training has never been clearly validated; its effects on some individuals have been quite harmful psychologically and many others have found it useless

295

because they have been unable to practise their newly found social skills in an unsympathetic working environment.

TRAINING IN SKILL

3. Definition

The Department of Employment's *Glossary of Training Terms* gives the following definition of skill:

> An organised and co-ordinated pattern of mental and/or physical activity in relation to an object or other display of information, usually involving both receptor and effector processes. It is built up gradually in the course of repeated training or other experience. It is serial, each part from second to second is dependent on the last and influences the next. Skills may be described as perceptual, motor, manual, intellectual, social, etc. according to the context or the most important aspect of the skill pattern.

(Receptor processes provide the sensory input and effector processes the output or response.)

More briefly, skill may be defined as a practised, expert way of perceiving a relevant stimulus and then responding to it. Skill training therefore comprises the following:

(a) Recognition of stimuli, e.g. the sensation of the material feeling smooth

(b) Appropriate responses, e.g. the correct angle at which the carpenter should hold the chisel

(c) Establishing serial performance, each response providing a new stimulus which in turn evokes a new response and so on.

Skills differ from 'tasks' or 'functions' in that whereas a skill is a pattern of behaviour, a function is an activity (e.g. selecting staff, organising decision making, appraising the performances of others) normally requiring several (possibly disparate) skills. Thus, although we sometimes refer to 'interviewing skills', interviewing is really a function requiring a number of skills – communication skills, listening, analysis and interpretation of information, etc.

Employment skills may be categorised as follows:

(a) *Technical skills* that involve working with physical objects or processes

(b) *Interpersonal skills* needed to operate as a member of a team, to lead others and to communicate effectively

(c) *Decision-taking skills* and techniques for solving problems

(d) *Information processing* related to the discovery and dissemination of information.

Education, training and skill

Education is not the same as training. The former is valued for its own sake; the latter for its practical uses. Education seeks to develop within the individual an awareness of cause and effect and the ability to appraise and criticise information; it need not be instrumental in attaining practical objectives. Thus, the educated person is (or should be) capable of: (*i*) understanding the wider contexts of particular tasks; (*ii*) appreciating the implications of various pieces of knowledge and the foundations upon which they are based; (*iii*) constructive criticism and independent thought.

Training, on the other hand, is utilitarian and intended to improve the skills that individuals use in their daily lives. Note, however, that training is not the same as 'teaching', since the latter concerns a range of activities, e.g. influencing, motivating and conditioning, as well as 'instruction' *per se*.

4. Methods of skill training

The traditional method of training in skill is usually known as 'sitting next to Nellie', i.e. the trainee is told to watch and copy an experienced worker. If 'Nellie' uses poor working methods, or if the job includes much that cannot be understood simply by observation, then the method is a bad one. If Nellie uses good methods and if the job is visible, i.e. it can be readily understood simply by observation, then the method can be effective and economical.

Since a very large number of jobs contain non-visible elements and many 'Nellies' use poor methods of work, it is preferable on most occasions to use more organised means of training. One approach is to analyse the key elements of jobs by breaking them down into their essential components. The method proceeds as follows:

(a) A supervisor performs the job him or herself and divides it into reasonably self-contained stages, each of which can be taught as a unit.

(b) He or she examines each stage to identify and describe 'key points', e.g. special difficulties or dangers. An example of a breakdown (taken from *Recommendations for Training Operatives* published by the Ceramics Industry Training Organisation) is given in Table 22.1. Permission to reproduce the example is gratefully acknowledged.

(c) He or she makes sure that the materials and equipment required for training are properly arranged.

(d) The supervisor talks to the trainee to find out what is already known about the job and arouses the trainee's interest in learning it.

(e) The job is then demonstrated to the trainee in stages, explained slowly and carefully, with particular emphasis on the key points.

(f) The trainee performs the job, the supervisor observing to see that no mistakes are made and asking questions to ensure that the trainee has

Table 22.1 Job breakdown

Replacing tap washer

Element no.	Stage	Key points
1	Unscrew spindle cover (ferrule) to expose spindle assembly retaining nut	Turn in anti-clockwise direction
2	Support spindle cover (ferrule) in left hand, unscrew spindle assembly from tap body and lift out	Ensure correct size spanner, unscrew in anti-clockwise direction
3	Remove washer assembly and inspect valve seat	Ensure no ingress of foreign bodies
4	Unscrew washer retaining nut and remove – remove damaged washer	
5	Fit new washer, replace retaining nut and tighten	Do not overtighten – might damage new washer
6	Replace washer assembly in tap	Ensure correct seating
7	Replace spindle assembly in tap body and tighten	Ensure washer assembly spindle is located in body of spindle assembly, tighten in clockwise direction
8	Replace spindle cover and tighten	Tighten in clockwise direction

understood it. It may be necessary for the supervisor to repeat some of the instructions given in **(e)**. The trainee repeats the job until the supervisor is satisfied that performance is adequate.

(g) The supervisor puts the trainee to work, watching fairly closely at first but gradually relaxing supervision as the trainee gains confidence and skill.

The method is cheap, and is suitable for small numbers of trainees. It begins by being off-job, though usually very near the scene of production, but soon becomes on-job. A separate training department with specialist staff is not required. The analysis of the job in **(a)** and **(b)** cannot go very deep, and the method is therefore not appropriate for difficult skills, i.e. where the stimulus-perception-response sequence is not obvious. Also, supervisors transmit current working practices from one generation of workers to the next even if the practices are outdated.

It is successful with 'visible' jobs where everything of importance in the job can be observed, the mental processes being relatively unimportant; good examples would be packing or most forms of assembly work. Jobs of this kind contain a low proportion of skill and a high proportion of procedural knowledge.

Further approaches to skills training are the technique of skills analysis (*see* below) and the discovery method (*see* **6**).

5. Skills analysis

This method of training has been developed for those jobs which require a high degree of dexterity and co-ordination of senses and bodily movements. The actions of a highly skilled worker are analysed in great detail to identify and describe:

(a) What actions are performed with each finger, each hand and each foot

(b) How these actions are combined

(c) The stimuli he or she recognises which give the signals to begin and end these actions

(d) The senses by which these stimuli reach the worker

(e) The possible faults that may occur in the article being produced; these are classified, the reasons for them determined and methods of rectifying and avoiding them analysed.

From this information is compiled a skills analysis breakdown (*see* Table 22.2) and a faults analysis. Exercises are developed to train employees in the recognition of stimuli, the perfection of difficult movements and the co-ordination of those movements.

Skills analysis training has been successful in reducing training times and increasing proficiency. It claims to abolish the learning plateau (*see* 3:**7(c)**) because its carefully graded exercises allow the trainee to make steady uninterrupted progress.

It is an off-job training method, for obvious reasons, and is expensive and lengthy to prepare because a detailed job analysis must be carried out by expert consultants. A company is only justified in using it, therefore, when there is a large intake of trainees and when training by simpler methods is fairly long, i.e. over one month. In such cases the heavy initial outlay in consultants' fees, special equipment and training premises may be amply justified.

6. The discovery method

This is a technique of skill training which has been developed in recent years and applied with particular success to the retraining of older workers. It is similar in many ways to the newer methods used in primary education.

Table 22.2 Extract from skills analysis breakdown

Job: Linishing of television lenses
Element: Removing surface

Equipment – linishing belt

Left hand	Right hand	Vision	Other senses	Comments
AP to start grind	AP to start grind	Watch build up of ground glass appearing as a white curved line above point of contact with wheel. Density of line indicates amount being ground off. Red area shows point of contact.	K to exert pressure and correct. Vibration of wheel indicates degree of pressure. Touch checks correct pressure being applied	Pressure exerted in a rocking motion to bring radius of face into even contact with belt
Hold	Hold	Check grind off of shear mark Check extent of grind up face ¾ approx	K to reduce pressure in centre of screen	Extend grind to centre of screen holding elbows as grind reaches top half of screen. Increase rate of locking across centre of screen
RG. Slide hand to bottom L/H side 3" from corner	Hold	Follow white line	K to reduce pressure in L/H, increase in R/H	
Push elbow away from body to assist rotation of screen	Pull screen towards body rotating screen through 180°	Follow white line to ensure smooth rotation		Weight of screen being taken by belt. Pivot for rotation of screen on belt at crown of screen face
RL and move	RG to top R/H corner, Th. inside touching angle of inside face and edge – 1234 wrap over top edge	Follow white line to ensure smooth rotation	K & T to increase pressure in L/H group	
RG top L/H corner, Th. inside touching angle of inside face and edge – 1234 wrap over edge	Hold	Follow white line to ensure smooth rotation		White line to be horizontal to belt – if at another angle a cross cut grinding ridge may occur

AP – Apply pressure   RL – Release   K – Kinaesthesis   RG – Re-grasp   T – Touch   Th – Thumb

Discovery learning occurs when the trainee finds out for him or herself the principles of the job and the correct method of performing it; it is claimed to be more motivating than other forms of training because it offers the trainee a challenge followed by the gratification of a discovered solution. The trainer is comparatively passive, giving little formal instruction or demonstration. Another advantage claimed for this method is that it is trainee-centred; it tries to approach training problems from the point of view of a worker who does not yet possess the skill rather than by taking an expert worker as a model, as in skills analysis. During a discovery training programme it becomes very obvious if a trainee does not understand, but when in contrast an instructor explains or demonstrates a task he or she can never be sure if the trainee has understood or not.

An illustration of discovery learning is the training scheme for menders of worsted cloth described in *Training the Adult Worker* by Eunice Belbin (HMSO). The trainees first learned the detailed patterns of the weaves by copying them using thick elastic instead of thread and then discovered how to mend faults which were introduced into the weaves. The size of the weaves was gradually reduced until it reached actual size; by then the trainees had reached in 12 weeks a standard of proficiency formerly attained in a year to 18 months. According to Belbin, training needs to address five basic requirements: comprehension by the worker of what has to be done, reflex development, attitude formation, memorising, and learning the procedures attached to a job. This is sometimes referred to as the CRAMP approach to training (the acronym for the five elements).

The discovery method, like skills analysis, is an off-job training technique and requires a large intake of trainees if it is to be economically justifiable. It can be used successfully not only for skill but for knowledge training, by presenting the trainee with the opportunity to deduce for him or herself the answer to a problem, or indicating where to find out necessary information. Further advantages are that:

(a) Trainees learn how to ask the right questions as well as find answers.

(b) The training is perceived as immediately relevant to trainees' jobs.

(c) Results of exercises may be useful for improving the firm's overall efficiency.

On the other hand, discovery training can be difficult and expensive to administer, and positive results cannot be guaranteed.

TRAINING IN KNOWLEDGE

7. Knowledge requirements

No employee can work well without adequate job knowledge; in some cases it can be acquired in informal ways by experience in the job but usually it is imparted more quickly and accurately by formal training. Job analysis will show what knowledge is required, for example under the following headings:

(a) Purpose – the function of the job within the total process.

(b) Background information – the history, traditions and policies of the company, which may help the employee to understand the significance of the job.

(c) Legal requirements.

(d) Quality standards – how accurate or how approximate the work should be.

(e) Materials of work, e.g. for a salesperson what goods are available, their prices and qualities, for a manual worker the physical properties of the materials being used.

(f) Tools and equipment.

(g) Technical, e.g. accountancy, scientific or engineering knowledge.

(h) Personal contacts – job relationships with other employees.

(i) Procedures – the order in which things are done.

In contrast to attitudes and skills, knowledge may be imparted in many different ways, most of which are inexpensive and convenient. The most important methods of knowledge training are described below.

8. Coaching

This may vary from a rather casual 'sitting next to Nellie' approach to formal regular sessions in which an experienced employee, usually a manager, explains the job, asks the trainee questions to test his or her knowledge and often exercises general supervision over the trainee to check that he or she is making correct use of the knowledge. The instruction is immediate, direct, inexpensive, convenient and allows two-way communi-cation. Account may be taken of the trainee's special needs, and the pace of the instruction may be varied.

Often, coaching consists of a demonstration followed by the trainee imitat-ing the instructor's actions. The trainee can repeat difficult operations, ask questions, and progressively attain higher levels of skill. Simple tasks should be demonstrated first; then more complex tasks once the simple ones have been mastered. There is intimate involvement in the training process and the instructor is available to remedy mistakes as they occur.

Two problems arise:

(a) Success depends on the instructor's ability to coach (an incompetent instructor will transmit incorrect working methods).

(b) Coaching is wasted if the trainee fails to pay attention at crucial moments.

A related approach is for the trainee to learn things independently and then be questioned by the instructor in order to expose gaps in the trainee's knowledge. However, such an approach could severely damage a trainee's self-confidence and should not be used unless a congenial rapport exists between coach and trainee before the interrogation.

Mentoring

This is a relatively informal process whereby an older, more experienced member of an organisation counsels a younger colleague about the way the organisation works. The mentor might advise the mentee about the firm's informal political system, act as a 'sounding board' for the mentee's ideas, and provide information of a mundane nature which the mentee would feel embarrassed seeking from other sources (e.g. appropriate styles of dress, the degrees of formality with which to approach various members of the organisation, etc.). Potential benefits of mentoring include enhanced employee motivation, job performance, and organisational culture. People learn what is expected of them and what it is reasonable to expect from the organisation. Mentors themselves receive valuable feedback on what is happening at lower levels.

In some companies new employees are allocated a mentor as an integral part of the induction process. Typically, someone other than the recruit's immediate supervisor assumes this role, on the grounds that the mentee may have confidential personal queries that he or she might not wish to disclose to a section leader or head of department. The person appointed needs to be mature, experienced, and willing to complete the task. Problems here are that mentor and mentee may not get on; that the mentor might be keen but not in fact psychologically suitable for mentoring work; or that the mentor could transmit to the mentee bad attitudes towards the organisation. Also the mentee might not consider the mentor to be sufficiently well-qualified to undertake the job.

9. Formal lectures

When a company has a number of trainees in the same kind of work simultaneously, it may arrange for the group to have lectures on the subjects **(a)** to **(f)** in 7 by one of its senior employees. When this cannot be done, trainees may attend lectures outside the company, for example at a technical college, though the knowledge they learn here will be more general, and less specific to the company's needs.

Lectures are transmissions of predetermined sets of facts and opinions within a controlled environment. A good lecture will emphasise major points, since only a minority of the points mentioned (about 25 per cent at most) will be remembered by trainees. Most people find it difficult to concentrate for more than an hour at a time. Another possible problem is lack of motivation to learn among trainees.

Technical knowledge (*see* **7(g)**) is usually acquired outside the company. As in coaching, the effectiveness of formal lectures depends on their perceived relevance, the ability of the lecturer, the care with which the lectures are prepared, and the extent to which the trainees are encouraged to participate in discussions. Films and other visual aids can make the lecture more effective, and it is customary to give the trainee a hand-out covering the main points of the lecture.

10. Other methods

A number of other devices may be used to help trainees acquire knowledge under **7(a)**, **(b)** and **(h)**. Examples are:

(a) *Visits and tours* whereby arrangements are made for trainees to visit other departments or establishments of the company and talk to employees with whom he or she would normally only deal by letter or telephone. The trainee often benefits by seeing the stages of work preliminary and subsequent to his or her own.

(b) *Manuals and charts.* The trainee is sometimes given a detailed written description of the job, perhaps incorporating charts which show the route the work takes or explain the decisions the employee has to make. Many employees prefer to learn by this method instead of by personal contact, though it is still necessary for someone to be responsible for the trainee, introduce him or her to the work and check progress.

(c) *Simulation.* Instead of putting the trainee immediately to work, he or she may be asked to simulate the job using dummy materials or documents. A programme is devised which grades tasks from the easy and obvious to the more complex. This method often makes formal instruction unnecessary, because skillfully applied it can become very similar to discovery learning (*see* **6**).

(d) *In-tray.* A special version of simulation is in-tray training, in which the trainee is asked to deal with a batch of miscellaneous documents which he or she is supposed to find in each day's in-tray. Decisions of various kinds have to be made, though not of course actually put into effect.

The value of this technique for training depends on the review which should follow, when the trainer discusses with the trainee the decisions made. It is used in management training and occasionally as a means of selecting managers, though the exercise is difficult to score objectively.

(e) *Auto-instruction.* To benefit from this method, trainees need above-average intelligence, persistence and motivation. They are given a programme of assignments or tasks which take them to various parts of the company and require them to obtain information from departmental managers or from company files. The trainees are required to report back to their trainer periodically for a discussion and review.

Like the discovery method, auto-instruction is based on the principle that knowledge gained by exploration and discovery is more likely to be permanent than knowledge imparted by instructors.

11. Programmed learning

This consists of a carefully ordered sequence of units or frames arranged so that the trainee masters each unit before proceeding to the next. It is individual instruction, each trainee working at his or her own pace, and can be presented as a teaching book, teaching machine or a visual display unit controlled by a computer which holds the programme.

Each frame contains some information; the trainee is then asked a question to test whether he or she has learned or understood it. If the answer is correct the trainee moves on to the next frame. Programmed learning thus follows the principles of operant conditioning (*see* 3:**5**) developed by B. F. Skinner, who has been mainly responsible for this method of instruction. The stimulus is the unit of information with its question, the response is the answer to the question, and the reinforcement is the immediate knowledge of results and in most cases the gratification of having made the correct answer.

(a) *Advantages*. Besides the advantages usually found in off-job training, programmed learning also offers the following:

(*i*) Trainees go at their own pace.
(*ii*) The training can be decentralised, i.e. the teaching book or the teaching machine can be sent to the trainee instead of bringing him or her to a training school.
(*iii*) Most trainees find the method interesting; research has also shown that its effects are long-lasting.
(*iv*) It can be designed to meet specified performance standards and is continually being validated by the questions it contains.
(*v*) It is quicker than most other methods of knowledge training.

(b) *Disadvantages*. These are few but important:

(*i*) Learning programmes are expensive to produce and therefore are economically justifiable only when many trainees will use them.
(*ii*) If the subject is changing rapidly the investment in a learning programme will not be justified.
(*iii*) It is suitable above all for teaching facts and procedures; it is not appropriate for subjects where some discussion and flexibility of approach is desirable, e.g. literary criticism.

12. Computer-based training (CBT)

This is training based on computer software packages. Most CBT programs are 'menu driven', meaning that the user selects from various options that appear on a visual display unit about how the training is to proceed. Typically, packages contain numerous self-check exercises and provide for continuous interaction between user and program. If the user makes a mistake, the program automatically scrolls back to the relevant part of the preceding text. 'Adaptive testing' packages enable trainees to predetermine the depth of the material they wish to cover. For instance, one user might require only a brief overview of a certain subject, while someone else may need extensive and detailed coverage and so would select the option providing this level of depth. Training is thus directly linked to individual training needs.

The advantages of CBT are that trainees usually find it interesting as well as instructional, and that users can work through a package at their own pace. However, much time may be lost as users become familiar with the proclivities of a particular package, and self-discipline is necessary to complete all the exercises from beginning to end.

13. Interactive video

These are videos of simulated interpersonal communication situations in which actors portray various characters in workplace scenes. The background to a situation is mapped out, developing to a climax at which the video stops, leaving the viewer to pretend that he or she is one of the characters in the film, and having to provide the next step. For instance, the video might show a production operative just about to lose his or her temper and then, just at the crucial moment, invite viewers to say how *they* would resolve the problem. The action may, of course, be slowed down or frozen to highlight critical events.

MANAGEMENT DEVELOPMENT

14. Definition

The *Glossary of Training Terms* gives the following definition of management development:

> A systematic process of development of effective managers at all levels to meet the requirements of an organisation, involving an analysis of the present and future management requirements, assessing the existing and potential skills of managers and devising the best means for their development to meet these requirements.

The definition shows that management development includes:

(a) Human resources planning to assess the demand for managers.

(b) Appraisal of managers' present abilities, sometimes using a management by objectives programme.

(c) Appropriate development methods.

It is sometimes regarded as part of *organisation development* – a planned attempt to improve the effectiveness of a company by examining and reforming the way it is organised, its communications and its management style. The systematic approach (*see* 21:3) cannot be applied to development, which aims to prepare for future jobs whereas training is concerned with improving performance in present jobs. Validation of a management development programme is therefore very difficult.

15. Development needs

These can be divided into three categories:

(a) Knowledge required to perform a manager's job in the company concerned, including:

(*i*) background of company, its organisation and practices
(*ii*) company resources available
(*iii*) company technology
(*iv*) specialist management techniques, e.g. operational research
(*v*) relevant law
(*vi*) general, social and economic environment.

(b) Planning, analytical and creative skills, which include the following:

(*i*) recognising objectives and putting them in order of importance
(*ii*) assessing the value of available resources, e.g. human, material, technological and financial
(*iii*) formulating and administering plans, delegating as necessary
(*iv*) discerning and solving day-to-day management problems.

(c) Social skills (sometimes called interpersonal or interactive skills), important because managers may easily spend two-thirds of their time working with and trying to influence others. They include:

(*i*) communication upwards, downwards and laterally
(*ii*) co-ordination within a department or between departments
(*iii*) motivation of subordinates
(*iv*) awareness of others' needs, attitudes and perceptions.

16. Development methods

Needs may be met either by activities arranged within the company or by external courses. The latter appear to be losing favour because they are unable to take into account a company's particular systems, traditions or general management style. In-company programmes are growing in popularity, especially those which include a team of people who normally work together, or even a whole department. It is, however, often difficult in practice to release a whole team or department at the same time unless the programme is held outside normal working hours.

Development methods often used in management development fall into three areas:

(a) *Knowledge.* As in training, this is the easiest area to deal with. Company matters are dealt with by secondment, coaching or auto-instruction (*see* **10**), while outside courses are appropriate for specialist techniques and the general environment.

(b) *Planning, analytical and creative skills.* This is the most difficult of the three categories. To a certain extent the acquisition of knowledge will help the manager by showing the factors to be considered and the techniques available, but it seems that planning, analytical and creative skills can only be developed by practice, either in a real job or in a situation which attempts to simulate reality.

In the first case, the manager will feel fully responsible, will take genuine decisions and will deal with their consequences, though the mistakes of an inexpert manager can be disastrous.

In the second case, the manager may be more enterprising but will have little sense of responsibility; his or her behaviour in real life may be entirely different. A simulated situation, however carefully it is described, can never depict, for example, the personalities and organisational climate which are so important in management decision making. Some simulated methods which are used to try to develop these skills are:

(*i*) *Case studies and role-playing* (*see* **2**)

(*ii*) *In-tray exercises* (*see* **10**)

(*iii*) *Business games* in which two or more teams attempt, for example, to market an imaginary product using the information supplied to them. The effects of their decisions are evaluated (usually by a computer) and fed back to them. The team which has made the largest profit will be the winner.

The following are real-life methods:

(*i*) *Projects*, i.e. special assignments given to managers, who must enquire into a company problem, make recommendations and sometimes put them into practice.

(*ii*) *Junior boards*, in which a group of young managers is given decisions of fairly low importance to make which have been delegated to the group by the main board.

(*iii*) *Action learning*, in which a manager takes over a different job and through doing it learns a new set of management skills. The manager must analyse the problems associated with a job, formulate a solution, implement the solution (under the guidance of an experienced superior) and monitor its consequences.

(*iv*) *Training companies*, usually small subsidiaries of a large group, which are intended to trade profitably, yet give opportunities for young managers to develop their skills in a somewhat protected environment.

(*v*) *Coaching* (*see* **8**) is often used and is frequently successful, but sometimes the experienced manager who is coaching may make decisions so automatically that either he or she does not realise they have been made or cannot explain the reasons for them.

(c) *Social skills*. These have received much attention in recent years and are always dealt with in special courses. The main methods are as follows:

(*i*) *Attitude change*, e.g. by T-groups or role-playing (*see* **2**).

(*ii*) *Team-work and management-style courses*, usually given by consultants, in which groups are formed to carry out simple tasks together and then discuss what lessons about their behaviour can be learned. Examples are:

- Coverdale training, which is a group-training application of the principles of action learning in which a specialist instructor directs a group in completing a straightforward task and then leads discussion after the task's completion.
- Group discussions about normal working behaviour in the context of a theoretical framework, e.g. the managerial grid (*see* **8:6**).

(*iii*) *Analysing individual behaviour* following a formal system, sometimes with a theoretical basis, e.g. transactional analysis.

(*iv*) *Training in social techniques*. This is the reverse of method (*i*) in which it is assumed that a change in attitudes will modify behaviour. Instead, training is given in the techniques of hand-shaking, smiling, eye contact, etc. in situations which are as near to reality as possible, e.g. a simulated appraisal interview. The trainee becomes aware of the benefits of the improved techniques in his or her social contacts, and thus modifies basic attitudes.

(*v*) *Lectures* in the psychology of perception, motivation, groups, etc. usually in conjunction with one of the above methods.

(*vi*) *Outdoor management training*. This assumes that the qualities needed for successful management may be cultivated through short management development courses involving outdoor pursuits such as rockclimbing, canoeing or orienteering. Such activities are said to enhance participants' abilities to plan, organise, create and manage teams, control others and handle uncertainty.

17. Arguments against management training

Academic management training has been criticised for having few practical applications, for encouraging technical specialisation rather than the overall ability to lead, and for creating unrealistic job and career expectations among junior managerial employees. Opponents of management training allege that the environments in which training occurs are necessarily artificial, and too remote from real life managerial situations to be of practical value. Arguably, most aspects of management can only be learned by doing. In particular, the entrepreneurial attitudes that are essential for commercial success cannot be inculcated through academic management training; many of the most innovative of all entrepreneurs and managers have received no management training whatsoever. Normal competition between managerial employees should ensure the emergence of the most able at the top. Further arguments against management training are that:

(a) The dimensions of managerial competence encompass a vast range of tasks, so that it is not possible to devise courses that comprehensively cover the entire management field.

(b) Individuals enter management in so many different ways and from such varied backgrounds that no single programme of studies can meet the highly specified needs of each participant.

(c) Management is by its very nature a fast changing subject, so that the contents of any management training course could quickly become out of date, especially if the course does not devote sufficient attention to underlying management principles.

Progress test 22

1. What methods may be used for attitude training?
2. What are the disadvantages of the 'sitting next to Nellie' method of skill training?
3. Why does skills analysis training sometimes eliminate the learning plateau?
4. What are the principles of the discovery method of training?
5. State three methods of knowledge training.
6. What are the advantages and disadvantages of programmed learning?
7. What are the advantages of computer-based training?
8. What are a manager's main development needs?

Part Four

INTERNATIONAL COMPARISONS

23

EUROPEAN TRAINING AND MANAGEMENT DEVELOPMENT

VOCATIONAL TRAINING

1. Importance of vocational education and training

The European countries with the best general and vocational education systems will increasingly possess a competitive advantage as West European economic integration progresses. Well-trained labour forces are productive (hence offsetting the higher wages that trained workers normally command), cohesive, motivated and (most importantly) capable of accommodating change and introducing new technologies.

Management training is equally important. Trained and competent manager's make superior operational decisions, choose the most efficient systems, purchase the correct inputs, apply relevant criteria when recruiting staff, control and appraise their subordinates more effectively, and so on. Badly trained managers, conversely, demotivate their workforces, make costly mistakes, and are unable to identify the need for new methods.

It follows that long-term neglect of industrial training in any European nation is sure to put its businesses at a disadvantage when faced with intense competition from rival countries. Note how a convergence of national European training practices is likely to occur as companies with the worst trained workforces go to the wall and the training, recruitment and staff development policies of successful firms are copied by other businesses.

2. General and vocational education

European youngsters are increasingly well educated. According to Eurostat (the statistical service of the European Union) about 23 per cent of the EU's population is now in full-time education, a figure comparable to that of Japan (but two per cent lower than in the US). Students, moreover, are spending more years at school and college: today a quarter of European students remain in education after the age of 19.

Portugal and the UK have the lowest percentage of their 5 to 24 year olds in full-time education (at around 65 per cent). Top EU countries in this respect are Germany, Sweden and France (about 83 per cent), with the rest of the Union's nations having between 70 and 77 per cent of the 5 to 24 age group as full-time students. About 12 per cent of all Danes have a third-level educational qualification, as do 11 per cent of Belgians and 10 per cent of the Dutch. Portugal, Ireland and Britain are the worst countries on this criterion, with between 5.5 and 7 per cent of their populations qualified at a high level (although these low figures do not necessarily reflect the *standard* of education provided). The representation of females in higher education has risen sharply over the last 20 years, and is roughly on a par with males in most Union states.

Education and training systems in the European Union are characterised by their diversity. Major differences in national approaches include the following:

(a) The status afforded to vocational education and training (VET) in a nation's overall educational system

(b) Quality assurance procedures for attesting individual competence

(c) The financing of training

(d) Workplace relationships between those who have experienced VET and those with other types of educational qualifications

(e) Whether basic general education is broadly based or specialised.

A further important difference in national approaches concerns the role of vocational education *within* the basic school system. In some EU countries a vocational qualification obtained at school can serve as a means for entry to higher education on exactly the same basis as an 'academic' school-leaving certificate. Also, vocational education begins at a much earlier age in some countries than elsewhere. Note how certain nations maintain the tradition whereby any student in possession of basic matriculation qualifications has the legal *right* to enter higher education (subject of course to space availability in various institutions), whereas selection by colleges is practised in other states. The former approach results in large classes and high failure and drop-out rates, which are accepted as normal and inevitable consequences of the system. Selection procedures and other key characteristics of the higher education systems of EU countries are given in Table 23.1.

Academic titles

Much confusion arises from the diversity of titles for academic and vocational qualifications of approximately similar level in various EU nations. The term 'university' or 'degree level' means different things in different countries. Britain, for instance, has a long tradition of institutions other than universities teaching at the undergraduate level. In Germany and the Netherlands the

Table 23.1 Higher education systems in EU countries

	Austria	Belgium	Denmark	Finland
Types of H E institution	Twelve universities Six art schools (university status)	Four state universities Two private ('free') universities Eleven H E colleges	Five universities One technical university Three H E business schools Ten technical colleges	21 universities 22 polytechnics
Military service for males	Yes	Yes	Yes	Yes*
Types of award	Diplom Doktoratsstudien	Legal degrees Scientific degrees **(1)**	Candidatus (basic degree) Teknikum Ingeniores (3 year engineering diploma) Magister Artium (post-graduate) Licentiatgrad (Ph.D)	Bachelors degree Masters degree Licentiate or Doctors degree
Lengths of H E courses	Four years (Diplom) Six years (Doktoratsstudien)	Four to five years	Five years	Four to six years [Five or six years – first degree; three to four years – new kind of professional degree]
Entry requirements	Open entry for all with matriculation qualifications	Open access for all with matriculation qualifications	Selection by college, subject to guidelines issued by the Ministry of Education	Students passing the matriculation exam or completing vocational studies at college or higher levels are eligible to enter higher education

*Recently women have been given the right to complete military service on a voluntary basis

Table 23.1 Higher education systems in EU countries (continued)

	France	Germany	Greece	Ireland
Types of H E institution	Universities Grandes écoles (high level vocational institutions) IUTs (university level technical institutes)	General universities Technical universities Fachhochschulen (technical institutions)	17 universities and TEIs (technical institutes (2))	6 universities Regional technical colleges
Military service for males	Yes	Yes	Yes	No
Types of award	Diplôme (Grandes écoles) Licence (3 year university course) Maîtrise (4 year university course) DEUG } 2 year university DEUST } courses DE (post-graduate diploma) Doctorat (Ph.D)	Diplom (undergraduate degree) Magister Artium (post-graduate degree) Staatsexamen (state awarded professional qualification) Fachhochschule (technical qualification)	Ptichio (basic degree) Didaktoriko (Ph.D)	Bachelor's degree National certificates and diplomas (technical colleges) Master's degree Ph.D
Lengths of H E course	Five years (Diplôme) Four years (Maîtrise)	Four years	Four to six years (universities) Three years (TEIs)	Three to four years
Entry requirements	Open entry to all universities with a Baccalauréat Competitive examination for entry to the Grandes écoles	Open entry for all with matriculation qualifications (the Abitur)	Competitive allocation of students to colleges by the Ministry of Education according to marks gained in national entrance examinations	Selection by colleges

Table 23.1 Higher education systems in EU countries (continued)

	Italy	Luxembourg	Netherlands
Types of H E institution	Universities (3)	One university One technical college	13 universities 3 technical universities Institutes of Higher Education (Hogescholen)
Military service for males	Yes	No	Yes
Types of award	Laurea (basic degree (4)) Diploma (three year course)	Diplôme (technical college) University certificate of entry to universities in France, Belgium and Germany	Doctorandus (masters degree) Ingenieur (engineering masters degree (5)) Meester in de Rechten (masters degree in law) Baccalaureas (Hogescholen qualifications)
Lengths of H E courses	Four to six years	Three years (Diplôme) One year (certificate of entry)	Four years
Entry requirements	Selection by colleges	Selection by college	Open entry to all with matriculation qualifications

Table 23.1 Higher education systems in EU countries (continued)

	Portugal	Spain	Sweden	United Kingdom
Types of H E institution	14 universities Institutos Politécnicos (sub-degree institutions)	31 state universities 4 Church universities 4 technical universities Technical high schools	Twelve universities 16 university colleges	Universities Institutes of Higher Education
Military service for males	Yes	Yes	Yes	No
Types of award	Licenciatura (basic degree) Bacharelato (technician qualification) MBA Ph.D	Licenciado (university degree) Ingeniero Arquitecto } Technical high school qualification Diplomado (three year course)	Two kinds of first degree: professional degrees (for careers in specific professions – medicine, fine arts, design) and non-professional (divided into 3 levels, depending on points awarded)	Bachelor's degree Higher national diploma (2 year course) BTEC diploma (2 year course) Master's degree Ph.D
Lengths of HE Courses	Four to six years (Licenciatura) Three to four years (Bacharelato)	Five to six years	Three to four years	Three to four years (degree)
Entry requirements	As Greece, with additional college entrance examinations in some cases	Selection by colleges **(6)**	Open access for students with upper secondary schooling equivalent to a 3 year upper secondary school diploma	Selection by colleges

Notes
(1) See text.
(2) Greek engineering technical institutes are commonly called 'Polytechnics'.
(3) An Italian Politecnico is a university specialising in engineering.
(4) Anyone with a Laurea may use the title Dottore or Dottoressa.
(5) Technical college graduates carry the same title but abbreviate it to Ing., rather than to Ir. as for university engineers.
(6) Students are expected to attend their local university unless it does not offer the course they desire.

term 'high school' is often used to describe a technical university. Belgian higher education courses that follow a national curriculum are called 'legal degrees' (which include most of the sciences and engineering); whereas programmes based on institution-based curricula lead to 'scientific' degrees. Courses in economics, politics and psychology usually result in scientific degrees being awarded.

3. An aging European workforce

Europe's workforce is aging rapidly. A consequence of this (according to estimates prepared by the European Commission) is that as older workers retire the size of the EU's total labour force will be shrinking by around one million per annum by the year 2005. At the same time, the bulk of the Union's workforce will be between 45 and 64 years of age; a cohort that has received minimal industrial training and will have experienced long bouts of (de-motivating) unemployment. Lack of skill, moreover, leads to lack of self-confidence when confronted with new technologies.

Equally however Commission forecasts predict that four in ten European workers will require university entrance level qualifications by the end of the century. This will badly affect employment prospects in countries which have not bothered to invest in the education of their young people. Possible consequences of the impending situation include:

(a) Greatly increased training efforts by companies

(b) Large-scale migrations of skilled labour across national frontiers

(c) Higher levels of participation in the labour force by (educated) women and ethnic minority workers

(d) Widespread use of loyalty bonuses to discourage skilled employees from changing their employer

(e) Further pressures to use robotics and other fully automated production methods.

4. European management training

Effective management training *necessarily* builds upon the basic education received by managers at school and college. Hence, the sounder the educational infrastructure within a country the firmer the foundation on which good quality management training may be constructed. Thereafter, the quality and extent of a country's management education typically depends on a mixture of state intervention and private provision by large corporations (it has always been the case in all EU countries that big and well-established companies undertake a disproportionately high proportion of management training).

Management training affects how managers define problems, choose strategies and determine the range of the options to be considered when formulating policies. It influences the organisational structures of enterprises (number of levels of authority, delegation patterns, ratios of supervisors to operatives, control systems, etc.); and the attitudes, creativities, industriousness and capacities of individual executives. In turn these factors determine productivity levels within businesses and hence the economic performances of nations. A highly significant fact is that within a few years the majority of European managers will be employed by firms engaged in the provision of services rather than the manufacture of products. It is essential therefore that the management theories that underlie training reflect this and not be based entirely on the experiences of manufacturing enterprises.

Terminology

The English word 'manager' is today widely used in Continental European countries to describe a business executive, although in France the term 'cadre' and in Germany the titles 'Unternehmer' and 'Führungskräfte' have wide circulation. However, a French cadre could be a doctor, civil servant, or indeed anyone with a professional background; while an Unternehmer is in principle an entrepreneur and a Führungskräfte a 'business leader'. As the word 'management' has a common and precise meaning that avoids such ambiguities it has naturally assumed pre-eminence as the Continental description of executive activity.

NATIONAL DIFFERENCES

Essential differences in the education and training systems of European Union countries are outlined below.

5. Austria

Austrian children complete four years's primary education at a Volksschule, after which they choose between vocationally oriented or broad-based educational streams. Education is compulsory and free to all between the ages of six and 15 years. Vocational education involves attendance at a Hauptschule for four years, followed by a course at one of a variety of technical or other specialised training schools. Some of the latter provide qualifications which enable the student to apply to a university. More general secondary education is available from an Allgemeinbildende hoher Schule, which offers an eight-year programme covering a wide range of subjects and which culminates in the Reifeprufung or Matura. Possession of these qualifications gives access to all Austrian universities.

The country has 18 'traditional' universities (including six Art Schools) plus 13 Colleges of Technology (Fachhochschules) which possess university status. Fachhochschules differ from other university-level institutions by offering academically sound technical and vocational education at the tertiary level. Their programmes last for a minimum of three years and include the requirement to complete a thesis. Graduates of Fachhochschules receive either a Magister or a Diplom-Ingenieur degree, and put the letters FH after their degree titles to distinguish them from other graduates. Five of the 12 traditional non-Art School universities (Vienna, Graz, Innsbruck, Linz and Salzburg) are multidisciplinary institutions offering broadly based academic programmes. The other seven specialise in particular subject areas such as agriculture, metallurgy, economics, or teacher training. Art Schools provide a wide range of courses concerned with music, drama and industrial design. Austrian degrees comprise two stages: the four-year (minimum) Diplom; and the Doktorat, which takes a further two years and involves the submission of a thesis.

All Austrian citizens over the age of 24 and possessing professional experience may attend prespecified university courses connected with their professional career or trade. Additionally Colleges of Technology, Institutes of Adult Education and centres operated by the Austrian Trade Union Federation offer part-time vocational education courses. Apprenticeships are available which last for two years and involve periods of work experience interspersed with training at a vocational school. The duration of an apprenticeship may be shortened for individuals who received large amounts of vocational instruction while they were at school. Around 350 'practice firms' operate within Austria, mostly attached to colleges and industry training organisations. A practice firm is a simulated company that functions in exactly the same way as a true-life business, with 'employees' (students) who complete all the tasks (marketing, purchasing, personnel, etc.) that have to be undertaken in a genuine company. Practice firms 'transact' with each other, buying and selling fictitious goods and exchanging artificial money. The aim is to mirror exactly the operations of a real business, even down to dealing with the tax authorities and state national insurance.

6. Belgium

Belgium's education and training system is divided linguistically, with each community (Flemish and Walloon) financing and controlling its schools, colleges and state vocational training organisations (which have trade union and employers' association representatives on their boards of management). Full-time education is compulsory until age 16. Students who leave school at 16 must continue their education on a part-time basis until they are 18. Secondary schools stream students into general ('academic'), technical, arts, and vocational programmes. All the latter provide successful students with a means of entry to higher education, although vocational students require an extra year of study before they can progress to HE. There are no national examinations; all leaving certificates are awarded by individual schools.

Part-time vocational education for those leaving school at age 16 occurs in

321

90 training centres scattered around the country. A limited number of 16 year olds obtain one to three year apprenticeships that involve 120 hours per year of off-job theoretical training. More commonly, however, individuals undertake 'industrial apprenticeships' which last from six months to two years and are organised by joint industry boards that include trade union and employers' association representatives. Higher education courses last four or five years and segment into two parts: the Candidat, followed by the Licence. Examinations are graded as satisfactory (satisfecit), distinction (cum laude), or exceptional distinction (summa cum laude). About one third of all Belgian degrees are awarded for scientific or engineering subjects.

A law of 1985 requires firms to grant one hour off work on full pay (to a maximum of 240 hours per year) to any employee for each period of 50 minutes spent on a *bona-fide* vocational training course outside normal working hours. Firms reclaim 50 per cent of the cost from the Belgian Ministry of Labour. Much of this training takes place in training centres run by the local governments of the two linguistic communities. About 40 of these centres offer management training courses which comprise 128 hours of instruction, normally spread over a 12 month period.

7. Denmark

Denmark is noted for the high quality of its basic education system, and is well served by universities, technical colleges and higher education business schools. Secondary education is compulsory until age 16 (although only about ten per cent of pupils leave at this stage). Schools provide a broadly based general education. An interesting feature of the Danish system is that 16 year olds take school examinations in a very limited range of subjects. There is a change of school for those continuing beyond age 16, with streams for science, arts, or technical subjects. The upper secondary schools also offer two-year part-time adult education courses, the successful completion of which enable students to enter further education.

Denmark has three universities offering five or six year undergraduate (Kandidat) degree programmes. Additionally there are business schools and technical universities, plus 'engineering academies' providing two to three year sub-degree courses. Engineering, computing and business studies are the most popular subjects. In Denmark the title 'civil engineer' refers to the *level* of qualification achieved rather than type of subject. University trained engineers are known as Akademiingeniorer; those produced in technical colleges as Teiknikum Ingeniører. Graduate engineers frequently go into general business management.

A unified system of vocational training (including apprenticeships) operates, financed in part by a training levy imposed on employing businesses. The national scheme involves a minimum of 20 weeks full-time training in theoretical aspects of the relevant subject, followed by work experience and thereafter a mixture of classroom and workplace instruction. The educational components of the scheme are state funded. Training can require up to 80 weeks' attendance at a commercial or technical college. Successful completion of the scheme leads to the award of a nationally recognised certificate. Grants are available to public sector colleges and to private trainers for the organisation of courses for non-managerial employees and for self-employed people for certain approved purposes (notably those relating to quality management and the application of new technology). Under a national industrial relations agreement, any Danish worker with at least 12 months' service who is made redundant by new technology is entitled to four weeks off work to attend retraining courses, at the employer's expense.

8. Finland

Basic education is compulsory for nine years, divided into a six-year lower stage (starting at age seven) followed by a three-year upper stage. The system is comprehensive and free, and provides the same core curriculum to all students. After comprehensive school the student may continue his or her studies either at a 'general' senior secondary school or through vocational training. General schools take about 40% of all students and provide courses that last for three years and lead to a matriculation examination, success in which offers entry to university. Vocational programmes are between two and five years in duration and may give a tertiary diploma that permits the holder to apply for a university course. There are 21 universities, 22 polytechnics and a large number of vocational colleges. Ten of the country's universities are multidisciplinary; the remainder specialise in particular fields such as business, administration, technology, economics, or art and design. First degree courses last five or six years, although many Finnish students take considerably longer to complete their undergraduate programmes. Large universities have separate research institutions affiliated to them. The standard polytechnic degree lasts three or four years and is highly vocational (the degree is recognised as a professional qualification in its own right). Polytechnics have very close relationships with businesses and industry. A notable feature of the Finnish higher education system is that a significant number of units, courses, and sometimes entire degrees are offered in English.

Adult vocational education in Finland occurs mainly within colleges. Apprenticeships play only a minor role: less that 3% of young Finnish people are enrolled on apprenticeship programmes. There is much government involvement in the provision of adult training and education. The state funds around 300 municipal Vocational Adult Education Centres, and imposes legally binding requirements that only appropriately qualified and registered persons may practice certain trades or professions. All universities are required to maintain Centres for Continuing Education with branches outside university towns. There are three main types of work-related training in Finland: 'in-service', 'adult vocational', and 'labour market'. In-service training is carried out by various training institutions which enter into contracts with individual firms. It is extremely popular, with more than one-third of the employed workforce participating in the short courses that are offered. Firms are charged the full cost of the training, although small public subsidies might be available. Adult vocational training is financed entirely by national and local government on a 50-50 basis. It is open to all Finnish citizens free of charge. Each year around 10% of the employed labour force is enrolled on adult education courses. Labour market training is managed by Finland's public employment service and is intended to improve the skills of unemployed workers. Enrolment on labour market programmes is free of charge, but otherwise there are no financial incentives. The schemes offer financial assistance to firms wishing to set up company-based training courses. Most of the people participating in labour market training are at the bottom end of the skills spectrum, about a third of them having received only lower secondary level education.

9. France

Secondary education begins at age eleven, on a comprehensive basis. The only private schools are religious and not a significant influence within the system. At the age of 14, about 15 per cent of pupils transfer to technical school, being joined at age 15 by a further 25 per cent of their cohort. The first set of transferees normally obtain a skilled worker certificate (CAP); the second a technical baccalauréat. Courses are full time and school based, although industry is requested to advise on the curriculum.

Those who do not enter the vocational stream at 15 study for a further two years in order to obtain a general education certificate (BEPC). Successful completion of a third year gives the student a baccalauréat and hence the automatic right to enter university. The baccalauréat subject combination based on mathematics and science (Bac C) has great prestige, and is often sought by students intending to pursue careers not remotely related to science or mathematics.

At university, students can take a two-year diploma, followed if they wish by a third-year 'licence' (bachelor's degree) and perhaps a fourth-year maitrise (master's degree). Sandwich courses containing three to five month industrial placements are common. In addition to the universities, France has nearly 200 grandes écoles, which take about ten per cent of all entrants to higher education. Competition for places in the grandes écoles is fierce and involves extensive testing of candidates (in contrast to the universities, which are obliged to offer places to anyone possessing the baccalauréat). An estimated 75 per cent of senior executives in large French companies have a grandes écoles qualification, and there is much social contact between these individuals and civil servants and public sector managers with a similar educational background.

Criticisms of the French system

The French educational system places a great deal of emphasis on formal intellect and academic qualifications. And since there is a long tradition in

France of graduates from elite grandes écoles going into industrial management the system has led perhaps to a French management style that is logical, intellectual, and lacking in intuition. Manifestations of this are evident in the sophisticated planning mechanisms common in large French organisations, a high level of abstraction, and careful attention to organisation.

Alleged deficiencies in the French system are that:

(a) Its inherent elitism excludes many talented people outside the orthodox hierarchy, especially those from working class backgrounds.

(b) Selection of entrants to management on the basis of high-level academic achievement can cause company administrations to lack common sense and to lose touch with the objective needs of the market.

(c) It encourages back-scratching, nepotism and old boy networks.

(d) The heavy concentration on mathematics distorts the *entire* education system.

(e) It produces 'jacks-of-all-trades' without specialist qualifications.

(f) There is insufficient emphasis on marketing and selling, especially international marketing.

Management training

French business was transformed in the 1960s and 1970s, with rapid economic growth and a general restructuring of firms away from traditional small- to medium-sized family enterprises and towards larger corporations. The removal of protectionist trade barriers, state investment in education and training and the general deregulation of business brought about by the country's membership of the (then) EEC encouraged these larger firms to adopt outward-looking internationalist perspectives. Annual growth rates approached six per cent on average during the 1960s, and exports became an important part of French gross national product. Labour productivity, living standards and educational levels rose to become among the highest in the world.

This expansion led to an upsurge of interest in management training and development, which itself has been encouraged by a law that requires companies to devote 1.5 per cent of the value of their payrolls to training or to forfeit this money to the government. Part of the levy must be used to finance training leave (see below), and some for the training of young workers. The levy requirement is reduced to 0.15 per cent of the wage bill for firms employing fewer than ten workers. Tax credits are available for companies that spend more than the statutory minimum on training.

The same law compels firms to publish their training and staff development plans and to grant paid leave (up to a certain limit) to employees wishing to undertake approved courses in further education. Training plans have to specify how the firm proposes spending its training budget and must be

325

submitted for consideration by the company's works council (see Chapter 24). The actual training can be undertaken in-house or *via* external bodies. In-house training is most popular, leading to criticisms that the levy has encouraged training that is too narrow and firm specific. It has also been argued that the levy encourages companies *not* to provide training on a voluntary basis. External courses financed by the levy are provided by Chambers of Commerce (to which a part of the training levy is recycled for this purpose), and by private consultants and industry trade associations. These courses often last for several weeks.

Any employee with at least two years' service in an industry and six months with a particular company within it can apply to take a year off work (or 1,200 hours part time) on 80 per cent of salary for approved training. The firm recovers its outlay from a central government fund. Workers under 26 years of age with no previous training and three months service with a firm are eligible for 200 hours of training per annum. Employers can refuse requests for training leave if the absences created would account for more than one per cent of total working hours.

Apprenticeships are available, but are few and far between and have much less status than in Germany. They usually last for two years and focus primarily on lower-level technical training.

10. Germany

The destruction of Germany's industrial capacity during the Second World War enabled the country to re-equip with up-to-date technology and to refocus its production towards high-quality advanced technology products specifically designed for international (rather than domestic) markets. This was made possible by the existence of a technically skilled industrial work-force, general consensus between management and labour on the need for improved methods, and government commitment to low inflation and the creation of a stable economic environment. Germany today can boast a first-class public education and vocational training system, a strong R&D orientation within its leading firms, and a commitment to developing human resources within industry unparalleled in the European Union.

German school students cover an extremely broad basic curriculum. They may leave school at age 15, but if they do so must then undertake part-time vocational education until they are at least 18. There are three types of school, catering for academic, intermediate and lower-ability students respectively. A few comprehensive schools operate, mostly in the Berlin area. About a quarter of German 19-year-olds take the Abitur examination, success in which gives the right to attend university. Note however that there are several other routes into German higher education. Student numbers in HE have more than doubled since 1975. Student loans are available; otherwise state support for university students is minimal.

A confusion arises in Germany in that whereas the basic undergraduate qualification is called the Diplom, the Diplom from a technical institute (Fachhochschulen – as opposed to the higher-ranking 'technical high schools' or 'technical universities') does not of itself give admission to postgraduate study. Graduates from Fachhochschulen are supposed to state their qualification as being a DIPL(FH), whereas university graduates write Diplom, or sometimes DIPL(U) or (if they are from a technical school or technical university) DIPL(TH) or DIPL(TU). Fachhochschule courses are shorter than university programmes, and much more vocationally orientated. The most popular subjects are mechanical and production engineering, business economics, computing and information technology, and public administration. Sandwich courses are common. The majority of (West) German managers have received a polytechnic or university education, completing their studies at about 27 years of age.

Germans are interested in education generally, and the concept of 'lifelong education' has much currency (up to a quarter of all German adults are estimated to participate in continuing education annually). An interesting feature of the German approach is that it does not apply the same distinctions between arts and sciences that characterise educational divisions in some other countries. Applied technology ('technik') embraces a number of subjects that elsewhere would be viewed as 'theoretical'. 'Technik' is *everything* concerned with manufacture, and technical competence is greatly admired in this nation.

The apprenticeship system

Apprenticeships are available in a wide range of occupations, and a large number of senior German managers have served an apprenticeship at some time during their careers (older people with academic backgrounds sometimes complete apprenticeships in order to obtain an additional and marketable qualification). The full German apprenticeship lasts three years; or two years for semi-skilled work. It comprises practical on-job experience plus day release study. Importantly, technical apprenticeships teach *management and administrative* skills (especially planning and cost accounting) as well as purely technical competencies.

The three-year apprenticeship combines in-company training with general education undertaken in a vocational school (Berufsschulen). Most apprentices are from general and intermediate schools, with a minority (five to ten per cent) from Gymnasia (Grammar Schools). Entrants from the latter will have completed 13 years of basic education; compared with ten and eight years for people from intermediate and general schools respectively. In-company apprenticeship training (which occurs in about half a million firms) is inspected and accredited by Germany's Chambers of Commerce, which register apprentices and conduct examinations. Vocational schools are financed and run by local government (Laender). Drop-out rates are low (less than ten per cent) and nine out of ten students pass the examinations.

Each year in excess of half a million apprentices embark on a three-year training programme. Many of the trainees will not be subsequently employed by their training companies. One important consequence of the availability of high-calibre apprenticeships in Germany is that many young people (up to 15 per cent of all school leavers possessing university entrance qualifications in some years) choose not to attend university right away but rather to complete a three-year industrial apprenticeship as their initial post-school qualification. A feature of the system is the low wage paid to apprentices while they are undergoing training (but also producing output), which in part compensates companies for their expenditures on apprentice training.

Apprenticeships might spend short periods with other firms as part of their programme. Examinations cover both theoretical and practical aspects of the apprentice's work and both must be passed in order to receive a completion certificate (Facharbeiterbrief). The latter is a valuable possession, acting as a passport to well paid work and responsible positions. Also the fact that the German system is standardised means that all employers know *precisely* what a person with a Facharbeiterbrief is able to do, creating thereby a national market for people with these qualifications. Two years after the Facharbeiterbrief has been acquired, a worker can undertake further (examined and certified) courses lasting 2–3 years in order to become a Meister and qualify for higher-level technical occupations. Administrative and organisational skills are taught in the Meister programme. In practice few people sit for higher qualifications until they are about 30 years of age. Possession of higher vocational qualifications can act as a passport to a managerial job.

Vocational education generally

Germany has a long tradition of technical education, stretching back to the medieval guild system. Many vocational education and training (VET) options are available to young (and not so young) people and a variety of vocational schools cater for basic intermediate and higher level vocational studies. Importantly, there is a *legal obligation* on German employers (a) to release young workers for technical education, and (b) to grant up to one week's training leave per year to any employee demanding the facility. Also there is legislation guaranteeing equality of financial support for students in vocational and 'academic' education.

Vocational schools and colleges are financed by the local governments of the German regions (Laender). On-the-job training is organised jointly by employers (who pay for it), unions and central government. It is supervised and appraised by local Chambers of Commerce and Industry. The implementation of training programmes within a company is subject to control and discussion by its works council (*see* 24:3). Recipients of vocational education are highly regarded in German society; there does not exist the perception that vocational subjects are somehow inferior to non-vocational studies (an affliction prevalent in certain other EU countries). VET is standardised and formal, with attention being paid to theoretical as well as practical aspects. There is a structured hierarchy of vocational qualifications, with advanced work building on lower-level competencies (as opposed to teaching vocational skills as self-contained units). High-level vocational education is available in universities, technical universities, and technical institutes.

Management training

German managers are noted for their immobility between companies. Internal promotion is the norm and few executives change employers more than a couple of times during their careers. Headhunting is discouraged by the German authorities, although it is not explicitly unlawful.

Not surprisingly, therefore, most management training and development is conducted in-house, although external courses are sometimes used by smaller companies. Programmes tend to be company or industry specific, with more general aspects of management (decision making, employee selection and appraisal, time management, human relations, etc.) being dealt with in higher-level management courses. In-company foreign language courses are common. It is unusual for courses to last longer than a couple of weeks. All German companies have to belong to Chambers of Commerce, which use part of the membership fees they receive to provide management training courses. Chambers of Commerce sometimes possess their own training centres. Also, employers' associations and local government education authorities of certain Laender have established 'management academies' that provide in-house company-specific management development programmes. Courses given by these academies cover such topics as sales management, presentation techniques, and human and industrial relations.

On average a third of executive board members (see 2:17) in German public companies (AGs) have doctorates; 50 per cent for the country's top 100 businesses.

11. Greece

Greeks complete nine years of compulsory basic education, thereafter opting either to seek a job or to continue their studies in a 'general' (academic), comprehensive, or technical school. The general school course lasts three years (or four years part time), leading to a leaving certificate the acquisition of which qualifies the holder to sit for the Greek higher education entrance examination. Technical schools prepare students for specific occupations. Courses last two years full time; three years part time.

Three-year apprenticeships are available from the state employment service. They are based in state-run Vocational Training Centres, where students spend all their first year. Thereafter, apprentices mix attendance at college with practical work experience. The state pays for apprentices' meals and lodging; employers pay apprentices a low wage (50 per cent of the national permitted minimum) during their periods of work experience.

Although Greece has a number of universities and technical institutions many Greek students opt to study abroad, especially in Britain and the United

States. Greece is one of the less-developed EU countries and this is reflected in the limited extent of its higher education system although this is improving annually. There is a big demand for English language business courses. Undergraduate degrees at Greek universities last a minimum of four years. Technical colleges offer three or four years sub-degree level courses which include eight months of compulsory work experience.

A system of national vocational qualifications was introduced in 1993 based on Vocational Training Institutes, which can be public or private sector institutions. National vocational qualifications are at three levels, depending on the relevant study period. Additionally, the state finances a plethora of short courses. Employees under 25 years of age are entitled to take up to 14 days a year leave in order to sit examinations. Grants towards the cost of this are available from the state authorities.

Greek firms are required to pay a training levy of 0.45 per cent of their total wage costs. The money is collected through the state social insurance system and the resulting fund administered by a committee consisting of trade union and employer's association representatives.

12. Ireland

Ireland's young are well-educated, enterprising, energetic, and prone to emigrate! About 30,000 Irish workers have left the Republic annually over recent years – a large number for a country with a work force of only 1.3 million. Arguably the need to emigrate creates incentives for young Irish people to do well in education and acquire saleable educational qualifications.

Secondary education (which is compulsory to the age of 15) occurs in state comprehensive or private church-owned schools. Those who stay at school beyond the age of 15 take a School Leaving Certificate at age 18. Students' performance in this determines whether they may progress to higher education. Three-year degree programmes are available in universities and in certain technical institutions.

An Act of 1987 empowers the Irish government to impose training levies on firms in particular industries if it believes this to be appropriate. The 1987 Act also set up a state agency to oversee and accredit company apprenticeship programmes. Completion of an accredited apprenticeship leads to the award of a nationally recognised Craft Certificate. The state bears the cost of the periods that apprentices spend at college, financed in part by 0.25 per cent levy on the payrolls of all Irish industrial companies. General vocational education is available *via* one-year full-time courses in technical colleges. A variety of special training opportunities are offered to the long-term unemployed.

Management training occurs predominantly in-house within large multinational firms. Forty per cent of the country's non-agricultural workforce is employed in about 900 foreign-owned companies, the aggregate turnover of which is half the turnover for all Irish businesses.

13. Italy

Secondary education in schools is compulsory until the age of 14. State schools are run on a comprehensive basis. Students who continue in education beyond 14 (and nearly 95 per cent do so) are streamed into academic, scientific and technical programmes. The latter lasts for four years; the others for five years.

Large numbers of young Italians begin a university course (including about three quarters of each year's high school graduates), but more than two thirds drop out subsequently. A problem for Italian industry is that the numbers of science and engineering graduates are low compared with litera-ture (which accounts for a fifth of all Italian graduates), medicine and the arts. Vocational training is controlled and organised by the Italian Ministry of Labour, and firms offering in-house vocational courses can claim large public subsidies. Educational leave is available to Italian workers covered by a wide-ranging wage agreement. Also, a statute of 1970 gave Italian workers employed by firms with more than 15 people the right to have their working hours scheduled to enable them to attend classes and examinations. Paid leave is obligatory for employees sitting examinations.

Apprenticeships are not a feature of the Italian training scene, except (to a limited extent) in craft industries. A craft apprenticeship lasts five years and is supposed to involve eight hours a week classroom instruction.

Management training occurs in-company in large organisations; smaller firms tend not to bother with such activities. This means that there is perhaps less management training in Italy than in comparable industrial countries, since about 60 per cent of all Italian workers work in small firms that employ fewer than 100 people.

The family tradition of Italian business has led, perhaps, to paternalistic approaches to management, with flexible organisation structures and a strong 'cult of the personality' in many firms.

14. Luxembourg

As Luxembourg is such a small country, its basic education system seeks mainly to prepare students for advanced study in institutions based in surrounding countries. There is just one university and one technical college.

Not surprisingly in a tiny nation, business leaders, bankers, government ministers and senior civil servants often know each other well, were educated together and mix freely. Organisations are formal and hierarchical. Also there is a strong internationalist ethic, due in part to the large numbers of foreigners working in the country.

15. Netherlands

The Netherlands has a comprehensive and meritocratic education system. All primary and secondary education is financed by the government, even though about 70 per cent of all Dutch schools are privately managed (often by religious foundations). Secondary education is compulsory until the age of 16. Students who leave at 16 are compelled to undertake part-time vocational training for at least one day per week for a further two years. Children are tested at age 12 and recommended for grammar school or general or vocational educational establishments. Parents are free to ignore the recommendation and send their offspring to any one of the three streams, although there are compulsory end-of-year examinations which, if failed twice (students may repeat a year), result in a compulsory move to the next lowest stream.

Entry to one of the country's nine conventional or three technical universities is automatically available to anyone passing the appropriate (grammar) school examinations. Around 15 per cent of school-leavers go into higher vocational training (hoger beroepsondewijs) and complete a three-year course, normally including a six-month industrial placement.

Apprenticeships are available, and are regulated by statute. A substantial part of the first two years of an apprenticeship *must* be spent at an accredited training institution. The state has set up and finances a number of industry-specific committees responsible for co-ordinating apprentice training, monitoring standards, and setting examinations. As in Germany (see above), older people sometimes undertake industrial apprenticeships as an extra qualification.

Dutch managers invariably speak two or three languages, enabling them quickly to pick up fresh ideas from other countries. The majority of Dutch executives have high-level educational qualifications, typically in vocational subjects. Management training tends to occur in-house and, compared to other industrially advanced countries, there is relatively little executive mobility between companies. Immobility is encouraged by the high company-specific pension benefits frequently available to long-serving managers in Dutch enterprises. Dutch managers tend to adopt more informal styles than (say) their German, French or UK counterparts, due perhaps to the acceptance of change associated with international perspectives. They are noted also for their egalitarian attitudes and indifference to status differentials. Internal company communications systems are perhaps more open than in surrounding countries, with less hierarchical organisation structures – reflecting perhaps the country's democratic traditions.

16. Portugal

Secondary education is compulsory until the age of 15. Students follow a common and broadly based curriculum until that age, thereafter entering the labour market or beginning a three-year academic or vocational course. Vocational programmes can be completed at school or in a special training college. Access to higher education is available to graduates of vocational courses on the same basis as students who attain 'academic' school leaving qualifications. Portugal has 14 universities and over 50 higher education technical training institutions. University degree courses last four to six years. Non-university degrees can be obtained in three years. There is easy transfer between university and non-university institutions. A quarter of Portuguese undergraduates study scientific subjects.

Portugal has not in the past possessed a coherent post-school vocational training system but, at the time of writing, the government of the country is trying to introduce one as quickly as possible. New training centres are to be set up and official course validation and certification procedures implemented. Currently the only state provision of post-school vocational training consists of:

(a) Twenty technical training establishments offering six to 12 month courses for literate students aged 18 or more but who do not possess formal qualifications

(b) Twenty-seven state-funded industry-specific training centres

(c) Grants to companies covering 75 per cent of the running costs of training facilities, plus low interest loans of 50 per cent of the cost of premises and equipment.

Employees who attend vocational further education courses are statutorily entitled to paid leave in order to sit examinations.

Apprenticeship training is co-ordinated by the Portuguese Ministry of Employment, which contributes to apprentices' wages and pays their travel and subsistence expenses. Schemes last from one to four years. Additionally there exist one or two year pre-apprenticeship courses for people whose basic educational qualifications are not adequate to begin a full apprenticeship.

In the past there has been very little management education or training in this country, arguably because of the dominance of small firms in the Portuguese economy and family traditions leading to paternalistic management styles with loose organisation structures and a heavy emphasis on control through personal charisma. Today however there exists a state-funded management training scheme which offers nine to 12 month college-based programmes that include a company placement. Trainees are paid a (low) basic wage by the companies to which they are attached during work experience periods. If the employing company then offers the trainee a permanent job the firm receives a (substantial) cash grant from the government. The state pays the trainee's expenses while he or she is at college.

17. Spain

All Spanish youngsters pursue a common course of study (the EGB) until the age of 14, when they split into academic and vocational streams for the next three years of their schooling. Secondary education is compulsory to the age of 16. School students must pass their end-of-year examinations in order to progress to the next year of study. Otherwise they have to repeat the year. This happens to about one in five Spanish pupils at some time during their schooling, especially those in the vocational stream.

The country has around 400 university-level institutions, although large numbers of Spanish students today seek higher education courses in other EU nations. Spanish university fees are high and the range of courses available is limited. Students may enter Spanish universities on the basis of vocational qualifications. Undergraduate degrees can be completed in three years. Spain has a number of business schools, many offering MBA type qualifications. Note however that an extremely high proportion of Spanish undergraduates (nearly 50 per cent) study law, social sciences and the humanities; with relatively few (15 per cent) graduating in science or engineering. This is causing much concern to the Spanish authorities, as is the high drop-out rate prevalent on university courses.

The 1939–1975 dictatorship not only isolated Spain from the Western commercial world; it also left the incoming democratic government with one of the least well-educated workforces in Europe. In particular, the huge expansion in economic activity resulting from Spain's accession to the EU has led to shortages of trained and qualified personnel at all levels of management. Successive Spanish governments have sought to tackle these problems; notably *via* a 1985 law on University Reform plus a 1985 statute that guaranteed the right to basic education. Consequently, there have been big increases in the numbers of skilled workers and well educated administrative managers, although the country has yet to catch up with the majority of EU members in this respect.

The Spanish Ministry of Education and Science pays subsidies to any firm that provides accredited training to young workers under the age of 20. Schemes last from three months to three years. Between a quarter and a half of the trainee's time must be spent receiving instruction rather than simply completing a job. The Ministry also finances a variety of special training programmes for unemployed workers. Employees undertaking approved training courses are legally entitled to unpaid time off work to attend examinations and to insist that their working hours be modified to enable them to attend college.

Much of the country's management training occurs in-house within large multi-national enterprises. Spain has attracted large amounts of foreign investment over the last quarter century, much of it in high technology sectors. Foreign multi-nationals brought with them modern approaches to organisational structuring, based on decentralisation, management by objectives, etc.; contrasting sharply with the bureaucratic traditions of older Spanish companies.

18. Sweden

Sweden has a comprehensive basic education system which is compulsory for nine years, starting at the age of six or seven years. The nine-year period is split into three 3-year stages: junior, intermediate and senior. After comprehensive school a student may enter an 'integrated upper secondary school' (gymnasieskolan) the courses at which last for three years and are organised into 16 government-specified study programmes. The latter comprise two university entrance courses and 14 vocational schemes. Sweden has 12 universities, the oldest of which date back to the 15th century. In 1995 legislation was introduced to transfer responsibility for course provision, admission regulations, entrance requirements, etc., from central government to individual institutions. In addition to the universities, Sweden has 25 university colleges and teacher training institutes. Most of the country's higher education institutions offer a wide range of undergraduate and post-graduate programmes. First degree courses usually last three or four years and comprise one of two types of qualification: 'professional' or 'non-professional'. A professional degree is awarded following completion of a programme designed for a career in a specific area such as engineering, medicine or teaching. All Swedish degrees are awarded under a points system. A one year (40 week) course usually earns around 40 points. To qualify for an undergraduate degree it is normally necessary to accumulate 120–160 points. Degrees are divided into three levels depending on the number of points awarded. University colleges (the majority of which were founded in the 1970s) offer a limited number of specialised undergraduate programmes.

Since the early 1980s the Swedish government has been anxious to encour-age research and technical development and, in line with this objective, has substantially increased its spending on university research programmes. Postgraduate training is offered at seven universities and at specialised research institutions. The normal qualification awarded to persons who successfully complete a postgraduate programme is the doctorate, which takes a minimum of 4 years. Additionally, a number of universities offer 'licentiate' degrees based on shorter periods of research training (normally between two and two and a half years). The licentiate can be complemented at a later date by further studies leading to the award of a doctor's degree. State funding for research is concentrated on natural sciences and technology. Special emphasis is placed on international co-operation in research.

Swedish adult education has expanded continuously since the 1960s, with one in three adults now enrolled on some kind of educational programme. Adult education is available through courses run by employers, 'folk high schools', government agencies or one of the eleven national adult education associations (which receive subsidies from central and local government). Sweden has 128 folk high schools, mostly residential and catering primarily for young adults. They are owned by private organisations or municipal authorities and have roots going back to the 19th century. The majority of programmes at folk high schools involve short courses lasting just a few days or a couple of weeks, although some take a full term to complete. There is extensive on-the-job training in Sweden provided by employers under government auspices. Typically, firms purchase customised training pack-ages from the public education system.

19. United Kingdom

According to a number of surveys, British companies spend far less on training than French and German firms. Four in five UK manual and three in five non-manual employees have received no training whatsoever since leaving school. Less than 25 per cent of British senior managers possess university degrees, compared to 60 to 65 per cent in France and Germany. A third of a sample of British companies surveyed by C. Handy and others confessed to having no training budget. High-level vocational training in Britain, moreover, has suffered badly through the decline in the country's manufacturing base, and especially during the deep recessions of the early 1980s and 1990s. Today, very few genuine apprenticeship schemes operate within British companies.

UK vocational training is fragmented and, many argue, unable to meet the demands of rapid technological change. Major problems have included the lack of meaningful standardised certification in many occupational areas, absence of liaison and co-ordination among training providers, and the short periods that individuals spend on courses. The British approach leaves industrial training to market forces, without any legal requirements compelling companies to train their employees. British vocational training tends to be firm or industry specific, hence tying the individual to a particular firm or occupation. The British system has also been criticised for focusing on skills, occupations and industries without a future and for being inflexible and generally resistant to change. Weaknesses in the system prompted the British government to introduce in the late 1980s a new framework for vocational education based on National Vocational Qualifications (NVQs), intended to rationalise and consolidate the system, determine national standards of occupational competence, and validate vocational qualifications. NVQs are discussed in 21:**14**.

General education

The UK system is largely comprehensive, although the private sector (accounting for about ten per cent of all school students) is extremely influential and provides a disproportionately high proportion of entrants to higher education. British universities and other higher education institutions attract large numbers of overseas students, including a rapidly increasing intake from other EU countries. Foreign students are attracted by (i) the desire to improve their English (the universal language of business and technology) while acquiring useful skills, (ii) the wide range of courses available in British institutions, and (iii) low fees in comparison with other EU nations. At lower levels however the British educational system has experienced a number of serious problems, including:

(a) A smaller proportion of students entering higher education than in leading competitor nations. In 1995 less than a quarter of British 18 years olds began an HE course, compared with nearly 40 per cent in France and about

30 per cent in Germany, Italy and the Netherlands. (Note however that the student drop-out rate is much lower in the UK than in many other European countries.)

(b) Lower levels of achievement, on average, in mathematics and science than in other major industrial countries (especially Germany, France, Japan and the USA).

(c) Severe teacher shortages in critical subject areas, notably mathematics and science.

(d) Weaknesses in basic literacy and numeracy among a substantial number of school-leavers. Tests conducted on entrants to the UK Youth Training Scheme (a government programme set up to provide vocational training and work experience for unemployed young people) in the late 80s revealed that a quarter of trainees had difficulty with elementary arithmetic and nearly a fifth were persistently unable to spell.

Management education

British approaches to management have their philosophical origins in United States business practices, and involve a heavy emphasis on the interpersonal skills aspects of company administration. Short courses are popular, and a number of very large UK companies have their own management training centres. It is probably the case, however, that managers in smaller enterprises receive fewer days of training annually than their counterparts in France or Germany.

Business studies is an extremely popular subject in British universities and colleges, and large numbers of students prepare for accountancy and other professional qualifications on a part-time basis. Training for the professions has a long and prestigious history in this country, and large numbers of young people take this particular route to a management career. The popularity of professional qualifications is due perhaps to:

(a) their practical orientation

(b) the ability of a professionally qualified person to make an *immediate* contribution to the work of a firm, without need for extensive further training

(c) the fact that individuals 'learn while they earn', hence ensuring that they have relevant work experience by the time they qualify

(d) their widespread recognition among employers, making a professional qualification an 'entry ticket' to well paid and interesting jobs.

Arguably, too high a premium has in the past been placed on 'gifted amateurism' and the ability to muddle through in chaotic situations. Competition arising from the country's involvement with the Single Market is changing this, however, and the country's increasing dependence on free EU trade is making it potentially adaptive and receptive to new ideas. Note for example the ease with which Japanese companies have been able to inject new business cultures and working methods into their UK operations.

Progress test 23

1. What are the main differences in the education and training systems of EU nations?
2. List the consequences for business management of national differences in management training systems.
3. What are the likely consequences of an aging European workforce?
4. How does the German apprenticeship system operate?
5. What are the main criticisms of the French education system?

24

EMPLOYEE RELATIONS IN WEST EUROPEAN NATIONS

INTRODUCTION

1. National differences

The essential difference between employee relations systems in Britain and in other West European countries is that, whereas in the UK collective agreements are binding 'in honour only', in most European nations they are *legally binding* so that workers or employers who break a collective agreement can be sued for damages by the other side. And there are many other significant disparities in employee relations laws and practices among European states, particularly in relation to the extent and nature of worker representation in management decisions, the role of trade unions, and methods for resolving disputes. Note moreover that not only might collective agreements be legally binding in Continental states, but it could also be the case that national collective agreements automatically extend to and legally bind other firms and workers who were not party to the agreement. Thus an agreement could cover the bulk of the workforce even though trade union membership is minimal in the industry or country concerned. The major differences in national laws on collective agreements and related matters in the European Union are shown in Table 24.1 (pp. 347-49).

2. Trade unions

The position concerning trade unions in each European country is the outcome of complex and specific historical, cultural, political, economic and (sometimes) religious factors. Union density (i.e. the proportion of the workforce belonging to a union) in various EU nations is shown in Table 24.2 (pp. 350-52). Overall, it is generally true to conclude that unionisation is today much less important in West European countries than in the past, except for Denmark and the Scandinavian nations of Norway and Sweden (where union membership has risen in recent years). (Note however that Scandinavian unions are involved in the distribution of social security benefits; so that workers in these countries have a powerful inducement to join trade unions.) Aggregate union membership has declined especially sharply in Ireland and the UK. Reasons for the decline of union membership in the EU include high unemployment and the recessions that have occurred in all states plus, it seems, a fundamental change in social *attitudes* towards trade unions. Table 24.2 outlines the main trade union groupings in each EU state. It also gives the names of the major EU employers' associations and other key information on industrial relations. Note the wide range of restrictions on the right to strike, and that secret ballots prior to calling a strike, compulsory arbitration and cooling-off periods may also be necessary. Lockouts and/or the dismissal of strikers may or may not be lawful.

Tripartite industrial relations bodies exist in the majority of EU nations. 'Tripartism' means the bringing together of the government, major national trade union organisations and employers' associations in order to establish mutually acceptable frameworks for the conduct of wage and other negotiations, possibly to conclude collective agreements applicable to a wide range of major industries, and to resolve national labour disputes. In Belgium, the Netherlands, and Portugal, tripartite bodies have a statutory position.

The right to strike is written into the Constitutions of 12 of the 15 EU states (Ireland, Britain and Denmark being the exceptions). In most years labour disputes account for (considerably) less than one per cent of all time lost to European industry. Sickness and accidents are responsible for a quarter of all time off; maternity leave and bad weather account for three and a half per cent each.

EMPLOYEE PARTICIPATION

Employee participation in management decisions is discussed in Chapter 2. The legal rights of employee representatives are extensive in some states. In Germany and the Netherlands for instance they can apply to Courts to prevent or delay certain important management decisions. Table 24.3 (pp. 353-54) gives details of employee representation on company boards of directors in countries where this is required.

3. Works councils

Information concerning the establishment, composition, rights and duties of compulsory works councils in countries which impose legal obligations above those required by the EU Directive (*see* **4**) is provided in Table 24.4. (pp. 355-57). Note from the table the large differences in the number of workers a firm needs to employ before it becomes necessary to set up a works council, and the widely differing extents of *(i)* the issues on which the council must (by law) be consulted, and *(ii)* the council's statutory decision-making powers. It can be seen that, very often, councils have a statutory right to receive and discuss large amounts of important management information regarding the work of the firm; including financial structures and plans, new investments, acquisitions, mergers and divestments, working practices, introduction of new technology, and so on. In Belgium, members of the works council are (legally) bound by confidentially and can be prohibited from disclosing sensitive information to other employees. Employers can apply to the Belgian Ministry of Labour to withhold certain information from the works council, although in practice this is extremely rare. German and Portuguese works council members are also statutorily bound by rules on confidentiality.

4. The Works Council Directive 1994

In 1991 the European Commission issued a Draft Directive that would require EU-wide companies with more than 1,000 European employees and at least two establishment in EU states to establish cross-border group or company-wide works councils. Management would be legally obliged to inform and consult these councils on matters relating to job reductions, the introduction of new technology, and changes in working practices. The proposal was vetoed by the British government, but the (then) other eleven EU countries decided to go ahead with the Directive under the procedures established by the Maastricht Protocol agreed in December 1991. Accordingly the UK exercised its opt-out so that when the Directive was finally adopted in 1994 it did not apply within the UK. Note however that British transnational companies employing substantial numbers of workers in subsidiaries in any two of the other 14 EU states (plus Iceland and Norway for this particular piece of legislation) were still bound by the Directive in respect of their operations in these states. Following the change in government in May 1997, UK opposition to the Directive ceased and measures were put in hand to apply the Directive within the United Kingdom.

Under the Directive a cross-frontier group or company-wide works council must have up to 30 members and the right to at least one meeting with management each year. A second meeting can be called in exceptional circumstances. A group or company is not compelled to form such a works council if its employees do not want one, but if the workers express a wish to have a cross-border works council and management fails to respond to a written request for a council to be implemented then legal processes can be invoked to force management to comply with the demand.

The Directive applies to:

(i) *EU scale undertakings*, i.e. those with at least 1,000 employees within the EU and at least 150 employees in at least two member states; *and*
(ii) *EU scale groups of companies*, i.e. groups controlled by a single parent and with at least 1,000 employees within the EU and possessing at least two undertakings in separate EU states each with at least 150 employees.

The nature, composition and *modus operandi* of a European works council must be set out in a written agreement between management and a 'special negotiating body' (SNB) elected by employee representatives and containing at least one worker representative from each EU state in which the company operates. Negotiations must begin within six months following a request from the SNB, and the council must be established within the next three years. The process of forming a works council is activated when the central management receives a written request from at least 100 employees or their representatives in at least two EU states (or Norway and/or Iceland).

The written agreement itself needs to cover the scope and powers of the council, number of members and their durations of office, election procedures, consultation mechanisms, and the resources and assistance to be given to the council by central management (such assistance is required by law to be of 'appropriate' dimensions). Council members are entitled to paid time off work to attend meetings. Consultations must be 'timely', and conducted on the basis of a report prepared by the central management. However, confidential information that if disclosed would 'substantially damage' the business may be withheld from the council. Whether a specific item of information might cause substantial damage is open to legal challenge. All council members are obliged not to disclose confidential information to third parties. The council is entitled to have professional help of its own choosing, paid for by the management. Even if a workforce decides not to have a works council, its representatives must still be informed of any management proposal likely to have serious consequences for employees in more than one EU state; notably in relation to mergers, relocations, planned redundancies and intended closures of establishments, organisation changes, and/or the introduction of substantially new technologies or working methods.

NATIONAL DIFFERENCES

5. Belgium and France

The diversity of national approaches to industrial relations can be illustrated by comparing the systems of a handful of EU countries. *Belgium*, for example, represents the extreme of legal regulation. Here, employee relations are highly developed, sophisticated, and generally stable. There is a National Labour Council comprising representatives of employers' association and trade unions plus an independent chair, which oversees national collective agreements and advises the Minister of Labour on industrial relations issues. Unions are well-established, with the overwhelming majority of Belgian workers in union membership. Each of the country's two main union confederations (Socialist and Christian Democrat) are structured on industry lines. There are negligible restrictions on the rights to strike, picket or take secondary action, except for essential national services. Strikers may be dismissed, provided they receive normal statutory notice or payment in lieu. Strike ballots are not legally necessary, but invariably occur in practice.

France's industrial relations scene is characterised by extensive inter-union rivalry (French workers often choose a union according to political or religious orientation rather than occupational criteria) which, it is sometimes alleged, weakens unions in their dealings with managements. French trade unionism developed much later than in Britain. It failed to achieve organisational unity, resulting in the French unions dividing into several political federations. This has impeded their ability to take joint action or (with a number of notable exceptions) to influence national institutions. Employers are often able to choose the set of unions with whom they will negotiate.

6. Germany

Germany has less than 20 major unions, which co-ordinate their policies and tactics centrally *via* the DGB. The DGB itself has a staff of trained permanent officials and a large administrative bureaucracy. The DGB does not finance any political party: it has links with the Social Democratic Party, but also maintains close relations with the right-of-centre Christian Democratic Union. Unions recruit by industry, representing all occupations and grades in the relevant industry. The country has had two union movements. The first emerged in consequence of German industrialisation in the mid-nineteenth century; the second following World War II, when the nation's entire collective bargaining machinery was reconstructed at the insistence of the occupying powers. Post-Second World War German approaches to employee relations have perceived labour and capital as 'social partners' and there is much cooperation (legally enforced in some cases) between the two sides. Plant-level negotiations occur through a Works Council. Agreements on wages and conditions emerging from these negotiations have the force of law.

Over 80 per cent of employee representatives on works councils are also union representatives, so that management/union relations are *implicitly* considered at works council meetings. Works councils may take issues to the local Labour Court for compulsory arbitration, but *cannot* call strikes. Apprentices' interests are represented in large organisations by a special body (Jugendvertretung) which reports direct to the enterprise's works council.

Several legal restrictions apply to a German union's ability to take industrial action. A strike is lawful *only* if all other means for resolving the dispute have been attempted and proved unsuccessful. Workers have to be balloted and a substantial majority (normally 75 per cent, otherwise according to the written constitution of the union) in favour of the strike obtained. Political strikes (i.e. strikes not related to issues conventionally determined through collective bargaining) are illegal, as are those which seek to damage 'common social welfare'. Once a deal has been concluded it is *legally binding* for the specified duration of the agreement, so that strikes within this period which attempt to overturn the deal are unlawful *per se*.

Advantages claimed for the German system are as follows.

(a) Employers typically deal with only one union, thus expediting the process of collective bargaining.

(b) There are numerous mechanisms to help settle disputes prior to industrial action.

(c) The formality of the system and the large number of legal rules means that situations are clear and that both sides to a dispute are fully aware of what actions are permitted.

(d) Two-way communication between management and labour creates mutual trust, leading to lasting agreements.

It has been argued that, through having problems dealt with *via* Works Councils and co-determination (i.e. the name given to the German system for co-decision-making *via* works councils and employee representation on supervisory boards), the German system favours employers by sidestepping and possibly undermining trade unions, thus preventing them from mobilising workers for head-on confrontations with management. The national strikes of 1992, however, suggest that this need not be true.

Germany has been the main protagonist of the proposition that employee participation in the management of European Companies (SEs) be made compulsory. This results perhaps from government sensitivity to the fact that certain large German businesses are known to oppose the co-determination system legally imposed on them. A European Company statute *without* worker representation on supervisory boards would provide German managements with the option of reconstituting their firms as European Companies which did not have to apply co-determination.

7. Austria

Austrian industrial relations are characterised by a close relationship (referred to as The Social Partnership) between government, business associations, and the Austrian Trade Union Federation. There is much legislation on terms of employment and working conditions, and on the procedures to be followed for settling industrial disputes. Every Austrian business with five or more employees must have a works council elected by the workforce using proportional representation. The works council is legally entitled to be consulted and informed on *all* matters concerning employees, and to veto management proposals relating to performance-related pay or to demotions. Additionally, the works council is empowered to conclude plant-level pay agreements. One third of the seats on the Supervisory Board of an Austrian company are reserved for works council members. Collective agreements are legally binding, and automatically apply to non-unionised employees within enterprises.

A notable feature of Austrian labour law is that collective agreements can only be concluded by firms, trade unions and employers' associations *licensed* for this purpose. To obtain a licence to undertake collective bargaining a trade union must be independent of employing companies. A state arbitration service is available. About 60 per cent of the male Austrian labour force and 35 per cent of all female workers belong to a trade union. However, all public sector and over 90 per cent of all private sector employees are covered by collective agreements. To date the Austrian industrial relations system has operated with a high degree of harmony between employers and unions, and strikes are very unusual.

8. Scandinavia

The *Finnish* workforce is highly unionised, with eight in ten employees belonging to an independent trade union. Note how the Finnish trade unions are partly responsible for the payment of social welfare benefits to members, creating a big incentive for workers to join trade unions. (This is also the case in Norway and Sweden, though to a lesser extent.) Finland has experienced a significantly higher rate of strikes than other West European countries since the early 1970s. There are four national trade union federations, each representing member unions in specific industry sectors. Three large employers' associations operate: for manufacturing and transport, commerce and services, and the public sector respectively. Over three quarters of all Finnish employees work for firms that are attached to an employers' association. Collective bargaining is highly centralised; with the government, union and employers' associations negotiating package deals on an annual basis. Firms with more than 150 employees must have worker directors.

Swedish approaches to industrial relations, based on compromise, voluntary self-regulation and highly centralised collective bargaining, attracted a great deal of attention for many years – resulting as they did in a stable and strike-free system. More recently however a number of pressures (notably a big increase in unemployment) have led to (*i*) increased legislation in the industrial relations field, (*ii*) decentralised bargaining, and (*iii*) state intervention in the settlement of industrial disputes.

Union density is among the highest in the world, with around 85 per cent of manual and 80 per cent of all white collar workers belonging to a trade union. There is a single dominant Swedish Employers' Federation, and a number of national union blocs. The largest union confederation is the Swedish Federation of Trade Unions, which recruits only private sector workers. Additionally there is a (private sector) Federation of Salaried Employees plus two public sector and two local government union federations.

Swedish law compels firms to inform employees of important plans and to discuss these with trade unions (although management retains the ultimate right to take decisions). Any company with more than 25 employees must appoint two trade union representatives to its board of directors. Also in Sweden there is compulsory employee representation on the boards of central and regional government agencies concerned with labour matters. Worker directors may not become involved in collective bargaining or negotiations to settle industrial disputes, and do not receive remuneration (other than expenses) for being a director. Swedish law offers a high level of security of employment to workers. In particular:

(a) Workers may not be dismissed without 'objective reason' (which cannot include illness or mental or physical handicap).

(b) Selection for redundancy must normally proceed on a 'last-in first-out' basis.

(c) Workers who believe they are being unfairly dismissed may remain at work until a court has heard their appeals.

Progress test 24

1. What is the main difference between the employee relations systems of the UK and the majority of other West European countries?
2. Define tripartism.
3. Give four examples of matters about which works councils in certain continental European countries have to be consulted.
4. What are the main characteristics of the French trade union situation?
5. Why is trade union density higher in Scandinavia than in the rest of Western Europe?
6. Examine the view that the completion of the Single Market will necessarily lead to a harmonisation of employee relations policies among firms throughout the European Union.

Table 24.1 Collective agreements

	Austria	Belgium	Denmark	Finland	France
Is there a national labour / management consultative body?	Yes, the Federal Chamber of Labour	Yes, the Conseil National du Travail	Yes, the Økonomiske Råd	No	Yes, the National Collective Bargaining Board
Are collective agreements legally binding?	Yes	Yes	Yes	Yes	Yes
Do national collective agreements legally bind non-signatories?	Yes, by Ministerial discretion	Yes, at the government's discretion	No, but signatory employers must impose the agreement on all their employees	Yes, by Ministerial discretion	Yes, by Ministerial discretion
Is employee consultation compulsory?	Yes, on Supervisory Boards and through Works Councils	Yes, *via* Works Councils	Yes, *via*, a government backed national agreement between unions and employers' associations	Yes, *via* Works Councils	Yes, *via* Works Councils

Table 24.1 Collective agreements (continued)

	Germany	Greece	Ireland	Italy	Luxembourg
Is there a national labour / management consultative body?	No	Yes, *via* the Ministry of Labour	Yes, the PESP (Programme for Economic and Social Progress)	No	No
Are collective agreements legally binding	Yes	Yes	Yes, but only on participants	Yes	Yes
Do national collective agreements legally bind non-signatories?	Yes, by Ministerial discretion	Yes, by Ministerial discretion provided at least 51% of workers in an industry are already covered	No	Yes, throughout the relevant industry	Yes, by Ministerial discretion
Is employee consultation compulsory?	Yes, on Supervisory Boards and through Works Councils	Yes, *via* Works Councils	Only in the public sector	No	Yes, through worker directors and Works Councils

Table 24.1 Collective agreements (continued)

	Netherlands	Portugal	Spain	Sweden	UK
Is there a national labour / management consultative body?	Yes, the Stichting van de Arbeid	No	No	No	No
Are collective agreements legally binding?	Yes	Yes	Yes	Yes	No
Do national collective agreements legally bind non-signatories?	Yes, by Ministerial discretion	Yes, by Ministerial discretion	Yes, to all firms in the same trade in the local area	Yes, by Ministerial discretion	No
Is employee consultation compulsory?	Yes, through Works Councils	Yes, through Works Councils	Yes, through Works Councils	Yes, through Works Councils	No

Table 24.2 Trade Unions

	Austria	Belgium	Denmark	Finland	France
Main trade union organisations	ÖSTERREICHISCHER GEWERKSCHAFTSBUND – OGB (close ties with Social Democratic Party) OEAAB (Austrian Worker and Employee Union; ties with the Conservative People's Party)	FGTB (Socialist) CSC (Christian Democrat) CGSLB (Liberal	LO (Social Democrat) FTF (White collar) AC (Professional workers)	SAK – Central Organisation of FinnishTrade Unions (covers manufacturing, construction & transport union & public sector workers) TVK – Confederation of Salaried Employees – white collar workers only AKAVA – Confederation of Unions for Academic and Professional Workers in Finland (organised according to educational background) STTK – Confederation of Technical Employees' Organisations in Finland (supervisors and technical specialists)	CGT (left wing) [1] CGT-FO (a break off from the CGT) CFDT (originally a Christian trade union organisation) CFTC (Christian) CGC (Professional workers)
Approximate union density	57.5 per cent	70 per cent	80 per cent	78 per cent	10 per cent
Main employers' association	BWK Bundeskammer der gewerblichen Wirtschaft (Federal Chamber of Business)	FEB (Fédération des Enterprises Belgique)	DA (Dansk Arbejdsgiverforening)	STK (Suomen Tyonantajain Keskusliitto) LTK – Liiketyonantajain Keskusliitto (Commerce and service industries)	CNPF (Conseil Nationale du Patronat Français)
Is there a state conciliation system?	Yes, the ArbVG provides public mediation or arbitration procedures for disputes over the content of collective agreements	Yes, the Bureau de Conciliation run by the Ministry of Labour	Yes, the Conciliation Board run by the Ministry of Labour	Yes, the Arbitration Committee which operates in connection with the central Chamber of Commerce to appoint arbitrators to settle business disputes	Yes, the Regional or National Conciliation Committee
Restrictions on the right to strike	Austrian law does not explicitly cover industrial disputes or internal union affairs	Port workers and certain essential services	A three quarters majority vote and seven days notice is required. Two 14 day cooling off periods may be imposed by the Ministry of Labour. Unofficial strikers can be fined	None	None other than for the police and security services. Compulsory arbitration can be imposed.
Can strikers be dismissed?	There are no legal provisions relating to strikes. Strikers can be dismissed but only in accordance with legal provisions on dismissal in general	Yes, but only after due notice	No	No	No
Are lockouts lawful?	Lockouts are lawful but employers are required to continue to pay salaries throughout the period	Yes	Yes, but only after seven days' notice, and two 14 day delays may be imposed.	Yes	No

Table 24.2 Trade Unions (continued)

	Germany	Greece	Ireland
Main trade union organisations	DGB (non-political but usually supports the Social Democrats) DAG (white collar) CGB (Christian)	GSEE (General confederation of labour)	ICTU (Irish Congress of Trade Unions)
Approximate union density	40 per cent	35 per cent	50 per cent
Main employers' association	BDA (Bundesvereinigung der Deutschen Arbeitgeberbände)	SEB (Federation of Greek Industries) ESE (Commerce and Trade)	FIE (Federation of Irish Employers)
Is there a state conciliation system?	No	Yes, the Ministry of Labour	Yes, the Labour Relations Commission
Restrictions on the right to strike	Notice must be given. A 75 per cent majority vote is required	Twenty-four hours' written notice must be given (four days for workers in essential services). A secret ballot is necessary	Political strikes Strikes to establish a closed shop Secret ballot necessary
Can strikers be dismissed?	No	No	Yes, provided all strikers are dismissed
Are lockouts lawful?	Yes	No	Yes, provided all employees are then reinstated

	Italy	Luxembourg	Netherlands
Main trade union organisations	CGIL (left wing) CISL (Christian Democrat) UIL (Social Democrat)	LCTU (Confederation of Trade Unions)	FNV (Catholic) CNV (Protestant) MHP (White collar)
Approximate union density	40 per cent	60 per cent	30 per cent
Main employers' association	Confindustria	Luxembourg Chamber of Commerce	VNO (Non-denominational Confederation of Dutch Enterprises) NCW (Christian Democrat) KNOV (Small firms) [2]
Is there a state conciliation system?	No	Yes, through the Ministry of the Economy	No
Restrictions on the right to strike	No statutory restriction, but skeleton services must be maintained in essential public industries	Notice must be given. Cooling off periods may be imposed	No statutory restrictions
Can strikers be dismissed?	No	No	No
Are lockouts lawful?	Yes	Yes	No

Table 24.2 Trade Unions (continued)

	Portugal	Spain	Sweden	UK
Main trade union organisations	CGTP (Left wing) UGT (Socialist)	CCO (Left wing) UGT (Socialist)	LO – Swedish Trade Union Federation (blue collar) SACO – Swedish Confederation of Professional Associations (professional) TCO – Central Government Organisation of Salaried Employees (white collar)	TUC (Trades Union Congress)
Approximate union density	40 per cent	15 per cent	81 per cent	35 per cent
Main employers' association	CIP (Industry) CCP (Trade and Commerce)	CEOE (Confederation of Spanish Employers) CEPYME (small businesses)	SAF (Svenska Arbetsgivareforeningen)	CBI (Confederation of British Industry)
Is there a state conciliation system?	Yes, *via* the Ministry of Labour	No	Yes, the Labour court (Arbetsdomstolen)	Yes, the Advisory, Conciliation and Arbitration Service
Restrictions on the right to strike	Strikes can only be called by trade unions or workers representing at least 20 per cent of the firm's employees. Two days' notice must be given. Five days for essential services.	Five days' notice must be given (ten days in the public sector) Workplace occupations are illegal Go slows are illegal	A strike or lockout is permissable only if the court finds that the matter is not covered by the current contract, and even then a week's notice must be given	Secondary actions Strikes in support of a closed shop Strikes called without a ballot of union members
Can strikers be dismissed?	No	No	Dismissal is possible if workers participate in illegal strikes	Yes, but only if all strikers are dismissed
Are lockouts lawful?	No	Yes	A strike or lockout is permissable only if the court finds that the matter is not covered by the current contract, and even then a week's notice must be given	Yes

NOTES

[1] The term 'left wing' is used to describe union groupings which prior to the events of 1991 had predominantly Communist affiliations.
[2] Five multinationals, Philips, Unilever, Shell, Akzo and DSM employ a fifth of the Dutch labour force.

Table 24.3 Employee representation on company boards

	Austria	Denmark	France	Germany
Type of board	Compulsory employee representation on Supervisory Boards	Compulsory employee representation on Supervisory or any other type of Board	Voluntary arrangements are possible, which are then backed by law	Compulsory employee representation on Supervisory Boards
Eligibility criteria	AGs and limited liability companies (GmbHs) with more than 300 workers (unless the GmbH is a subsidiary of a joint stock company that already has labour representation, in which case the threshold for the subsidiary is raised to 500 workers)	All firms employing more than 35 workers	None specified	AGs and any business employing more than 500 workers
Number of employee representatives	One third of the Board's seats is delegated from the Works Council	Between two and half the number of ' shareholders representatives	Four (or five in a quoted company) or one third of the total size of the board	Between one third and one half of the Board depending on the size of the company. The casting vote lies with the chair in the latter situation
Period of office	Five years maximum but reappointment is possible	4 years	6 years	No statutory requirement
Method of appointment	Chosen by Works Council	Direct election	Direct election	Direct election

Table 24.3 Employee representation on company boards (continued)

	Luxembourg	Netherlands	Sweden
Type of board	Compulsory employee representation on the main board	Compulsory employee representation on Supervisory Boards	Compulsory representation on the main Board of Directors
Eligibility criteria	SAs employing more than 1000 workers	Public companies with more than 100 workers and assets exceeding a certain value	Any company with more than 25 employees must appoint two union representatives to its Board of Directors
Number of employee representatives	One third of the Board	Must contain at least one person nominated by the firm's Works Council but who is not an employee of the enterprise	At least two
Period of office	3 years	Not relevant	Same as any other board member
Method of appointment	Direct election	Not relevant. Works Councils can legally object to any appointment to a Supervisory Board	Appointed by trade union(s)

Table 24.4 Works councils in EU nations

	Austria	Belgium	Denmark	Finland	France
Name *Establishment criteria*	Works Councils Firms with 5 or more employees	Conseils d'enterprise All firms with at least 100 workers	Co-operation committees All firms with at least 35 workers	Works Councils Workplaces with 30 or more people	Comités d'enterprise (1) All firms with at least 50 workers
Composition	Proportional representation (e.g. 4 members for 50–100 employees; 14 for 1,000–1,400	Equal numbers of employee and management representatives	Between two and six members depending on the size of the enterprise. Equal management/labour representation	At least one employee representative	Between two and twenty members with two extra for every 250 workers in firms with more than 1000 employees. Equal management/labour representation
Method of appointment	Direct election by workers in each plant	Secret ballot of all employees	Direct vote of employees	Direct election	Secret ballot on lists proposed by trade unions plus direct election of non-union employees
Term of office *Frequency of meetings (minimum)*	Four years Four times a year	Four years Monthly	Two years Every two months	No restriction None specified	Two years Monthly (fortnightly if a majority of workers so decide)
Range of issues discussed	Rights apply to all matters affecting the establishment's employees. Right to information and a hearing on all changes affecting more than one group subsidiary. Must be given advance notice of planned dismissals and plant closures & of reorganisations or mergers that could affect employment. The Works Council is legally entitled to be consulted and informed on all matters concerning employees, and to veto management proposals relating to performance related pay or demotions.	Financial data; Investment plans; Production levels and prices; Takeovers; Introduction of new technology; Plans likely to affect the workforce; Working methods and organisation; Personnel practices	Training; Implementation of change; Effects of new incentive schemes; Financial prospects	Significant changes of operations affecting the number of employees, working conditions and social conditions, financial position and profitability of the company; Annual personnel plan and statistics on wages and salaries	Health and safety; Redundancy and dismissals; Training; Introduction of new technology; New working methods; Changes in working conditions; Mergers and acquisitions
Right to take decisions	Management decisions are dependent on the Works Council's approval for matters such as the introduction of control systems that affect human dignity, for the introduction of performance related pay, and for internal transfers that downgrade the position of employees within the firm	Internal rules; Criteria for hiring temporary staff; Criteria for selecting workers for redundancy	None	Decisions on the use of funds reserved by the board of directors for employee welfare and the allocation of employer-owned accommodation	Profit sharing agreements; Imposition of a four day working week

Table 24.4 Works councils in EU nations (continued)

	Germany	Greece	Luxembourg
Name Establishment criteria	Betriebsträte All firms with at least five workers	Works Councils All firms with at least 50 workers, or 20 if there is a workplace union	Conseils d'enterprise All firms with at least 150 workers
Composition	Varies according to the size of the enterprise. Employees only.	Between three and seven	Equal numbers of management and employee representatives
Method of appointment	Direct election	Direct election	Secret ballot of all employees
Term of office	Four years	Two years	Three years
Frequency of meetings (minimum)	Monthly	Every two months	Monthly
Range of issues discussed	Health and safety; Working hours and methods; Wage systems; Company structure; Changes in plant or premises; Recruitment practices; Company finance; Redundancy and dismissal; New investments; Mergers and acquisitions	Mergers and acquisitions; Introduction of new technology; Redundancy; Investment and other business plans	Changes in working conditions; Health and safety; Welfare; Personnel policies
Right to take decisions	Changes in working hours; Holiday arrangements; Training; Disciplinary procedures; Recruitment procedures	Internal works and health and safety rules; Scheduling of training	Recruitment and appraisal procedures

Table 24.4 Works councils in EU nations (continued)

	Netherlands	Portugal	Spain
Name	Ondernemingsraad	Commissões de trabalhadores	Comités de empresa
Establishment criteria	All firms employing at least 100 workers or 35 workers doing more than one third of full time hours	No minimum size of firm specified	All firms with at least 50 workers
Composition	Three to 25 depending on the size of the company. Employees only.	Between two and eleven depending on the size of the enterprise	Between five and 75 depending on the number of workers employed
Method of appointment	Secret ballot on lists proposed by trade unions or other employee groups accounting for one third of the workforce	Direct election of candidates endorsed by at least 10 per cent of the work force or 100 persons	Secret ballot
Term of office	Three years	Decided by employees	Four years
Frequency of meetings	Every two months	Monthly	Every two months
Range of issues discussed	Mergers and acquisitions; Plant closures; Redundancy; Recruitment of temporary employees	Internal rules; Working conditions; Job evaluation; Promotion systems; Redundancy; Plant closures	Health and safety; Financial data; Redundancy; Personnel management; Training; Overtime working
Right to take decisions	Working hours; Internal rules; Job evaluation systems; Regulations concerning recruitment, training and appraisal; Grievance procedures	None	None

Note
(1) By law, firms with more than ten employees are required to have 'works delegates' (délégues du personnel) who may or may not be associated with a union. Délégues are elected annually by secret ballot. Their role is to handle individual employee grievances and problems relating to the implementation of collective agreements. 'Works Committees' have been compulsory since 1945 for enterprises employing more than 50 people.

25

EUROPEAN UNION DIMENSIONS OF PERSONNEL MANAGEMENT

FUNDAMENTALS

1. Introduction

British membership of the European Union affects personnel management in several important areas, particularly *vis-à-vis* possibilities for the cross-border recruitment of employees (*see* **2**); new training requirements (*see* **3**); redundancy (*see* **11**); and compulsory employee participation in management decision making.

EU law on matters pertaining to personnel management overrides UK legislation, and comes in three forms: Regulations, Directives and Decisions.

(a) *Regulations* are precise laws that apply immediately and equally in all member states.

(b) *Directives* are edicts which specify a necessary outcome (e.g. to have equal pay for work of equal value completed by men and women) but then allow each EU member to introduce its own specific legislation to achieve the desired objective.

(c) *Decisions* are rulings of the European Court of Justice on test cases, and have the same effect as Regulations.

Additionally, *Draft Directives* are issued. These are proposals of the European Commission, accepted in principle by most EU nations, but not yet implemented in consequence of opposition by one or more EU members.

2. Cross-border recruitment

A major consequence of the Single Market is that EU citizens may freely reside in any EU country of their choice and seek employment in that state. They are entitled to unemployment and retirement benefit in the nation of their employment, and to equal access to public housing and education for their children on a par with local workers. Free mobility of labour makes possible the recruitment of workers from other EU countries, particularly of workers possessing skills and competencies not available locally. This will lead to the following consequences:

(a) Personnel managers will require knowledge of recruitment practices in various EU countries and need to be familiar with:

(*i*) pan-European job advertising media capable of reaching good quality foreign EU workers
(*ii*) levels of pay and conditions of service necessary to attract high calibre Continental applicants
(*iii*) foreign EU educational and other qualifications.

(b) Possibilities for training staff *via* courses held in other EU countries, especially for training in European business practices, European transport and distribution systems, negotiation and tendering procedures in various EU states, etc.

(c) EU-wide headhunting (*see* 15:**5**).

Cross-border recruitment can occur through placing job advertisements in foreign newspapers or trade magazines, personal recommendations from foreign business contacts (such as suppliers, customers or banks), extension of a firm's 'milk-round' to include Continental educational institutions, and by taking foreign EU students for sandwich-course or other work-experience placements.

3. Free movement of workers

The Treaty of Rome does *not* establish an absolute right to freedom of migration for EU citizens, but does guarantee freedom of movement for 'workers' and their families. This is supposed to enable labour to move from high unemployment areas to places where there are labour shortages. Three Directives passed in 1990 extend the right of freedom of movement to (*i*) persons of independent means, (*ii*) retired people, and *(iii)* students undertaking courses in other EU countries. In all areas the individuals involved *must not be economically dependent on the social security system of the host nation.* Hence it is definitely not the situation that a long-term unemployed person can choose to reside in whichever country offers the highest rate of social security benefit. Rather, workers are free to move to another member country in order to accept offers of employment, and thereafter to remain in that country to continue employment.

A 'worker', according to the European Court of Justice, is 'someone who performs services for another during a certain period of time and under the direction of another in return for remuneration' (*Lawrie* v. *Blum* 1987). Part-time as well as full-time work falls within the definition. Self-employed persons are also guaranteed freedom of movement, provided they are economically active. The period allowed a person to look for work in another country has not been specified in any Directive or Regulation, but was set at a minimum of three months by the ECJ in a case heard in 1982 – subject to the individual being able to support him or her self without recourse to public assistance. A number of countries (including the UK) allow six months for job hunting. Once a person has found a job he or she has the right of residence, unless the job is given up voluntarily. Residence permits are issued for renewable five-year periods. When the worker retires he or she has the right to remain in the host country provided the person has reached the normal age of retirement for that nation and has lived there for at least three years, the last one of which must have been spent in employment. If a worker is incapacitated by an industrial disease or accident that entitles the person to a pension, then the right of residency applies regardless of the duration of previous residence. Persons incapacitated by causes other than employment are entitled to remain if they have two years' previous residence.

All residency rights apply to workers' dependants and family members, i.e.

- the spouse and descendants under the age of 21 or descendants over 21 who are dependants; *or*
- dependant parents and grandparents of the worker and spouse.

The family must receive equivalent treatment *vis-à-vis* education, welfare, access to public housing, etc., as natives of the host country. Family rights end when (*i*) the worker loses his or her residence rights, or (*ii*) a person ceases to be a family member (e.g. on divorce or on the marriage of a child). At the time of writing it is unclear whether co-habitees qualify as 'spouses' in all EU countries. A worker's death does not deprive his or her family of the right to residence provided the family has lived in the country for at least two years *or* the worker died from an industrial disease or accident. Social security contributions paid by a worker during employment in one country must be taken into account when calculating benefits receivable in another.

Article 48 of the Treaty of Rome makes it unlawful to discriminate against job applications on the grounds of an EU applicant's nationality, *except* for public sector employment. However, public sector employers are required to justify such discrimination, and if a person from another EU country is given a public sector job then he or she must thereafter be treated in the same manner as local nationals.

The Posted Worker Proposal

A 1995 Draft Directive on the temporary posting of workers seeks to prescribe which country's employment protection rules shall apply to workers temporarily posted from their home base to another EU nation, e.g. from a country with extensive employment protection to one with only the basic rules required by agreed EU Directives. The purpose of the proposal is to prevent the high levels of employment protection currently in force in northern Europe from being undermined *via* the widespread use of sub-contracted labour recruited in nations with poor employment conditions. Under the Draft Directive any employee posted to a foreign country for more than three months is entitled to the protection of all the employment laws of the *host* rather than his or her home country. Hence the posted worker must be given at least the legal minimum wage of the host nation and observe that country's laws on working hours, notice periods, sick leave, etc.

EXPATRIATE MANAGERS

4. Euro-executives

These are multi-lingual managers who feel at home in any European country, are familiar with EU business laws and practices, and regularly move between companies and countries. Qualities of Euro-executives include:

(a) Cultural adaptability, i.e. the ability to blend quickly into the local culture of any EU member nation

(b) Wide-ranging experience of European business management resulting from several changes of jobs and location

(c) Possession of generalist rather than function-specific management competencies

(d) Ability to communicate effectively and to exercise interpersonal management skills

(e) Knowledge of individual EU markets

(f) Selling and negotiating skills, and the ability to conduct hostile negotiations in more than one language

(g) Familiarity with EU product standards

(h) Knowledge of the documentation and procedures attached to cross-border EU marketing, including those needed for transport and distribution across the Union

(i) Willingness and ability to cope with rapid technical, organisational and environmental change

(j) Capacity to get on with fellow workers of different nationalities and to contribute to multinational project teams

(k) Acceptance of a lifestyle involving much foreign travel, frequent relocation and disruptions to normal family routines.

Problems attached to the employment and use of Euro-executives are:

(a) Their high salaries (resulting from their short supply) which create large differentials between Euro-executives and other managers. Euro-executives are hired in consequence of their superior competencies and will demand remuneration packages comparable to those available in other countries. Additionally, they could demand compensation for the high cost of accommodation in prosperous areas (London, for instance), for the cost of sending children to private schools that cater for a particular nationality, and for the loss of a spouse's earnings.

(b) Fitting them into conventional line and staff organisation systems, which might stifle their initiative and creativity.

(c) A high probability of their being headhunted by other firms.

(d) Their lack of intimate knowledge of their employing companies and associated products or of the local economy and local business cultures. Euro-executives might not stay in a country long enough to develop networks of contacts with local business people, banks, ancillary services, etc.

(e) Possible conflicts arising from different approaches to business adopted by Euro-executives compared to locally-recruited managers.

Euro-executives, moreover, could experience significant domestic problems that might reduce their usefulness to employing firms, for example:

(a) Reluctance to accept a fresh assignment in another EU country because the manager's children have only just settled into a local school

(b) Opposition to an intended move from the manager's spouse, who may regard it as interference with his or her own career

(c) Traumas and tribulations attached to regularly moving house and resettling in other cultures

(d) Practical problems connected with finding suitable housing, arranging for pension transfers, tax arrangements, etc.

5. Management of expatriate staff

Another consequence of the completion of the Single Market is the ability of an EU business to set up subsidiaries and operate in any EU state, leading to an increase in the number of expatriate European employees working abroad for significant periods. This creates special problems for human resource management, as follows:

(a) Determining the remuneration package to be offered, taking account of all the extra costs involved (removal and accommodation, school fees for children, etc.) and the need to offer a higher salary to induce people to live in a foreign and unfamiliar country.

(b) Difficulties arising from failure of expatriates to settle-in to their new environment, resulting perhaps from:

(*i*) the expatriate's family not adjusting to local physical and cultural conditions

(*ii*) children not making progress at school

(*iii*) a spouse not finding local employment.

(c) Arranging for the orderly re-absorption of a former expatriate following his or her return to head office.

Note moreover that the use of expatriates in senior positions within the foreign subsidiary necessarily blocks promotion opportunities for locally recruited staff, the most able of whom will thus not remain with the firm for very long. Initial job specifications should detail the company's expectations of performance while abroad, and foreign placements need to be carefully dovetailed into an overall staff development plan, making sure that they do not impede career development. Training is necessary prior to the person being sent abroad; both in the business methods and the local culture of the foreign country concerned. This might include visits to the country, briefings by other employees recently returned from abroad, and the supply of information to family members who will accompany the person to the new location. While abroad, the expatriate might be kept in touch with head office affairs via the appointment of a mentor (typically a senior head office manager) who periodically meets with the expatriate to discuss the latter's progress and what is likely to happen to the expatriate on his or her return. Further training might be needed to prepare the person and his or her family for repatriation.

6. Higher Education Diplomas (HEDs)

These are professional qualifications obtained after at least three years' study and recognised in all EU countries. Their purpose is to facilitate the mobility of professionally-qualified workers within the Union. In the past, member states restricted the right of entry to certain professions (e.g. accountancy, law, medicine) to persons who studied and qualified within their own national territories. HEDs, however, should enable these restrictions to be lifted. The training, examination and other requirements for specific professions are being harmonised across member states, and anyone possessing the appropriate HED will be free to practise his or her profession in any EU country (although some 'topping-up' of qualifications may be required in certain specified circumstances). Accordingly, professionally-qualified people will be able to offer their services on a European scale, possibly resulting in:

(a) Greater competitiveness among professionals, and an increased supply of professionals in job markets offering the highest reward

(b) Recruiting companies advertising for professionally qualified staff throughout the Union

(c) Rapid transmission among professionals in different countries of new ideas and working methods.

Moreover, a number of Directives are in force which compel member states to recognise 'Certificates of Experience' relating to experience obtained in a particular industry in another member state and issued by the authorities of that country.

LEGAL OBLIGATIONS

7. Equal rights for men and women

Perhaps the most significant of EU interventions in the personnel field lies in its continued promotion of (gender) equal opportunities. Article 119 of the Treaty of Rome demanded equal pay for equal work, and this (in principle, at least) is mandatory in all member countries. The Council of Ministers has also directed that there shall be equal pension rights and social security benefits for men and women – this has been interpreted by the Court of Justice to mean equal retirement ages for men and women. Equal opportunity considerations are further discussed in Chapter 26.

8. Health and safety at work

UK health and safety legislation is extensive, detailed, and not normally affected by minimum EU standards because UK requirements are generally above these basic levels. Nevertheless, the number of EU Directives concerning health and safety is increasing rapidly, partly since EU health and safety Directives may be approved by a majority (rather than unanimous) vote of EU members. Already there exist important Directives on visual display units (*see* below), eye protection, the manual lifting of heavy loads, protective equipment, and workplace safety. More are expected soon, possibly increasing the complexity of bureaucratic rules and the costs to employers of complying with health and safety laws.

9. Directive on visual display units

This specifies minimum health and safety requirements for work with display screen equipment. The UK is incorporating the requirements of the Directive *via* amendments to the Health and Safety at Work, etc. Act 1974. Under the Directive, employers must:

(a) Analyse display screen workstations to identify potential hazards and take measures to remedy any health and safety problem discovered

(b) Train employees in the proper use of display screen equipment, inform workers of relevant facts, and consult employee representatives about VDU matters

(c) Plan VDU operators' daily schedules in order to interrupt long periods of screen work and to create changes of activity

(d) Ensure that workstations satisfy the technical requirements of the Directive in relation to screen sizes and luminosity, keyboard design, working environment, etc.

(e) Provide employees with eye and eyesight tests prior to their commencing VDU work and at regular intervals thereafter. Firms must supply special spectacles if employees' normal spectacles are not suitable for display screen jobs.

10. The Framework Directive

In addition to *specific* Directives on health and safety, the Union enacted in 1989 a Framework Directive which contained a statement of *general principles* concerning the protection of employees' health and safety at work. It obliged employers to take 'appropriate measures' to satisfy these principles, according to detailed rules imposed by national authorities. Under the Framework Directive, employers must ensure the prevention of occupational risks, eliminate dangers, inform and consult with workers, and invite the 'balanced participation' of employee representatives when dealing with health and safety matters. The British government considers the UK Health and Safety at Work, etc. Act 1974 to meet the essential requirements of the Framework Directive.

11. Directive on the protection of pregnant employees 1992

Under this Directive, all pregnant workers are protected against dismissal on the grounds of pregnancy (regardless of length of service) and maintain all their contractual employment rights during maternity leave (of which a minimum of 14 weeks must be granted) and associated absences. State financial support is payable during maternity leave. Further entitlements are that:

(a) A pregnant worker may refuse to work at night if a doctor certifies that night working could endanger the woman's health. An alternative day job must be offered for a 16 week period, of which eight weeks must be prior to the expected date of birth of the child.

(b) The employer must assess the risks of particular jobs to the health of pregnant workers and inform the person of any potential hazards. Working conditions must be adjusted to protect the woman's health and safety. The exposure of pregnant employees to certain specified harmful substances and processes is illegal.

365

(c) Pregnant women may take paid time off to attend ante-natal examinations during working hours.

Most of these provisions were already in force in the UK when the Directive was agreed. Alterations in UK law needed to satisfy the Directives' remaining requirements were included in the Trade Union Reform and Employment Rights Bill 1993.

12. Directive on mass redundancies

This 1975 Directive requires that companies give prior notification of group redundancies scheduled for implementation over a period of 30 days or less. Additionally, consultation with employee representatives concerning the mechanics of imposing large-scale redundancies and on measures for avoiding them (e.g. through natural wastage or redeployment) is required. All the provisions of the Directive were embodied in the UK Employment Protection Act 1975, and in the Employment Protection (Consolidation) Act 1978 (which actually go considerably further than the Directive demands).

13. Directive on safeguarding employees' rights following the transfer of ownership of undertakings

The purpose of this Directive is to protect employees' rights and to compel management to inform and consult with employee representatives on the transfer of the ownership of a business. General information about the transfer must be disclosed, plus specific facts regarding its effects (redundancies, for example) on particular groups of workers. Information must be transmitted early enough to permit proper discussions with employee representatives to occur. Employees terms and conditions of service cannot be altered at the time of transfer, and workers may only be declared redundant if this can be objectively justified at the moment the business changes hands. If redundancies are necessary, the new owner *automatically* assumes full responsibility for making statutory redundancy payments to the people involved.

14. Directive on the protection of employees following an employer's insolvency

All the requirements of this 1990 Directive had already been incorporated into domestic UK legislation by the time of its implementation. The Directive obliges the state to pay to workers dismissed in consequence of an employing firm's insolvency all outstanding maternity pay, holiday pay for up to six weeks accumulated over the previous twelve months, up to eight weeks' arrears of wages, amounts due as compensation for redundancy or unfair dismissal, and pay for employees' statutory minimum periods of notice.

366

THE SOCIAL FRAMEWORK

15. The social dimension of the European Single Market

A major requisite of the Treaty of Rome is that EU countries actively seek to raise the living standards of their citizens. Measures adopted to achieve this aim are collectively known as the 'social dimension' policies of the EU. Such policies include:

(a) Job creation and training schemes

(b) Equal opportunities programmes

(c) Provision of information on opportunities for employment and training

(d) Legislation on industrial health and safety.

16. The European Social Charter

In December 1989 the European Council voted by eleven to one (the UK being the dissenting member) for the adoption of a Community Charter of fundamental social rights. The effect of this Social Charter is to establish uniform employment conditions throughout the EU, including matters relating to remuneration, training, living and working conditions, access to company information, consultation, and participation in management decision making. The philosophy underlying the Charter is the belief that the Single Market will only succeed if both sides of industry (employers and labour) are fully involved in creating a new united Europe.

It is important to note that under the Single European Act 1987 (which amended the Treaty of Rome so as to facilitate the rapid completion of the Single Market), any proposal regarding employee rights and interests, and/or the free movement of people, requires unanimous agreement among member nations before it becomes legally binding. Accordingly, acceptance of the Social Charter is *voluntary*, and may not be imposed on an EU state against its wishes, although all 15 EU member nations have now agreed that the Charter be implemented. The Charter itself guarantees individual rights to the following:

(a) Fair remuneration. This involves the specification of rules for establishing a fair wage.

(b) Health, protection and safety at the workplace.

(c) Access to vocational training throughout a person's working life, including the right to retraining.

(d) Freedom of association and collective bargaining, i.e. to belong or not belong to a trade union and for unions to have the right to bargain with employing firms.

(e) Integration into working life of disabled people. The provision of training for the disabled, accessibility to work premises, availability of special transport, and explicit consideration of disabled people during the ergonomic design of equipment.

(f) Information, consultation and worker participation in company decision making, especially in enterprises that operate in more than one EU country.

(g) Freedom of occupation, residence and movement of workers, including equal treatment *vis-à- vis* local taxes and social security entitlements.

(h) Improvement in living and working conditions. This embraces equality of treatment for part-time and temporary workers, controls on night working, and requirements for weekly rest periods and paid holidays.

(i) Social protection, including adequate unemployment and other social security benefits.

(j) Equal treatment of men and women.

(k) Protection of young people, with a minimum working age of 15 years (16 for full-time employment) and a ban on night work for those under 18.

(l) Reasonable living standards for senior citizens, with a specified minimum income underwritten by the state.

17. Advantages and problems of the Social Charter

Implementation of the Charter will create a social partnership between the two sides of industry and will improve social cohesion within the European Union, hence raising living standards and the skill levels of workers and greatly contributing to increased productivity.

Some of the subjects dealt with in the Charter are already covered by existing EU Directives, but the Charter will pull together into a unified whole a variety of currently fragmented employment and social policies.

When adopted, the Charter will be more than a statement of intentions; it will become *legally binding* in all EU states – which will have to legislate to ensure that the rights it embodies are guaranteed within their frontiers. Also, the draft Charter insists that member countries commit themselves to 'mobilise all the resources necessary' to implement its provisions.

Objections to the Social Charter have included:

(a) Some of its requirements violate the 'principle of subsidiarity', i.e. the EU's agreed position that laws be imposed at the EU level *only* if social policy objectives *cannot* be achieved *via* government action within each member state.

(b) Matters pertaining to consultation, employee representation, etc. are perhaps best resolved through *voluntary* collective bargaining between employers and trade unions.

(c) The operating costs of certain businesses will increase following the Charter's implementation, making EU companies uncompetitive compared to companies in Pacific rim countries and the USA.

(d) Application of some of the Charter's provisions will necessitate the creation of large bureaucracies within government departments and much administrative inconvenience within firms.

(e) Intervention and control go against the spirit of free enterprise that supposedly underlies the decision to create a Single European Market.

(f) Currently, social protection is greatest in the more affluent EU states. As laws on social protection are harmonised there could be a tendency to 'harmonise upwards' towards higher (and more expensive) common standards, thus imposing unbearable additional costs on poorer EU countries.

Social dumping

The European Trade Union Confederation (ETUC) has alleged that without the pan-European application of minimum social and employment conditions, 'social dumping' will occur, i.e. that there will be unfair undercutting of the price of labour by certain countries. Absence of a minimum wage, lack of employment protection for part-time and casual labour, no minimum working week, and the general denial of Social Charter benefits enable employers to pay low wages, reduce other employment costs and hence charge lower prices for their outputs. This is seen as a violation of Single Market principles. The counter-argument to the proposition that social dumping leads to the countries involved having a competitive advantage is that a low-wage low-productivity labour-intensive economy is only suitable for the production of certain types of item. In the long term it could lack the high technology skills, education and training systems, and the dynamics needed for sustainable growth. Also, industrial relations problems may be more severe in low-wage countries.

Progress test 25

1. Explain the difference between an EU Regulation and an EU Directive.
2. What are the characteristics of Euro-executives?
3. List the main requirements of the Framework Directive on health and safety in employment.
4. Describe the disadvantages of the European Social Charter.
5. What are the special HRM problems associated with the employment of expatriate staff?
6. What is meant by social dumping?
7. Is the ultimate aim of European integration to create a people's Europe or a business persons' Europe?
8. Outline the main elements of the European Social Charter and discuss its implications for businesses.

26

INTERNATIONAL COMPARISONS OF HUMAN RESOURCES MANAGEMENT PRACTICE

1. Differences in HRM practice

The needs to recruit, motivate, appraise and control employees are common to organisations throughout the world. How HRM is implemented, however, differs substantially from state to state. Major disparities in national HRM practice might be attributable to:

(a) *Cultural factors* including attitudes towards work, perceptions of the relationship between the individual and his or her working group, concepts of justice and fairness *vis-à-vis* employment situations, and the role of wages and other material rewards as a motivating influence. Arguably, cultural considerations are becoming less important as business methods harmonise and as successful business management assumes an increasingly technical aspect independent of the cultures of particular nations.

(b) *Legal frameworks.* Laws and regulations on equal opportunities in employment, dismissal procedures, health and safety at work, the protection afforded to part-time and casual employees, plus many other key elements of the employment relationship vary markedly from country to country.

(c) *National economic situations*, e.g. unemployment levels, rates of economic growth, and the extent of competition in the local market. Intense competition forces companies to apply flexible working practices and constantly to look for fresh HRM techniques that might give the firm a competitive edge.

(d) *Employee relations systems* including the degree of state involvement in employee relations affairs, the extent of the unionisation of the workforce, relationships between trade unions and employing firms, etc.

(e) *State provision of vocational training.* If little state-funded technical and

370

vocational training is available then firms requiring skilled labour need to devote more of their resources to training than in countries with extensive government training programmes.

HUMAN RESOURCES MANAGEMENT IN THE EUROPEAN UNION

Although the European Union imposes much legislation affecting personnel and human resource management (health and safety standards, gender equal opportunities requirements and minimum employee protection measures, for example), national laws and business practices in the HRM field differ significantly between EU countries. Major disparities occur in relation to terms and conditions of employment; the extent of the casualisation of national workforces; the availability of special leave for maternity, career breaks and for compassionate matters; and in recruitment and dismissal procedures. The essential characteristics of EU countries' workforces and the main differences in working conditions are shown in Table 26.1 (pp. 373-77). Here it will be seen that there are big differences in the degrees of protection afforded to employees.

2. Recruitment and dismissal

Laws on recruitment differ from state to state. In France and Belgium for instance it is illegal to use press advertisements for job vacancies for implicit corporate image advertising (offering jobs that in reality do not exist). Additionally, French job advertisements cannot lawfully specify an upper age limit for applicants for the vacant post. Small fines may be imposed on advertisers ignoring this legislation. Application forms for French jobs cannot lawfully include questions concerning union membership, religion, politics, or family situation.

German firms' selection methods must be approved by their works councils (see Chapter 24) and are subject to much Federal legislation. Applicants are legally entitled to privacy, the right to be treated with dignity, payment of interview expenses, and not to be asked 'improper' questions. The latter include questions concerning the candidate's politics or family situation. Italian job advertisements have to comply with the state Workers' Statute, which forbids mention of political views, union membership, racial or religious criteria. In Spain, a law of 1982 guarantees job applicants freedom from invasion of privacy. Also the Spanish state employment service is supposed to vet all job advertisements appearing in the press in order to weed out any that are sexually discriminatory, although this rarely happens in practice. In Belgium a legally binding national collective agreement between unions and employers' associations entitles job applicants to total privacy during the recruitment process. Questions concerning marriage or family plans are unlawful. The agreement requires employers to return to unsuccessful candidates all documents accompanying an application.

Statutory notice periods on termination of employment differ widely from state to state, as does the compensation available for unfair dismissal. Further information on national differences in termination procedures is given in Table 26.2 (pp. 378-80).

3. Part-time and temporary work

According to Eurostat (the statistical service of the EU), about 15 per cent of all EU workers are on part-time contracts. Part-time work is concentrated among females, with nearly 30 per cent of women employees working part-time (five per cent of men). In the Netherlands about 80 per cent of working women have part-time jobs; for Britain and Denmark the figure is around 43 per cent. The lowest percentages are in Italy, Portugal and Greece (ten per cent) and in Spain and Luxembourg (14 per cent). Spain and Portugal have the highest proportions of their workforces on temporary contracts (22 and 19 per cent respectively). Luxembourg and Belgium have the lowest (four per cent and five per cent).

In Belgium, part-time employees must be provided with work lasting at least one third of the hours of a full-time employee, and have at least three consecutive hours of work at a stretch. Employers are legally obliged to pay part-time workers pro-rata to full-time employees. French part-timers have exactly the same legal rights *vis-à-vis* working conditions: protection against unfair dismissal, the use of temporary contracts, which must specify details of the employee who is temporarily replaced (if appropriate) and the expected duration of the assignment, which may not exceed 18 months in normal circumstances. The law restricts temporary employment to seasonal work, *ad hoc* projects, unexpected increases in workload, and filling-in for sick workers. Firms imposing redundancy cannot hire temporaries for six months after the redundancies have taken place. A 15 per cent end-of-contract bonus must be paid to compensate a temporary worker for the eventual loss of his or her job. Essentially similar provisions apply in Germany and Portugal.

Germany has laws which have prevented the widespread casualisation of the labour force that has happened in some other countries. This inhibits management's ability to discard labour as demand reduces, but does compel businesses to devise long-term human resource plans – usually to the benefit of the employing organisation. A 1987 Court case (*Bilka Kaufhaus* v. *Weber von Hartz*) ruled that occupational pension schemes which exclude part-timers are unlawful because they discriminate indirectly against women (who form the bulk of the part-time work labour force). This principle has been extended by other German Court cases which have determined that any employment provisions that exclude part-timers are illegal unless they can be justified by objective factors. The same qualifying periods for access to benefits, legal protection, etc. must be applied to part-time and full-time employees.

Table 26.1 Labour force characteristics and working conditions in EU countries

LABOUR FORCE CHARACTERISTICS	Austria	Belgium	Denmark	Finland
Approximate size of labour force (millions)	3.0	4.1	2.8	2.4
Percentage of the labour force that works part time	11	10	25	8
Legal restrictions on the use of temporary staff	There are no restrictions on the use of part-time or temporary employees	Temps may only be used as cover for sick workers, for exceptional workloads, or to cover for a dismissed worker for up to three months	No statutory restrictions	There are no legal restrictions on the use of temporary staff

	France	Germany	Greece	Ireland	Italy
Approximate size of labour force (millions)	24.1	39.9	4.0	1.3	23.8
Percentage of the labour force that works part time	10	13	4	8	3
Legal restrictions on the use of temporary staff	Temps may only be used for seasonal and urgent work or for exceptional workloads	Agency temps may not work for more than six months in any one establishment	No statutory restrictions	No statutory restrictions	No statutory restrictions, but temp agencies are banned

	Portugal	Spain	Sweden	UK	Netherlands
Approximate size of labour force (millions)	4.6	15	4.3	27.4	6.7
Percentage of the labour force that works part time	4	5	23	22	28
Legal restrictions on the use of temporary staff	Temps may only be used as cover for dismissed workers, for seasonal work, exceptional workloads, or ad-hoc tasks	Temps may only be used for exceptional workloads, ad-hoc tasks lasting no longer than six months, or as cover for sick workers	No restrictions on part-time working (no minimum number of hours, but strong presumption towards 18–20 hours)	No statutory restrictions	As Germany. Some industry collective agreements restrict the use of temporary staff

Table 26.1 Labour force characteristics and working conditions in EU countries (continued)

WORKING CONDITIONS	Austria	Belgium	Denmark	Finland	France
Statutory probationary period	One month	Seven days for blue collar workers. One to 12 months for white collar workers, depending on earnings	Three months for white collar workers (only)	A trial period is only possible if specifically agreed upon. As a general rule, the maximum length of a trial period is four months. If the employer provides special work-related training lasting more than four months, the trial period can be six months	No statutory provision
Maximum legal working week	40 hours. In most sectors negotiations over collective agreements have included a reduction of the average industrial working week to 38.5 hours	40 hours (no more than eight hours a day)	None	Eight-hour days within a 40-hour week	46 hours (no more than ten hours a day, 12 in exceptional circumstances)
Restrictions on Sunday working?	None	Yes	None	Double pay for Sunday working	None
Maximum overtime allowed	Ten hours per week	65 hours per three month period *provided* equivalent time off is granted the following quarter	No statutory restrictions	Defined by law – 200 hours of daily overtime and 120 hours of weekly overtime per annum. The Labour Council may permit up to a 50% increase in overtime. Therefore the maximum possible overtime is 480 hours.	Nine hours per week

Table 26.1 Labour force characteristics and working conditions in EU countries (continued)

WORKING CONDITIONS	Austria	Belgium	Denmark	Finland	France
Statutory paid leave for compassionate purposes	Seven days per annum	Up to ten days	One day	Temporary care leave (for children who fall sick) of up to four days per case of sickness	Up to four days
Statutory career breaks	Two years parental leave for either (but not both) parents	Six to 12 months for public sector employees. Pro-rata for part-time workers. Private sector subject to industry agreements	No statutory provision	An employee who has been employed full-time by the same employer in one or more periods is entitled to Study Leave. Maximum length during any five year period is two years, which can be used in one or more periods.	Up to one year full time or 1200 hours part time on 80 per cent pay for training purposes. Six to eleven months unpaid in other cases
Statutory holiday entitlement	Five weeks, increasing to six weeks after 20 years service with the same employer. Employees who have changed employers during the past 20 years may receive up to five years credit for such service.	Four weeks	Five weeks	Every employee has the right to an annual paid vacation of two to two and one-half working days for each full month worked	Five weeks
Number of days of public holidays per year	13	10	10	10	11
Statutory maternity leave	Eight weeks before and 8 weeks after the birth. The mother/father is eligible for up to 2 years' leave at a monthly compensation of Sch. 4,700 with full job guarantee during the second year. 3 years' leave is negotiable with part-time work during last 2 years.	15 weeks	18 weeks plus ten further weeks to be taken by either parent (Paternity leave of two weeks is also available)	Six months on state benefit at 66% of normal earnings plus childcare leave at a flat rate of payment until the child's third birthday	16 weeks (up to 32 weeks in exceptional circumstances)
Retirement age	65 years	Between 60 and 65 at the discretion of the worker	67	65	60

Table 26.1 Labour force characteristics and working conditions in EU countries (continued)

WORKING CONDITIONS	Germany	Greece	Ireland	Italy
Statutory probationary period	No statutory provision	No statutory provision	No statutory provision	12 days to six months depending on type of job
Maximum legal working week	48 hours	48 hours (no more than nine hours a day)	48 hours (no more than nine hours a day)	48 hours (no more than nine hours a day)
Restrictions on Sunday working?	Yes	None	None	Yes
Maximum overtime allowed	No statutory restrictions	Not allowed without special permission from the Ministry of Labour	Two hours per day 240 hours per year	Two hours per day
Statutory paid leave for compassionate purposes	Up to three days	Up to ten days	No statutory provision	15 days for marriage Otherwise no statutory provision
Statutory career breaks	Three years parental leave for either parent	Parents of either sex working in companies with more than 100 employees may take up three months parental leave	No statutory provision	No statutory provision
Statutory holiday entitlement	18 days	20 to 22 days depending on length of service	Three weeks	No statutory minimum
Number of days of public holidays per year	10	4	8	10
Statutory maternity leave	12 weeks	16 weeks	14 weeks	Five months
Retirement age	60	65 for men 60 for women	65	60 for men 55 for women

Table 26.1 Labour force characteristics and working conditions in EU countries (continued)

WORKING CONDITIONS	Netherlands	Portugal	Spain	Sweden	UK
Statutory probationary period	Two months	60 days	Two weeks (unskilled workers) Three months (skilled) Six to nine months (professional)	One year	No statutory provision
Maximum legal working week	48 hours (no more than nine hours a day)	44 hours (no more than eight hours daily)	40 hours (no more than nine hours daily)	40 hours per week	None
Restrictions on Sunday working?	Yes	None	None	None	Yes
Maximum overtime allowed	Up to 14 hours per week, subject to authorisation by the Labour Inspectorate	Two hours per day 160 hours per year	80 hours per year	Legal overtime beyond 40 hours per week must be registered and limited to 200 hours per year	No statutory restrictions
Statutory paid leave for compassionate purposes	Up to four days	Up to 30 days	Up to four days	None	No statutory provision
Statutory career breaks	No statutory provision	No statutory provision	Up to three years for parents of either sex	Unlimited period of unpaid leave for educational purposes	No statutory provision
Statutory holiday entitlement	Four times the number of days worked each week	At least 21 days and not more than 30 days	22 days	25 days	No statutory minimum
Number of days of public holidays per year	8	12	14	9	8
Statutory maternity leave	16 weeks	90 days	16 weeks	State paid leave of 15 months is available to either parent of a new-born infant with the first 12 months paid at 100% salary. Either parent is entitled to stay home on sick leave for up to 90 days per year for each child below the age of 12 if the child is ill.	18 weeks
Retirement age	65	No statutory requirement	69 maximum (state pensions payable from age 65)	65	65

Table 26.2 Termination of employment

	Austria	Belgium	Denmark	Finland	France
Statutory notice period(1)	White collar workers: Up to two years service– six weeks Two to five years – two months Five to 15 years – three months 15 to 25 years – four months Over 25 years – five months Blue collar workers – 14 days	Seven to 56 days for blue collar workers, depending on length of service. Three to 15 months for white collar employees	One to six months	Two months for under five years service Three months for five to eight years service Four months for nine to eleven years Five months for 12 to 14 years Six months thereafter	One to two months
Statutory appeals against dismissal	Labour and Social Court (Arbeits- und Sozialgericht)	District Labour Court	Tribunal on Dismissals	Labour Court	Labour Tribunal
Compensation for unfair dismissal (2)	Resume employment or be paid a sum in compensation equal to the worker's earnings between the time of dismissal and the final legal settlement of the case.	At least six months' wages, but not reinstatement	Reinstatement or up to 39 weeks' wages	At least three and up to 24 months salary if dismissal is found to be unlawful. There is no statutory requirement to pay additional severance pay. Employer is required to compensate employee for any losses from unjustified notice given for financial or production-related reasons or from illegal termination of employment.	At least six months wages

Table 26.2 Termination of employment (continued)

	Germany	Greece	Ireland	Italy	Netherlands
Statutory notice period (1)	During the first six months of employment, two to 4 weeks according to age and length of service. Thereafter up to six months.	Two to six months (white collar) Five to 60 days (blue collar)	One to eight weeks	No statutory provision	One to 26 weeks depending on age and length of service
Statutory appeals against dismissal	Labour Court *via* a Works Council	Civil remedies only	Employment Appeals Tribunal	Labour Court	Department of Employment (GAB)
Compensation for unfair dismissal (2)	Reinstatement or up to 18 months' wages according to age and length of service	Civil remedies only	Reinstatement or up to 104 weeks' pay	Reinstatement or up to 15 months' pay	Reinstatement and civil damages

Table 26.2 Termination of employment (continued)

	Portugal	Spain	Sweden	UK
Statutory notice period (1)	No statutory provision	One to three months according to length of service	Age-related. One month's notice after six month's service, rises with age to between two (age 25) and six months (45).	One to 12 weeks according to length of service
Statutory appeals against dismissal	Labour Court	Labour Court	Labour Court (*Arbetsdomstolen*)	Industrial Tribunal
Compensation for unfair dismissal (2)	Reinstatement or one month's pay for each year of service (minimum of three months' wages is payable)	Up to 42 months' pay according to length of service	Damages are payable only if employer refuses to reinstate the employee. Amounts are (employees over 60 years of age in parenthesis): • 16 (25) month's pay for workers with less than five years service • 24 (36) month's pay for service between five and ten years • 32 (48) month's pay for workers with ten or more years' service	Varies according to the nature of the unfair dismissal and the age of the worker. Normally up to 30 weeks' pay.

Notes

(1) This refers to the period to be given by employers, which in most countries differs from the notice period to be given by resigning employees. The latter is normally shorter than the durations stated in the table. In France, no period of notice (other than that specified in the worker's contract of employment) need be given by a person quitting his or her job. In most countries there is no eligibility period, or short periods of up to six months. France and Britain require workers to have been employed by the same firm for more than two years before being able to register a claim.

(2) Eligibility periods prior to unfair dismissal claims vary from state to state.

Italian part-timers and temporary workers must be given pay and benefits pro-rata to whose who work full-time. In Spain a part-timer is not legally entitled to pro-rata pay but does have the same statutory employment protection rights as a full-time employee.

CONDITIONS OF EMPLOYMENT

4. Working conditions

Night work is strictly controlled in a number of EU states. Greek night workers must be paid at least time and a quarter of normal rates; double time at weekends. Spain and Portugal also have a statutory minimum rate of 125 per cent for night work. Spain bans night work for anyone under the age of 18. The Netherlands prohibits night work entirely unless the firm involved obtains a special licence from the Dutch Ministry of Labour. In Belgium night work has to be voluntary, approved by employee representatives, and only undertaken by permanent full-time workers. Pregnant workers have the legal right to be temporarily transferred from night to day working. Overtime is also subject to legislation in many countries (see Table 26.1).

Additionally, some countries set down minimum wage premiums for overtime working. French, Greek, German and Irish workers are entitled to at least time and a quarter for overtime; Portuguese employees have to be paid at least time and a half for the first hour of extra working and time and three-quarters from then on. Until 1994, all overtime worked in Spain attracted a 75 per cent statutory bonus. Since 1994 overtime rates have been subject to negotiation between managements and workers, but typically involve a 75 per cent premium.

5. Equal opportunities

Article 119 of the Treaty of Rome demanded equal pay for equal work completed by men and women, and this (in principle, at least) is mandatory in all member countries. The Council of Ministers has also directed that there shall be equal pension rights and social security benefits for men and women. This has been interpreted by the European Court of Justice to mean equal retirement ages for men and women. Article 119 encompasses wages, fringe benefits, payments in kind, access to pension schemes, etc. Equal work means work of equal value (not just people engaged in identical duties) and the onus is on the employer to prove that any discrepancy between male and female rates of pay is not due to sex discrimination.

Equal opportunities legislation exists in all EU countries. In Belgium a victim of unfair sex or race discrimination can seek compensation (of up to six month's pay or the actual value of damages suffered) from a Labour Court. Criminal penalties ranging from small fines to one month's imprisonment are also available. France also has criminal penalties for sex discrimination.

Additionally, French firms employing more than 50 workers must prepare and submit to union representatives and the Labour Inspectorate an annual report on the degree of equality of men and women within the enterprise. In Germany, job applicants rejected on the grounds of sex may claim four months pay for the work they would have done had their applications been successful. The legislation also covers internal promotion.

Greek victims of acts of unfair discrimination must seek damages through the civil courts, although small fines can also be imposed by the Ministry of Labour. Irish victims can claim up to 104 weeks' pay, and courts may impose daily fines for as long as discriminatory practices continue.

Denmark, Greece and Belgium draw an important statutory distinction between white collar (salaried) and blue collar (manual) employees. Under Belgium's 1978 Contract of Employment Act, for example, a worker's status as white or blue collar affects *(i)* his or her probationary and notice periods and *(ii)* when notice of termination begins to take effect (the Monday following notification of dismissal for manual workers, the month following notification for white collar staff). Denmark also has distinct legislation for specific employee groups which determines sick pay entitlements and notice periods. In Greece, blue collar workers cannot lawfully be instructed to undertake clerical work.

The EU Code of Practice on the prevention of sexual harassment at work 1992

This is a broadly based set of recommendations that advises employers to produce a policy statement on the subject of sexual harassment, to establish complaints procedures and to communicate these to employees. Persistent offenders should be subject to the firm's internal disciplinary procedures and the necessary sanctions applied. However there is no requirement for EU member countries to introduce legislation on this matter, although several actually have.

Race discrimination

Ten EU countries have laws that prohibit race discrimination in employment (Britain, Finland, France, Germany, Ireland, Italy, Netherlands, Portugal, Spain and Sweden). Finland and Spain restrict protection to persons *already* in employment, while Irish legislation only applies to dismissals. In the other countries the law extends to recruitment processes as well as treatment within employment. 'Race' can refer to ethnic origin, nationality or skin colour. Six of the nine have anti-race discrimination provisions written into their constitutions (France, Germany, Italy, Netherlands, Portugal and Spain); the other three rely on *ad hoc* legislation. Note however that all EU nations apart from Ireland have ratified the 1965 United Nations International Convention on the Elimination of all Forms of Racial Discrimination, which requires governments to undertake to prohibit and eliminate racial discrimination in all its forms and to guarantee the right of everybody to equality before the law in relation to conditions of employment, free choice of employment, fair treatment at work, equal pay for equal work, etc. EU countries other than Ireland, Luxembourg and the United Kingdom, moreover, have signed the 1958 International Labour Organisation Convention on Discrimination in Respect of Employment and Occupation, which imposes on governments the obligation to 'declare and pursue a national policy designed to promote equality of opportunity in respect of employment and occupation with a view to eliminating discrimination.' Acceptance of such Conventions puts pressures on national governments to legislate in order to meet agreed international standards, but does not guarantee that they will do so.

To date, EU institutions have expressed concern about racism, although no substantial legislation has emerged. At the time of writing however a proposed Draft Directive on the matter is under discussion, which if adopted will effectively outlaw all forms of racial discrimination. The United Kingdom's stated intention to veto the proposal was reversed following the change in government of 1997. At present the only protection available *via* EU law is on the grounds of *nationality* rather than race or colour, since discrimination related to nationality is prohibited by Article 7 of the Treaty of Rome. Thus, for example, a black or Asian UK citizen seeking a job in an EU country outside the UK is not protected against discrimination on the basis of colour (as opposed to nationality). This lack of concern with race discrimination is in sharp contrast with the comprehensive EU legislation against sex discrimination that has been in place since 1975.

6. Parental leave

The term 'parental leave' is used to describe leave taken by women *after* the expiry of maternity leave and which is unpaid (or paid at a very low rate) and carries the right to re-engagement in a similar position in the former employing firm. Statutory provision for parental leave varies widely across the European Union. In Ireland there is no statutory right to parental leave whatsoever. Thereafter there are large differences in conditions and benefits, ranging from:

- Zero length of service requirements in five EU countries, four weeks' service in Germany, six months in three nations, and one year in the remaining half dozen
- Leave durations of three months (in Greece) to three years (in France, Germany, Norway and Spain)
- No financial payment in four countries, a flat rate monthly sum in five others, through varying percentages of previous earnings elsewhere.

Nine EU nations give people returning from parental leave the legal right to insist that they be employed part time.

The issue of parental leave is important because of the huge increase in the number of working women in EU countries that has occurred over the last couple of decades, in combination with the rise of single person households.

Advantages claimed for the practice of granting employees parental leave are:

(a) Employment and family responsibilities may be reconciled.

(b) Equal opportunities for women are promoted (through enabling women to remain in the labour force).

(c) Women are encouraged to have more children. This is a critical factor in countries where the birth rate is in sharp decline.

(d) Unemployment is reduced as fresh workers are engaged to cover for people who are away on leave.

(e) Firms retain trained and competent staff for longer periods.

(f) Mothers have more time to spend with their families. Equal sharing of family responsibilities between men and women is facilitated, as women are relieved of the (stressful) burden of having to return quickly to a job while caring for an infant at the same time.

(g) The state formally recognises the social importance of parenting.

Criticisms of statutory parental leave are:

(a) It is more efficient to allow market forces to determine whether parental leave is necessary. If firms really require the long-term services of the women involved they will be prepared to pay the appropriate rate to retain them.

(b) Employers' wage bills are higher than otherwise would be the case, possibly helping to make European firms uncompetitive in world markets.

(c) The long-term absence of key employees can severely disrupt an organisation's work.

(d) Having to find replacements for people away on parental leave is troublesome and expensive. Replacements have to be inducted and trained, only to be dismissed on the return of the absent worker.

Paternity leave

Seven EU countries give fathers the statutory right to a few days' paid leave at the times their children are born. The period involved varies from two days in Spain to ten days in Sweden. Additionally eleven EU states allow fathers to take, by law, a longer period of unpaid leave for parenting purposes, provided the mother waives her entitlement to all or part of her statutory parental leave. The shortest duration of this kind of paternity leave applies in Denmark (ten weeks); the longest in France, Austria and Germany (two to three years): six months is the commonest period. In 1994 the UK government vetoed an EU Draft Directive on parental leave giving all employees the right to at least three months' unpaid leave (whether working full time or part time) following the birth or adoption of a child. Nevertheless the other 14 EU member states went ahead with the measure. Following the change in government in 1997 the UK decided to introduce unpaid paternity leave on the same basis as in all other EU countries.

Benefits resulting from the practice of granting paternity leave are:

(a) Employees are helped to reconcile their work and family responsibilities.

(b) Gender equal opportunities are facilitated: women are allowed greater flexibility in their working lives and hence can better pursue and develop their own careers.

(c) Beneficiaries are likely to be more loyal to the firm.

(d) Companies can plan ahead to avoid possible disruptions caused by men taking time off work (through formal leave or deliberate absenteeism) when a child is being born.

The disadvantages include:

- The final costs imposed on employers
- Reductions in productivity caused by the use of inexperienced temporary replacement workers
- Adverse effects on individual career development.

THE USA

US personnel management practices emphasise the importance of individual initiative and responsibility, selection and promotion on merit, the assumption that employees should and will be loyal to the employing organisation, and willingness to dismiss workers whose performance does not come up to scratch. Motivation often depends on (substantial) rewards and penalties. There is open vertical and horizontal communication compared with many other countries, and relatively informal personal relationships.

7. Employment at will

United States employment law and practice is based on the doctrine of 'employment at will,' i.e. the freedom of employers to hire and fire as they please and to terminate an employee's job at any time and for any reason – subject to that person's contract of employment. It follows that contracts of employment with terms and conditions determined by collective bargaining assume great importance within the system. They are legally binding and provide the basis for a worker's security of employment, with terms and conditions typically renegotiated every two or three years (via collective bargaining in unionised firms).

8. Trends in employment

The American Department of Labor predicts that by the year 2000 less than five per cent of new jobs in the US labour force will be for unskilled people. As in other western countries, the proportion of the US labour force employed in manufacturing has declined, while the proportion engaged in services is continuously increasing. Since 1980, fewer people have been employed in US manufacturing than in wholesaling and retailing. This has greatly reduced the bargaining power of (unionised) manufacturing workers, whose wage levels relative to other employee categories have deteriorated. The new jobs created over the last 20 years have tended to be in office administration and catering, and are frequently low paid and part-time. Jobs lost have been in well-paid skilled and semi-skilled manual occupations. In the 1970s only 20 per cent on average of the new jobs created each year fell within the Federal Department of Labour's lowest category of income. Through the 1980s the figure was 60 per cent, and one-third were part-time. Unemployment is unevenly distributed. Black people, Hispanics and the poorly educated experience the highest rates of unemployment (around 30 per cent for black youths).

9. Cultural influences

The USA is ethnically diverse and religiously multi-denominational. It is a large country both in terms of its geographical size (it covers twice the area of the EU countries combined) and its population (250 million). Parts of the US have a sub-tropical climate (Florida for example); parts of Alaska lie within the Arctic Circle. Size and ethnic diversity mean that employees in various regions may have widely different cultural traditions, attitudes and perspectives. Note moreover that each of America's 50 states has its own laws, many of which impinge on personnel management.

Market forces determine the pattern of most US economic activity (apart from the nation's extensive defence industries). Vigorous competition and the regular business shut-downs/start-ups that it implies have led perhaps to a greater willingness to accept change than in some other countries and to a workforce that is prepared, on the whole, to move to areas and industries where jobs are available. Another important fact is that the US continues to accept large numbers of immigrants from other countries, with the consequence that the skilled labour force has been supplemented even when birth rates were down. Also the US has a younger workforce than either Europe or Japan.

10. Labour relations

Collective bargaining (*see* 20:7) has traditionally taken place at the enterprise rather than the industry or national level. Also, American unions negotiate on a far wider range of matters than their West European counterparts, especially regarding fringe benefits (health and welfare schemes, extended holidays, occupational pension, etc). US unions' successes in negotiating with managements in relation to fringe benefits derive in part from the Wagner Act which empowers the US National Labour Relations Board (NLRB) to compel employers to bargain with unions on a multitude of issues.

To gain recognition against a management's wishes a union must petition the NLRB which then organises a ballot to establish the wishes of the firm's workforce. If the ballot goes in favour of the union then management is legally obliged to negotiate with that union. Only one union is entitled to negotiating rights within a particular workplace. If another union gains a foothold in the firm it must approach the NLRB and ask for a fresh ballot to determine which union shall be recognised. There is no legislation compelling employee representation on company boards.

Certain US business sectors have a long history of 'union avoidance', and the practice has been pursued vigorously by some American companies. Measures intended to prevent union involvement with a firm have included:

(a) Referring *all* labour relations matters to company lawyers, so that union members must discuss issues with a lawyer rather than a line executive.

(b) Identification and intimidation of potential union supporters.

(c) Unfair (and unlawful) sacking of union representatives knowing that the costs to the company in fines and compensation to the affected individuals will be lower than the possible effects on the wages bill if the firm is unionised.

(d) Encouraging non-union employees of unionised businesses to file derecognition petitions with the NLRB.

11. The Taft–Hartley Act 1947

This contained the following provisions:

(a) The US President was given the right to obtain from the Congress an injunction banning for 80 days any strike which the President considered a threat to national health and safety. Intervention occurs when a stalemate in negotiations has been reached. A report on the dispute is commissioned and the two sides are instructed to co-operate with the Federal Mediation and Conciliation Service. The NLRB ballots the workers in the dispute to establish whether they wish to accept the employer's latest offer. If the answer is negative the dispute continues without further interference.

(b) Individual states were allowed to ban the closed shop (i.e. a situation in which a firm will only employ union members). Such prohibitions were called 'right to work' laws and inhibited union organisation, especially in Southern states.

(c) Secondary actions were outlawed, as were strikes relating to inter-union disputes.

(d) Collective agreements became legally enforceable.

(e) Workers refusing to join a union were given legal protection.

HUMAN RESOURCES MANAGEMENT IN JAPAN

12. Theory Z

This is the label applied to the Japanese approach to HRM by William Ouchi, a westerner, who suggested that the approach comprised three strategies and six associated techniques. The strategies are as follows:

1. Commitment to life-long employment
2. Projection of the philosophy and objectives of the organisation to the individual worker. Making workers feel they belong in a clearly defined corporate entity.
3. Careful selection of new entrants and intensive socialisation of recruits into the existing value system.

These strategies are implemented through six techniques:

1. Seniority-based promotion systems. Recruits expect to spend their entire careers with a single firm. They acquire experience of various aspects of the business through job rotation and steady (but slow) progression through the management hierarchy. Since there is but limited opportunity for promotion, most transfers are lateral. This develops generalist rather than specialist management skills, and well-rounded management personalities.
2. Continuous training and appraisal which, combined with guaranteed job security, enable managers to construct long-term career plans. Managers might experience less stress than their Western counterparts.
3. Group-centred activities. Tasks are assigned to groups rather than individuals.
4. Open communications both within the work groups and between management and labour. Managers and workers dress alike and eat in the same works canteen.
5. Worker participation in decision making, based on consultation with all who will be affected by a proposed change.
6. A production-centred approach with, nonetheless, great concern for the welfare of the employee. There is no great social divide between management and workers.

In Japan, payments systems are seniority based. The longer an employee has been with the firm the more he or she is paid. Another important feature of the Japanese corporation is that it will usually have just one trade union representing all its employees. For more information on the origins and nature of enterprise unionism in Japan see *Employee Relations*, Chapter 18, in this series.

Workers within a privately owned firm have the right to form a union, and management must recognise the union for the purpose of collective bargaining. If several unions exist within a firm then management must deal with each of them (though this is extremely rare in practice). Management is legally obliged to negotiate with the union in relation to the determination of works rules, but only with the union that represents most employees. The specific rules that must be discussed include shift-work management, starting and finishing times, holiday entitlements and wage payment systems. If a company refuses to negotiate with a union then the latter may sue for financial damages caused by the refusal. Note the differences involved in assessing the value of such damages. Managements are at liberty to require that all employees be union members as part of their contracts of employment. However, it is illegal for firms to apply contractual terms which forbid workers from joining trade unions.

13. Working practices

Japanese approaches to employee relations have attracted much attention in recent years because of formidable successes achieved by Japanese industry and the contrasts offered by Japanese management styles relative to those applied in Western countries. Japanese firms, moreover, seem to have obtained the co-operation of foreign workers, even in countries where industrial strife is commonplace.

The basic practice is to organise work around teams which exercise some discretion over how they complete tasks, and which assume responsibility for the quality of their outputs. Each team receives clearly defined inputs from other working units and is given a range of productivity and quality targets. Five to ten minute team meetings between supervisors and workers might occur twice a day, usually at the beginning and end of each shift. Some Japanese companies have abandoned the use of the term 'worker' or 'operative', or even 'employee' when referring to their people, preferring instead to call them 'associates' or 'partners'. This supposedly helps break the attitude that lower-grade workers are somehow less important for the firm's survival than is management, but can lead to charges of managerial hypocrisy: employees in Japanese enterprises do *not* share power or profits on equal terms with the owners and managers of the company.

It is important to note that despite the large amount of consensus decision making that occurs at the workplace level, Japanese firms are in many respects highly authoritarian. They demand strict conformity with company rules and unquestioning compliance with cultural norms. However, the exercise of authority is limited to matters necessary for the organisation's survival and success.

14. Advantages and problems of the Japanese approach

Benefits claimed for the Japanese approach are:

(a) To the extent that the workforce is involved in taking decisions, the decisions taken will be speedily and wholeheartedly implemented.

(b) The fact that employees invest so much of their life energy in a single employing organisation results in their becoming totally committed to its long-term survival.

(c) Emphasis on group work rather than individual discretion encourages harmony within the workforce, consensus between management and labour, and a high degree of employee co-operation.

(d) Workers are able to develop their skills and are given the opportunity to be creative and to assume responsibility for output. Individuals are offered the chance to be recognised and rewarded for their efforts, to learn a wide variety of competencies, and to receive constant feedback on their performance.

(e) Single status for all employees (Japanese managers and other workers dress alike and eat in the same canteen) can significantly improve loyalty to the organisation, morale and team spirit.

Criticisms of Japanese approaches include:

(a) The emphasis on conformity and obedience to authority might itself eventually become a barrier to the introduction of new methods and the acceptance of change.

(b) Job satisfaction among the employees of Japanese firms need not be greater than in other enterprises. The pace of work is intensive and workers are expected to give their all to the company; Japanese production operatives are subject to large amounts of stress.

(c) Trade unions become an instrument of management rather than a means for furthering the interests of workers.

(d) Arguably the Japanese approach is nothing more than a managerial confidence trick intended to brainwash workers into subservient obedience to management's wishes.

(e) There is much discrimination against women in Japanese industry.

(f) Young managers may resent restrictions on the speed at which they can progress through an organisation and thus might themselves eventually become the agents of change who will disrupt the system.

Reference

Ouchi, W. (1981), *Theory Z: How American Business Can Meet the Japanese Challenge*, Addison-Wesley.

Progress test 26

1. What are the main areas in which national differences in HRM practice are most evident?
2. List the major differences in the treatment of part-time employees in EU nations.
3. Define the doctrine of 'employment at will'.
4. Outline the role of the US National Labour Relations Board.
5. What are the main problems associated with the Japanese approach to human resources management?
6. Discuss the likely impact on UK industrial relations of current industrial relations practices within the European Union.

Appendix 1

EXAMPLE OF A JOB SPECIFICATION

Job description

Cement mixer operator   **XYZ Pre-cast Concrete Ltd**

Operates a cement mixing process which is largely automatic but requires checking to see that it is functioning correctly.

Manually adds colour to the mix when required.

Cleans interior of mixer at end of each day.

Keeps record of coloured mixes (normal mixes are recorded automatically).

Responsible to the plant supervisor.

Not responsible for any other operators.

Job specification

Major responsibilities

The operator is responsible for the production of satisfactory mixes and for the routine cleaning of the equipment. About 120 mixes should be produced per day, including colour mixes when required. The operator must be prepared to correct or stop the process manually if it is apparent that unsatisfactory mixes are being produced or if mechanical or electrical faults occur.

Routine duties

Starts process each day by operating controls.

By observing mixer control panel and appearance of mix, judges whether process is working correctly or if manual adjustments need to be made.

When instructed by supervisor produces coloured mixes by adding colour from small pre-weighed bags. Enters details in record book daily.

Cleans equipment in last hour of the day.

Training (off-job, with an experienced operator) lasts two weeks. Should be able to work unsupervised after a further four weeks.

No unusual physical demands are made on the operator except that cleaning the equipment necessitates some bending and stretching.

Non-routine or infrequent duties

During annual overhaul of plant assists for about a week in cleaning and dismantling.

May occasionally be required for general labouring duties, e.g. snow clearing.

Working conditions

A seat is provided by the mixer control panel but the operator frequently needs to stand or walk short distances to inspect the quality of the mix or to prepare coloured mixes.

There is some heating in winter from a hot water pipe running through the control area, which is under cover but draughty because of the entrance and exit points for the materials used in the process.

The work is occasionally dusty while the process is operating but very dusty while the equipment is being cleaned, necessitating the wearing of a mask.

There is a moderate noise and vibration, but it does not impede communication because the operator receives instructions re coloured mixes in writing. The work area is adequately lit.

Tools and materials used

The materials for the mix (except colour) are delivered and controlled automatically.

No tools are used except a hose, brushes and scrapers when cleaning.

Personal contacts

The operator is isolated except for very occasional visits from the supervisor. The operator can see operators in other parts of the plant through the windows.

Performance standards

120 mixes per day.
Colour mixes as required.
Satisfactory quality of mix.
No breakdowns due to inadequate cleaning.
Records of coloured mixes legible, accurate and up to date.

Appendix 2

EXAMPLE OF AN APPRAISAL RATING SCALE

Name_____ Department_____
Job _____ How long in dept._____
Date of birth _____How long in company_____

Please tick the ratings you think appropriate, after reading carefully the definitions of the factors and grades. You should add any general remarks in the space provided at the end of the form. Base your judgment on the requirements of the job and the employee's performance in the job.

1. KNOWLEDGE OF JOB
(Present knowledge of job and of work related to it.)

Knows only routine repetitive work. Will not learn	_____
Knows routine work and some parts of other jobs	_____
Knows most jobs but relies on others for special knowledge	_____
Good knowledge of practically all aspects of the work	_____
Complete grasp of all aspects of the work	_____

2. ACCURACY
(Standard of work compared with standard expected, degree to which work must be checked.)

Work is inaccurate; requires constant checking	_____
Careless at times; requires frequent checking	_____
Usually accurate; requires occasional checking	_____
Accurate except on very difficult jobs	_____
Accurate on all jobs	_____

3. SPEED OF WORK
(Speed at which work is accomplished in relation to the standard expected in the job.)

Very slow; always fails to meet requirements	_____
Slow; often below requirements	_____
Average speed; meets requirements as a rule	_____
Above average speed; usually exceeds requirements	_____
Fast; always exceeds requirements	_____

4. CO-OPERATION

(Ability to work with others at all levels; readiness to try out new ideas and methods; response when asked for a special effort.)

Difficult to work with; often touchy and unco-operative	_____
Occasionally difficult to work with	_____
Normally co-operative; raises few difficulties	_____
Always tries hard to co-operate; easy to work with	_____
Co-operates extremely well with others at all levels	_____

5. INITIATIVE

(Resourcefulness; ability to work without detailed instructions; readiness to offer ideas and suggestions about work.)

Requires detailed supervision; waits to be told	_____
Requires frequent supervision; asks for instructions	_____
Requires occasional supervision, sometimes offers ideas	_____
Rarely requires supervision; resourceful, offers ideas	_____
Never requires supervision; has many ideas, solves problems unaided	_____

TRAINING NEEDS

(Suggest any training course or in-company experience which might improve the employee's performance.)

PROMOTION POTENTIAL

The employee is an excellent promotion candidate because	_____
The employee is a good promotion candidate because	_____
The employee is a border-line promotion candidate because	_____
The employee is unlikely to be promoted because	_____

GENERAL REMARKS

GENERAL RATING

Assess employee's job performance in his or her *present* job:

Poor		Average		Excellent
□	□	□	□	□

Signed_____ Position_____ Date_____

Countersigned_____ Position_____ Date_____

Appendix 3

EXAMPLES OF JOB EVALUATION SCHEMES

OFFICE JOB EVALUATION

The Institute of Administrative Management has developed a grading scheme for office staff which is described fully in its publication *Office Job Evaluation*. Extracts from the scheme are shown below, by kind permission of the Institute.

Nine job grades are defined as follows:

A. Jobs which require no previous work experience and are either
(a) simple enough to require very limited training; *or*
(b) simple but still require a training period and will be closely controlled by supervision or self-checking procedures.

B. Jobs which by virtue of their composition remain simple but develop the ability of the job holder beyond the initial level through extended training both theoretical and on the job. Will consist of standard routines less closely controlled.

C. Jobs which necessitate a length of experience to enable a special aptitude to be used. Routines will continue to be standardised but rulings can start to be relaxed to allow for initiative to be developed.

D. Jobs requiring considerable experience thereby relaxing standardised routines but remaining within predetermined procedures. Limited initiative is to be encouraged resulting in a material reduction in control procedures.

E. Jobs which require either or both of the following, dependent upon the percentages of total time spent on specialist, technical and work control activities:
(a) technical or specialised knowledge applied where the occasional use of discretion and initiative is necessary;
(b) control of work procedures distributed over up to, say, five lower-grade staff.

F. Jobs which require the application of both knowledge and experience in one or more of the following:
(a) technical or professional operations at intermediate qualification level of an appropriate professional institute;
(b) performance or control of work of developing complexity whether secretarial, technical or administrative where judgment and initiative are called for;
(c) supervision requiring leadership, guidance on work procedures, training of others and motivation covering a team where control of work alone is delegated to a lower-level grade.

M 1. Jobs where requirements equate to one or more of the following:
(a) professional or specialised knowledge beyond the Intermediate level examination

of an appropriate professional institute but not necessarily to a final qualification of such institutes;

(b) performance or control of work of wide complexity including non-routine decisions and regular use of judgment within determined policy;

(c) management of sufficient numbers of staff to require F-level activities carried out by more than one position.

M 2. Jobs requiring one or more of the following:

(a) the final qualification of an appropriate professional institute equivalent to a university degree;

(b) performance or control of work of significant complexity and importance requiring regular non-routine decisions based upon initiative leading to the development of policy changes;

(c) management of specialist functions where more than one level of supervision is necessary to control the range of activities involved.

M 3. Jobs requiring one or more of the following:

(a) in addition to a final qualification and/or equivalent university degree a period of experience consistent with the level of authority;

(b) performance or control of work over a series of functions demanding a high level of generalist expertise and involved in policy-making at the highest level.

(c) management of a series of specialist functions where management level jobs report in for guidance, control and monitoring.

The Institute gives examples of the application of the grading scheme to various types of office jobs. The following show how a variety of office jobs might be graded.

Typing and secretarial

A. –

B. Preparation of straightforward documents by copy-typing from a clear statement, including manuscript, at about 35 words per minute.

C. Word processor operation requiring the organising of adequate space on storage systems in a single word processor unit requiring an understanding of standard records and systems.

D. Preparation of statements which require careful layout of both words and figures from author's draft, including the correction of grammar and punctuation, in order to produce a finished document.

E. Secretarial work requiring the receipt of dictation and its transcription for members of management covering correspondence, reports, etc. Other activities include making appointments, filing and generally working on own initiative.

F. Supervision of a group of typists including training, distribution of work and maintenance of standards.

M 1. –

M 2. –

M 3. –

397

Accounting

A. –

B. Sorting documents, preparing ledger entries and assisting with the filing thereof after input. Processing details of new accounts for authorisation, changes of address, etc., all under the control of higher-grade staff.

C. Checking input documents, in that quantities and terms are accurate, calculating extensions and discounts agree with orders and contract terms, etc.

D. Maintaining control accounts to ensure that all ledger input has been correctly processed. Making necessary corrections within knowledge and experience, referring other queries to higher grade staff.

E. Preparing cost and departmental accounts, having responsibility for investigating queries and noting abnormal resulting figures for attention.

F. Supervision of work of a section of clerical staff dealing with the administration of customers' or suppliers' accounts involving dealing with queries which emerge.

M 1. Preparation of statements on the effects of price increases on profit margins which involve knowledge of products and processes as well as management accounting principles and practices.

M 2. Preparing reports to develop complex annual budgets requiring a detailed knowledge of both financial and management accountancy.

M 3. –

Computing

A. –

B. Microcomputer operation: entering data and/or text using the keyboard and simple commands under the guidance of an experienced operator and where input is subject to check.

C. Computer operation: loading disks onto disk drives, paper into printers, operating VDUs to give simple operating commands in accordance with prescribed procedures.

D. Writing specialist programs for particular systems, e.g., personal computers, optical mark/character readers, etc.

E. Investigating current systems which are straightforward and expected to need a small computer to improve flow of work and productivity. Examining alternatives and preparing statements of requirements.

F. Supervising and operating with a team or shift of computer operators for a medium-sized installation. Ensuring that procedures are adhered to, records are maintained, faults reported and work scheduled in accordance with priorities.

M 1. Defining systems requirements for major projects. Controlling the work of a section of programmers, liaising with systems analysts and designers together with senior management and users.

M 2. Planning large scale or complex data processing systems covering a significant area of the operations of an organisation, including negotiations with departments about projects.

M 3. Control and management of a computer system comprising mini and main-frame computers together with a complex network of more than 250 VDUs.

Miscellaneous

A. Collecting and assembling outgoing mail, collecting and delivering internal mail to a timetable.

B. Sorting and filing in alphabetical and numerical order, preparation of files and extraction of files, etc.

C. Share registration activities involving despatching completed certificates after sealing and maintaining records accordingly. Distribution operations, taking orders over the telephone and responding to delivery queries.

D. Personnel records involving compiling regular statistics for management on sickness and overtime, etc.

Maintenance of insurance registers of policies to ensure renewal within the prescribed period.

E. Maintaining statistical records of sales performance and circulating such information to appropriate departments.

Control of work of a small team of purchasing clerks, progressing orders and maintaining records.

F. In property management, calculating maintenance claims and preparing information on property values.

Supervision of staff involved in the calculation and payment of pension benefits.

M 1. Evolving and running suitable training courses for staff up to supervisory level, assessing success and maintaining records of a financial and personnel nature related to the courses.

M 2. Preparing complex reports on major aspects of business activity which involve the interpretation of information and calculation of forecasts for discussion at senior management meetings.

M 3. Management of multi-discipline activities whereby monitoring and control procedures result in policy formulation.

The examples shown above are brief, and only provide a rough guide to the type or level of job in each grade. Fuller information may be found in the Institute's book *Office Job Evaluation*.

POINTS RATING SCHEME FOR MANUAL JOBS

The following is an example of a scheme used in industry for evaluating manual jobs. Note that the sub-factors under the heading 'working conditions' are intended to cover outdoor as well as indoor jobs. A company in which nearly all manual jobs were under cover or free from contamination and noise would have a different set of sub-factors under this heading. The reader may wish to use this scheme to evaluate the job described in Appendix 1.

		Max points	
Skill and knowledge			
	Education and training required	25	
	Experience required	60	
	Dexterity	15	
		–	100
Effort			
	Energy and stamina required	60	
	Working position	40	
		–	100
Responsibility and mental requirements			
	For material and equipment	20	
	For the work of others	25	
	Concentration and alertness	20	
	Need to act on own initiative	15	
	Need to work steadily	20	
		–	100
Working conditions			
	Temperature and humidity	20	
	Exposure to climatic conditions	20	
	Atmospheric contamination (dust, dirt, smell, etc.)	25	
	Noise and vibration	15	
	Monotony and isolation	10	
	Nervous strain, hazards	10	
		–	100

Appendix 4

GLOSSARY OF HUMAN RESOURCES MANAGEMENT TERMS

ACAS (Advisory, Conciliation and Arbitration Service). A government agency established to improve UK industrial relations. It mediates in industrial disputes, seeks out-of-court settlements in cases of alleged unfair dismissal, and publishes *Codes of Practice* on employment matters.

Access to Medical Reports Act 1988. Legislation compelling firms to obtain the consent of employees prior to their being required to take medical examinations.

Achievement test. A selection test intended to establish whether a person possesses a particular *skill* or ability (e.g. typing or driving).

Action learning. An approach to training that requires trainees to collect, evaluate and deal with information relevant to real-life problems.

Actions short of dismissal. Disciplinary sanctions other than the sack (e.g. demotion, denial of pay increases, loss of fringe benefits, or refusal of requests for time off).

Actuarial selection. Employee selection based on objective statistical data about candidates.

Additional award. Extra compensation awarded by *industrial tribunals* to unfairly dismissed workers whose ex-employers refuse to re-engage them.

Affect structure. A pattern of interpersonal attractions which determines the extent and nature of associations within a group.

Affirmative action programmes. United States federal and local government purchasing policies under which a supplying firm's continuing access to public sector contracts is made conditional on the supplier achieving certain prespecified equal opportunity targets, e.g. to increase ethnic minority representation in the workforce by 20 per cent within the next 18 months.

Alienation. Extreme job dissatisfaction that causes an employee to feel that work is neither important nor relevant to his or her life.

Alternance. According to the European Commission, the extent to which a training programme mixes off-job training and work experience (e.g. within a sandwich course).

Analogous tests. *Achievement tests* that seek to replicate key aspects of a certain type of employment (e.g. shorthand tests for applicants for secretarial jobs).

Analytical job evaluation. Techniques of *job evaluation* which attempt to quantify the effort, skill and responsibility attached to a job.

Annualised-hours contract. A contract of employment whereby an employee works a certain number of hours during the year; the actual weekly hours varying from week to week within the 12-month period.

Any difference rule. The legal principle that a dismissal is fair even if the procedures leading up to it were unfair (e.g. an employer failing to give proper warnings), provided the outcome would have been exactly the same had no procedural defect occurred.

APL (assessment of prior learning). Pre-testing of trainees to ascertain how much they already know and to evaluate their past activities and achievements.

Apprentice. An employee who receives substantial on-job training for a craft or trade. In return, the apprentice accepts a relatively low wage until he or she is fully competent.

Arbitration. Resolution of a dispute through having an independent outsider examine all its aspects and impose a ruling.

Associated employers. Any pair of companies where one is directly or indirectly controlled by the other or where both are controlled by a third party.

Attitude. An inclination to perceive, interpret and evaluate people, events and issues in a certain manner.

Attribution. The mental processes through which individuals explain their own or other people's behaviour.

Authority. Formal rights to control others that result from appointment to a management position.

Automatically unfair dismissal. Dismissal for joining or refusing to join a trade union; for being pregnant; or because a business has changed hands. *Industrial tribunals* will automatically award compensation to the victims of such sackings.

Autonomous team working. A group work system whereby teams of employees are given self-contained tasks and the authority to implement team decisions. Each group member is trained to be able to undertake all jobs performed within the group, so that frequent job rotation is possible.

Banded day work. A wage payment system in which management sets a series of bands for pay and performance, each band carrying a certain flat-rate wage.

Bargaining unit. The sections, departments and/or grades of employee to which a collective agreement is to apply.

Basic award. Compensation awarded by an *industrial tribunal* to an unfairly dismissed worker just equal in value to the amount of a statutory redundancy payment.

Behaviour-modelling training. An application of the social learning approach to training wherein the trainee is encouraged to observe and copy the attitudes and behaviour of carefully-selected role models.

Behaviourism. The proposition that human actions are mainly determined by stimulus–response factors.

Benchmark job. A job against which the duties and responsibilities associated with other jobs are compared.

Biodata. Information on a job applicant's lifetime experiences and current personal circumstances.

Blacking of work. Refusing to complete work normally undertaken by striking employees.

Blackleg. A term of abuse directed against strikebreaking workers.

Blue collar workers. A term commonly used to describe manual workers. The name derives from the blue overalls that many manual employees wear.

Branch committee. A committee comprising key members of a branch of a trade union, responsible for dealing with routine branch administration.

Bridlington agreement. An agreement among member unions of the Trades Union Congress not to poach each other's members.

CAC (Central Arbitration Committee). A government body established to arbitrate in disputes referred to it by *ACAS*, and which hears complaints from trade unions over employers' alleged refusals to disclose information reasonably required for *collective bargaining.*

Cafeteria benefits. Packages of company fringe benefits which allow employees to select whichever elements suit them personally, given their particular circumstances at a certain time (e.g. trading off additional maternity leave against reduced pension benefits).

Card vote. A ballot taken at the annual Trades Union Congress whereby each representative of a member union casts a number of votes proportional to the size of his or her union.

Career. A series of jobs that follow a hierarchy of levels of difficulty, responsibility and status.

Cell working. A way of organising the workforce of a manufacturing company. Workers in each cell are made responsible for quality, production control and the movements of work from one cell to the next. They are expected to function as a team and to cover for each other's absences, late-comings, etc.

Certification Officer. A government official responsible for registering independent trade unions and for hearing union members' complaints about their union's conduct of ballots and elections.

Chaos theory. The proposition that since disorder and confusion are endemic to business situations, managements should accept that 'anything can happen' and hence not attempt to plan and control long-term future activities. Rather, organisations need to be able to learn from past and current events and develop rapid and flexible responses to fast-changing environments.

Chunking. Grouping together items to be learned into meaningful segments in order to facilitate their memorisation.

CIRO method. A training evaluation technique that analyses the effectiveness of an instructional programme under four main headings: context, input, reaction and output.

Classical conditioning. Association of a neutral stimulus with a reflexive response (i.e. one controlled by the autonomic nervous system).

Clinical selection. Employment interviews that rely on judgmental, impressionistic criteria to select the successful candidate.

Closed question. An interview or written question with fixed alternative answers.

Codes of Practice. Documents published by government agencies (e.g. *ACAS* or the Equal Opportunities Commission), or by professional bodies or trade associations to outline model procedures for good practice in a particular field (e.g. health and safety at work, or the removal of unfair discrimination in employment).

Co-determination. The German system of worker participation in management. It provides for employee representatives on supervisory boards, plus works councils and the provision of management information to employees.

Cognition. The mental processes concerned with thinking, reasoning, language, problem solving and perception.

Cognitive dissonance. Inconsistencies in an individual's perceptions of related objects, events or circumstances (e.g. believing that it is raining but not feeling wet).

Collective bargaining. Negotiations between managements and trade unions intended to establish pay and conditions for a large number of workers.

Collectivism. The proposition that since society is an aggregation of groups with conflicting interests then institutions (e.g. trade unions) which represent group interests make important and useful contributions to social welfare overall. According to this view, governments should constrain and regulate individual activities and actively seek to protect disadvantaged groups.

Commissioner for the Rights of Trade Union Members. A government official appointed to assist trade unionists obtain redress following unlawful acts committed by their unions.

Compa ratio. An index showing the degree to which pay levels are clustered around the mid-point of a particular grade.

Compensatory award. Compensation awarded by an *industrial tribunal* to an unfairly dismissed worker and fixed at a level just sufficient to offset his or her lost wages and benefits.

Conciliation. Use of a third party to help settle an industrial dispute (e.g. by suggesting solutions and advising each disputant of the other side's negotiating position).

Concurrent validity. The property of certain selection tests that they have already been tried on employees actually performing the work for which applicants are being tested and have been proven to identify characteristics genuinely relevant to that type of job.

Conflict cycle. The stages through which industrial disputes typically develop; starting with the issue that triggers the conflict, through negotiations, reassessment of each party's position, the emergence of compromises, and final settlement of the dispute.

Conjunctive negotiations. Negotiating situations where the parties have no alternative but to settle.

Conjunctive task. A group task which depends for its successful completion on each group member finishing one or more subsidiary and highly-interdependent operations.

Consideration leadership style. An approach to leadership which focuses on the need for *two-way communications*, concern for subordinates' feelings, and mutual respect between subordinate and boss.

Consolidation of wages. Incorporation into an employee's basic wage of existing fringe benefits, *ad-hoc* bonuses, etc., that were previously regarded as privileges rather than rights.

Conspiracy. A secret plan to commit an unlawful act by two or more persons.

Construct validity. The characteristic of certain selection tests that there exist significant relationships between the test scores achieved by candidates and other evidence regarding their abilities (e.g. possession of academic qualifications).

Constructive dismissal. The resignation of an employee caused by the employer's unreasonable behaviour (e.g. sexual harassment) that represents a fundamental breach of the employee's contract of employment. The aggrieved worker may then claim to have been unfairly dismissed.

Content theories. *Motivation* theories that seek to define and explain the needs the attempted fulfilment of which is assumed to motivate workers.

Content validity. The desirable property of a selection test that the questions it asks (or the tasks it requires be performed) directly relate to the personal qualities the test is attempting to measure (e.g. a numeracy test for applicants for trainee accountancy positions).

Contract for services. A contract to engage a self-employed person to provide *ad-hoc* services, as opposed to a 'contract of service' for hiring a waged employee.

Contracted-out national insurance contributions. Class I state national insurance contributions paid by individuals who also belong to a private occupational pension scheme. Such contributions are slightly lower than the normal Class I rate.

Contracting out. An individual's decision not to contribute to a trade union's political fund, and instructing the union not to use any part of his or her union subscription for political purposes.

Control theories of motivation. Approaches to *motivation* which claim that employees typically compare their actual job situations with desired standards and then behave in ways intended to reduce discrepancies.

Convenor. The senior *shop steward* in a company or major division of a firm.

Core workers. Permanent full-time employees, usually super-annuated.

Counselling. Assisting employees recognise and accurately define their own problems, find solutions, or learn to live with a situation.

Coverdale training. A self-discovery group training method that focuses on the emotional aspects of intra-group behaviour.

CRAMP approach to training. A fivefold classification of the personal competencies that trainees are said to need to develop during an instructional programme (i.e. comprehension, reflex response, attitude formation, memorising, and procedural learning).

Criterion behaviour. All the tasks, procedures, techniques and skills that a trainee should have mastered by the end of a course.

Criterion-referenced assessment. Evaluation of a trainee's abilities against his or her capacity to complete particular specified duties at a predefined level of competence.

Critical incidents. Specific examples of an employee's exceptionally good or bad performance considered in a *performance appraisal* exercise.

Decentralised bargaining. The practice within some large companies (with numerous divisions, subsidiaries, units and sections spread throughout the nation) of empowering the management of each subsidiary, division, etc. to conclude separate deals with the union(s) in that unit, independent of agreements struck by 'local' managers and unions in the firm's other subsidiaries and divisions elsewhere.

Decision band method. A *job evaluation* technique that ranks jobs according to the amounts of responsibility and decision making they carry.

Delayering. The removal of an entire level of management within an organisation in order to improve vertical communication and shorten the chain of command. It is frequently accompanied by an *empowerment* programme.

405

Demarcation disputes. Conflicts between different unions and/or grades of employee within the same organisation regarding which tasks should be completed by which category of worker. For example, is changing a light bulb an electrician's job or a cleaner's?

Derecognition of trade unions. Either (i) the removal of collective bargaining rights from employees, or (ii) the derecognition of particular unions in certain parts of a firm in consequence of the rationalisation of its overall management/worker negotiation procedures.

Differential bonus scheme. A wage incentive system whereby workers' remunerations rise by very large amounts for increased output at high levels of efficiency, but by low amounts for improvements at low levels of efficiency.

Dilutees. Unskilled workers employed to complete jobs previously undertaken by trained and skilled employees.

DISC test. A psychological test developed from research on American soldiers in the 1920s. It purports to identify four basic aspects of test subjects' personalities: dominance, influence, submission and compliance.

Discouraged workers. Unemployed workers who remain out of work for longer than is objectively necessary because of depression caused by repeated rejections from job applications, resulting in their ceasing to look for work, even when the labour market has improved substantially.

Discovery learning. An approach to training that requires trainees to ascertain for themselves the basic principles of their jobs and how best to complete them.

Distributive negotiation. Bargaining over the distribution of shares in a fixed amount of resources.

Division of labour. Breaking work into small and simple units that can be completed quickly by unskilled operatives.

Double loop learning. Learning that involves challenging the basic assumptions about how tasks should be undertaken and whether particular standards and objectives are relevant to a job.

Downsizing. Reduction of the size of a firm's workforce, typically involving voluntary or involuntary redundancies. It is sometimes referred to as 'right-sizing'.

Dynamic adaptive testing. Tests of achievement, intelligence or other mental ability whereby the difficulty of the questions asked automatically increases as test subjects continue to give correct answers.

EAT (Employment Appeal Tribunal). A court that hears appeals against the decisions of *industrial tribunals* and the government *Certification Officer*. It is chaired by a High Court judge who sits with two lay members, and may only consider appeals on questions of law (not points of fact).

Element of competence. According to the *NCVQ*, a description of an action, behaviour or outcome which a person should be able to demonstrate, or a piece of knowledge or understanding of what should be done in a workplace situation that a person needs to possess in order to complete a certain type of work proficiently.

Embezzlement. Theft from an employer.

Emolument. Any wage, salary, fee, profit or perquisite.

Employer-led standards. Criteria for evaluating the contents of training courses laid down by employers in a certain industry or group of occupations, normally through industry *lead bodies*.

Empowerment. The process of giving an employee the right to take executive decisions within certain specified limits, but requiring that person to assume full responsibility for his or her actions.

End-loaded wage agreement. A negotiated pay deal which provides a relatively modest wage increase on conclusion of the agreement followed by further substantial amounts towards the end of the period covered by the bargain.

Equality bargaining. Incorporation of equal opportunities issues into *collective bargaining*, accompanied by attempts by managements and unions to purge collective bargaining machinery of unfair discrimination and to amend existing collective agreements to make them non-discriminatory.

Equity theory. An approach to *motivation* which suggests that employees' perceptions of how they are treated relative to (*i*) their efforts, and (*ii*) other workers, are primary determinants of the enthusiasm they apply to their jobs.

ERG (existence, relatedness and growth) theory. A restructuring of Maslow's *hierarchy of needs*.

Ergonomics. Analysis of the relationships between people and their physical working environments and of how the latter can be adapted to meet human needs and capabilities.

Ethnic minority. A group distinguished from others by a combination of shared customs, beliefs, traditions and characteristics derived from a common or presumed common past, even if the distinctions are not biologically determined.

Euro-executives. Geographically mobile, multi-lingual EU managers capable of quickly adapting to the culture and business methods of any EU country.

Ex-gratia payment. An *ad-hoc* payment made without accepting any responsibility for the possible existence of a legally-binding obligation.

Exchange theory. The proposition that the structure of interpersonal relations depends primarily on the rewards (e.g. compliments or gestures of affection) exchanged, and the costs (e.g. humiliations, rebukes, etc.) incurred during social interactions.

Executive search. Use of external consultants to identify and confidentially approach potential candidates for senior management positions.

Exit interview. An interview conducted with a resigning employee in order to establish his or her reasons for leaving, hence enabling the firm to implement measures to prevent other workers resigning for similar reasons.

Expectancy theory. An approach to *motivation* which suggests that an individual's behaviour depends on his or her self-selected goals and what the person has learned or believes will help achieve them.

Expert system. A computer-software package that mimics the problem-solving methods of a human expert.

Face validity. The property of certain selection tests that they create the impression of measuring attributes directly relevant to the jobs for which candidates are being tested (e.g. a test for selecting trainee accountants might include questions that refer to practical financial situations).

Facilitating questions. Interview questions intended to ease the flow of conversation. Examples are friendly remarks phrased as questions, general questions not related to the job, or a summary in question form of previous comments.

Factor comparison method. An approach to *job evaluation* that seeks to identify the presence of certain common factors within jobs (e.g. mental ability, skill and physical requirements, responsibility, working conditions).

False negatives. Trainees who fail assessments not because they are incompetent but rather through faults in the assessment process. 'False positives', conversely, are trainees who pass an assessment which objectively they should have failed.

Fast tracking. Accelerated promotion systems whereby certain employees are placed on training, planned experience and management development programmes, and then presented with specific targets the attainment of which automatically leads to promotion.

Faults analysis. Investigation of the types of mistake commonly made by employees while undertaking certain kinds of duties.

Featherbedding. Use by employees of rules and working practices that cause overmanning and/or reduced output.

Felt fair methods. *Job evaluation* techniques that apply overall general assessments to the grading of employees' duties, in contrast to using analytical methods.

Field review. A method of *performance appraisal* in which a personnel officer interviews heads of department about their subordinates' qualities and then prepares appraisal reports (rather than heads of department doing this personally).

Flexibility agreement. A collective agreement whereby employees consent to do anything within their capabilities at the behest of management, in return for union involvement in decisions concerning how flexible practices are to be applied.

Force field analysis. Investigation of the elements most resistant to change within an organisation.

Forced-choice rating scale. A *performance appraisal* checklist comprising ordered pairs of statements from which the assessor is required to tick the alternatives considered most descriptive of the appraisee's performance.

Formative assessment. Evaluation of a trainee's performance using assessments that provide feedback to the trainee on his or her progress and which help the trainee correct mistakes and remedy weaknesses.

Four Cs model of human resources management. An approach to HRM that emphasises the importance of *stakeholders* in an organisation and the 'situational factors' of (i) the labour market, (ii) employee motivation, (iii) management style and (iv) the technologies used in production. The effectiveness of HRM policies are evaluated under four headings: employee commitment, employee competence, congruence (i.e. whether management and workers share the same perceptions of the organisation's goals), and cost-effectiveness.

Frame of reference. All the attitudes and psychological influences that determine how a person perceives events and issues.

Friend. In industrial relations, a person who accompanies a worker to a grievance or disciplinary interview.

Frustration. Feelings of anguish that result from interference with an individual's attempts to achieve his or her self-established objectives.

Functional analysis. A means for determining performance standards for *units of competence* in National Vocational Qualifications (NVQs). A 'function' in this context is a 'role expectation', i.e. an activity described in terms of what is expected of its outcomes (e.g. 'providing information', or 'performing calculations').

Functional job analysis. Categorisation of jobs according to two main criteria: nature of the work performed (contacts with other people, data analysis, environmental conditions, etc.), and the personal traits deemed necessary in the individual completing the job (aptitudes, intelligence, temperament, and so on).

Gatekeeper. Someone who communicates with the outside world on behalf of an organisation, who gathers information from external sources and who, in consequence of being able to alter or withhold this information, can significantly affect the organisation's decisions.

Generic skills. Skills that apply to a wide range of activities and hence are easily transferred from one job or occupation to others.

Genuine material factor. A legitimate reason for men and women not receiving equal pay for work of equal value.

Genuine occupational qualification. A legitimate reason for discriminating in favour of one of the sexes or a particular *ethnic group* in an employment situation (e.g. recruiting only Chinese waiters to work in a Chinese restaurant).

Golden handcuffs. Arrangements whereby firms withhold significant payments to senior employees until the latter have remained with their employing organisations for certain minimum periods. The aim is to prevent the *headhunting* of top managers.

Grandfather system. In *performance appraisal*, the practice whereby a manager's assessment of a subordinate is sent to the appraising manager's own boss for review and comment.

Grapevine. An informal and unofficial collection of communication channels that disseminate news and rumours within an organisation.

Green labour. School leavers or other fresh recruits who do not possess work experience.

Group cohesion. The extent to which the members of a group co-operate, share common goals, and possess common attitudes and perspectives.

Group norms. Shared perceptions of what constitutes correct behaviour, of how work should be completed, and of proper attitudes towards management and other workers.

Guarantee payments. Payments available to workers under the Employment Protection (Consolidation) Act 1978 for lay-offs of up to five days during any three-month period.

Half-life survival rate. The average period that elapses before half a particular group of recruits, all of whom started at the same time, leave the firm.

Halo effect. The situation that arises when interviewers wrongly assume that because certain job applicants possess one desirable characteristic (e.g. attractive physical appearance) they must be equally worthy in several other areas.

Harvard model. See *Four Cs model*.

Hay-MSL method. A job evaluation technique that breaks jobs down into three basic factors: know-how, problem solving, and accountability.

Headhunting. Another term for *executive search*.

Hersey–Blanchard model. A leadership theory which asserts that managers should adjust their leadership styles according to subordinates' work experience, levels of ability, and willingness to accept responsibility.

Hierarchy of needs. According to the American psychologist A.H. Maslow, a rank order of needs which individuals attempt to satisfy sequentially. There are five levels: physiological, security, affection, esteem and *self-actualisation*.

Horizontal fast track. A planned experience job rotation scheme intended to give selected employees numerous postings – all at the same level of responsibility – thus enabling them to acquire quickly the experience and broader perspectives needed for senior management positions.

House party method. Employee selection through observing how candidates interact with each other at an assessment centre.

Human resource accounting. Systematic measurement, analysis and recording of the costs and financial benefits of hiring and utilising human resources (e.g. estimation of recruitment and training costs, assessment of the effects of staff development programmes, investigation of the consequences for output of various types of wage incentive system, etc.).

Hygiene factor. An element of the working environment which, if it is satisfactory, will not be noticed but which, if it is unsatisfactory, will demotivate workers. However, the adequacy of a hygiene factor will not of itself motivate employees.

Impingement pay. Additional payments to employees who work during their contractual holiday entitlements.

Incapability. A reason for fair dismissal. Examples are incompetence, and incapacity for work caused by ill health or injury.

Indenture. A special contract of employment for an *apprentice*.

Independent trade union. A trade union not controlled by an employer or subject to interference by an employer *via* the latter's provision or withdrawal of financial support.

Indirect discrimination. Unfair race or sex discrimination resulting from the imposition of a special requirement for the occupancy of a job (e.g. insisting that job applicants be over six feet tall, which automatically discriminates against the great majority of women).

Indirect labour. Workers who do not contribute directly to the production of goods. Examples are secretaries, cleaners and maintenance workers.

Individualism. The proposition that people work best when left alone to pursue their own self-interest. An implication of the principle is that individuals should not be subjected to state regulation or control by institutions such as trade unions.

Industrial engineering. The application to industrial operations of analytical techniques such as work study, quality control, network analysis and production planning.

Industrial relations. All the rules, practices and conventions that govern interrelations between managements and organised labour.

Industrial tribunal. A three-person court comprising a qualified lawyer plus two lay members (each representing one of the two sides of industry – i.e. employers' associations and trade unions) that hears cases concerning unfair dismissal, health and safety at work, violations of equal opportunities legislation, and related employment matters.

Information agreement. A collective agreement between management and unions regarding the precise extent of the information that management will disclose to employee representatives on a regular basis.

Initiating structure. A leadership style that involves close supervision of subordinates and extensive application of the *division of labour*.

Inner directedness. Personal qualities associated with creativity, individualism and independence. This contrasts with 'other directedness' which involves conformism and easy submission to external influences.

Input-driven learning. Training that follows a preset syllabus, using predetermined training methods. The aim is to guarantee that learners acquire certain knowledge and/or abilities.

Instrumental attitudes. Employee orientations towards work that focus on pay and job security rather than on job satisfaction or the quality of working life.

Instrumentality. In motivation theory, how a worker perceives the correlation between reward and performance.

Integrative negotiations. Bargaining situations in which the parties seek common positions on issues.

Interactive video. A training film which outlines the background to a stimulated interpersonal communication situation and then leaves the trainee to specify how he or she would deal with critical aspects of the problems depicted.

Interview funnel. A method for conducting employment interviews which begins by asking broad, open-ended questions and then systematically narrows down the scope of the questions asked, eventually focusing on specific job related topics.

Intrinsic reinforcement. In *classical* and *operant conditioning, reinforcement* caused by positive inner feelings that result from performing a particular activity.

Inventory, personal. A test intended to measure a person's characteristics in a certain dimension (e.g. personality, intelligence or vocational interests). Personal inventories differ from conventional tests in that they do not have pass/fail cut-off marks. Their sole purpose is to enable participants to identify their own strengths and weaknesses.

Involuntary absenteeism. Non-attendance at work through factors entirely beyond an employee's control (e.g. bad weather leading to transport difficulties).

Ipsative tests. Psychometric tests that require candidates to express a preference from several specified alternatives outlined in each question.

Item information. Data on employees which describes their personal biographical details, qualifications, training courses attended, etc.

Job characteristics model. A means for evaluating the impact of *job enrichment* on employee attitudes and behaviour. The psychological consequences of the measures taken are predicted and then compared with actual changes in workers' perceptions and attitudes.

Job depth. The degrees of decision making and control over choice of working methods exerted by an employee while completing a job.

Job enlargement. The process of giving a worker a wider variety of tasks to perform, all at approximately the same level of difficulty.

Job enrichment. Allocation to a worker of additional responsibilities and/or more difficult and complex tasks in order to make his or her job more interesting.

Job evaluation. Analysis of the characteristics of jobs so as to rank them according to their relative value. It focuses on the elements of each job rather than the personal attributes of job occupants.

Joint consultation. Meetings between management and employee representatives to discuss matters of mutual concern. It does *not* involve negotiations, but rather the exchange of information and views in order that management may take mutually acceptable decisions. Note that employee representatives do not control managerial decision making.

Kaizen system. A form of *quality circle* based on a cycle of 'planning, doing, checking and actioning'.

Key time workers. Employees who are called-in as required at the busiest times of the week, month or year.

Kinaesthetics. In *motion study*, the study of the body movements needed to perform work.

Knowledge-based assessment. Evaluation of a trainee's possession of knowledge, rather than his or her ability to apply knowledge in a work situation.

Knowledge of results. Feedback given to trainees regarding their level of performance.

Labour stability index. A labour-turnover measure which shows the proportion of a firm's employees with more than one year's service.

Lead body. A committee comprising representatives of professional bodies, government departments and employers' associations concerned with a particular industry or occupation. The role of a lead body is to work out criteria for measuring the competence of employees in that industry or occupation in order to devise National Vocational Qualifications (*NVQs*) for its workers.

Lean production. Manufacturing processes that minimise waste while maximising the quality of output. Examples include just-in-time systems, *quality circles*, flexible working methods and the extensive use of robots.

Leapfrogging. Constantly escalating pay awards in various industries as unions in each industry use the immediately preceding pay awards obtained by unions in other industries as the basis for their own claims for wage increases.

Learned helplessness. The situation that arises when an individual who is unemployed for a long period 'learns' that it is futile applying for any more jobs.

Learner-centred learning. Training which seeks to impart only the knowledge and skills that trainees need to learn, rather than sticking rigidly to institutional syllabuses.

Learning family, creation of. The grouping together of training and job experiences into broad occupational categories so that trainees learn a variety of skills within a particular 'family' (e.g. 'manufacturing and assembly'). This should enable them to transfer the *skills* acquired in one job to others in the same family.

Learning organisation. A business operating in a turbulent environment that requires regular transformations in working methods, so that the firm needs continuously to train and develop its employees in order to facilitate the introduction of new systems.

Like work. Jobs done by men and women that are broadly similar in terms of the work involved and the effort, *skill* and knowledge needed for their completion.

Local collective bargaining. *Collective bargaining* to determine pay and working conditions in particular workplaces.

Lock-out. A firm's decision to bar employees from entering their place of work, normally in retaliation for workers having taken industrial action.

Lump labour. Workers who offer their services as self-employed sub-contractors rather than as 'employees' to enable employers to avoid paying national insurance and/or assume any other legal obligations.

Managerial grid. A technique of management training intended to assist managers identify their leadership style and hence improve their managerial effectiveness. Managers are categorised according to their concern for production and concern for subordinates' welfare.

Managerial ideology. Beliefs held by some senior managers which inwardly support and legitimise their elite status within organisations.

Managerial prerogative. The right of management to manage without interference from employees or their representatives. Advocates of this view justify its propriety against the fact that managers represent the owners of the business.

Manifest need theory. The proposition that most human needs are learned rather than inherited and come to be felt only when triggered by events in external environments.

Maturity curve. A graph showing the median salaries of various groups of workers against their average age, thus enabling a firm to forecast its future salary bills as the average age of its workforce increases.

Measured day work. A wage-payment system whereby employees must produce a prespecified daily output for a fixed daily wage.

Mediation. Attempts to settle an industrial dispute through the intervention of a third party who informs each side of the views and requirements of the other.

Mentor. A senior manager who provides help, encouragement and psychological support to a favoured subordinate so as to promote the latter's career development.

Merit rating. Appraisal of the performances of manual and clerical workers.

Method study. Analysis of working methods in order to simplify procedures and eliminate duplication of effort.

Methods time measurement (MTM). A form of *predetermined motion time system* based on published tables of *standard times* used to predict the periods in which basic operations should be completed, given various working environments.

Modernism. A term used to describe the manner in which modern society is organised and the belief that the rational application of scientific research is capable of solving the world's problems.

Moonlighters. Employees who simultaneously hold more than one job, often without any one employer knowing the individual is also working elsewhere.

Motion study. Analysis of the human body movements needed for work.

Motivating factor. According to F. Herzberg, something responsible for creating satisfaction at work, as opposed to a *hygiene factor*. Examples of motivators in the *two factor theory* are recognition, interesting work, responsibility, and prospects for promotion.

Motor responses. Limb and other body movements that result from receipt of messages from the brain.

Motor skills. *Skills* needed for repetitive manual activities.

Multi-skilling. Working systems in which employees regularly exchange and share tasks. No job is undertaken exclusively by a single individual.

Multi-unionism. The presence within an organisation of several trade unions, each demanding separate negotiations with management.

Mutuality agreement. An agreement negotiated between management and a firm's trade unions whereby management promises not to alter any aspect of working methods or conditions without the consent of shop stewards or other union representatives.

National Executive Committee (NEC). The highest level of authority in a trade union. Under the Trade Union Act 1984, every member of a union's NEC must be elected by the entire union membership.

Natural justice. Rules that courts expect employers to apply when implementing disciplinary procedures. Examples are informing an accused person of the full details of complaints, allowing the worker to be represented by a third party, not prejudging the issue, etc.

NCVQ (National Council for Vocational Qualifications). A government body set up to implement a national framework for vocational qualifications and to determine national standards of occupational competence.

Negligence. Failure to exercise the amount of care that an average reasonable person would exercise in a given situation. For negligence to be legally actionable there has to exist a duty of care, a breach of that duty by the negligent person, and resulting damage.

Networking, employment. Organising a business in such a manner that employees work from home, communicating with the head office *via* a computer, telephone, and occasional visits.

Non-compliance award. Additional compensation awarded by an *industrial tribunal* to an unfairly dismissed worker whose employer refuses to take back that person.

Normative approach to industrial relations. The view that the best way to achieve order and stability in industrial relations is to have clear and binding laws that apply to all parties. Participants then know precisely what is expected of them, although possibilities for flexibility in negotiating agreements are lost.

Norm-based assessment. Evaluation of a trainee's abilities in comparison with other trainees, rather than against his or her capacity to complete certain prespecified tasks successfully.

NTTF (National Training Task Force). A government agency responsible for co-ordinating the activities of the *Training and Enterprise Councils (TECs)*.

Objective knowledge. Knowledge obtained by a worker in consequence of his or her employment in a particular firm and is therefore the intellectual property of the employing organisation, not the worker.

Occupational analysis inventory. A job-analysis method which categorises work activities and conditions under five main headings: information received, mental activities, observed behaviour, work outcomes, and work contexts.

Occupational personality questionnaire. A personality test similar to the *16PF test* but specifically related to occupational requirements, rather than to general personality characteristics.

Occupational standards. Performance or quality standards recognised by an industry, profession or training organisation as necessary for the satisfactory completion of work.

Official dispute. An industrial dispute formally sanctioned by a trade union.

Open question. An interview or written question to which any response may be given.

Operant conditioning theory. The proposition that learning occurs mainly through trial and error. According to the theory, behaviour that leads to reward will tend to be repeated, and vice versa. Hence, actual behaviour is regarded as being determined by its perceived consequences.

Organisational behaviour modification (OBM). Application of the principles of *operant conditioning theory* to organisational problems.

Organisational climate (culture). The totality of the attitudes, norms, beliefs and perspectives shared by the majority of the members of an organisation.

Organisational development. Analysis of the adequacy of a firm's organisation structures, communication networks, authority and responsibility systems, etc., and the implementation of measures for improving them.

Organisational politics. Negotiations and settlements that occur among the members of an organisation in consequence of the existence of conflicting interests between sections and employees of the firm.

Originating application. A form completed by an aggrieved person who wishes to initiate a case in an *industrial tribunal.*

Other directedness. See *inner directedness.*

Outplacement. Assistance given by firms to workers who are about to be made redundant, in an attempt to help them find other jobs. Outplacement activities include career counselling, informing suppliers and customer businesses of workers' availability, and *psychometric testing* intended to discover workers' aptitudes for alternative types of work.

Paired comparison method. A technique of *job evaluation* which involves the stepwise comparison of the characteristics of several jobs until a consistent hierarchy emerges.

Path-goal theory. A leadership theory which suggests that effective leadership requires managers to clarify to subordinates the actions they must take to obtain various rewards (higher wages, promotion, access to training, etc.).

Pay anomalies. Large differences in the remuneration levels of various occupational groups whose work, nevertheless, requires similar inputs of skill, effort, responsibility, educational qualifications and decision taking.

Pendulum arbitration. A wage *arbitration* method whereby management and union each submit to a third party a figure they believe appropriate for this year's pay increase. The arbitrator then chooses one figure or the other; there are no negotiations or haggling.

Perception. The mental processes through which individuals interpret sensory inputs such as sight, sound, smell, taste, etc.

Performance appraisal. Analysis of an employee's recent successes and failures, personal strengths and weaknesses, and suitability for promotion or further training.

Performance-based assessment. Evaluation of a trainee's knowledge, *skills* and competence while he or she is actually undertaking work-based tasks.

Performance criteria. In *NVQs*, definitions of expected levels of ability for *elements of competence.* Criteria relate to 'outcomes' in terms of what trainees need to be able to do, rather than to the process of learning.

Peripheral workers. Casual and/or part-time employees hired and fired according to a firm's immediate short-term requirements.

Person culture. An organisational culture sometimes found in organisations which exist to serve the people within them, e.g. consultancy firms or professional organisations.

Person specification. A written description of the ideal candidate for a vacant position.

Personal contract. An agreement on the wage and conditions of employment of a specific employee resulting from an individual bargain between the firm and that employee (as opposed to *collective bargaining*).

Personal effectiveness. Aspects of occupational competence determined by personal attributes rather than job knowledge (e.g. maturity, initiative, or self-confidence).

Personality. The totality of an individual's attitudes, perspectives, beliefs, values, motives, dispositions, mental and other personal characteristics.

Pickets. Striking workers who stand at the entrances of their firms in order to try and persuade fellow employees and others not to enter the premises.

Plant bargaining. Another term for *local collective bargaining*.

Pluralism. The view that the best way of avoiding industrial disputes is to recognise from the beginning that the two sides of industry (management and workers) necessarily possess conflicting interests, so that formal procedures are necessary for resolving (inevitable) disagreements.

Post-Fordism. Changes in working methods necessitated by the shift from standardised mass production towards customised production for niche markets using the techniques of *flexibility agreements*, *total quality management* and the employment of *peripheral workers*.

Postmodernism. The proposition that today's world is so different to how it used to be that there are few connections between what occurred in the past and what is likely to happen in the future.

Power. The ability to change the attitudes or behaviour of other people. Power can be exerted by unofficial as well as official leaders.

Power culture. An *organisational culture* based on a single authority figure, as in a small business that begins to expand. There are few rules or procedures and all important decisions are taken by a handful of people.

Predetermined motion time (PMT) system. A *motion study* technique which assumes that every job can be broken down into standard body movements for which average completion times have already been tabulated.

Predictive validity. The desirable property of a selection test that it generates high test scores among candidates who subsequently succeed in the job for which they were tested.

Pre-hearing assessment. A sitting of an *industrial tribunal* convened if a superficial examination of the facts of a situation indicates that one of the parties is bound to lose the case. Its purpose is to warn the appropriate party that its case is legally groundless.

Preliminary hearing. A sitting of an *industrial tribunal* convened to establish whether it has the authority to hear a case (e.g. whether a worker claiming unfair dismissal has completed the statutory period of continuous employment necessary to be able to register a claim).

Prescribed diseases. Industrial diseases the victims of which are automatically entitled to receive state industrial injury benefit.

Primary group. A group whose members regularly come into face-to-face contact.

Primary mental abilities. Aspects of intelligence involving spatial ability, numerical ability, memory, inductive reasoning, speed of perception, and verbal fluency.

Principal executive committees. The key decision-making committees of a trade union. Under the Trade Union Act 1984, every voting member of a principal executive committee must be elected by the union's entire membership.

Proactive inhibition. The situation that arises when a person's past learning inhibits his or her ability to learn new things (e.g. a two-finger typist who has difficulty learning how to touchtype). 'Retroactive inhibition', conversely, means that freshly acquired skills interfere with a trainee's capacity to apply previously learned methods.

Procedural agreements. Agreed procedures concerning rules, methods and institutions to be used for settling management/union disputes.

Process theories. *Motivation* theories which examine the thought processes underlying individual propensities to behave in certain ways.

Product skills. Skills that can be measured quantitatively (e.g. the ability to type at 40 words per minute). This contrasts with 'process' skills, which do not have quantifiable outcomes (e.g. organisational ability).

Productivity bargaining. Management/union negotiations concerning the introduction of radical changes in working methods in exchange for a package of output-related pay increases.

Profile information. Data extracted from employee records to enable a firm to define the main characteristics of typical incumbents of various types of position.

Programmed learning. Instructional materials that present trainees with a series of small units of information ('frames') each immediately followed by a list of questions that have to be answered prior to attempting more advanced work.

Progressive discipline. Increasingly severe penalties imposed on errant employees for persistent latecoming, unauthorised absence, substandard work, etc. For example, the first offence might result in a verbal warning, the second in a written warning, followed by deductions from pay, suspension and, ultimately, dismissal from the firm.

Protective award. Payments of wages for up to 90 days ordered by an *industrial tribunal* to employees whose union has complained that a firm has not followed statutory procedures when declaring the workers redundant.

Psychological contract. An informal unwritten understanding between a worker and his or her employing firm concerning how the person should be treated and how he or she should interrelate with company management.

Psychometric tests. Tests which attempt to measure the psychological dimensions of job applicants or current employees. Examples include intelligence tests, personality tests, and tests of individual *motivation*.

Psychomotor skills. *Skills* which require the co-ordination of thought and physical action.

Quality champion. An influential individual within a firm's workforce selected by management to champion the cause of quality management. This person might be invited to participate in planning the implementation of intended systems and in solving problems as they arise.

Quality circle. An employee discussion group that meets periodically to consider, analyse and resolve quality and production control difficulties.

Quality of working life (QWL). The totality of human satisfactions at work. Determinants of QWL include working conditions, extent of participation in management decision making, interpersonal relations, and the *organisational climate* of the employing business.

Range statements. Descriptions of the activities, processes, equipment and contexts to which NVQ *elements of competence* apply.

Ranking system. A non-analytical method of *job evaluation* which involves an overall assessment of jobs rather than attempting to quantify the particular elements of each position.

Rating, work study. A work study officer's subjective assessment of the degree of effort an employee is putting into his or her work.

Receptor processes. The mechanisms through which individuals sense cues and stimuli from their external environments.

Recognised trade union. Any independent trade union with which an employer is prepared to bargain over employment matters. Once recognised, a union enjoys certain legal rights (e.g. to appoint *safety representatives*).

Record of achievement. A document issued to a school leaver listing his or her achievements and progress within and outside the classroom, including activities not tested by formal examinations.

Red circling. The practice following the completion of *job evaluation* exercises of continuing to pay current salary levels to individuals whose jobs have been downgraded. However, a lower rate will be paid to employees who eventually replace red-circled workers.

Re-engineering. The radical redesign of business processes in order to improve their efficiency. Out-of-date systems are replaced in their entirety, rather than simply attempting to automate and speed-up existing methods for completing work.

Reference groups. Informal groups against which individuals evaluate their attitudes, beliefs, feelings and behaviour.

Reinforcements. Rewards (positive reinforcement) and punishments (negative reinforcement) that motivate people to behave in certain ways.

Reliability of assessment. The extent to which an assessment method generates consistent results over time and among assessors.

Reliability of selection tests. The extent to which selection tests generate consistent spreads of results when repeated on different groups of people.

Repetitive strain injury (RSI). Upper limb disorders (e.g. cramp or tenosynovitis) resulting from prolonged work at a keyboard.

Reportable accidents. Accidents causing death or more than three days' absence from employment. By law such accidents must be reported to the Health and Safety Executive.

Respondent. An employer who defends an action in an *industrial tribunal*.

Retroactive inhibition. See *Proactive inhibition*.

Role. A total and self-contained pattern of behaviour typical of a person who occupies a particular social position.

Role culture. An *organisational culture* based on highly bureaucratic rules and procedures.

Safety officer. A manager appointed by a firm to be responsible for implementing its health and safety policies.

Safety representative. An employee selected by his or her trade union to deal with workplace health and safety. Duties of a safety representative include the inspection of premises, liaison with outside inspectors, and the investigation of hazards, accidents and dangerous occurrences.

Salary attrition. Cost savings resulting from long delays in replacing highly-paid employees who leave the firm.

Secondary actions. Industrial actions (e.g. picketing) taken against firms (such as suppliers or major customers) which are not directly involved in a trade dispute.

Secondary rewards. *Reinforcements* that are earned and not connected with characteristics innate to the individual. Examples are recognition, job satisfaction, social approval, pay rises, etc.

Self-actualisation. The highest level of need allegedly felt by a human being, i.e. the need to fulfil one's potential to the maximum level.

Self-managed learning. Training courses in which participants are themselves responsible for deciding what they need to know and, in liaison with an instructor, for selecting appropriate learning methods.

Shamrock form of organisation. An organisation system based on three distinct groups of employee: *core workers*, *peripheral workers*, and outside contractors.

Shop steward. A lay workplace trade union representative.

Single loop learning. The learning necessary to enable an employee to apply existing methods to the completion of a job.

Single status. The situation in which all grades of management and other workers share the same canteen, use the same car park, wear similar clothes, and enjoy equal access to *superannuation* and other fringe benefits.

Single table bargaining. Negotiating situations wherein the terms and conditions of an entire category of employee (e.g. manual workers) are settled at a single sitting.

Single-union agreement. A situation in which management only recognises one trade union for the purpose of *collective bargaining*.

Situational interview. An employment interview which asks questions about how the candidate would handle specific incidents likely to arise in the course of the vacant job.

[Sixteen] 16 PF test. A widely used personality test which assumes the existence within test subjects of 16 clusters of behavioural factors (e.g. emotional stability, intelligence, assertiveness, etc.).

Skill. A capacity to perform a task competently, normally involving a co-ordinated sequence of mental and/or physical activities.

Skills analysis. Observation and recording of the methods used by a competent, skilled and experienced worker while completing tasks. Its aim is to analyse these methods as a basis for training other workers.

Skills inventory. A listing of all the qualifications, competencies and work experiences possessed by a firm's employees in order to inform management of all the alternative jobs that its current workforce is capable of undertaking.

Skittle effects. The consequences of training one group of workers for the training needs of others. For example, training manual workers in new skills could necessitate extra training for their supervisors, which in turn could require better trained middle managers, etc.

Soft criteria. Subjective judgmental criteria used in employee selection, as opposed to 'hard' criteria involving factual information.

Spearhead negotiator. A spokesperson for a negotiating team who intentionally does most of the talking on behalf of the team and generally tries to dominate the proceedings.

419

Special compensation. A form of compensation awarded by *industrial tribunals* to workers unfairly dismissed for joining or refusing to join a trade union.

Speculative training. Another term for *training for stock.*

Spent conviction. A criminal conviction which the offending person is not obliged to disclose – even if asked to do so – following the expiry of a certain period after the imposition of a fine or the offender's release from prison.

Staff association. An association of employees (which is not a trade union) formed to represent workers' interests in a company.

Stakeholder. A person or group with a vested interest in the behaviour of a business.

Standard time. The period needed by a competent, experienced and motivated worker to complete a task, allowing for contingencies and employee relaxation.

Status congruence. Consistency of opinion among the members of a group regarding the status assigned to each participant.

Stereotyping. The attribution to an individual by other people of a number of characteristics assumed typical of the group to which the person belongs.

Substantive agreement. A negotiated agreement which relates to pay, working hours, holiday entitlement or some other specific term or condition of employment.

Summary dismissal. Dismissal on the spot, without notice.

Summative assessment. An evaluation of a trainee's performance on a course, undertaken purely for recording purposes (e.g. to qualify for the award of a certificate), rather than to help the trainee identify personal strengths and weaknesses and hence improve his or her work.

Sunlighter. A person who continues in full-time employment beyond the normal age for retirement.

Superannuation schemes. Company pension schemes, normally requiring both the employer and the employee to contribute about six per cent of the employee's salary to a central fund.

Synchropay. A suggested means (never implemented) for avoiding *leapfrogging.* Under the scheme all unions and employers would negotiate annual pay deals on the same day each year.

Systematic training. A term used to describe logical, analytical approaches to training, involving the identification of training needs, planning and implementing programmes, and the careful evaluation of the effectiveness of courses.

Task and finish system. A wage payment scheme whereby employees receive a fixed wage but are allowed to leave work as soon as an agreed task has been completed (as happens with some local authority refuse collectors, for example).

Task culture. An *organisational culture* that is project orientated, flexible and responsive to change. Job satisfaction is high and there is much group cohesion.

Team spirit. High motivation within a group resulting from feelings of loyalty, *group cohesion*, effective leadership and extensive interaction among group members.

Theory X and theory Y. Assumptions about human nature supposedly held by managers. Theory X assumptions are that workers are naturally lazy and must be coerced into working hard; theory Y assumptions assert that individuals are naturally industrious, may be relied upon to exercise self-direction and do not require close supervision.

Theory Z. A term coined by W. Ouchi to describe the Japanese approach to management. According to Ouchi, this involves long-term employment, seniority-based promotion, intense socialisation of recruits, production orientation, employee participation in decision making and great concern for the quality of output.

Threshold agreements. Pay deals whereby employees' wages automatically increase by a predetermined amount whenever the rate of inflation exceeds a certain level.

Time span of discretion method. A technique of *job evaluation* which relates employees' remunerations to the time periods that elapse between checks or evaluations of their work. The longer the intervals, the greater the level of responsibility assumed to be involved in the job.

Total loss control. An approach to accident prevention and consequent losses to production. It involves the systematic analysis of potential hazards, safety training, safety audits, spot checks, and the development of reporting procedures.

Total quality management (TQM). Integration of practical techniques of quality control (inspection, sampling, etc.) with a firm's overall strategies and tactics in order to create an *organisational culture* that is conducive to the continuous improvement of quality.

Trade dispute. A dispute between an employer and workers which is immune from civil liability, i.e. the workers or unions involved cannot be sued for breach of contract or conspiracy to induce a breach of contract.

Training and Enterprise Councils (TECs). Government-appointed bodies consisting of local business people charged with the task of identifying training needs in various geographical areas and then contracting training providers (e.g. local colleges) to deliver courses corresponding to specifications laid down by the area TEC.

Training for stock (speculative training). Training undertaken in anticipation of new *skills* requirements and/or cyclical upturns in the economy.

Transactional leadership. A leadership style based on the provision to subordinates of the resources they need and on helping subordinates complete their duties. This differs from 'transformational' leadership, which seeks to motivate workers to look beyond mundane short-term work requirements.

Transfer of learning. The ability to transfer competencies learned in one situation to others. For example, someone who has learned one wordprocessing package can usually pick up very quickly how to operate another.

Tripartism. The proposition that government, the Trades Union Congress and the Confederation of British Industry should jointly determine national industrial relations (and perhaps even economic) policies.

Triple I organisation. A *learning organisation* based on 'ideas, information and intelligence'.

Two-factor theory. A motivation theory that distinguishes between 'motivators' and *'hygiene factors'*.

Two-way communications. Communications that involve a response from message recipients.

Unconditioned stimulus. A stimulus that naturally evokes a response (e.g. a presentation of food to a hungry dog, causing the dog's mouth to water).

Unfair dismissal. Dismissal of a worker who is covered by the Employment Protection (Consolidation) Act 1978, for anything other than incapability, genuine redundancy, gross misconduct or some other substantial reason.

Union density. The percentage of employees who belong to a trade union in a particular workplace, firm or industry.

Unit of competence. A collection of NVQ *elements of competence*.

Unitarism. The belief that management and workers have identical interests and thus may be expected naturally to work as a team and in a harmonious manner towards the achievement of common objectives.

Utility analysis. Estimation of the monetary costs and benefits of various techniques of employee selection so as to compare alternative recruitment strategies. Costs include job advertising, the effects of underperformance by a badly-selected person, and the replacement costs of unsatisfactory workers who are dismissed or resign. Benefits encompass the ability to promote satisfactory recruits, improved organisational performance, *group cohesion*, etc.

Valence. The strength of a person's desire for a particular outcome or occurrence of a certain event.

Vertical job enlargement. Another term for *job enrichment*.

Vertical loading. Another term for *job enrichment*.

Vestibule training. Training that takes place in a room specially set up to replicate the conditions of a workplace.

Vicarious liability. A legal doctrine which requires employers to assume general responsibility for breaches of contract, common law or statutory obligations committed by employees in the course of their employment.

Victimisation. Unfavourable treatment of an individual because he or she complains of being denied a statutory right or helps another person complain about such treatment.

Voluntarism. A philosophy of industrial relations which asserts that employers and unions should be left to resolve disputes and reach collective agreements voluntarily, without the existence of laws governing industrial relations or the ability of one of the parties to a dispute to take the other to court.

Wage drift. The tendency of locally negotiated wage rates to rise above minimum levels determined nationally by panels of unions and employers' associations.

Wage–effort bargain. A person's perception of how much work is to be done for an agreed wage, including the effort put into the job as well as the number of hours of employment.

Wastage curve. A graph showing the proportions of a firm's employees who resign in various age categories. Normally the highest wastage rates occur among young workers and those approaching the normal age of retirement.

Whistleblowing. The practice of an employee reporting to the police or other outside authority the illegal practices or improper actions of the employing organisation.

Work-factor method. A *motion study* technique which analyses the times needed to perform operations in terms of body member used, distance travelled, extent of manual control needed, and weight or resistance encountered.

Work-profiling system. A method for generating *person specifications* based on answers to questionnaires issued to job occupants. Jobs are analysed according to the time spent on various duties, the importance of each task, the work environment, organisational involvement, and job autonomy.

Work to rule. Refusal by employees to undertake any tasks not strictly covered by their contracts of employment.

Wrongful dismissal. Dismissal without proper notice or in breach of a clause in a worker's contract of employment.

Zero-sum bargaining. A negotiating situation in which each party trades concessions to the extent that total gains and losses add up to zero.

INDEX